SPELL

CHECK

✔

SPELL
CHECK

based on

The American Heritage® Dictionary

of the English Language,

Third Edition

Houghton Mifflin Company

Boston   New York

Library of Congress Cataloging-in-Publication Data

Spell check : based on The American Heritage dictionary
   of the English language, third edition.
        p.   cm.
   ISBN 0-395-75691-X
   1. Spellers.   2. English language — Syllabication — Dictionaries.
I. American Heritage dictionary of the English language.
PE1146.S78   1996   96-55
428.1 — dc20   CIP

For information about this and other Houghton Mifflin trade and reference books
and multimedia products, visit The Bookstore at Houghton Mifflin on the World
Wide Web at http://www.hmco.com/trade/.

Manufactured in the United States of America

BP   10   9   8   7   6   5   4   3   2   1

CONTENTS

How to Use This Book   vii

Guide to Spelling   xi

Sound-Spelling Correspondence Table   xxii

A-Z Word List   1

EDITORIAL AND PRODUCTION STAFF

Editorial Staff

Managing Editor
Marion Severynse

Senior Lexicographer
Joseph P. Pickett

Editor
Ann-Marie Imbornoni, *Project Director*

Associate Editor
James J. Boyle

Assistant Editors
Beth Anderson
Susan S. Chicoski

Production Staff

Production and Manufacturing Manager
Christopher Leonesio

Production Supervisor
Elizabeth Rubè

Senior Art & Production Coordinator
Margaret Anne Miles

Text Design
Melodie Wertelet

HOW TO USE THIS BOOK

Spell Check is a useful guide to spelling and dividing into syllables the most commonly used words in the English language. In addition, *Spell Check* also functions as a guide to basic pronunciation, showing which syllables are stressed when a word is pronounced. The body of the book comprises a list of approximately 40,000 words, the core of which was taken from *The American Heritage Student Dictionary,* including many new words and technical and scientific terms from *The American Heritage College Dictionary, Third Edition.*

Spell Check has several special features that will save you time and effort: an explanation of some basic rules of spelling; a section on forming plurals; a section on forming compounds and hyphenation. There is also a sound-spelling correspondence table to help those who know the pronunciation of a word but are having difficulty finding it under the correct spelling.

Although *Spell Check* is simple to use, the following guide will help you make the most of its special benefits and features.

Division of Words

Spell Check clearly shows how a word may be divided into syllables. Such divisions are indicated by a centered dot, a stress mark, or a hyphen:

com•put′er	screen′writ′er
dou′ble-check′	right′-an′gled

At the end of a line of type, a word may be broken wherever a syllable division is indicated. However, many editors, compositors, and typesetters observe the following general principles:

1. A syllable consisting of a single letter should not be separated from the rest of the word:

>   abide, not a-bide
>   stealthy, not stealth-y
>   uto-pia, not u-topia or utopi-a

2. A syllable consisting of a single letter that is embedded in the word should not be separated from the preceding syllable:

>   oxy-gen, not ox-ygen
>   visi-tation, not vis-itation

3. The preceding rule does not apply to the suffixes *-able* and *-ible* or to words in which the vowel standing alone is the first syllable of a root word:

>   account-able, not accounta-ble
>   flex-ible, not flexi-ble
>   un-aware, not una-ware

4. Compound words, if possible, are divided between their elements:

>   any-body   over-estimate   type-writer

5. A hyphenated word should be divided only at the hyphen.

Stress

Spell Check indicates the relative degree of stress that a syllable has when it is pronounced. Two different stress marks are used. The first, a boldface stress, indicates the syllable that receives the primary stress in the word:

>   cen′ter   in•ven′tion   sin•cere′

The second mark, a lighter stress, indicates syllables that are not as strong as the one marked with a primary stress, but are still stronger than unmarked syllables:

>   bi′o•log′i•cal   dic′tion•ar′y

Inflected Forms

Inflected forms are given for every entry word exhibiting any irregularity or unpredictable stress or spelling changes in the inflected forms. These forms include the plurals of nouns; the past tense, past participle, and present participle of verbs; and comparative and superlative forms of adjectives. Many inflected forms have been cut back, or shortened, to save space:

fish *pl.* fish *or*
   fish′es

po′di•um *pl.* -di•a
   or -di•ums

mad, mad′der,
   mad′dest

shy, shi′er *or* shy′er,
   shi′est *or* shy′est

bake, baked,
   bak′ing

fly, flew, flown,
   fly′ing

Note that verbs may have two or three inflected forms. If only two forms are given, the first is both the past tense and the past participle (*baked*). If three forms are given, the first is the past tense (*flew*) and the second is the past participle (*flown*). Variant inflected forms are also shown (*shyer, shyest*).

If a word has more than one part of speech, usually only one part of speech is entered (the one with the most complicated spelling changes in the inflected forms):

cry, cried, cry′ing

slide, slid, slid′ing

If, however, a word's stress pattern changes depending on whether it is used as a noun or verb, both forms are entered:

rec′ord *n.*
re•cord′ *v.*

Variants

Spell Check includes variant spellings of words whenever these are in common use. Such variant spellings appear only at the main entry for that word. If the variants are used almost equally, they are separated by an *or:*

aes•thet'ic *or* es•thet'ic

When one form is preferred over another form, the preferred form is entered first and the two forms are separated by an *also:*

ge'o•graph'ic *also* ge'o•graph'i•cal

Words Likely to Be Confused

In *Spell Check*, glosses, or brief definitions, are given for all pairs or sets of words that are likely to be confused, including homographs (words that are spelled the same but have different meanings), homophones (words that are pronounced the same but spelled differently), words that have similar spellings or pronunciations, and troublesome words that are often used incorrectly. A check mark precedes a cross-reference to the word or words with which the entry word may be confused:

smelt *(fish), pl.* smelts
  or smelt

smelt *(to melt)*

hoard *(cache)*
  ✔ horde

horde *(throng)*
  ✔ hoard

ac•cept' *(to receive)*
  ✔ except

ex•cept' *(to leave out)*
  ✔ accept

bi•week'ly *(once in
two weeks)*
  ✔ semiweekly

sem'i•week'ly *(twice a
week)*
  ✔ biweekly

Should such words fall in regular alphabetical order, only the gloss is shown:

bloc *(group)*
block *(solid substance)*

GUIDE TO SPELLING

Although it would be impossible to formulate a set of rules that would cover the spelling of all English words, the seven basic rules given here are intended as an aid in learning and understanding the correct spelling of a large number of English words.

Seven Basic Rules of Spelling

1. Adding a suffix to a one-syllable word.

a. Words of one syllable that end in a single consonant preceded by a single vowel double the final consonant before a suffix beginning with a vowel: *bag, baggage; hop, hopper; red, redder; stop, stopped*. There are two notable exceptions to this rule: *bus* (*buses* or *busses; busing* or *bussing*) and *gas* (*gasses* or *gases; gassing; gassy*).

b. If a word ends with two or more consonants or if it ends with one consonant preceded by two or more vowels instead of one, the final consonant is not doubled: *debt, debtor; lick, licking; mail, mailed; sweet, sweetest*.

2. Adding a suffix to a word with two or more syllables.

a. Words of two or more syllables that have the accent on the last syllable and end in a single consonant preceded by a single vowel double the final consonant before a suffix beginning with a vowel: *admit, admitted; confer, conferring; control, controller; regret, regrettable*. There are a few exceptions: *chagrin, chagrined; transfer, transferred, transferring* but *transferable, transference*.

b. When the accent shifts to the first syllable of the word after the suffix is added, the final consonant is not doubled: *prefer, preference; refer, reference*.

c. If the word ends with two consonants or if the final consonant is preceded by more than one vowel, the final consonant
is not doubled: *perform, performance; repeal, repealing.*

d. If the word is accented on any syllable except the last, the
final consonant is not doubled: *develop, developed; market, mar-
keted.* However, some words like *cobweb, handicap,* and *outfit*
follow the models of *web, cap,* and *fit,* even though these
words may not be true compounds. A few others ending in *g*
double the final *g* so that it will not be pronounced like *j*:
zigzag, zigzagged.

3. Adding a suffix beginning with a vowel to a word ending in
a silent *e.* Words ending with a silent *e* usually drop the *e* before a suffix beginning with a vowel: *force, forcible; glide, glid-
ing; operate, operator; trifle, trifler.* However, there are many exceptions to this rule:

a. Many words of this type have alternative forms: *blamable* or
blameable; bluish or *blueish.* And in certain cases, alternative
forms have different meanings: *linage* or *lineage* (number of
lines) but *lineage* (ancestry).

b. Many words ending in *ce* or *ge* keep the *e* before the suffixes
-able and *-ous: advantage, advantageous; trace, traceable.*

c. Words ending in a silent *e* keep the *e* if the word could be
mistaken for another word: *dye, dyeing; singe, singeing.*

d. If the word ends in *ie,* the *e* is dropped and the *i* changed to
y before the suffix *-ing.* A word ending in *i* remains unchanged
before *-ing: die, dying; ski, skiing.*

e. *Mile* and *acre* do not drop the *e* before the suffix *-age:
mileage, acreage.*

4. Adding a suffix beginning with a consonant to a word ending in a silent *e.* Words ending with a silent *e* generally retain
the *e* before a suffix that begins with a consonant: *plate, plate-
ful; shoe, shoeless; arrange, arrangement; white, whiteness.* However, there are many exceptions to this rule. Some of the most

common are: *abridge, abridgment; acknowledge, acknowledgment; argue, argument; awe, awful; due, duly; judge, judgment; nine, ninth; true, truly; whole, wholly; wise, wisdom.*

5. Adding a suffix to a word ending in *y*.

a. Words ending in *y* preceded by a consonant generally change the *y* to *i* before the addition of a suffix, except when the suffix begins with an *i: accompany, accompaniment; beauty, beautiful; icy, icier, iciest, icily, iciness;* but *reply, replying.*

b. The *y* is retained in derivatives of *baby, city,* and *lady* and before the suffixes -*ship* and -*like: babyhood, cityscape, ladyship, ladylike.*

c. Adjectives of one syllable ending in *y* preceded by a consonant usually retain the *y* when a suffix beginning with a consonant is added: *shy, shyly, shyness; sly, slyly, slyness; wry, wryly, wryness;* but *dryly* or *drily, dryness.* These adjectives usually also retain the *y* when a suffix beginning with a vowel is added, although most have variants where the *y* has changed to *i: dry, drier* or *dryer, driest* or *dryest; shy, shier* or *shyer, shiest* or *shyest.*

d. Words ending in *y* preceded by a vowel usually retain the *y* before a suffix: *buy, buyer; key, keyless; coy, coyer, coyest; gay, gayer, gayest;* but *day, daily; gay, gaily* or *gayly.*

e. Some words drop the final *y* before the addition of the suffix -*eous: beauty, beauteous.*

6. Adding a suffix to a word ending in *c*. Words ending in *c* almost always have the letter *k* inserted after the *c* when a suffix beginning with *e, i,* or *y* is added: *panic, panicky; picnic, picnicker.*

7. The problem of "*ie*" or "*ei.*"

a. When the two letters have a long *e* sound (as in *feet*), *i* generally comes before *e*, except after *c: believe, chief, grieve, niece, siege, shield;* but *either, leisure, neither, seize, sheik.*

b. After *c*, *e* generally comes before *i: ceiling, conceit, deceive, perceive, receive, receipt;* but *ancient, financier, specie.*

c. When the two letters have a long *a* sound (as in *cake*), a short *e* sound (as in *pet*), a short *i* sound (as in *fit*), or a long *i* sound (as in *mine*), *e* generally comes before *i: Fahrenheit, foreign, forfeit, height, neighbor, sleight, sovereign, surfeit;* but *friend, handkerchief, mischief, sieve.*

Many words spelled with *ie* or *ei* present no difficulties because the vowels are pronounced separately: *deity, piety.*

Forming Plurals

1. The plural of most nouns is formed by adding *s* to the singular: *apples, epochs, griefs, months, Georges, the Romanos.*

2. a. Common nouns ending in *ch* (soft), *sh, s, ss, x, z* or *zz* usually form their plurals by adding *es: churches, slashes, gases, classes, foxes, buzzes.*

b. Proper nouns of this type add *es: Charles, the Charleses; the Keaches; the Joneses; the Coxes.*

3. a. Common nouns ending in *y* preceded by a vowel usually form their plurals by adding *s: bays, guys, keys, toys.*

b. Common nouns ending in *y* preceded by a consonant or by *qu* change the *y* to *i* and add *es: baby, babies; city, cities; faculty, faculties; soliloquy, soliloquies.*

c. Proper nouns ending in *y* form their plurals regularly, and do not change the *y* to *i* as common nouns do: *the two Kathys; the Connallys; the two Kansas Citys.* There are a few well-known exceptions to this rule: *the Alleghenies, the Ptolemies, the Rockies, the Two Sicilies.*

4. Most nouns ending in *f, ff,* or *fe* form their plurals regularly by adding *s* to the singular: *chief, chiefs; proof, proofs; roof, roofs; sheriff, sheriffs; fife, fifes.* However, some nouns ending in *f* or *fe* change the *f* or *fe* to *v* and add *es: calf, calves; elf, elves; half, halves; knife, knives; life, lives; loaf, loaves; self, selves; shelf, shelves; thief, thieves; wife, wives; wolf, wolves.* A few nouns ending in *f* or *ff,* including *beef, dwarf, hoof, scarf, wharf,* and *staff* have two plural forms: *beefs, beeves; dwarfs* or *dwarves; hoofs* or *hooves; scarfs* or *scarves; wharfs* or *wharves; staffs* or *staves*. In this case, sometimes different forms have different meanings, as *beefs* (complaints) and *beeves* (animals) or *staffs* (people) and *staves* (long poles).

5. a. Nouns ending in *o* preceded by a vowel form their plurals by adding *s* to the singular: *cameos, duos, studios, zoos*.

b. Most nouns ending in *o* preceded by a consonant also usually add *s* to form the plural: *altos, casinos, egos, Latinos*. However, some nouns ending in *o* preceded by a consonant add *es*: *echoes, heroes, jingoes, noes, potatoes, tomatoes*. Some nouns ending in *o* preceded by a consonant have two plural forms: *buffaloes* or *buffalos; cargoes* or *cargos; desperadoes* or *desperados; halos* or *haloes; mosquitoes* or *mosquitos; zeros* or *zeroes*.

6. Most nouns ending in *i* form their plurals by adding *s: alibis, khakis, rabbis, skis*. Three exceptions are *alkali, taxi*, and *chili: alkalis* or *alkalies; taxis* or *taxies; chilies*.

7. a. A few nouns undergo a vowel change in the stem: *foot, feet; goose, geese; louse, lice; man, men; mouse, mice; tooth, teeth; woman, women*. Usually compounds in which one of these nouns is the final element form their plurals in the same way: *webfoot, webfeet; gentleman, gentlemen; dormouse, dormice; Englishwoman, Englishwomen*. Note, however, that *mongoose* and many words ending in *man*, such as *German* and *human*, are not compounds. These words forms their plurals by adding *s: mongooses; Germans, humans*.

b. Three nouns have plurals ending in *en: ox, oxen; child, children; brother, brothers* (of the same parent) or *brethren* (a fellow member).

8. a. Compounds written as a single word form their plurals the same way that the final element of the compound does: *cloths, dishcloths; brushes, hairbrushes; wives, midwives; men, anchormen; women, businesswomen*.

b. In rare cases both parts of the compound are made plural: *manservant, menservants.*

c. Compounds ending in *-ful* normally form their plurals by adding *s* at the end: *cupfuls, handfuls, tablespoonfuls.*

d. Compound words, written with or without a hyphen, that consist of a noun followed by an adjective or other qualifying expression form their plurals by making the same change in the noun as when the noun stands alone: *daughter-in-law, daughters-in-law; man-of-war, men-of-war; heir apparent, heirs apparent; notary public, notaries public.*

9. Some nouns, mainly names of birds, fishes, and mammals, have the same form in the plural as in the singular: *bison, deer, moose, sheep, swine.* Some words that follow this pattern, such as *antelope, cod, crab, elk, fish, flounder, grouse, herring, quail, reindeer, salmon, shrimp,* and *trout,* also have regular plurals ending in *-s: antelope, antelopes; fish, fishes; salmon, salmons.* Normally in such cases the unchanged plural denotes that the animal in question is being considered collectively, while the plural ending in *s* is used specifically to denote different varieties or species or kinds: *We caught six fish* but *Half a dozen fishes inhabit the lake.* By far, however, most animal names take a regular plural: *dogs, cats, lions, monkeys, whales.*

10. a. Many words indicating nationality or place of origin have the same form in the plural as in the singular: *Japanese, Milanese, Swiss.*

b. Similarly a few names of tribes or peoples have the same form in the plural as in the singular: *Iroquois; Sioux.* Many other such names have both an unchanged plural form and a regular plural form ending in *s: Apache* or *Apaches; Cherokee* or *Cherokees; Eskimo* or *Eskimos; Zulu* or *Zulus.*

11. Many nouns derived from a foreign language retain their foreign plurals: (from Latin) *alumna, alumnae; bacillus, bacilli; genus, genera; series, series;* (from Greek) *analysis, analyses; basis,* *bases; crisis, crises; criterion, criteria* or *criterions; phenomenon, phenomena* or *phenomenons;* (from French) *adieu, adieux* or *adieus; beau, beaux* or *beaus; madame, mesdames;* (from Italian) *paparrazzo, papparazzi;* (from Hebrew) *cherub, cherubim* or *cherubs; kibbutz, kibbutzim.* As you can see, many words of this type also have a regular plural ending in *s* or *es,* in which case the English plural is usually the one used in everyday speech, and the foreign plural is reserved for a technical sense or for use by a specialist: *antennas* (TV or radio part) or *antennae* (physiological structure).

12. a. Usage with regard to forming the plurals of letters, numbers, and abbreviations varies. In some cases you have a choice between adding *s* or *'s: three As* or *three A's; the ABCs* or *the ABC's; the 1900s* or *the 1900's; PhDs* or *PhD's; several IOUs* or *several IOU's.* With lowercase letters, symbols, abbreviations with periods, and in cases where confusion might arise without an apostrophe, use *'s* to form the plural: *p's and q's; +'s; -'s; M.A.'s; A's and I's; 2's.*

b. The plural of a word being used as a word is indicated by *'s: underline all the* but's.

Word Compounding

A compound word is made up of two or more words that together express a single idea. There are three types of compound words. An *open compound* consists of two or more words written separately, such as *salad dressing* or *April Fools' Day.* A *hyphenated compound* has words connected by a hyphen, such as *mother-in-law* or *force-feed.* A *solid compound* is two words that are written as one word, such as *keyboard* or *typewriter.* In addition, a compound may be classified as permanent or temporary. A *permanent compound* is fixed by common usage and can usually be found in the dictionary, whereas a *temporary compound* consists of two or more words joined by a hyphen as needed, usually to modify another word or to avoid ambiguity. The following general rules apply to forming compounds.

Prefixes and suffixes

1. Normally, prefixes and suffixes are joined with a second element without a hyphen, unless doing so would double a vowel or triple a consonant: *antianxiety, anticrime, antiwar* but *anti-intellectual; childlike, taillike* but *bell-like*. Even so, many common prefixes, such as *co-, de-, pre-, pro-,* and *re-,* are added without a hyphen although a double vowel is the result: *coordinate, preeminent, reenter*.

2. A hyphen is also used when the element following a prefix is capitalized, or when the element preceding a suffix is a proper noun: *anti-American, America-like*.

3. The hyphen is usually retained in words that begin with *all-, ex-* (meaning "former"), *half-, quasi-* (in adjective constructions), and *self-*: *all-around; ex-governor; half-life* but *halfhearted, halfpenny, halftone, halfway; quasi-scientific* but *a quasi success; self-defense* but *selfhood, selfish, selfless, selfsame*.

4. Certain homographs require a hyphen to prevent mistakes in pronunciation and meaning: *recreation* (enjoyment), *recreation* (new creation).

When the compound is a noun or adjective

5. In order to avoid confusion, compound modifiers are generally hyphenated: *fine-wine tasting; high-school teacher; hot-water bottle; minimum-wage worker; rare-book store; real-life experiences*. If there is no possibility of confusion, or if the hyphen would look clumsy, omit the hyphen: *bubonic plague outbreak, chemical engineering degree, temp agency employee*.

6. When a noun that is an open compound is preceded by an adjective, the compound is often hyphenated to avoid confusion: *wine cellar, damp wine-cellar; broom closet, tiny broom-closet; house cat, old house-cat*.

7. Compound adjectives formed with *high-* or *low-* are generally hyphenated: *high-quality programming; low-budget films.*

8. Compound adjectives formed with an adverb plus an adjective or a participle are often hyphenated when they occur before the noun they modify: *a well-known actor, an ill-advised move, best-loved poems, a much-improved situation, the so-called cure.* However, when these compounds occur after the noun, or when they are modified, the hyphen is usually omitted: *the actor is well known; an extremely well known actor.* Many compounds of this type are permanent hyphenated compounds: *a well-done steak; the steak was well-done.*

9. If the adverb ends in *-ly* in an adverb-adjective compound, the hyphen is omitted: *a finely tuned mechanism; a carefully worked canvas.*

10. Compound adjectives formed with a noun and a past participle are always hyphenated when they precede the noun they modify: *helium-filled balloons, snow-capped mountains.* Many compounds of this type have become permanent and are hyphenated whether they precede or follow the noun they modify: *the tongue-tied winner; She remained tongue-tied.*

11. Also hyphenate compound adjectives formed with an adjective and a noun to which *-d* or *-ed* has been added: *yellow-eyed cat, fine-grained wood, many-tiered cake, stout-limbed toddler.* Many such compounds have become permanent hyphenated or solid compounds: *middle-aged, old-fashioned, lightheaded, kindhearted.*

12. Compound adjectives formed with a noun, adjective, or adverb and a present participle are hyphenated when the compound precedes the noun it modifies: *a bone-chilling tale, two good-looking sons, long-lasting friendship.* Many such compounds have become permanent solid compounds: *earsplitting, farseeing.* Many such compounds have become permanent and are hyphenated whether they precede or follow the noun they modify: *far-reaching consequences; The consequences are far-reaching.*

13. Compound nouns formed with a noun and a gerund are generally open: *crime solving, house hunting, trout fishing.* Many such compounds, however, have become permanent solid compounds: *faultfinding, housekeeping.*

14. Compound modifiers formed of capitalized words should not be hyphenated: *Old English poetry; Iron Age manufacture; New World plants.*

15. Usage is divided with regard to compounds that are proper names used to designate ethnic groups. Under normal circumstances such terms when used as nouns or adjectives should appear without a hyphen: *a group of African Americans, many Native Americans, French Canadians in Boston; a Jewish American organization, Latin American countries.* However, many (but not all) compounds of this type are now frequently hyphenated: *African-Americans, French-Canadian music.*

16. Nouns or adjectives consisting of a short verb and a preposition are either hyphenated or solid depending on current usage. The same words used as verbs are written separately: *a breakup* but *break up a fight; a bang-up job* but *bang up the car.*

17. Two nouns of equal value are hyphenated when the person or thing is considered to have the characteristics of both nouns: *secretary-treasurer, city-state, time-motion study.*

18. Compound forms must always reflect meaning. Consequently, some compounds may change in form depending on how they are used: *Anyone may go* but *Any one of these will do; Everyone is here* but *Every one of these is good.*

19. Scientific compounds are usually not hyphenated: *carbon monoxide poisoning; dichromic acid solution.*

Phrases

20. Phrases used as modifiers are normally hyphenated: *a happy-go-lucky person; a here-today-gone-tomorrow attitude.*

21. A foreign phrase used as a modifier is not hyphenated: *a bona fide offer; a per diem allowance.*

Numbers

22. Numbers from twenty-one to ninety-nine and adjective compounds with a numerical first element (whether spelled out or written in figures) are hyphenated: *twenty-one, thirty-first, second-rate movie, third-story window, three-dimensional figure, six-sided polygon, 13-piece band, 19th-century novel, decades-old newspapers.*

23. Spelled-out numbers used with *-fold* are not hyphenated; figures and *-fold* are hyphenated: *tenfold; 20-fold.*

24. Compounds of a number and *-odd* are hyphenated: *four-odd, 60-odd.*

25. Modifying compounds consisting of a number and a possessive noun are not hyphenated: *one week's pay; 35 hours' work.*

26. Fractions used as modifiers are hyphenated unless the numerator or denominator of the fraction contains a hyphen: *three-eighths inch; twenty-four hundredths part; The pie was one-half eaten.* Fractions used as nouns are usually not hyphenated: *He ate one half of the pie.*

Color

27. Compound color adjectives are hyphenated: *a red-gold sunset; a cherry-red sweater.*

28. Color compounds whose first element ends in *-ish* are hyphenated when they precede the noun, but not when they follow the noun: *a reddish-gold sunset; The sky is reddish gold.*

SOUND-SPELLING CORRESPONDENCES

This table, which is designed to help the user find a word known only through its pronunciation, lists the speech sounds of English and matches them with their possible spellings. Note that the letter *x* spells six sounds in English: ks, as in box, exit; gz, as in exact; sh, as in anxious; gzh, as in luxury; ksh, also as in luxury; and z, as in anxiety, xerography.

SOUND	SPELLING	SAMPLE WORDS
a (as in pat)	ai	plaid
	au	laugh
a (as in mane)	ae	maelstrom
	ai	pain
	ao	gaol
	au	gauge
	ay	pay
	e	suede
	ea	break
	ee	matinee, melee
	ei	vein, feign
	ey	prey
a (as in father)	ah	**ah**
	e	sergeant
	ea	heart
b (as in **bib**)	bb	blubber
	pb	cupboard
ch (as in **church**)	c	cello
	Cz	Czech
	tch	patch, stitch

SOUND	SPELLING	SAMPLE WORDS
ch (as in **church**)	ti	question
	tu	denture
d (as in **deed**)	dd	la**dd**er
	ed	mail**ed**
e (as in **pet**)	a	**a**ny
	ae	**ae**sthetic
	ai	s**ai**d
	ay	s**ay**s
	ea	thr**ea**d
	ei	h**ei**fer
	eo	l**eo**pard
	ie	fr**ie**ndly
	oe	r**oe**ntgen
	u	b**u**rial
e (as in **be**)	ae	C**ae**sar
	ay	qu**ay**
	ea	**ea**ch, b**ea**ch
	ee	b**ee**t
	ei	conc**ei**t
	eo	p**eo**ple
	ey	k**ey**
	i	p**i**ano, card**i**ac
	ie	s**ie**ge
	oe	ph**oe**nix
	y	ichth**y**osis, cit**y**
er (as in **certain**)	ear	p**ear**l, y**ear**n
	eur	restaurat**eur**
	ir	b**ir**d, f**ir**st
	or	w**or**k
	our	j**our**ney
	ur	b**ur**den
	yr	m**yr**tle

SOUND	SPELLING	SAMPLE WORDS
f (as in **fife**)	ff	sti**ff**
	gh	enou**gh**
	lf	ha**lf**
	ph	**ph**os**ph**ate
g (as in **gag**)	gg	bra**gg**ed
	gh	**gh**ost
	gu	**gu**est
h (as in **hat**)	wh	**wh**ole
	g	**G**ila monster
	j	**j**ai alai
i (as in **pit**)	a	vill**a**ge, clim**a**te
	e	**e**nough
	ee	b**ee**n
	ia	carr**ia**ge
	ie	s**ie**ve
	o	w**o**men
	u	b**u**sy
	ui	b**ui**lt
	y	c**y**st, phar**y**nx
i (as in **idle**)	ai	gu**ai**ac, **ai**sle
	ay	b**ay**ou
	ei	h**ei**ght, m**ei**osis
	ie	l**ie**
	uy	b**uy**
	y	sk**y**, l**y**re
	ye	r**ye**
j (as in **jar**)	d	gra**d**ual
	dg	lo**dg**ing
	di	sol**di**er
	dj	a**dj**ective
	g	**g**eriatric
	gg	exa**gg**erate

SOUND	SPELLING	SAMPLE WORDS
k (as in **k**ite)	c	**c**all, e**c**stasy
	cc	a**cc**ount
	cch	sa**cch**arin
	ch	**ch**orus
	ck	acknowledge
	cqu	la**cqu**er
	cu	bis**cu**it
	lk	ta**lk**
	q	Ira**q**i
	qu	**qu**ay
	que	pla**que**
l (as in **l**id)	ll	ta**ll**, **ll**ama
	lh	**Lh**asa apso
m (as in **m**um)	chm	dra**chm**
	gm	paradi**gm**
	lm	ba**lm**
	mb	plu**mb**
	mm	ha**mm**er
	mn	sole**mn**
n (as in **n**o)	gn	**gn**at, ali**gn**
	kn	**kn**ife
	mn	**mn**emonic
	nn	ca**nn**y, i**nn**
	pn	**pn**eumonia
o (as in **p**ot)	a	w**a**ffle, w**a**tch
	ho	**ho**nest
	ou	tr**ou**gh
o (as in n**o**)	au	m**au**ve
	eau	b**eau**, bur**eau**
	eo	y**eo**man
	ew	s**ew**
	oa	f**oa**l, f**oa**m
	oe	f**oe**

SOUND	SPELLING	SAMPLE WORDS
o (as in no)	oh	ohm
	oo	brooch
	ou	shoulder
	ough	borough, dough
	ow	low, row
	owe	owe
o (as in for)	a	all
	ah	Utahan
	au	caught, gaunt
	aw	awful
	oa	broad
	ough	bought
oi (as in noise)	oy	boy
ou (as in out)	au	sauerkraut
	hou	hour
	ough	bough
	ow	scowl, sow
oo (as in took)	o	woman, wolf
	ou	should
	u	cushion, full
oo (as in boot)	eu	leukemia
	ew	shrew
	ieu	lieutenant
	o	do, move, two
	oe	canoe
	ou	group, soup
	u	rude
	ue	blue, flue
	ui	bruise, fruit
p (as in pop)	pp	happy
r (as in roar)	rh	rhythm
	rr	cherry

SOUND	SPELLING	SAMPLE WORDS
r (as in **roar**)	rrh	cirrhosis
	wr	write
s (as in **say**)	c	cellar, medicine
	ps	psychology
	sc	sciatic, abscess
	sch	schism
	ss	pass, sassafras
	sth	isthmus
sh (as in **ship**)	ce	oceanic
	ch	chandelier
	ci	special
	s	sugar
	sc	conscience
	sch	schist
	se	nauseous
	si	pension
	ss	tissue, mission
	ti	election, nation
t (as in **tie**)	bt	debt
	ed	stopped
	ght	caught
	pt	ptomaine, receipt
	th	thyme
	tt	letter
u (as in **cut**)	o	son, income
	oe	does
	oo	blood
	ou	couple, trouble
u (as in **use**)	eau	beautiful
	eu	feud, eugenic
	eue	queue
	ew	pew
	ieu	adieu

SOUND	SPELLING	SAMPLE WORDS
u (as in **use**)	iew	**v**iew
	ue	c**ue**
	you	**you**th
	yu	**yu**le
v (as in **valve**)	f	o**f**
w (as in **with**)	o	**o**ne
	u	g**u**anese, q**u**ick
y (as in **yes**)	i	on**i**on
	j	hallelu**j**ah
z (as in **zebra**)	cz	**cz**ar
	s	ri**s**e, her**s**
	ss	de**ss**ert
	x	**x**ylem
	zz	fu**zz**

SPELL

CHECK

✔

A

aard'vark'
ab'a•ca'
a•back'
ab'a•cus *pl.* -cus•es
  or -ci'
a•baft'
ab'a•lo'ne
a•ban'don
a•ban'doned
a•base', a•based',
  a•bas'ing
a•base'ment
a•bash'
a•bate', a•bat'ed,
  a•bat'ing
a•bate'ment
ab'at•toir'
ab'bess
ab'bey *pl.* -beys
ab'bot
ab•bre'vi•ate',
  -at'ed, -at'ing
ab•bre'vi•a'tion
ab'di•cate', -cat'ed,
  -cat'ing
ab'di•ca'tion
ab'di•ca'tor
ab'do•men
ab•dom'i•nal
ab•duct'
ab•duc'tion
ab•duc'tor
a•beam'
a•bed'

Ab'e•na'ki *pl.* -ki *or*
  -kis
ab•er'rant
ab'er•ra'tion
a•bet', a•bet'ted,
  a•bet'ting
a•bet'tor *or*
  a•bet'ter
a•bey'ance
ab•hor', -horred',
  -hor'ring
ab•hor'rence
ab•hor'rent
a•bide', a•bode' *or*
  a•bid'ed, a•bid'ing
a•bil'i•ty
ab'ject'
ab'ju•ra'tion
ab•jure' *(to re-*
  nounce), -jured',
  -jur'ing
  ✓ *adjure*
ab•la'tion
a•blaze'
a'ble, a'bler, a'blest
a'ble-bod'ied
a•bloom'
ab•lu'tion
a'bly
ab'ne•gate',
  -gat'ed, -gat'ing
ab'ne•ga'tion
ab•nor'mal
ab'nor•mal'i•ty
a•board'
a•bode'

a•bol'ish
ab'o•li'tion
ab'o•li'tion•ist
A'-bomb'
a•bom'i•na•ble
a•bom'i•na•bly
a•bom'i•nate',
  -nat'ed, -nat'ing
a•bom'i•na'tion
ab'o•rig'i•nal
ab'o•rig'i•ne
a•bort'
a•bor'tion
a•bor'tive
a•bound'
a•bout'
a•bout'-face',
  -faced', -fac'ing
a•bove'
a•bove'board'
ab'ra•ca•dab'ra
a•brade', a•brad'ed,
  a•brad'ing
ab•ra'sion
ab•ra'sive
a•breast'
a•bridge',
  a•bridged',
  a•bridg'ing
a•bridg'ment *also*
  a•bridge'ment
a•broad'
ab'ro•gate', -gat'ed,
  -gat'ing
ab'ro•ga'tion
a•brupt'

ab'scess'
ab'scessed'
ab·scis'sa *pl.*
  -scis'sas *or* -scis'sae
ab·scis'sion
ab·scond'
ab'sence
ab'sent *adj.*
ab·sent' *v.*
ab'sen·tee'
ab'sen·tee'ism
ab'sent-mind'ed
ab'sinthe *also*
  ab'sinth
ab'so·lute'
ab'so·lute'ly
ab'so·lu'tion
ab'so·lut'ism
ab·solv'a·ble
ab·solve', -solved',
  -solv'ing
ab·sorb' *(to soak up)*
  ✔ adsorb
ab·sorbed'
ab·sorb'ent
ab·sorb'ing
ab·sorp'tion
ab·stain'
ab·ste'mi·ous
ab·sten'tion
ab'sti·nence
ab'sti·nent
ab'stract' *n.*
ab·stract' *v.*
ab·stract'ed
ab·strac'tion
ab·struse'

ab·surd'
ab·surd'i·ty
a·bun'dance
a·bun'dant
a·buse', a·bused',
  a·bus'ing
a·bus'er
a·bu'sive
a·but', a·but'ted,
  a·but'ting
a·but'ment
a·but'ter
a·buzz'
a·bys'mal *(deep,*
  limitless, bad)
  ✔ abyssal
a·byss'
a·bys'sal *(deep, relat-*
  ing to ocean depths)
  ✔ abysmal
a·ca'cia
ac'a·deme'
ac'a·de'mi·a
ac'a·dem'ic
ac'a·de·mi'cian
ac'a·dem'i·cism
  also a·cad'e·mism
a·cad'e·my
A·ca'di·an
a·can'thus *pl.*
  -thus·es *or* -thi'
a' cap·pel'la
ac·cede' *(to agree),*
  -ced'ed, -ced'ing
  ✔ exceed
ac·ced'ence
ac·cel'er·an'do

ac·cel'er·ant
ac·cel'er·ate',
  -at'ed, -at'ing
ac·cel'er·a'tion
ac·cel'er·a'tor
ac·cel'er·om'e·ter
ac'cent'
ac·cen'tu·al
ac·cen'tu·ate',
  -at'ed, -at'ing
ac·cen'tu·a'tion
ac·cept' *(to receive)*
  ✔ except
ac·cept'a·bil'i·ty
ac·cept'a·ble
ac·cept'a·bly
ac·cep'tance
ac·cep'tant
ac'cep·ta'tion
ac'cess *(entrance)*
  ✔ excess
ac·ces'si·bil'i·ty
ac·ces'si·ble
ac·ces'si·bly
ac·ces'sion
ac·ces·so'ri·al
ac·ces·so'ri·ly
ac·ces'so·rize',
  -ized', -iz'ing
ac·ces'so·ry
ac'ci·dent
ac'ci·den'tal
ac'ci·dent-prone'
ac·claim'
ac'cla·ma'tion
  (acclaim)
  ✔ acclimation

ac•clam′a•to′ry
ac′cli•mate′,
-mat′ed, -mat′ing
ac′cli•ma′tion
(adaptation)
✔ acclamation
ac•cli′ma•ti•za′tion
ac•cli′ma•tize′,
-tized′, -tiz′ing
ac•cliv′i•ty
ac′co•lade′
ac•com′mo•date′,
-dat′ed, -dat′ing
ac•com′mo•da′-
tion
ac•com′pa•ni•
ment
ac•com′pa•nist
ac•com′pa•ny,
-nied, -ny•ing
ac•com′plice
ac•com′plish
ac•com′plish•ment
ac•cord′
ac•cor′dance
ac•cord′ing•ly
ac•cor′di•on
ac•cost′
ac•count′
ac•count′a•bil′i•ty
ac•count′a•ble
ac•count′ant
ac•count′ing
ac•cou′ter or
ac•cou′tre, -tered or
-tred, -ter•ing or
-tre•ing

ac•cou′ter•ments
or ac•cou′tre•ments
ac•cred′it
ac•cred′i•ta′tion
ac•cre′tion
ac•cru′al
ac•crue′, -crued′,
-cru′ing
ac•cul′tur•ate′
ac•cul′tur•a′tion
ac•cu′mu•late′,
-lat′ed, -lat′ing
ac•cu′mu•la′tion
ac•cu′mu•la′tive
ac•cu′mu•la′tor
ac′cu•ra•cy
ac′cu•rate
ac•curs′ed also
ac•curst′
ac′cu•sa′tion
ac•cu′sa•tive
ac•cuse′, -cused′,
-cus′ing
ac•cus′er
ac•cus′tom
ace, aced, ac′ing
a•cer′bic also
a•cerb′
a•cer′bi•ty
ac′e•tal′
ac′et•al′de•hyde′
a•cet′a•min′o•
phen
ac′e•tate′
a•ce′tic (relating to
acetic acid)
✔ ascetic

ac′e•tone′
a•ce′tyl
a•cet′y•lene′
a•ce′tyl•sal′i•cyl′ic
ac′id
ache, ached, ach′ing
a•chieve′,
a•chieved′,
a•chiev′ing
a•chiev′er
a•chieve′ment
A•chil′les′ heel′
ach′ro•mat′ic
ach′y
ac′id
a•cid′ic
a•cid′i•fi•ca′tion
a•cid′i•fy′, -fied′,
-fy′ing
a•cid′i•ty
ac′i•do•phil′ic also
ac′i•doph′i•lus
a•cid′u•late′,
-lat′ed, -lat′ing
a•cid′u•la′tion
a•cid′u•lous
ac•knowl′edge,
-edged, -edg•ing
ac•knowl′edge•
a•ble
ac•knowl′edg•
ment or ac•knowl′-
edge•ment
ac′me
ac′ne
ac′o•lyte′
ac′o•nite′

a'corn'
a·cous'tic *also*
  a·cous'ti·cal
a·cous'tics
ac·quaint'
ac·quain'tance
ac·quain'tance·
  ship'
ac·quaint'ed
ac'qui·esce',
  -esced', -esc'ing
ac'qui·es'cence
ac'qui·es'cent
ac·quir'a·ble
ac·quire', -quired',
  -quir'ing
ac·quire'ment
ac'qui·si'tion
ac·quis'i·tive
ac·quis'i·tor
ac·quit', -quit'ted,
  -quit'ting
ac·quit'tal
ac·quit'tance
ac·quit'ter
a'cre
a'cre·age
a'cre-foot'
ac'rid
ac'ri·mo'ni·ous
ac'ri·mo'ny
ac'ro·bat'
ac'ro·bat'ic
ac'ro·nym'
a·crop'o·lis
a·cross'
a·cros'tic

a·cryl'ic
ACTH
ac'tin
act'ing
ac·tin'ic
ac'ti·nide'
ac'ti·nism
ac·tin'i·um
ac'tion
ac'tion·a·ble
ac'ti·vate', -vat'ed,
  -vat'ing
ac'ti·va'tion
ac'ti·va'tor
ac'tive
ac'tive·ly
ac'tiv·ism
ac'tiv·ist
ac·tiv'i·ty
ac'tor
ac'tress
ac'tu·al
ac'tu·al'i·ty
ac'tu·al·ly
ac'tu·ar'y
ac'tu·ate', -at'ed,
  -at'ing
ac'tu·a'tion
ac'tu·a'tor
a·cu'i·ty
a·cu'men
ac'u·punc'ture
a·cute'
ad *(advertisement)*
  ✔ add
ad'age
a·da'gio

ad'a·mant
Ad'am's ap'ple
a·dapt' *(to adjust)*
  ✔ adept, adopt
a·dapt'a·bil'i·ty
a·dapt'a·ble
ad'ap·ta'tion
a·dapt'ed
a·dapt'er *also*
  a·dap'tor
a·dap'tive
add *(to combine)*
  ✔ ad
ad'dax'
ad'dend'
ad·den'dum *pl.* -da
add'er *(one that
  adds)*
ad'der *(snake)*
ad·dict' *v.*
ad'dict' *n.*
ad·dict'ed
ad·dic'tion
ad·dic'tive
ad·di'tion *(adding)*
  ✔ edition
ad·di'tion·al
ad'di·tive
ad'dle, -dled, -dling
ad·dress'
ad'dress·ee'
ad·duce', -duced',
  -duc'ing
ad·duct'
ad·duc'tion
ad'e·nine'
ad'e·noi'dal

ad'e•noids'
a•dept' *(skillful)*
  ✔ adapt, adopt
ad'ept' *(skilled person)*
ad'e•qua•cy
ad'e•quate
ad'e•quate•ly
ad•here' *(to stick)*,
  -hered', -her'ing
  ✔ cohere
ad•her'ence
ad•her'ent
ad•he'sion
ad•he'sive
ad hoc'
ad'i•a•bat'ic
a•dieu' *(farewell)*, pl.
  a•dieus' or a•dieux'
  ✔ ado
ad in'fi•ni'tum
ad'i•os'
ad'i•pose'
ad•ja'cent
ad'jec•ti'val
ad'jec•tive
ad•join'
ad•join'ing
ad•journ'
ad•journ'ment
ad•judge',
  -judged', -judg'ing
ad•ju'di•cate',
  -cat'ed, -cat'ing
ad•ju'di•ca'tion
ad•ju'di•ca'tive
ad•ju'di•ca'tor

ad'junct'
ad'ju•ra'tion
ad•jure' *(to command)*, -jured',
  -jur'ing
  ✔ abjure
ad•just'
ad•just'a•ble
ad•just'er
ad•just'ment
ad'ju•tant
ad-lib', -libbed',
  -lib'bing
ad•min'is•ter
ad•min'is•trate',
  -trat'ed, -trat'ing
ad•min'is•tra'tion
ad•min'is•tra'tive
ad•min'is•tra'tor
ad'mi•ra•ble
ad'mi•ra•bly
ad'mi•ral
ad'mi•ral•ty
ad'mi•ra'tion
ad•mire', -mired',
  -mir'ing
ad•mir'er
ad•mis'si•bil'i•ty
ad•mis'si•ble
ad•mis'si•bly
ad•mis'sion
ad•mit', -mit'ted,
  -mit'ting
ad•mit'tance
ad•mit'ted•ly
ad•mix'
ad•mix'ture

ad•mon'ish
ad•mon'ish•ment
ad'mo•ni'tion
ad•mon'i•to'ry
ad nau'se•am
a•do' *(fuss)*
  ✔ adieu
a•do'be
ad'o•les'cence
ad'o•les'cent
A•don'is or a•don'is
a•dopt' *(to take as one's own)*
  ✔ adapt, adept
a•dopt'a•ble
a•dop'tion
a•dop'tive
a•dor'a•ble
a•dor'a•bly
ad'o•ra'tion
a•dore', a•dored',
  a•dor'ing
a•dor'er
a•dorn'
ad•re'nal
a•dren'a•line
a•drift'
a•droit'
ad•sorb' *(to accumulate on a surface)*
  ✔ absorb
ad•sorp'tion
ad'u•late', -lat'ed,
  -lat'ing
ad'u•la'tion
ad'u•la'tor
ad'u•la•to'ry

a·dult'
a·dul'ter·ant
a·dul'ter·ate',
  -at'ed, -at'ing
a·dul'ter·a'tion
a·dul'ter·er
a·dul'ter·ess
a·dul'ter·ous
a·dul'ter·y
a·dult'hood'
ad'um·brate'
ad'um·bra'tion
ad·vance',
  -vanced', -vanc'ing
ad·vance'ment
ad·van'tage
ad'van·ta'geous
ad'vent'
Ad'vent·ism
Ad'vent·ist
ad'ven·ti'tious
ad·ven'ture, -tured,
  -tur·ing
ad·ven'tur·er
ad·ven'ture·some
ad·ven'tur·ous
ad'verb
ad·ver'bi·al
ad'ver·sar'y
ad·verse' *(hostile)*
  ✔ *averse*
ad·ver'si·ty
ad·vert'
ad'ver·tise, -tised',
  -tis'ing
ad'ver·tise'ment
ad'ver·tis'er

ad'ver·tis'ing
ad·vice' *(guidance)*
  ✔ *advise*
ad·vis'a·bil'i·ty
ad·vis'a·ble
ad·vis'a·bly
ad·vise' *(to give
  advice)*, -vised',
  -vis'ing
  ✔ *advice*
ad·vis'ed·ly
ad·vise'ment
ad·vis'er *or* ad·vi'-
  sor
ad·vi'so·ry
ad'vo·ca·cy
ad'vo·cate', -cat'ed,
  -cat'ing
ad'vo·cate *n.*
ad'vo·ca'tion
ad'vo·ca'tor
adz *or* adze
ae'gis *also* e'gis
aer'ate', -at'ed,
  -at'ing
aer·a'tion
aer'a'tor
aer'i·al
aer'i·al·ist
aer'ie *or* aer'y *also*
  ey'rie *or* ey'ry
  (nest), pl. aer'ies
  also ey'ries
  ✔ *airy, eerie*
aer'obe'
aer·o'bic
aer'o·dy·nam'ic

also aer'o·dy·
  nam'i·cal
aer·ol'o·gy
aer'o·nau'tic *also*
  aer'o·nau'ti·cal
aer'o·pause'
aer'o·sol'
aer'o·space'
aes'thete *or*
  es'thete
aes·thet'ic *or*
  es·thet'ic
aes'the·ti'cian *or*
  es'the·ti'cian
aes·thet'i·cism *or*
  es·thet'i·cism
aes·thet'ics *or*
  es·thet'ics
a·far'
af'fa·bil'i·ty
af'fa·ble
af'fa·bly
af·fair'
af·fect' *(to influence,
  to pretend)*
  ✔ *effect*
af'fec·ta'tion
af·fect'ed
af·fect'ing
af·fec'tion
af·fec'tion·ate
af·fec'tive
af·fer'ent
af·fi'ance, -anced,
  -anc·ing
af·fi·da'vit
af·fil'i·ate', -at'ed,

-at'ing
af·fil'i·a'tion
af·fin'i·ty
af·firm'
af·fir·ma'tion
af·fir'ma·tive
af·fix' *v.*
af·fix' *n.*
af·flict'
af·flic'tion
af·flu·ence
af·flu·ent
af·ford'
af·ford'a·ble
af·fray'
at·fright'
af·front'
Af'ghan' *(person, dog)*
af'ghan' *(blanket)*
a·fi'cio·na'do *pl. -dos*
a·field'
a·fire'
a·flame'
a·float'
a·flut'ter
a·foot'
a·fore'
a·fore'men'tioned
a·fore'said'
a·fore'thought'
a for'ti·o'ri
a·foul'
a·fraid'
A'-frame'
a·fresh'

Af'ri·can
Af'ri·can-
   A·mer'i·can *or*
   Af'ri·can
   A·mer'i·can
Af'ri·kaans'
Af'ri·ka'ner
Af'ro *pl. -ros*
Af'ro-A·mer'i·can
Af'ro-A'si·at'ic
af'ter
af'ter all' *also*
   af'ter·all'
af'ter·birth'
af'ter·burn'er
af'ter·care'
af'ter·deck'
af'ter·ef·fect'
af'ter·glow'
af'ter·im'age
af'ter·life'
af'ter·math'
af'ter·noon'
af'ter·shock'
af'ter·taste'
af'ter·thought'
af'ter·ward *also*
   af'ter·wards
af'ter·world'
a·gain'
a·gainst'
a·gape'
a'gar' *also*
   a'gar'-a'gar'
ag'ate
a·ga've
age, aged, ag'ing

aged *(of the age of)*
ag'ed *(elderly)*
age'ism *also* ag'ism
age'ist
age'less
a'gen·cy
a·gen'da *pl. -das*
a·gen'dum *pl. -da*
   also -dums
a'gent
age'-old'
ag·glom'er·ate',
   -at'ed, -at'ing
ag·glom'er·a'tion
ag·glu'ti·nate',
   -nat'ed, -nat'ing
ag·glu'ti·na'tion
ag·glu'ti·na'tive
ag·gran'dize',
   -dized', -diz'ing
ag·gran'dize·ment
ag·gran'diz'er
ag'gra·vate',
   -vat'ed, -vat'ing
ag'gra·va'tion
ag'gra·va'tor
ag'gre·gate',
   -gat'ed, -gat'ing
ag'gre·ga'tion
ag·gres'sion
ag·gres'sive
ag·gres'sor
ag·grieved'
a·ghast'
ag'ile
ag'ile·ly
a·gil'i·ty

ag′i•tate′, -tat′ed,
  -tat′ing
ag′i•ta′tion
ag′i•ta′tor
a•gleam′
a•glit′ter
a•glow′
ag•nos′tic
ag•nos′ti•cal•ly
ag•nos′ti•cism
a•go′
a•gog′
ag′o•nize′, -nized′,
  -niz′ing
ag′o•ny
ag′o•ra pl. -o•rae′ or
  -o•ras
ag′o•ra•pho′bi•a
ag′o•ra•pho′bic
a•gou′ti pl. -tis
a•grar′i•an
a•gree′, a•greed′,
  a•gree′ing
a•gree′a•ble
a•gree′a•bly
a•gree′ment
ag′ri•busi′ness
ag′ri•cul′tur•al
ag′ri•cul′ture
ag′ri•cul′tur•ist
ag′ro•nom′ic or
  ag′ro•nom′i•cal
a•gron′o•mist
a•gron′o•my
a•ground′
a′gue
ah

a•ha′
a•head′
a•hem′
a•hoy′
aid (to help)
aide (assistant)
aide′-de-camp′ pl.
  aides′-de-camp′
AIDS
ai•grette′ or ai•gret′
ai′ki•do′
ail (to be ill)
  ✔ ale
ai•lan′thus
ai′le•ron′
ail′ment
aim
aim′less
Ai′nu pl. -nu or -nus
air (gas)
  ✔ are, e′er, ere, heir
air′ bag′
air′ base′
air′ blad′der
air′borne′
air′ brake′
air′brush′
air′-con•di′tion
air′-con•di′tioned
air′ con•di′tion•er
air′ con•di′tion•ing
air′-cooled′
air′craft′ pl.
  -craft′
air′craft car′rier
air′drome′
air′drop′, -dropped′,

-drop′ping
Aire′dale′
air′field′
air′flow′
air′foil′
air′ force′
air′ glow′
air′ gun′
air′ hammer′
air′ hole′
air′i•ly
air′i•ness
air′ing
air′ lane′
air′ let′ter
air′lift′
air′line′
air′lin′er
air′ lock′
air′mail′ v.
air′mail′ or air′
  mail′ n.
air′man
air′plane′
air′port′
air′pow′er or air′
  pow′er
air′ shaft′
air′ship′
air′sick′
air′sick′ness
air′space′ or air′
  space′
air′ speed′
air′strip′
air′tight′
air′time′

air'-to-air'
air'-to-sur'face
air'waves'
air'way'
air'wor'thi·ness
air'wor'thy
air'y *(relating to air)*
  ✔ aerie
aisle *(passageway)*
  ✔ isle
a·jar'
a·kim'bo
a·kin'
Al'a·ba'mi·an *or*
  Al'a·bam'an
al'a·bas'ter
à' la carte' *also* a' la
  carte'
a·lack'
a·lac'ri·ty
al'a·me'da
à' la mode'
a·larm'
a·larm'ing
a·larm'ist
a·la'rum
a·las'
A·las'kan
alb
al'ba·core' *pl.* -core'
  or -cores'
Al·ba'ni·an
al'ba·tross' *pl.*
  -tross' *or*
  -tross'es
al·be'it
al'bi·nism

al·bi'no *pl.* -nos
al'bum
al·bu'men *(egg*
  white)
al·bu'min *(protein)*
al·chem'i·cal *or*
  al·chem'ic
al'che·mist
al'che·my
al'co·hol'
al'co·hol'ic
al'co·hol·ism
al'cove'
al'de·hyde'
al'der
al'der·man
ale *(beverage)*
  ✔ ail
a·lee'
a·lert'
A·leut' *pl.* A·leut' *or*
  A·leuts'
A·leu'tian
ale'wife' *pl.* -wives'
Al'ex·an'dri·an
al·fal'fa
al·fres'co
al'ga *pl.* -gae
al'ge·bra
al'ge·bra'ic
Al·ge'ri·an
Al·gon'quin *pl.*
  -quin *or* -quins
al'go·rithm
a'li·as
al'i·bi' *pl.* -bis'
a'li·en

al'ien·a·ble
al'ien·ate', -at'ed,
  -at'ing
al'ien·a'tion
al'ien·a'tor
a·light', a·light'ed
  or a·lit', a·light'ing
a·lign' *also* a·line',
  a·ligned' *also*
  a·lined', a·lign'ing
  also a·lin'ing
a·lign'ment *also*
  a·line'ment
a·like'
al'i·men'ta·ry
al'i·mo'ny
al'i·phat'ic
a·live'
al'ka·li' *pl.* -lis' *or*
  -lies'
al'ka·line
al'ka·line-earth'
  met'al
al'ka·lin'i·ty
al'ka·lize' *also*
  al'ka·lin·ize', -lized'
  also -lin·ized',
  -liz'ing *also*
  -lin·iz'ing
al'ka·loid'
all *(total)*
  ✔ awl
all'-A·mer'i·can
al·lan'to·is *pl.*
  al'lan·to'i·des'
al'lan·to'i·des'
all'-a·round' *also*
  all'-round'

al·lay'
al·le·ga'tion
al·leg'a·ble
al·lege' -leged',
 -leg'ing
al·leged'
al·leg'ed·ly
al·le'giance
al·le·gor'i·cal
al·le·gor'ist
al·le'go'ry
al·le·gret'to
al·le'gro
al·lele'
al·le'lic
al·le·lu'ia
al'ler·gen
al·ler·gen'ic
al·ler'gic
al'ler·gist
al'ler·gy
al·le'vi·ate' -at'ed,
 -at'ing
al·le'vi·a'tion
al·le'vi·a'tor
al'ley (passageway),
 pl. -leys
 ✔ ally
al'ley·way'
al·li'ance
al·lied'
al'li·ga'tor
all'-im·por'tant
al·lit'er·ate' -at'ed,
 -at'ing
al·lit'er·a'tion
al·lit'er·a'tive

all'-night'
al'lo·cate', -cat'ed,
 -cat'ing
al'lo·ca'tion
al·lot', -lot'ted,
 -lot'ting
al·lot'ment
al'lo·trope'
al'lo·trop'ic
al·lot'ro·py
al·lot'ter
all' out' adv.
all'-out' adj.
all' o'ver adv.
all'-o'ver also
 all'o'ver adj.
al·low'
al·low'a·ble
al·low'a·bly
al·low'ance
al'loy' n.
al·loy' v.
all'-pur'pose
all read'y (com-
 pletely prepared)
 ✔ already
all' right'
all'spice'
all'-star' adj. & n.
all'-time' adj.
all' to·geth'er
 (collectively)
 ✔ altogether
al·lude' (to refer to),
 -lud'ed, -lud'ing
 ✔ elude
al·lure', -lured',

-lur'ing
al·lu'sion (reference)
 ✔ illusion
al·lu'sive (sugges-
 tive)
 ✔ elusive, illusive
al·lu'vi·al
al·lu'vi·um pl.
 -vi·ums or -vi·a
al·ly', -lied', -ly'ing
al'ly (friend)
 ✔ alley
al'ma ma'ter
al'ma·nac'
al·might'y
al'mond
al'mo·ner
al'most'
alms
alms'house'
al·ni'co'
al'oe
al'oe ver'a
a·loft'
a·lo'ha
a·lone'
a·long'
a·long'side'
a·loof'
a·loud'
alp
al·pac'a pl. -pac'a or
 -pac'as
al'pen·horn'
al'pen·stock'
al'pha
al'pha·bet'

al'pha•bet'i•cal
  also al'pha•bet'ic
al'pha•bet'i•za'-
  tion
al'pha•bet•ize',
  -ized', -iz'ing
al'pha•bet•iz'er
al'pha•nu•mer'ic
al'pine' *(relating to*
  high mountains)
Al'pine' *(relating to*
  the Alps)
al•read'y *(by this*
  time)
  ✔ all ready
Al•sa'tian
al'so
al'so•ran'
al'tar *(religious table)*
  ✔ alter
al'tar•piece'
al'ter *(to change)*
  ✔ altar
al'ter•a•ble
al'ter•a•bly
al'ter•a'tion
al'ter•ca'tion
al'ter e'go
al'ter•nate',
  -nat'ed, -nat'ing
al'ter•nate *adj.*
al'ter•na'tion
al•ter'na•tive
al'ter•na'tor
al•though' *also*
  al•tho'
al•tim'e•ter

al'ti•tude'
al'to *pl.* -tos
al'to•cu'mu•lus
al'to•geth'er
  (completely)
  ✔ all together
al'to•stra'tus
al'tru•ism
al'tru•ist
al'tru•is'tic
al'um
a•lu'mi•na
a•lu'mi•num
a•lum'na *pl.* -nae'
a•lum'nus *pl.* -ni'
al•ve'o•lar
al•ve'o•lus *pl.* -li'
al'ways
a•lys'sum
Alz'heim•er's
  dis•ease'
a•mal'gam
a•mal'ga•mate',
  -mat'ed, -mat'ing
a•mal'ga•ma'tion
a•mal'ga•ma'tor
am'a•ni'ta
a•man'u•en'sis *pl.*
  -ses
am'a•ranth'
am'a•ryl'lis
a•mass'
a•mass'a•ble
a•mass'er
am'a•teur'
am'a•teur'ish
am'a•to'ry

a•maze', a•mazed',
  a•maz'ing
a•maz'ed•ly
a•maze'ment
Am'a•zon' *also*
  am'a•zon'
Am'a•zo'ni•an
  (relating to the
  Amazon River)
am'a•zo'ni•an
  (resembling an
  Amazon)
am•bas'sa•dor
am'ber
am'ber•gris'
am'bi•ance *also*
  am'bi•ence
am'bi•dex•ter'i•ty
am'bi•dex'trous
am'bi•ent
am'bi•gu'i•ty
am•big'u•ous
am•bi'tion
am•bi'tious
am•biv'a•lence
am•biv'a•lent
am'ble, -bled, -bling
am'bler
am•bro'sia
am•bro'sial
am'bu•lance
am'bu•la•to'ry
am'bus•cade'
  -cad'ed, -cad'ing
am'bush
a•me'lio•rate',
  -rat'ed, -rat'ing

a•me'lio•ra'tion
a•me'lio•ra'tor
a•men'
a•me'na•bil'i•ty *or*
  a•me'na•ble•ness
a•me'na•ble
a•me'na•bly
a•mend' *(to improve)*
  ✔ emend
a•mend'ment
a•mends'
a•men'i•ty
Am'er•a'sian
A•mer'i•can
A•mer'i•ca'na
A•mer'i•can
  In'di•an *n.*
A•mer'i•can-
  In'di•an *adj.*
A•mer'i•can•ism
A•mer'i•can•i•za'-
  tion
A•mer'i•can•ize',
  -ized', -iz'ing
am'er•i'ci•um
Am'er•in'di•an *also*
  Am'er•ind'
am'e•thyst
a'mi•a•bil'i•ty
a'mi•a•ble
a'mi•a•bly
am'i•ca•bil'i•ty
am'i•ca•ble
am'i•ca•bly
a•mid' *also* a•midst'
am'ide'
a•mid'ships' *also*

a•mid'ship'
a•mi'go *pl.* -gos
a•mine'
a•mi'no ac'id
A'mish
a•miss'
am'i•ty
am'me'ter
am'mo
am•mo'nia
am•mo'ni•um
am'mu•ni'tion
am•ne'sia
am•nes•ty
am'ni•o•cen•te'sis
  pl. -ses
am'ni•on *pl.*
  -ni•ons *or* -ni•a
am'ni•ot'ic
a•moe'ba *also*
  a•me'ba *pl.* -bas *or*
  -bae
a•moe'bic
a•mong' *also*
  a•mongst'
a•mor'al
a'mo•ral'i•ty
a•mor'ous
a•mor'phous
am•or•ti•za'tion
am•or•tize', -tized',
  -tiz'ing
a•mount'
a•mour'
amp
am'per•age
am'pere'

am'per•sand'
am•phet'a•mine'
am•phib'i•an
am•phib'i•ous
am'phi•bole'
am'phi•the'a•ter
am•phor•a *pl.*
  -pho•rae' *or*
  -pho•ras
am'ple, -pler, -plest
am'pli•fi•ca'tion
am'pli•fi'er
am'pli•fy', -fied',
  -fy'ing
am'pli•tude'
am'ply
am'poule *also*
  am'pule *or* am'pul
am'pu•tate',
  -tat'ed, -tat'ing
am'pu•ta'tion
am'pu•ta'tor
am'pu•tee'
a•muck' *also*
  a•mok'
am'u•let
a•mus'a•ble
a•muse', a•mused',
  a•mus'ing
a•muse'ment
a•mus'ing
am'yl
am'y•lase'
An'a•bap'tist
an'a•bol'ic
a•nab'o•lism
a•nach'ro•nism

a•nach'ro•nis'tic
an'a•con'da
an'aer•obe'
an'aer•o'bic
an'a•gram'
a'nal
an'al•ge'si•a
an'al•ge'sic
an'a•log'
  com•pu'ter
a•nal'o•gous
an'a•logue' *also*
  an'a•log'
a•nal'o•gy
a•nal'y•sis *pl.*
  -ses'
an'a•lyst
an'a•lyt'ic *or*
  an'a•lyt'i•cal
an'a•lyz'a•ble
an'a•ly•za'tion
an'a•lyze', -lyzed',
  -lyz'ing
an'a•lyz'er
an'a•pest'
an'a•phase'
an'a•phy•lac'tic
an'a•phy•lax'is
an•ar'chic *or*
  an•ar'chi•cal
an'ar•chism
an'ar•chist
an'ar•chis'tic
an'ar•chy
A'na•sa'zi *pl.* -zi
a•nath'e•ma *pl.*
  -mas

a•nath'e•ma•ti•za'-
  tion
a•nath'e•ma•tize',
  -tized', -tiz'ing
an'a•tom'i•cal *also*
  an'a•tom'ic
a•nat'o•mist
a•nat'o•mi•za'tion
a•nat'o•mize',
  -mized', -miz'ing
a•nat'o•my
an'ces•tor
an•ces'tral
an'ces•try
an'chor
an'chor•age
an'cho•rite'
an'chor•man
an'chor•per'son
an'chor•wom'an
an'cho'vy *pl.* -vy
an'cient
an'cil•lar'y
an•dan'te
and'i'ron
an'dro•gen
an'dro•gen'ic
an•drog'y•nous
an•drog'y•ny
an'droid'
an'ec•dot'al
an'ec•dote'
a•ne'mi•a *also*
  a•nae'mi•a
a•ne'mic *also*
  a•nae'mic
an'e•mom'e•ter

a•nem'o•ne
an'es•the'sia *also*
  an'aes•the'sia
an'es•the•si•ol'o•
  gist *also* an'aes•
  the•si•ol'o•gist
an'es•the•si•ol'o•
  gy *also* an'aes•
  the•si•ol'o•gy
an'es•thet'ic *also*
  an'aes•thet'ic
a•nes'the•tist *also*
  a•naes'the•tist
a•nes'the•ti•za'tion
a•nes'the•tize' *also*
  a•naes'the•tize',
  -tized', -tiz'ing
an'eu•rysm *also*
  an'eu•rism
a•new'
an'gel
An'ge•le'no *pl.*
  -nos
an'gel•fish'
an'gel food' cake'
an•gel'ic *also*
  an•gel'i•cal
an'ger
an•gi'na
an•gi'na pec'to•ris
an'gi•o•sperm'
an'gle, -gled, -gling
an'gler
an'gler•fish'
an'gle•worm'
An'gli•can
An'gli•can•ism

An'gli•cize', -cized',
  -ciz'ing
an'gling
An'glo *pl.* -glos
An'glo-
  A•mer'i•can
An'glo-French'
An'glo-Nor'man
An'glo-Sax'on
An•go'ra *(animal)*
an•go'ra *(yarn)*
an'gri•ly
an'gri•ness
an'gry
angst
ang'strom
an'guish
an'guished
an'gu•lar
an'gu•lar'i•ty
an•hy'dride
an•hy'drous
an'i•line *also*
  an'i•lin
an'i•mad•ver'sion
an'i•mal
an'i•mal'cule
an'i•mate', -mat'ed,
  -mat'ing
an'i•mat'ed•ly
an'i•ma'tion
a'ni•ma'to
an'i•ma'tor
an'i•mism
an'i•mos'i•ty
an'i•mus
an'i•on

an'ise
an'ise seed' *or*
  an'i•seed'
an'kle
an'kle•bone'
an'klet
an'nals
an•neal'
an'ne•lid
an•nex' *v.*
an'nex' *n.*
an•nex•a'tion
an•ni'hi•late',
  -lat'ed, -lat'ing
an•ni'hi•la'tion
an•ni'hi•la'tive
an•ni'hi•la'tor
an'ni•ver'sa•ry
an'no Dom'i•ni'
an'no•tate', -tat'ed,
  -tat'ing
an'no•ta'tion
an'no•ta'tive
an'no•ta'tor
an•nounce',
  -nounced',
  -nounc'ing
an•nounce'ment
an•nounc'er
an•noy'
an•noy'ance
an•noy'er
an•noy'ing
an'nu•al
an•nu'i•ty
an•nul', -nulled',
  -nul'ling

an'nu•lar
an•nul'ment
an'nu•lus *pl.*
  -lus•es *or* -li'
an•nun'ci•ate' *(to*
  announce), -at'ed,
  -at'ing
  ✔ *enunciate*
an•nun'ci•a'tion
an'ode'
an'o•dyne'
a•noint'
a•noint'ment
a•nom'a•lous
a•nom'a•ly
a•non'
an'o•nym'i•ty
a•non'y•mous
a•noph'e•les'
an'o•rec'tic
an'o•rex'i•a
  nerv•o'sa
an'o•rex'ic
an•oth'er
an•ox'i•a
an'swer
an'swer•ing
  ma•chine'
ant *(insect)*
  ✔ *aunt*
ant•ac'id
an•tag'o•nism
an•tag'o•nist
an•tag'o•nis'tic
an•tag'o•nize',
  -nized', -niz'ing
Ant•arc'tic

an'te, -ted *or* -teed,
-te•ing
ant'eat'er
an'te•bel'lum
an'te•ce'dent
an'te•cham'ber
an'te•date', -dat'ed,
-dat'ing
an'te•di•lu'vi•an
an'te•lope' *pl.*
-lope' *or* -lopes'
an'te me•rid'i•em
an•ten'na *pl.* -nae
or -nas
an'te•pe'nult *n.*
an'te•pe•nul'ti•
mate *adj. & n.*
an•te'ri•or
an'te•room'
an'them
an'ther
ant'hill'
an•thol'o•gist
an•thol'o•gize',
-gized', -giz'ing
an•thol'o•gy
an'thra•cite'
an'thrax'
an'thro•po•cen'tric
an'thro•poid'
an'thro•po•log'i•
cal
an'thro•pol'o•gist
an'thro•pol'o•gy
an'thro•po•mor'-
phic
an'thro•po•mor'-

phism
an'ti•a•bor'tion
an'ti•air'craft'
an'ti•bal•lis'tic
mis'sile
an'ti•bi•ot'ic
an'ti•bod'y
an'tic
an'ti•christ'
an•tic'i•pate',
-pat'ed, -pat'ing
an•tic'i•pa'tion
an•tic'i•pa'tor
an•tic'i•pa•to'ry
an'ti•cler'i•cal
an'ti•cli•mac'tic
an'ti•cli'max
an'ti•cli'nal
an'ti•cline'
an'ti•co•ag'u•lant
an'ti•cy'clone'
an'ti•de•pres'sant
an'ti•do'tal
an'ti•dote'
an'ti•freeze'
an'ti•gen *also*
an'ti•gene'
an'ti•gen'ic
an'ti•grav'i•ty
an'ti•he'ro *pl.* -roes
an'ti•her'o•ine *or*
an'ti•her'o•ine
an'ti•his'ta•mine'
an'ti•knock'
an'ti•log'
an'ti•log'a•rithm
an'ti•ma•cas'sar

an'ti•mat'ter
an'ti•mis'sile
an'ti•mo'ny
an'ti•neu•tri'no *pl.*
-nos
an'ti•neu'tron'
an'ti•nu'cle•ar
an'ti•ox'i•dant
an'ti•par'ti•cle
an'ti•pas'to *pl.* -tos
or -ti
an•tip'a•thet'ic
also an•tip'a•thet'i•
cal
an•tip'a•thy
an'ti•per'spi•rant
an'ti•phon'
an•tiph'o•nal
an•tiph'o•ny
an•tip'o•dal
an•tip'o•des'
an'ti•pov'er•ty
an'ti•pro'ton
an'ti•py•ret'ic
an'ti•quar'i•an
an'ti•quar'y
an'ti•quate',
-quat'ed, -quat'ing
an•tique', -tiqued',
-tiqu'ing
an•tiq'ui•ty
an'ti-Se•mit'ic
an'ti-Sem'i•tism
an'ti•sep'tic
an'ti•slav'er•y
an'ti•so'cial
an'ti•tank'

an•tith'e•sis *pl.* -ses'
an'ti•thet'i•cal *also*
  an'ti•thet'ic
an'ti•tox'in
an'ti•trades'
an'ti•trust'
an'ti•ven'in
an'ti•vi'ral
an'ti•war'
ant'ler
an'to•nym'
ant'sy
a'nus *pl.* a'nus•es
an'vil
anx•i'e•ty
anx'ious
an'y
an'y•bod'y
an'y•how'
an'y•more'
an'y•one'
an'y•place'
an'y•thing'
an'y•time'
an'y•way'
an'y•where'
A'-OK'
A'-one'
a•or'ta *pl.* -tas *or* -tae
a•pace'
A•pach'e *pl.*
  A•pach'e *or* -es
a•part'
a•part'heid'
a•part'ment
ap'a•thet'ic
ap'a•thy

ape, aped, ap'ing
a•pé'ri•tif'
ap'er•ture
a'pex *pl.* a'pex•es *or*
  a'pi•ces'
a•pha'sia
a•pha'sic
a•phe'li•on *pl.* -li•a
a'phid
aph'o•rism
aph'o•ris'tic
aph•ro•dis'i•ac'
a'pi•ar'y
a'pi•cal
a•piece'
ap'ish
a•plen'ty
a•plomb'
a•poc'a•lypse'
a•poc'a•lyp'tic *also*
  a•poc'a•lyp'ti•cal
A•poc'ry•pha
  (Biblical books)
a•poc'ry•pha *(writ-*
  ings of questionable
  authority)
A•poc'ry•phal
  (relating to the
  Apocrypha)
a•poc'ry•phal *(of*
  questionable
  authority)
ap'o•gee
a•pol'o•get'ic
a•pol'o•gist
a•pol'o•gize',
  -gized', -giz'ing

a•pol'o•gy
ap'o•plec'tic
ap'o•plex'y
a•pos'ta•sy
a•pos'tate'
a•pos'tle
ap'os•tol'ic
a•pos'tro•phe
a•pos'tro•phize',
  -phized', -phiz'ing
a•poth'e•car'ies'
  meas'ure
a•poth'e•car'y
ap'o•thegm' *also*
  ap'o•phthegm'
  (maxim)
ap'o•them' *(geomet-*
  ric distance)
a•poth'e•o'sis *pl.*
  -ses'
ap•pall'
ap•pall'ing
ap•pa•loo'sa
ap•pa•ra'tus *pl.* -tus
  or -tus•es
ap•par'el, -eled *or*
  -elled, -el•ing *or*
  -el•ling
ap•par'ent
ap•pa•ri'tion
ap•peal'
ap•peal'ing
ap•pear'
ap•pear'ance
ap•pease', -peased',
  -peas'ing
ap•pease'ment

ap·pel'lant
ap·pel'late
ap'pel·la'tion
ap·pend'
ap·pend'age
ap·pen·dec'to·my
ap·pen'di·ci'tis
ap·pen'dix *pl.*
  -dix·es *or* -di·ces'
ap'per·tain'
ap'pe·tite'
ap'pe·tiz'er
ap'pe·tiz'ing
ap·plaud'
ap·plaud'a·ble
ap·plaud'er
ap·plause'
ap'ple
ap'ple but'ter
ap'ple·jack'
ap'ple·sauce'
ap·pli'ance
ap'pli·ca·bil'i·ty
ap'pli·ca·ble
ap'pli·ca·bly
ap'pli·cant
ap'pli·ca'tion
ap'pli·ca'tor
ap·plied'
ap·pli'er
ap'pli·qué', -quéd',
  -qué'ing
ap·ply', -plied',
  -ply'ing
ap·point'
ap·point'ee'
ap·point'ive

ap·point'ment
ap·por'tion
ap·por'tion·ment
ap·pose' *(to juxta-*
  pose), -posed',
  -pos'ing
  ✔ *oppose*
ap'po·site *(appro-*
  priate)
  ✔ *opposite*
ap'po·si'tion
ap·pos'i·tive
ap·prais'al
ap·praise',
  -praised', -prais'ing
ap·prais'er
ap·pre'cia·ble
ap·pre'cia·bly
ap·pre'ci·ate',
  -at'ed, -at'ing
ap·pre'ci·a'tion
ap·pre'cia·tive
ap·pre'ci·a'tor
ap'pre·hend'
ap'pre·hen'sion
ap'pre·hen'sive
ap·pren'tice, -ticed,
  -tic·ing
ap·pren'tice·ship'
ap·prise', -prised',
  -pris'ing
ap·proach'
ap·proach'a·bil'i·
  ty
ap·proach'a·ble
ap'pro·ba'tion
ap·pro'pri·ate',

-at'ed, -at'ing
ap·pro'pri·ate·ly
ap·pro'pri·a'tion
ap·pro'pri·a'tor
ap·prov'al
ap·prove', -proved',
  -prov'ing
ap·prox'i·mate',
  -mat'ed, -mat'ing
ap·prox'i·mate·ly
ap·prox'i·ma'tion
ap·pur'te·nance
a'pri·cot'
A'pril
a'pron
ap'ro·pos'
apse
ap'ti·tude'
apt'ly
aq'ua *pl.* -uae *or* -uas
aq'ua·cul'ture *also*
  aq'ui·cul'ture
aq'ua·ma·rine'
aq'ua·plane',
  -planed', -plan'ing
aq'ua re'gi·a
a·quar'i·um *pl.*
  -i·ums *or* -i·a
a·quat'ic
aq'ue·duct'
a'que·ous
aq'ui·fer
aq'ui·line'
Ar'ab
ar'a·besque'
A·ra'bi·an
Ar'a·bic

ar'a•ble
a•rach'nid
A•rap'a•ho' *pl.* -ho'
  or -hos'
Ar'au•ca'ni•an
Ar'a•wak *pl.* -wak'
  or -waks'
Ar'a•wa'kan *pl.*
  -kan *or* -kans
ar'bi•ter
ar'bi•trage'
ar'bi•tra•geur'
ar•bit'ra•ment
ar'bi•trar'i•ly
ar'bi•trar'i•ness
ar'bi•trar'y
ar'bi•trate', -trat'ed,
  -trat'ing
ar'bi•tra'tion
ar'bi•tra'tor
ar'bor
ar•bo're•al
ar'bo•re'tum *pl.*
  -tums *or* -ta
ar'bor•vi'tae
ar•bu'tus
arc *(to curve)*, arced
  or arcked, arc'ing *or*
  arck'ing
  ✔ *ark*
ar•cade'
arch
ar'chae•o•log'i•cal
  or ar'che•o•log'i•cal
ar'chae•ol'o•gist *or*
  ar'che•ol'o•gist
ar'chae•ol'o•gy *or*

ar'che•ol'o•gy
ar'chae•op'ter•yx
ar•cha'ic
ar'cha•ism
arch•an'gel
arch•bish'op
arch•dea'con
arch•di'o•cese
arch•duch'ess
arch•duke'
arched
arch•en'e•my
arch'er
arch'er•y
ar'che•type'
ar'chi•pel'a•go' *pl.*
  -goes' *or* -gos'
ar'chi•tect
ar'chi•tec'tur•al
ar'chi•tec'ture
ar'chi•trave'
ar•chi'val
ar'chive'
ar'chi•vist
arch'ly
arch'way'
arc'tic
ar'dent
ar'dor
ar'du•ous
are *form of* to be
are *(metric unit of*
  area)
  ✔ *air, e'er, ere, heir*
ar'e•a *(space)*
  ✔ *aria*
Ar'e•a Code' *also*

ar'e•a code'
ar'e•a•way'
a•re'na
aren't
Ar'gen•tine' *or*
  Ar'gen•tin'e•an
ar'gon'
ar'go•sy
ar'got
ar'gu•a•ble
ar'gu•a•bly
ar'gue, -gued,
  -gu•ing
ar'gu•er
ar'gu•ment
ar'gu•men'ta•tive
ar'gu•men'ta•tive•
  ly
ar'gyle' *also* ar'gyll'
a'ri•a *(melody)*
  ✔ *area*
ar'id
a•rid'i•ty
a•right'
A•rik'a•ra *pl.* -ra
a•rise', a•rose',
  a•ris'en, a•ris'ing
ar'is•toc'ra•cy
a•ris'to•crat'
a•ris'to•crat'ic
Ar'is•to•te'li•an
Ar'is•to•te'li•an•
  ism
a•rith'me•tic *n.*
ar'ith•met'ic *or*
  ar'ith•met'i•cal *adj.*
a•rith'me•ti'cian

Ar'i•zo'nan *or*
Ar'i•zo'ni•an
ark *(boat)*
  ✓ arc
Ar•kan'san
armed
ar•ma'da
ar'ma•dil'lo *pl.* -los
Ar'ma•ged'don
ar'ma•ment
ar'ma•ture
arm'band'
arm'chair'
Ar•me'ni•an
arm'ful'
arm'hole'
ar'mi•stice
arm'let
arm'load'
ar•moire'
ar'mor
ar'mored
ar•mo'ri•al
ar'mor•y
arm'pit'
arm'rest'
ar'my
ar'ni•ca
a•ro'ma
ar'o•mat'ic
a•round'
a•rous'a•ble
a•rous'al
a•rouse', a•roused',
  a•rous'ing
ar•peg'gi•o *pl.* -os

ar'que•bus
ar•raign'
ar•raign'ment
ar•range', -ranged',
  -rang'ing
ar•range'ment
ar'rant
ar'ras *pl.* -ras
ar•ray'
ar•ray'er
ar•rears'
ar•rest'
ar•rest'ing
ar•rhyth'mi•a
ar•ri'val
ar•rive', -rived',
  -riv'ing
ar•ri've•der'ci
ar'ro•gance
ar'ro•gant
ar'ro•gate', -gat'ed,
  -gat'ing
ar'ro•ga'tion
ar'row
ar'row•head'
ar'row•root'
ar•roy'o *pl.* -os
ar'se•nal
ar'se•nic
ar'son
ar'son•ist
art' dec'o *also* Art'
  Dec'o
ar•te'ri•al
ar•te'ri•ole'
ar•te'ri•o•scle•ro'sis
ar'ter•y

ar•te'sian well'
art'ful
ar•thrit'ic
ar•thri'tis
ar'thro•pod'
ar'thro•scope'
Ar•thu'ri•an
ar'ti•choke'
ar'ti•cle
ar•tic'u•la•ble
ar•tic'u•lar
ar•tic'u•late',
  -lat'ed, -lat'ing
ar•tic'u•late•ly
ar•tic'u•la'tion
ar•tic'u•la'tor
ar'ti•fact' *also*
  ar'te•fact'
ar'ti•fice
ar•tif'i•cer
ar'ti•fi'cial
ar'ti•fi'ci•al'i•ty
ar•til'ler•y
ar•til'ler•y•man
ar'ti•san
art'ist
ar•tis'tic
art'ist•ry
art'less
art' nou•veau'
art'work'
ar'um
Ar'y•an
as'a•fet'i•da
as•bes'tos *also*
  as•bes'tus
as•cend'

as•cen′dan•cy *also*
  as•cen′den•cy
as•cen′dant *also*
  as•cen′dent
as•cend′ing
as•cen′sion
as•cent′ *(upward*
  slope)
  ✓ *assent*
as′cer•tain′
as′cer•tain′a•ble
as′cer•tain′a•bly
as•cet′ic *(austere)*
  ✓ *acetic*
as•cet′i•cism
ASCII
a•scor′bic ac′id
as′cot
as•crib′a•ble
as•cribe′, -cribed′,
  -crib′ing
as•crip′tion
a•sep′sis
a•sep′tic
a•sex′u•al
a•shamed′
a•sham′ed•ly
A•shan′ti *pl.* -ti *or*
  -tis
ash′can′ *or* ash′
  can′
ash′en
a•shore′
ash′tray′
ash′y
A′sian
A′sian A•mer′i•

can *or* A′sian-
  A•mer′i•can
A′si•at′ic
a•side′
as′i•nine′
ask
a•skance′
a•skew′
a•slant′
a•sleep′
asp
as•par′a•gus
as′par•tame′
as′pect
as′pen
as•per′i•ty
as•per′sion
as′phalt′
as′pho•del′
as•phyx′i•a
as•phyx′i•ate′,
  -at′ed, -at′ing
as•phyx′i•a′tion
as•phyx′i•a′tor
as′pic
as′pi•rant
as′pi•rate′, -rat′ed,
  -rat′ing
as′pi•ra′tion
as′pi•ra′tor
as•pire′, -pired′,
  -pir′ing
as′pi•rin
ass *pl.* ass′es
as•sail′
as•sail′a•ble
as•sail′er

as•sail′ant
as•sas′sin
as•sas′si•nate′,
  -nat′ed, -nat′ing
as•sas′si•na′tion
as•sas′si•na′tor
as•sault′
as•sault′er
as•say′ *n.*
as•say′ *(to analyze)*
  ✓ *essay*
as•say′er
as•se•gai′ *or*
  as′sa•gai′ *pl.* -gais′
as•sem′blage
as•sem′ble, -bled,
  -bling
as•sem′bler
as•sem′bly
as•sem′bly line′
as•sem′bly•man
as•sem′bly•
  wom′an
as•sent′ *(agreement)*
  ✓ *ascent*
as•sert′
as•sert′er *or*
  as•ser′tor
as•ser′tion
as•ser′tive
as•sess′
as•sess′a•ble
as•sess′ment
as•ses′sor
as′set
as•sev′er•ate′,
  -at′ed, -at′ing

as'si·du'i·ty
as·sid'u·ous
as·sign'
as·sign'a·ble
as'sig·na'tion
as·sign·ee'
as·sign'er
as·sign'ment
as·sim'i·la·ble
as·sim'i·late', -lat'ed, -lat'ing
as·sim'i·la'tion
as·sim'i·la'tive *also* as·sim'i·la'to·ry
as·sim'i·la'tor
As·sin'i·boin' *pl.* -boin' *or* -boins'
as·sist'
as·sis'tance
as·sis'tant
as·siz'es
as·so'ci·ate', -at'ed, -at'ing
as·so'ci·a'tion
as·so'ci·a'tive
as·so'ci·a'tor
as'so·nance
as'so·nant
as·sort'
as·sort'ed
as·sort'ment
as·suage', -suaged', -suag'ing
as·suage'ment
as·sum'a·ble
as·sum'a·bly
as·sume' *(to sup-*

pose, to undertake), -sumed', -sum'ing ✔ *presume*
as·sump'tion
as·sur'ance
as·sure' *(to declare positively, to convince),* -sured', -sur'ing ✔ *ensure, insure*
as·sur'ed·ly
as'ta·tine'
as'ter
as'ter·isk'
a·stern'
as'ter·oid'
asth'ma
asth·mat'ic
as'tig·mat'ic
a·stig'ma·tism
a·stir'
a·ston'ish
a·ston'ish·ing
a·ston'ish·ment
a·stound'
a·stound'ing
a·strad'dle
as'tra·khan
as'tral
a·stray'
a·stride'
as·trin'gen·cy
as·trin'gent
as'tro·labe'
as'tro·log'i·cal *or* as'tro·log'ic
as·trol'o·ger

as·trol'o·gy
as·trom'e·try
as'tro·naut'
as'tro·nau'tic *or* as'tro·nau'ti·cal
as·tron'o·mer
as'tro·nom'i·cal *also* as'tro·nom'ic
as·tron'o·my
as'tro·phys'i·cal
as'tro·phys'i·cist
as'tro·phys'ics
as·tute'
as·tute'ly
a·sun'der
a·sy'lum
a·sym·met'ri·cal *also* a·sym·met'ric
a·sym'me·try
at'a·vism
at'a·vis'tic
a·tax'i·a *also* a·tax'y
a·tax'ic
at·el·ier'
a tem'po
Ath'a·bas'kan
a'the·ism
a'the·ist
a'the·is'tic
A·the'ni·an
ath'er·o·scle·ro'sis
a·thirst'
ath·lete'
ath·lete's foot'
ath·let'ic
a·thwart'
at'las *pl.* -las·es

at'mos•phere'
at'mos•pher'ic *also*
  at'mos•pher'i•cal
a'toll'
at'om
a•tom'ic
at'om•i•za'tion
at'om•ize', -ized',
  -iz'ing
at'om•iz'er
a•ton'al
a'to•nal'i•ty
a•tone', a•toned',
  a•ton'ing
a•tone'ment
a•top'
ATP
a'tri•um *pl.* a'tri•a
  or -ums
a•tro'cious
a•troc'i•ty
at'ro•phy, -phied,
  -phy•ing
at'ro•pine' *also*
  at'ro•pin
at•tach'
at•tach'a•ble
at'ta•ché'
at'ta•ché' case'
at•tach'ment
at•tack'
at•tack'er
at•tain'
at•tain'a•bil'i•ty
at•tain'a•ble
at•tain'der
at•tain'ment

at•taint'
at•tar'
at•tempt'
at•tempt'a•ble
at•tend'
at•ten'dance
at•ten'dant
at•ten'tion
at•ten'tive
at•ten'tive•ly
at•ten'u•ate',
  -at'ed, -at'ing
at•ten'u•a'tion
at•test'
at•test'ed
at'tic
at•tire', -tired',
  -tir'ing
at'ti•tude'
at•tor'ney *pl.* -neys
at•tor'ney at law'
  pl. at'torneys at
  law'
at•tor'ney
  gen'er•al *pl.*
  at•tor'neys
  gen'er•al *or*
  at•tor'ney
  gen'er•als
at•tract'
at•tract'er *or*
  at•trac'tor
at•trac'tion
at•trac'tive
at•trac'tive•ly
at•trib'ut•a•ble
at•trib'ute, -ut•ed,

  -ut•ing
at'tri•bute' *n.*
at•trib'ut•er *or*
  at•trib'u•tor
at'tri•bu'tion
at•trib'u•tive
at•tri'tion
at•tune', -tuned',
  -tun'ing
at•tune'ment
a•typ'i•cal
au'burn
auc'tion
auc'tion•eer'
au•da'cious
au•dac'i•ty
au'di•bil'i•ty *or*
  au'di•ble•ness
au'di•ble
au'di•bly
au'di•ence
au'di•o' *pl.* -di•os'
au'di•om'e•ter
au'di•o-vis'u•al
  also au'di•o•
  vis'u•al
au'dit
au•di'tion
au'di•tor
au'di•to'ri•um *pl.*
  -ri•ums *or* -ri•a
au'di•to'ry
auf Wie'der•
  seh'en
au'ger *(tool)*
  ✓ *augur*
aught *also* ought

(anything at all)
✔ ought
aught *also* ought
(zero)
✔ ought
aug·ment'
aug·ment'a·ble
aug'men·ta'tion
aug·ment'er
au gra'tin
au'gur *(to predict)*
✔ auger
au'gu·ry
au·gust' *(majestic)*
Au'gust *(month)*
au jus'
auk
auld' lang syne'
aunt *(female relative)*
✔ ant
au'ra *pl.* -ras *or* -rae
au'ral *(relating to the ear)*
✔ oral
au're·ole'
au' re·voir'
au'ri·cle *(part of the ear)*
✔ oracle
au·ric'u·lar
au'rochs' *pl.* -rochs'
au·ro'ra
au·ro'ra aus·tra'lis
au·ro'ra bo're·al'is
aus'pi·ces
aus·pi'cious
aus·tere', -ter'er,

-ter'est
aus·ter'i·ty
Aus·tra'lian
Aus'tri·an
au'tarch
au·teur'
au·teur'ism
au·then'tic
au·then'ti·cate', -cat'ed, -cat'ing
au·then·tic'i·ty
au·then'ti·ca'tion
au·then'ti·ca'tor
au'thor
au·thor'i·tar'i·an
au·thor'i·tar'i·an·ism
au·thor'i·ta'tive
au·thor'i·ty
au'thor·i·za'tion
au'thor·ize', -ized', -iz'ing
au'thor·iz'er
au'thor·ship'
au'tism
au'to *pl.* -tos
au'to·bi·og'ra·pher
au'to·bi'o·graph'i·cal *or* au'to·bi'o·graph'ic
au'to·bi·og'ra·phy
au'to·clave'
au·toc'ra·cy
au'to·crat'
au'to·crat'ic
au'to·graph'
au'to·graph'ic *or*

au'to·graph'i·cal
au'to·im·mune'
au'to·im·mu'ni·ty
au'to·mak'er
au'to·mate', -mat'ed, -mat'ing
au'to·mat'ed tel'ler ma·chine'
au'to·mat'ic
au'to·ma'tion
au·tom'a·ton *pl.* -tons *or* -ta
au'to·mo·bile'
au'to·mo'tive
au'to·nom'ic
au·ton'o·mous
au·ton'o·my
au'to·pi'lot
au'top·sy
au'tumn
au·tum'nal
aux·il'ia·ry
aux'in
a·vail'
a·vail'a·bil'i·ty *or* a·vail'a·ble·ness
a·vail'a·ble
a·vail'a·bly
av'a·lanche'
a·vant'-garde'
av'a·rice
av'a·ri'cious
a·vast'
av'a·tar'
a·venge', a·venged', a·veng'ing
a·veng'er

av′e•nue′
a•ver′, a•verred′,
 a•ver′ring
av′er•age, -aged,
 -ag•ing
a•verse′ *(opposed,
 reluctant)*
 ✔ *adverse*
a•verse′ly
a•ver′sion
a•vert′
a•vert′a•ble *or*
 a•vert′i•ble
a′vi•an
a′vi•ar′y
a′vi•a′tion
a′vi•a′tor
av′id
a•vid′i•ty
a′vi•on′ics
av′o•ca′do *pl.* -dos
av′o•ca′tion
a•void′
a•void′a•ble
a•void′a•bly
a•void′ance
av′oir•du•pois′
 weight′
a•vouch′
a•vow′
a•vow′al
a•vun′cu•lar
aw *interj.*
 ✔ *awe*
a•wait′
a•wake′, a•woke′ *or*
 a•waked′, a•waked′

or a•wok′en,
 a•wak′ing
a•wak′en
a•wak′en•er
a•wak′en•ing
a•ward′
a•ward′a•ble
a•ward′er
a•ware′
a•ware′ness
a•wash′
a•way′ *(at a dis-
 tance)*
 ✔ *aweigh*
awe *(to fill with won-
 der)*, awed, aw′ing
 ✔ *aw*
a•weigh′ *(free of the
 bottom)*
 ✔ *away*
awe′some
awe′struck′ *also*
 awe′strick′en
aw′ful *(horrible)*
 ✔ *offal*
aw′ful•ly
a•while′
awk′ward
awl *(tool)*
 ✔ *all*
awn′ing
AWOL
a•wry′
ax *or* axe, axed,
 ax′ing
ax′i•al
ax′i•om

ax′i•o•mat′ic
ax′is *pl.* ax′es
ax′le
ax′le•tree′
ax′on′
a′ya•tol′lah
aye *also* ay *(a vote of
 yes)*
 ✔ *eye, I*
Ay′ma•ra′ *pl.* -ra′
Ay′ma•ran′
Ayr′shire
a•zal′ea
az′i•muth
AZT
Az′tec′ *also*
 Az•tec′an
az′ure

B

baa, baaed, baa′ing
bab′bitt met′al
bab′ble, -bled,
 -bling
bab′bler
babe
ba′bel *also* Ba′bel
ba•boon′
ba•bush′ka
ba′by, -bied, -by′ing
ba′by•hood′
ba′by•ish
Bab′y•lo′ni•an
ba′by's breath′
ba′by-sit′, -sat′,

-sit'ting
bab'y sit'ter
bac'ca·lau're·ate
Bac'cha·na'lian
 also bac'cha·
 na'lian
bach'e·lor
bach'e·lor's but'-
 ton *pl.* bach'e·lor's
 but'tons
bach'e·lor's
 de·gree'
ba·cil'lus *pl.* -cil'li'
back
back'ache'
back'bite', -bit',
 -bit'ten, -bit'ing
back'bit'er
back'board'
back'bone'
back'break'ing
back'coun'try
back'drop'
back'er
back'field'
back'fire', -fired',
 -fir'ing
back'-for·ma'tion
 or back' for·ma'tion
back'gam'mon
back'ground'
back'hand'
back'hand'ed
back'hoe'
back'ing
back'lash'
back'list'

back'log'
back'pack'
back'pack'er
back'rest'
back'-seat' driv'er
back'side'
back'slide', -slid',
 -slid'ing
back'slid'er
back'space',
 -spaced', -spac'ing
back'spin'
back'stage'
back'stairs' *also*
 back'stair' *adj.*
back'stitch'
back'stop'
back'stretch'
back'stroke'
back' talk'
back'track'
back'up' *n. & adj.*
back'ward *or*
 back'wards *adv.*
back'wash'
back'wa'ter
back'woods'
back' yard' *also*
 back'yard'
ba'con
bac·te'ri·a *sing.*
 -ri·um
bac·te'ri·al
bac·te'ri·cid'al
bac·te'ri·cide'
bac·te'ri·o·log'i·cal
bac·te'ri·ol'o·gist

bac·te'ri·ol'o·gy
Bac'tri·an camel
bad, worse, worst
badge
badg'er
bad'i·nage'
bad'lands'
bad'min'ton
bad'mouth' *or*
 bad'-mouth'
baf'fle, -fled, -fling
baf'fler
bag, bagged,
 bag'ging
bag'a·telle'
ba'gel
bag'gage
bag'gi·ness
bag'gy
bag'pipe'
bag'pip'er
bah
Ba·ha'mi·an *or*
 Ba·ha'man
bail *(money, pail han-*
 dle)
 ✔ bale
bail *(to empty)*
 ✔ bale
bail'iff
bail'i·wick'
bail'out' *n.*
bails'man
bait *(lure)*
 ✔ bate
baize
bake, baked, bak'ing

bak′er's
bak′er's doz′en
bak′er•y
bak′ing pow′der
bak′ing so′da
ba•kla•va′
bal′a•lai′ka
bal′ance, -anced,
   -anc•ing
bal•bo′a
bal•brig′an
bal′co•ny
bald
bal′da•chin also
   bal′da•chi′no pl.
   -chins also -chi′nos
bal′der•dash′
bald′-faced′
bald′head′ed
bald′ing
bald′pate′
bal′dric
bale (to bundle
   tightly), baled,
   bal′ing
   ✔ bail
ba•leen′
bale′ful
bal′er
balk
Bal′kan
balk′y
ball (round object,
   dance)
   ✔ bawl
bal′lad
ball′-and-sock′et

joint′
bal′last
ball′ bear′ing
bal′le•ri′na
bal•let′
bal•lis′tic
bal•lis′tics
bal•loon′
bal•loon′ist
bal′lot
ball′park′
ball′play′er
ball′point′ pen′
ball′room′
bal′ly•hoo′ pl.
   -hoos′
bal′ly•hoo′,
   -hooed′, -hoo′ing
balm′y
ba•lo′ney (nonsense)
   ✔ bologna
bal′sa
bal′sam
Balt
Bal′tic
bal′us•ter
bal′us•trade′
bam•bi′no pl. -nos
   or -ni
bam•boo′ pl. -boos
bam•boo′zle, -zled,
   -zling
bam•boo′zler
ban, banned, ban′-
   ning
ba•nal′
ba•nal′i•ty

ba•nan′a
band′age, -aged,
   -ag•ing
ban•dan′na or
   ban•dan′a
band′box′
ban′di•coot′
ban′dit
ban′di•try
band′mas′ter
ban′do•leer′ or
   ban′do•lier′
band′ saw′
band′stand′
band′wag′on
ban′dy, -died,
   -dy•ing
ban′dy-leg′ged
bane
bane′ber′ry
bane′ful
bang
ban′gle
bang′-up′ adj.
ban′ish
ban′ish•ment
ban′is•ter also
   ban′nis•ter
ban′jo pl. -jos or
   -joes
bank′book′
bank′card′
bank′er
bank′ing
bank′ note′
bank′roll′
bank′rupt′

bank'rupt•cy
ban'ner
banns *also* bans
ban'quet
ban'shee
ban'tam
ban'tam•weight'
ban'ter
ban'ter•er
Ban'tu *pl.* Ban'tu
ban'yan
ban•zai'
ba'o•bab'
bap'tism
bap•tis'mal
Bap'tist
bap'tis•ter•y *also*
  bap'tis•try
bap'tize', -tized',
  -tiz'ing
bar, barred, bar'ring
barb
bar•bar'i•an
bar•bar'ic
bar'ba•rism
bar•bar'i•ty
bar'ba•rous
bar'be•cue', -cued',
  -cu'ing
barbed
barbed' wire'
bar'bel *(feeler)*
bar'bell' *(weight)*
bar'ber
bar'ber'ry
bar'ber•shop'
bar'bi•can

bar•bi'tu•rate
bar'ca•role' *also*
  bar'ca•rolle'
bar' code'
bard *(poet)*
  ✔ barred
bare *(naked)*, bar'er,
  bar'est
  ✔ bear
bare *(to uncover)*,
  bared, bar'ing
  ✔ bear
bare'back' *also*
  bare'backed'
bare'faced'
bare'foot' *also*
  bare'foot'ed
bare'hand'ed
bare'head'ed
bare'leg'ged
bare'ly
bar'gain
barge, barged,
  barg'ing
bar'ite
bar'i•tone'
bar'i•um
bark *(sound, outer*
  covering)
bark *also* barque
  (ship)
bar'keep'er
bar'ken•tine'
bark'er
bar'ley
bar'ley•corn'
bar'maid'

bar'man
bar mitz'vah,
  -vahed, vah•ing
barn
bar'na•cle
barn'storm'
barn'storm'er
barn'yard'
bar'o•gram'
bar'o•graph'
ba•rom'e•ter
bar'o•met'ric *or*
  bar'o•met'ri•cal
ba•rom'e•try
bar'on *(nobleman)*
  ✔ bar'ren
bar'on•ess
bar'on•et
bar'on•et•age
bar'on•et•cy
bar'on•et•ess
ba•ro'ni•al
bar'o•ny
ba•roque'
ba•rouche'
bar'rack
bar'ra•cu'da *pl.* -da
  or -das
bar'rage *(dam)*
bar•rage' *(to fire at)*,
  -raged', -rag'ing
barred *(having bars*
  or stripes)
  ✔ bard
bar'rel, -reled *or*
  -relled, -rel•ing *or*
  -rel•ling

bar′ren *(sterile)*
  ✔ baron
bar′ren·ness
bar·rette′ *(hair clasp)*
  ✔ burette
bar′ri·cade′, -cad′ed, -cad′ing
bar′ri·er
bar′ri·o′ *pl.* -os′
bar′ris·ter
bar′room′
bar′row
bar′tend′er
bar′ter
bas′al
ba·salt′
base *(to find a basis for)*, based, bas′ing
  ✔ bass
base *(contemptible)*, bas′er, bas′est
  ✔ bass
base′ball′
base′board′
base′ hit′
base′less
base′ line′
base′man
base′ment
base′ness
ba·sen′ji
base′ run′ner
bash
bash′ful
ba′sic *(fundamental)*
BA′SIC *(computer language)*
ba′si·cal·ly
bas′il
ba·sil′i·ca
bas′i·lisk′
ba′sin
ba′sis *pl.* -ses′
bask *(to take pleasure in)*
  ✔ basque, Basque
bas′ket
bas′ket·ball′
bas′ket·ry
basque *(bodice)*
  ✔ bask
Basque *(people)*
  ✔ bask
bas′-re·lief′
bass *(fish)*, *pl.* bass or bass′es
bass *(voice)*
  ✔ base
bas′set hound′
bas′si·net′
bas′so *pl.* -sos or -si
bas·soon′
bas·soon′ist
bass′ vi′ol′
bass′wood′
bast
bas′tard
baste, bast′ed, bast′ing
bas′ti·na′do *also* bas′ti·nade′ *pl.* -na′does *also* -nades′

bas′tion
bat, bat′ted, bat′ting
bat′boy′
batch
bate *(to lessen)*, bat′ed, bat′ing
  ✔ bait
ba·teau′ *pl.* -teaux′
bat′girl′
bath *n.*
bathe, bathed, bath′ing
bath′er
ba·thet′ic
bath′house′
bath′ing cap′
bath′ing suit′
bath′mat′
bath′o·lith′
ba′thos′
bath′robe′
bath′room′
bath′tub′
bath′y·scaph′ *also* bath′y·scaphe′
bath′y·sphere′
ba·tik′
ba·tiste′
bat mitz′vah *or* bas mitz′vah, -vahed, -vah·ing
ba·ton′
bats′man
bat·tal′ion
bat′ten
bat′ter
bat′ter·ing ram′

bat'ter•y
bat'ting
bat'tle, -tled, -tling
bat'tle-ax' *or* bat'tle-
  axe'
bat'tle cry'
bat'tle•dore'
bat'tle•field'
bat'tle•front'
bat'tle•ground'
bat'tle•ment
bat'tler
bat'tle roy'al *pl.*
  bat'tles roy'al
bat'tle•ship'
bat'ty
bau'ble
baud
baux'ite'
bawd'y
bawd'i•ness
bawl *(cry)*
  ✔ *ball*
bay *(water, recess,*
  color, tree)
  ✔ *bey*
bay *(to bark),* bayed,
  bay'ing
  ✔ *bey*
bay'ber•ry
bay' leaf'
bay'•o•net, -net•ed
  or -net•ted,
  -net•ing *or* -net•ting
bay'ou
ba•zaar' *also* ba•zar'
  (market)

✔ *bizarre*
ba•zoo'ka
BB gun
be *(to exist), singular*
  present tense forms,
  am, are, is *plural*
  present tense form,
  are *present participle,*
  be'ing *singular*
  past tense forms,
  was, were *plural*
  past tense form,
  were *past participle,*
  been
  ✔ *bee*
beach *(shore)*
  ✔ *beech*
beach'head'
bea'con
bead
bead'ing
bea'dle
bead'work'
bead'y
bea'gle
beak
beak'er
beam
bean
bean'bag'
bean' curd'
bean'ie
bean'pole'
bean' sprouts'
bean'stalk'
bear *(to hold up),*
  bore, borne *or*

born, bear'ing
  ✔ *bare*
bear *(animal)*
  ✔ *bare*
bear'a•ble
bear'a•bly
beard
bear'er
bear'ing
bear'ish
bé•ar•naise' sauce'
bear'skin'
beast
beast'li•ness
beat *(to hit),* beat,
  beat'en *or* beat,
  beat'ing
  ✔ *beet*
beat'er
be•a•tif'ic
be•at'i•fy', -fied',
  -fy'ing
be•at'i•tude'
beat'nik'
beat'-up' *adj.*
beau *(boyfriend), pl.*
  beaus *or* beaux
  ✔ *bow*
Beau'fort scale
beaut
beau'te•ous
beau•ti'cian
beau'ti•fi•ca'tion
beau'ti•fi'er
beau'ti•ful
beau'ti•fy', -fied',
  -fy'ing

beau′ty

beaux-arts′

bea′ver

bea′ver·board′

be·calmed′

be·cause′

beck′on

be·cloud′

be·come′, -came′,
-come′, -com′ing

bed, bed′ded, bed′-
ding

bed′-and-break′-
fast

be·daub′

be·daz′zle, -zled,
-zling

bed′bug′

bed′cham′ber

bed′clothes′

bed′ding

be·deck′

be·dev′il, -iled or
-illed, -il·ing or
-il·ling

be·dev′il·ment

be·dew′

bed′fel′low

be·di′zen

bed′lam

Bed′ou·in *pl.* -in or
-ins

bed′pan′

bed′post′

be·drag′gled

bed′rid′den

bed′rock′

bed′roll′

bed′room′

bed′side′

bed′sore′

bed′spread′

bed′spring′

bed′stead′

bed′time′

bee *(insect, gathering)*
✔ *be*

beech *(tree)*
✔ *beach*

beech′nut′

beef *(animal)*, *pl.*
beeves or beef

beef *(complaint)*, *pl.*
beefs

beef′i·ness

beef′steak′

beef′y

bee′hive′

bee′keep′er

bee′line′

beep′er

beer *(beverage)*
✔ *bier*

bees′wax′

beet *(plant)*
✔ *beat*

bee′tle *(insect, mal-
let)*
✔ *betel*

bee′tle *(to overhang)*,
-tled, -tling
✔ *betel*

bee′tle-browed′

be·fall′, -fell′,

-fall′en, -fall′ing

be·fit′, -fit′ted,
-fit′ting

be·fog′, -fogged′,
-fog′ging

be·fore′

be·fore′hand′

be·foul′

be·friend′

be·fud′dle, -dled,
-dling

beg, begged,
beg′ging

be·get′, -got′,
-got′ten or -got′,
-get′ting

be·get′ter

beg′gar

beg′gar·ly

beg′gar·y

be·gin′, -gan′,
-gun′, -gin′ning

be·gin′ner

be·gone′

be·go′nia

be·grime′,
-grimed′, -grim′ing

be·grudge′,
-grudged′,
-grudg′ing

be·guile′, -guiled′,
-guil′ing

be·guile′ment

be·guil′er

be·guine′

be·half′

be·have′, -haved′,

-hav′ing
be•hav′ior
be•hav′ior•al
be•hav′ior•ism
be•hav′ior•ist
be•head′
be•he′moth
be•hest′
be•hind′
be•hind′hand′
be•hold′, -held′,
 -hold′ing
be•hold′en
be•hold′er
be•hoove′,
 -hooved′,
 -hoov′ing
beige
be′ing
be•jew′eled
bel (*unit of measure-*
 ment)
 ✔ bell, belle
be•la′bor
be•lat′ed
be•lay′
bel can′to
belch
bel′dam *or* bel′dame
be•lea′guer
bel′fry
Bel′gian
be•lie′, -lied′,
 -ly′ing
be•lief′
be•liev′a•ble
be•lieve′, -lieved′,

-liev′ing
be•liev′er
be•lit′tle, -tled,
 -tling
bell (*instrument*)
 ✔ bel, belle
bel′la•don′na
bell′-bot′toms
bell′boy′
belle (*woman*)
 ✔ bel, bell
belles-let′tres
bell′flow′er
bell′hop′
bel′li•cose′
bel′li•cos′i•ty
bel•lig′er•ence
bel•lig′er•en•cy
bel•lig′er•ent
bell′ jar′
bel′low
bel′lows
bell′weth′er
bel′ly, -lied, -ly•ing
bel′ly•ache′,
 -ached′, -ach′ing
bel′ly•ach′er
bel′ly•band′
bel′ly•but′ton
bel′ly-land′,
 -land′ed, -land′ing
bel′ly land′ing
bel′ly laugh′
be•long′
be•long′ings
be•lov′ed
be•low′

belt
belt′ing
belt′way′
be•lu′ga
bel′ve•dere′
be′ma *pl.* -ma•ta
be•moan′
be•mused′
bench
bench′mark′
bend, bent,
 bend′ing
be•neath′
Ben′e•dic′tine
ben′e•dic′tion
ben′e•fac′tor
be•nef′ic
ben′e•fice
be•nef′i•cence
be•nef′i•cent
ben′e•fi′cial
ben′e•fi′ci•ar′y
ben′e•fit, -fit•ed *also*
 -fit•ted, -fit•ing *or*
 -fit•ting
be•nev′o•lence
be•nev′o•lent
Ben•ga′li
be•night′ed
be•nign′
be•nig′nant
be•nig′ni•ty
ben′i•son
bent
be•numb′
ben′zene′ (*hydrocar-*
 bon)

ben′zine′ *(mixture of hydrocarbons)*
ben′zo•ate′ of so′da
ben•zo′ic ac′id
ben′zo•in
ben′zol
be•queath′
be•quest′
be•rate′, -rat′ed, -rat′ing
Ber′ber
be•reave′, -reaved′ or -reft′, -reav′ing
be•reave′ment
be•reft′
be•ret′
berg *(iceberg)*
✔ *burg*
ber′i•ber′i
ber•ke′li•um
berm
Ber•mu′da shorts′
ber′ry *(fruit)*
✔ *bury*
ber•serk′
berth *(bed)*
✔ *birth*
ber′yl
be•ryl′li•um
be•seech′, -sought′ or -seeched′, -seech′ing
be•set′, -set′, -set′ting
be•side′ *(next to)*
be•sides′ *(in addi-tion)*

be•siege′, -sieged′, -sieg′ing
be•sieg′er
be•smirch′
be•sot′, be•sot′ted, be•sot′ting
be•spat′ter
be•speak′, -spoke′, -spo′ken or -spoke′, -speak′ing
be•spec′ta•cled
be•sprin′kle, -kled, -kling
Bes′semer proc′ess
best
bes′tial
bes′ti•al′i•ty
bes′ti•ar′y
be•stir′, -stirred′, -stir′ring
be•stow′
be•stow′al
be•strew′, -strewed′, -strewed′ or -strewn′, -strew′ing
be•stride′, -strode′, -strid′den, -strid′ing
best′sell′er
best′-sell′ing
bet, bet or bet′ted, bet′ting
be′ta
be•take′, -took′, -tak′en, -tak′ing
be′ta•tron′

be′tel *(plant)*
✔ *beetle*
be′tel nut′
bête noire′
be•think′, -thought′, -think′ing
be•tide′, -tid′ed, -tid′ing
be•times′
be•to′ken
be•tray′
be•tray′al
be•tray′er
be•troth′
be•troth′al
be•trothed′
bet′ter *(greater)*
✔ *bettor*
bet′ter•ment
bet′tor *also* bet′ter *(one who bets)*
✔ *better*
be•tween′
be•twixt′
bev′el, -eled or -elled, -el•ing or -el•ling
bev′er•age
bev′y
be•wail′
be•ware′, -wared′, -war′ing
be•wil′der
be•witch′
be•witch′ing
bey *(governor)*
✔ *bay*

be•yond′
bi•a′ly pl. -lys
bi•an′nu•al (*twice a year*)
  ✔ biennial, biyearly,
  semiannual,
  semiyearly
bi′as, -ased or -assed,
  -as•ing or -as•sing
bi•ath′lon
bi•ax′i•al
bib
Bi′ble
bib′li•cal
bib′li•og′ra•pher
bib′li•o•graph′i•cal
  or bib′li•o•graph′ic
bib′li•og′ra•phy
bib′u•lous
bi•cam′er•al
bi•car′bon•ate′
bi′cen•ten′a•ry
bi′cen•ten′ni•al
bi′ceps′ pl. -ceps′ or
  -ceps′es
bi•chlo′ride′
bick′er
bick′er•er
bi•coast′al or bi-
  coast′al
bi′con•cave′
bi′con•vex′
bi•cul′tur•al
bi•cus′pid
bi′cy•cle, -cled,
  -cling
bi′cy•cler or

bi′cy•clist
bid (*to order, to
  invite*), bade or bid,
  bid′den or bid,
  bid′ding
bid (*to make an
  offer*), bid, bid′ding
bid′der
bid′dy
bide, bid′ed or bode,
  bid′ed, bid′ing
bi•det′
bi•en′ni•al (*lasting
  two years, once every
  two years*)
  ✔ biannual, biyearly,
  semiannual,
  semiyearly
bier (*coffin stand*)
  ✔ beer
bi•fo′cal adj.
bi′fo•cals n.
bi′fur•ca′tion
bi′fur•cate′, -cat′ed,
  -cat′ing
big, big′ger, big′gest
big′a•mist
big′a•mous
big′a•my
big′-heart′ed
big′horn′ pl. -horn′
  or -horns′
bight (*loop, curve,
  bay*)
  ✔ bite, byte
big′ league′ n.
big′-league′ adj.

big′ot
big′ot•ed
big′ot•ry
big′ shot′
big′ time′ n.
big′time′ or
  big′-time′ adj.
big′wig′
bike, biked, bik′ing
bik′er
bike′way′
bi•ki′ni
bi•lat′er•al
bile
bilge
bi•lin′gual
bil′ious
bilk
bill
bill′board′
bil′let
bil′let-doux′ pl.
  bil′lets-doux′
bill′fold′
bil′liards
bill′ing
bil′lion
bil′lion•aire′
bil′lionth
bil′low
bil′ly
bil′ly club′
bil′ly goat′
bi•month′ly (*once
  every two months,
  twice a month*)
  ✔ semimonthly

bin
bi'na·ry
bin·au'ral
bind, bound,
  bind'ing
bind'er
bind'er·y
bind'ing
bind'weed'
binge, binged,
  bing'ing *or*
  binge'ing
bin'go *pl.* -goes
bin'na·cle
bin·oc'u·lar
bi·no'mi·al
bi'o·chem'i·cal
bi'o·chem'ist
bi'o·chem'is·try
bi'o·chip'
bi'o·com·pat'i·bil'-
  i·ty
bi'o·de·grad'a·ble
bi'o·di·ver'si·ty
bi'o·en·gi·neer'ing
bi'o·eth'ics
bi'o·feed'back'
bi'o·gen'e·sis
bi·og'ra·pher
bi'o·graph'i·cal
  also bi'o·graph'ic
bi·og'ra·phy
bi'o·haz'ard
bi'o·log'i·cal *also*
  bi'o·log'ic
bi·ol'o·gist
bi·ol'o·gy

bi'o·lu'mi·nes'-
  cence
bi'o·lu'mi·nes'-
  cent
bi'o·mass'
bi'ome'
bi'o·me·chan'ics
bi'o·med'i·cine
bi'o·met'rics
bi·on'ic
bi'o·phys'i·cist
bi'o·phys'ics
bi'op'sy
bi'o·rhythm
bi·os'co·py
bi'o·sphere'
bi'o·syn'the·sis
bi'o·syn·thet'ic
bi·o'ta
bi'o·tech'no·log'i·
  cal
bi'o·tech·nol'o·gy
bi·ot'ic
bi'o·tin
bi·par'ti·san
bi·par'ti·san·ism
bi·par'tite'
bi'ped'
bi'plane'
bi·po'lar
bi·ra'cial
birch
bird'bath'
bird'cage'
bird'call'
bird'er

bird'house'
bird'ie
bird'lime'
bird' of par'a·dise'
  pl. birds' of
  par'a·dise'
bird'seed'
bird's'-eye'
bird' watch'er
bird' watch'ing
bi·ret'ta
birr *(whirring sound)*
  ✓ bur
birth *(beginning)*
  ✓ berth
birth'day'
birth'mark'
birth'place'
birth'rate'
birth'right'
birth'stone'
bis'cuit *pl.* -cuits
bi'sect'
bi·sec'tion
bi·sec'tor
bi·sex'u·al
bi·sex·u·al'i·ty
bish'op
bish'op·ric
bis'muth
bi'son
bisque
bis'tro *pl.* -tros
bit
bitch
bite *(to grip or tear*
  with the teeth), bit,

bit'ten *or* bit,
bit'ing
✔ *bight, byte*
bit'er
bit'ter
bit'tern
bit'ter•root'
bit'ter•sweet'
bi•tu'men
bi•tu'mi•nous
bi'va'lent
bi'valve'
biv'ou•ac', -acked',
-ack'ing
bi•week'ly *(once
every two weeks,
twice a week)*
✔ *semiweekly*
biyearly *(once every
two years, twice a
year)*
✔ *biannual, bien-
nial, semiannual,
semiyearly*
bi•zarre' *(strange)*
✔ *bazaar*
blab, blabbed,
blab'bing
blab'ber•mouth'
black'-and-blue'
adj.
black'-and-white'
adj.
black'ball'
black'ber'ry
black'bird'
black'board'

black'bod'y
black' box'
black'damp'
black'en
black' eye'
black'-eyed' pea'
black'-eyed'
Su'san
Black'foot' *pl.* -foot'
or -feet'
black'guard
black'head'
black' hole'
black'ing
black'ish
black'jack'
black'list'
black'mail'
black'mail'er
black' mar'ket *n.*
black'-mar'ket *adj.*
& *v.*
black'-mar'ket•er
or black'-mar'ke•
teer'
black'out'
black'smith'
black'snake'
black'thorn'
black'-tie' *adj.*
black'top',
-topped', -top'ping
blad'der
blade
blah
blam'a•ble *also*
blame'a•ble

blame, blamed,
blam'ing
blame'less
blame'wor'thi•
ness
blame'wor'thy
blanch *also* blench
(to whiten)
✔ *blench*
bland
blan'dish
blank
blan'ket
blare, blared,
blar'ing
blar'ney
bla•sé'
blas•pheme',
-phemed,
-phem'ing
blas•phem'er
blas'phe•mous
blas'phe•my
blast
blas'to•coel' *or*
blas'to•coele'
blas'to•derm'
blast'off' *also*
blast'-off'
blas'tu•la *pl.* -las *or*
-lae'
bla'tan•cy
bla'tant
blaze, blazed,
blaz'ing
blaz'er
bla'zon

bleach
bleach'ers
bleak
blear
blear'i•ness
blear'y
bleat
bleat'er
bleed, bled,
  bleed'ing
bleed'er
bleed'ing heart' *n.*
bleed'ing-heart'
  adj.
bleep
blem'ish
blench *(to shy away)*
  ✔ *blanch*
blend, blend'ed *or*
  blent, blend'ing
blend'er
bless, blessed *or*
  blest, bless'ing
bless'ed *also* blest
  adj.
bless'ing
blight
blimp
blind
blind'ers
blind'fold'
blind'fold'ed
blind'man's buff'
blink'er
blintz *also* blin'tze
blip
bliss

bliss'ful
blis'ter
blis'ter•y
blis'ter•ing
blithe, blith'er,
  blith'est
blithe'ly
blithe'some
blitz
blitz'krieg'
bliz'zard
bloat
blob
bloc *(group)*
block *(solid sub-*
  stance)
block•ade', -ad'ed,
  -ad'ing
block•ad'er
block•ade'-run'ner
block'age
block'bust'er
block'head'
block'house'
bloke
blond *also* blonde
blood
blood' bank'
blood'bath'
blood' count'
blood'cur'dling
blood'ed
blood'hound'
blood'i•ness
blood'less
blood'let'ting
blood'line'

blood'mo•bile'
blood'root'
blood'shed'
blood'shot'
blood'stained'
blood'stone'
blood'stream' *also*
  blood' stream'
blood'suck'er
blood'thirst'i•ness
blood'thirst'y
blood'y, -ied, -y•ing
bloom
bloom'ers
bloom'ing
bloop'er
blos'som
blot, blot'ted,
  blot'ting
blotch
blotch'y
blot'ter
blouse
blow, blew, blown,
  blow'ing
blow'-dry', -dried',
  -dry'ing
blow' dry'er
blow'er
blow'fish' *pl.* -fish'
  or -fish'es
blow'fly'
blow'gun'
blow'hard'
blow'hole'
blow'off' *n.*
blow'out' *n.*

blow′pipe′
blow′torch′
blow′up′ *n.*
blow′zy *also*
  blow′sy
blub′ber
bludg′eon
blue, blu′er, blu′est
blue, blued, blu′ing
blue′ ba′by
blue′bell′ *also*
  blue′bells′
blue′ber′ry
blue′bird′
blue′ blood′ *(noble
  descent)*
blue′ blood′ *(a per-
  son of noble descent)*
blue′bon′net
blue′bot′tle
blue′ cheese′
blue′-col′lar *adj.*
blue′fish′ *pl.* -fish′
  or -fish′es
blue′grass′
blue′ jay′
blue′print′
blue′-rib′bon *adj.*
blues
blu′ets
bluff
bluff′er
blu′ing *also*
  blue′ing
blu′ish *also* blue′ish
blun′der
blun′der•buss′

blunt
blur, blurred,
  blur′ring
blurb
blur′ry
blurt
blush
blush′er
blus′ter
blus′ter•er
blus′ter•ous
blus′ter•y
bo′a
boar *(animal)*
  ✓ Boer, bore
board
board′er *(lodger)*
  ✓ border
board′ing house′
board′ing school′
board′walk′
boast
boast′er
boast′ful
boat
boat′house′
boat′man
boat′ peo′ple
boat′swain *also*
  bo's′n *or* bo′sun
bob, bobbed,
  bob′bing
bob′bin
bob′ble, -bled,
  -bling
bob′by
bob′by pin′

bob′by socks′ *also*
  bob′by sox′
bob′cat′
bob′o•link′
bob′sled′, -sled′ded,
  -sled′ding
bob′tail′
bob′white′
bode, bod′ed,
  bod′ing
bo•de′ga
bod′ice
bod′i•less
bod′i•ly
bod′kin
bod′y
bod′y•build′ing
bod′y•guard′
Boer *(Dutch South
  African)*
  ✓ boar, bore
bog, bogged,
  bog′ging
bo′gey *also* bo′gy *or*
  bo′gie *pl.* -geys *also*
  -gies
bo′gey•man′
bog′gle, -gled,
  -gling
bo′gus
bo•he′mi•an
boil
boil′er
boil′ing point′
bois′ter•ous
bo′la *also* bo′las
bold

bold′face′ *n. & adj.*
bold′-faced′ *adj.*
bole *(tree trunk)*
  ✔ *boll, bowl*
bo•le′ro *pl.* -ros
bo•li′var *pl.* -vars *or*
  -var•es′
Bo•liv′i•an
boll *(seed pod)*
  ✔ *bole, bowl*
bol′lix *also* bol′lox
bo•lo′gna *also*
  ba•lo′ney *or*
  bo•lo′ney *(meat)*
  ✔ *baloney*
Bol′she•vik *pl.* -viks′
  or Bol′she•vi′ki
Bol′she•vism
Bol′she•vist
bol′ster
bolt
bo′lus *pl.* -lus•es
bomb
bom•bard′
bom′bar•dier′
bom•bard′ment
bom′bast′
bom•bas′tic
bom′ba•zine′
bomb′er
bomb′shell′
bomb′sight′
bo′na fide′
bo•nan′za
bon′bon′
bond′age
bond′hold′er

bond′man
bond′ser′vant
bonds′man
bond′wom′an
bone, boned,
  bon′ing
bone′black′ *also*
  bone′ black′
bone′-dry′
bone′fish′ *pl.* -fish′
  or -fish′es
bone′head′
bone′ meal′
bon′er
bon′fire′
bon′go drums′
bon′gos
bon′ho•mie′
bo•ni′to *pl.* -to *or*
  -tos
bon mot′ *pl.* bons
  mots′
bon′net
bon′ny *also* bon′nie
bon•sai′ *pl.* bon•sai′
bo′nus *pl.* -nus•es
bon′ vi•vant′ *pl.*
  bons′ vi•vants′
bon′ voy•age′
bon′i•ness
bon′y *or* bon′ey,
  -i•er *or* -ey•er, -i•est
  or -ey•est
boo *pl.* boos
boo, booed, boo′ing
boob
boo′-boo *also* boo′-

boo *pl.* -boos
boo′by
boo′by prize′
boo′by trap′
boog′ie-woog′ie
book
book′bind′er
book′bind′er•y
book′bind′ing
book′case′
book′ club′
book′end′
book′ie
book′ing
book′ish
book′keep′er
book′keep′ing
book′let
book′mak′er
book′mak′ing
book′mark′
book′mo•bile′
book′plate′
book′sell′er
book′shelf′
book′shop′
book′stand′
book′store′
book′worm′
Bool′e•an
  al′ge•bra
boom
boo′mer•ang′
boom′town′
boon
boon′docks′
boor

boor'ish
boost
boost'er
boot'black'
boot' camp'
boot'ed
boo'tee *also* boo'tie
(*baby shoe*)
✓ *booty*
booth
boot'jack'
boot'leg', -legged',
-leg'ging
boot'leg'ger
boot'lick'
boot'lick'er
boot'strap'
boo'ty (*plunder*)
✓ *bootee*
booze, boozed,
booz'ing
booz'er
bop, bopped,
bop'ping
bo'rate'
bo'rax'
Bor·deaux' *pl.*
-deaux'
bor'der (*boundary*)
✓ *boarder*
bor'der·land'
bor'der·line'
bore (*to drill, to
weary*), bored,
bor'ing
✓ *boar, Boer*
bore (*wave*)

✓ *boar, Boer*
bore'dom
bor'er
bo'ric ac'id
bor'ing
born (*brought into
life*)
✓ *bourn*
born'-a·gain'
bo'ron
bor'ough (*town*)
✓ *burro, burrow*
bor'row
bor'row·er
bor'row·ing
borscht *also* borsch
bor'zoi'
bosk'y
bos'om
boss
boss'ism
boss'y
Bos'ton ter'ri·er
bo·tan'i·cal *also*
bo·tan'ic
bot'a·nist
bot'a·ny
botch
bot'fly' *also* bot' fly'
both
both'er
both'er·some
bot'tle, -tled, -tling
bot'tle·neck'
bot'tler
bot'tom
bot'tom·land'

bot'tom·less
bot'u·lism
bou'doir'
bouf·fant'
bou·gain·vil'le·a
also bou'gain·
vil'lae·a
bough (*branch*)
✓ *bow*
bouil'la·baisse'
bouil'lon' (*broth*)
✓ *bullion*
boul'der
boul'e·vard'
bounce, bounced,
bounc'ing
bounc'er
bounc'i·ly
bounc'y
bound
bound'a·ry
bound'en
bound'less
boun'te·ous
boun'ti·ful
boun'ty
bou·quet'
bour'bon
bour·geois' *pl.*
-geois'
bour'geoi·sie'
bourn *also* bourne
(*stream*)
✓ *born*
bourn *also* bourne
(*limit*)
✓ *born*

bour·rée′
bout
bou·tique′
bou′ton·niere′ also
  bou′ton·nière′
bo′vine′
bow *(front of a ship,*
  bending)
  ✔ bough
bow *(weapon)*
  ✔ beau
bowd′ler·ism
bowd′ler·i·za′tion
bowd′ler·ize′
bow′el
bow′er
bow′ie knife′
bowl *(dish, ball)*
  ✔ bole, boll
bow′leg′
bow′leg′ged
bowl′er
bow′line
bowl′ing
bow′man
bow′sprit′
bow′string′
bow′ tie′
box *(container, slap),*
  pl. box′es
box *(shrub), pl.* box
  or box·es
box′car′
box′er
box′ing
box′wood′
box′y

boy *(boy child)*
  ✔ buoy
boy′cott′
boy′friend′
boy′hood′
boy′ish
Boy′ Scout′
boy′sen·ber′ry
bra
brace, braced,
  brac′ing
brace′let
brac′er
bra′chi·o·pod′
brack′en
brack′et
brack′ish
bract
brad, brad′ded,
  brad′ding
brag, bragged,
  brag′ging
brag′ga·do′ci·o′
brag′gart
brag′ger
Brah′ma *(deity)*
Brah′man *also*
  Brah′ma *also*
  Brah′min *(cattle)*
Brah′man·ism
Brah′min *also*
  Brah·man *(class)*
braid
braid′er
Braille *or* braille
brain
brain′child′

brain′-dead′
brain′ death′
brain′less
brain′pan′
brain′ stem′ *also*
  brain′stem′
brain′storm′
brain′wash′
brain′wash′ing
brain′ wave′
brain′y
braise *(to cook),*
  braised, brais′ing
  ✔ braze
brake *(to slow or*
  stop), braked,
  brak′ing
  ✔ break
brake *(fern)*
  ✔ break
brake′man
bram′ble
bram′bly
bran
branch
brand
brand′er
bran′dish
brand′-new′
bran′dy, -died,
  -dy·ing
brant *pl.* brant *or*
  brants
brash
brass
bras′se·rie′
bras·siere′

brass'y
brat
brat'ty
brat'wurst'
bra·va'do *pl.* -dos *or* -does
brave, brav'er, brav'est
brave, braved, brav'ing
brave'ly
brav'er·y
bra'vo *pl.* -vos
bra·vu'ra
brawl
brawl'er
brawn
brawn'i·ness
brawn'y
bray
braze *(to solder),* brazed, braz'ing
✔ *braise*
bra'zen, -zened, -zen·ing
bra'zier
Bra·zil'ian
Bra·zil' nut'
breach *(gap, violation)*
✔ *breech*
bread
bread'-and-but'ter *adj.*
bread'bas'ket
bread'fruit'
bread' line'

bread'stuff'
breadth
bread'win'ner
break *(to make unusable),* broke, bro'ken, break'ing
✔ *brake*
break'a·ble
break'age
break'er
break'down' *n.*
break'fast
break'front'
break'neck'
break'point'
break'through' *n.*
break'up' *n.*
break'wa'ter
bream *pl.* bream *or* breams
breast
breast'bone'
breast'-feed', -fed', -feed'ing
breast'plate'
breast'stroke'
breast'work'
breath *n.*
breathe, breathed, breath'ing
breath'er
breath'less
breath'tak'ing
breath'y
breech *(buttocks)*
✔ *breach*
breech'cloth'

breech'es buoy'
breech'load'er
breed, bred, breed'ing
breed'er
breed'ing
breeze, breezed, breez'ing
breeze'way'
breez'i·ly
breez'y
breth'ren
Bret'on
breve
bre'vi·ar'y
brev'i·ty
brew
brew'er·y
brew'ing
bri'ar *also* bri'er *(shrub, pipe)*
✔ *brier*
bri'ar·wood'
bribe, bribed, brib'ing
brib'er·y
bric'-a-brac'
brick *pl.* bricks *or* brick
brick'bat'
brick'lay'er
brick'lay'ing
brick'work'
brick'yard'
bri'dal *(relating to a bride)*
✔ *bridle*

bride
bride'groom'
brides'maid'
bridge'a•ble
bridge, bridged,
 bridg'ing
bridge'head'
bridge'work'
bri'dle (to restrain),
 -dled, -dling
 ✔ bridal
bri'dle path'
brief
brief'case'
brief'ing
bri'er also bri'ar
 (thorny shrub)
 ✔ briar
brig
bri•gade'
brig'a•dier'
brig'a•dier'
 gen'er•al pl.
 brig'a•dier'
 gen'er•als
brig'and
brig'an•tine'
bright
bright'en
bril'liance
bril'lian•cy
bril'liant
brim, brimmed,
 brim'ming
brim'ful
brim'stone'
brin'dle

brin'dled
brine
bring, brought,
 bring'ing
brink
brin'y
bri•quette' also
 bri•quet'
brisk
bris'ket
bris'ling
bris'tle, -tled, -tling
bris'tly
britch'es
Brit'i•cism
Brit'ish
Brit'ish•er
Brit'on
brit'tle, -tler, -tlest
broach (to begin to
 discuss)
 ✔ brooch
broad
broad'ax' or
 broad'axe'
broad'cast', -cast'
 or -cast'ed, -cast'ing
broad'cast'er
broad'cloth'
broad'en
broad'loom'
broad'-mind'ed
broad'side'
broad'sword'
bro•cade', -cad'ed,
 -cad'ing
broc'co•li

bro•chure'
bro'gan
brogue
broil
broil'er
broke
bro'ken
bro'ken-down'
bro'ken•heart'ed
bro'ker
bro'ker•age
bro'mide'
bro'mine'
bron'chi•a sing.
 -chi•um
bron'chi•al
bron'chi•ole'
bron•chit'ic
bron•chi'tis
bron'cho•scope'
bron'chus pl. -chi'
bron'co pl. -cos
bron'to•saur' or
 bron'to•sau'rus
bronze, bronzed,
 bronz'ing
bronz'y
brooch (pin)
 ✔ broach
brood
brood'er
brook
brook'let
broom (implement
 for sweeping)
 ✔ brougham
broom'corn'

broom'stick'
broth
broth'er
broth'er•hood'
broth'er-in-law' *pl.*
  broth'ers-in-law'
broth'er•li•ness
broth'er•ly
brougham *(carriage)*
  ✔ *broom*
brow
brow'beat', -beat',
  -beat'en, -beat'ing
brown
brown' Bet'ty
brown'ie
brown'ish
brown'out'
brown'stone'
browse, browsed,
  brows'ing
brows'er
bru'in
bruise, bruised,
  bruis'ing
bruis'er
bruit *(to spread news)*
  ✔ *brute*
brunch
bru•nette' *also*
  bru•net'
brunt
brush
brush'fire' *also*
  brush' fire'
brush'land'
brush'off' *also*

brush'-off' *n.*
brush'wood'
brush'work'
brusque
brusque'ly
brusque'ness
Brus'sels sprouts'
bru'tal
bru•tal'i•ty
bru'tal•ize', -ized',
  -iz'ing
brute *(beast)*
  ✔ *bruit*
brut'ish
bub'ble, -bled, -bling
bub'ble gum'
bub'bly
bu'bo *pl.* -boes
bu•bon'ic plague'
buc'ca•neer'
buck
buck'a•roo' *pl.*
  -roos'
buck'board'
buck'et
buck'et•ful'
buck'et seat'
buck'eye'
buck'le, -led, -ling
buck'ler
buck'ram
buck'saw'
buck'shot'
buck'skin'
buck'tooth' *pl.*
  -teeth'
buck'toothed'

buck'wheat'
bu•col'ic
bud, bud'ded,
  bud'ding
Bud'dhism
Bud'dhist
bud'dy
budge, budged,
  budg'ing
budg'er•i•gar'
budg'et
bud'get•ar'y
budg'ie
buff
buf'fa•lo' *pl.* -lo' *or*
  -loes' *or* -los'
buff'er
buf•fet' *(furniture,*
  meal)
buf'fet *(blow)*
buf•foon'
buf•foon'er•y
bug, bugged,
  bug'ging
bug'a•boo' *pl.*
  -boos'
bug'bear'
bug'gy
bu'gle, -gled, -gling
bu'gler
build, built,
  build'ing
build'er
build'ing
build'up' *also*
  build'-up' *n.*
built'-in'

built'-up'
bulb
bul'bous
Bul•gar'i•an
bulge, bulged,
  bulg'ing
bulg'i•ness
bulg'y
bulk
bulk'head'
bulk'i•ness
bulk'y
bull
bull'dog'
bull'doze', -dozed',
  -doz'ing
bull'doz'er
bul'let
bul'le•tin
bul'le•tin board'
bul'let•proof'
bull'fight'
bull'fight'er
bull'fight'ing
bull'finch'
bull'frog'
bull'head'
bull'head'ed
bull'horn'
bul'lion *(gold or
  silver bars)*
  ✔ *bouillon*
bull'ish
bul'lock
bull'pen'
bull'ring'
bull's'-eye' *or* bull's'

eye'
bul'ly, -lied, -ly•ing
bul'rush'
bul'wark'
bum, bummed,
  bum'ming
bum'ble•bee'
bum'mer
bump
bump'er
bump'er stick'er
bump'i•ness
bump'kin
bump'y
bun
bunch
bun'dle, -dled,
  -dling
bung
bun'ga•low'
bung'hole'
bun'gle, -gled,
  -gling
bun'gler
bun'ion
bunk
bun'ker
bunk'house'
bun'ny
Bun'sen burn'er
bunt
bunt'er
bunt'ing
buoy *(float)*
  ✔ *boy*
buoy'an•cy
buoy'ant

bur *also* burr *(prickly
  seed)*
  ✔ *birr*
bur'ble, -bled,
  -bling
bur'den
bur'den•some
bur'dock'
bu'reau *pl.* -reaus *or*
  -reaux
bu•reauc'ra•cy
bu'reau•crat'
bu'reau•crat'ic
bu•rette' *also*
  bu•ret' *(glass tube)*
  ✔ *barrette*
burg *(city or town)*
  ✔ *berg*
bur'geon
burg'er *(hamburger)*
  ✔ *burgher*
bur'gess
burgh'er *(citizen)*
  ✔ *burger*
bur'glar
bur'glar•ize', -ized',
  -iz'ing
bur'gla•ry
bur'gle, bur'gled,
  bur'gling
bur'go•mas'ter
bur'gun•dy *(color)*
Bur'gun•dy *(wine)*
bur'i•al
burl
bur'lap'
bur•lesque',

-lesqued', -les'quing
bur'li·ness
bur'ly
Bur·mese' *pl.* -mese'
burn, burned *or*
  burnt, burn'ing
burn'a·ble
burn'er
burn'ing
bur'nish
bur·noose' *also*
  bur·nous'
burn'out' *n.*
burp
burr *(rough spot)*
burr *also* bur *(trill)*
bur·ri'to *pl.* -tos
bur'ro *(donkey), pl.*
  -ros
  ✔ borough
bur'row *(hole)*
  ✔ borough
bur'row·er
bur'sa *pl.* -sae *or* -sas
bur'sar
bur·si'tis
burst
bur'y *(to put in the*
  ground), -ied, -y·ing
  ✔ berry
bus *(vehicle), pl.*
  bus'es *or* bus'ses
bus *(to transport),*
  bused *or* bussed,
  bus'ing *or* bus'sing
bus'boy' *also* bus'
  boy'

bush
bushed
bush'el
bush'i·ness
bush'ing
Bush'man
bush'mas·ter
bush'whack'
bush'whack'er
bush'y
bus'i·ly
busi'ness
busi'ness·like'
busi'ness·man
busi'ness·per'son
busi'ness·wom'an
bus'load'
bust
bus'tard
bust'er
bus·tier'
bus'tle, -tled, -tling
bust'y
bus'y, -ied, -y·ing
bus'y·bod'y
bus'y·ness
bus'y·work'
but *conj.*
  ✔ butt
bu'ta·di'ene'
bu'tane'
butch'er
butch'er·y
but'ler
butt *(to hit or push)*
  ✔ but
butt *(target)*

✔ but
butte
but'ter
but'ter bean'
but'ter·cup'
but'ter·fat'
but'ter·fin'gers
but'ter·fish' *pl.*
  -fish' *or* -fish'es
but'ter·fly'
but'ter·milk'
but'ter·nut'
but'ter·scotch'
but'ter·y
but'tock
but'ton
but'ton·hole',
  -holed', -hol'ing
but'ton·wood'
but'tress
bu'tyl
bu·tyr'ic
bux'om
buy *(to purchase),*
  bought, buy'ing
  ✔ by
buy'er
buzz
buz'zard
buzz'er
buzz' saw'
by *prep.*
  ✔ buy
by' and by' *adv.*
by'-and-by' *n.*
bye'-bye'
by'gone'

by'law'
by'line'
by'pass' *also*
  by'-pass'
by'-path'
by'-play'
by'prod'uct *or*
  by'-prod'uct
by'road'
by'stand'er
byte *(computer unit)*
  ✔ *bight, bite*
by'way'
by'word'
Byz'an•tine'

C

cab
ca•bal', -balled',
  -bal'ling
cab'al•le'ro *pl.* -ros
ca•ban'a *also*
  ca•ba'ña
cab'a•ret'
cab'bage
cab'by *or* cab'bie
cab'driv'er
cab'in
cab'i•net'
cab'i•net•mak'er
cab'i•net•work'
ca'ble, -bled, -bling
ca'ble car'
ca'ble•gram'
ca•boose'

cab'ri•o•let'
ca•ca'o *pl.* -os
cach'a•lot'
cache *(to hide)*,
  cached, cach'ing
  ✔ *cash*
ca•chet'
cack'le, -led, -ling
ca•coph'o•nous
ca•coph'o•ny
cac'tus *pl.* -ti' *or*
  -tus•es
cad
ca•dav'er
ca•dav'er•ous
cad'die *also* cad'dy
  (to carry golf clubs),
  -died, -dy'ing
  ✔ *caddy*
cad'dis fly' *also*
  cad'dice fly'
Cad'do *pl.* Cad'do
  or -dos
Cad'do•an
cad'dy *(small con-*
  tainer)
  ✔ *caddie*
ca'dence
ca•den'za
ca•det'
cad'mi•um
cad're
ca•du'ce•us *pl.*
  -ce•i'
cae'sar *also* Cae'sar
cae•su'ra *pl.* -su'ras
  -su'rae

ca•fé' *also* ca•fe'
caf'e•te'ri•a
caf•feine' *also*
  caf•fein'
caf'tan' *or* kaf'tan'
cage, caged, cag'ing
ca'gey *also* ca'gy,
  -gi•er, -gi•est
cag'i•ness
ca•hoots'
cai'man *also*
  cay'man *pl.* -mans
cairn
cais'son'
ca•jole', -joled',
  -jol'ing
ca•jol'er•y
Ca'jun *also* Ca'jan
cake, caked, cak'ing
cake'walk'
cake'walk'er
cal'a•bash'
cal'a•boose'
cal'a•mine'
ca•lam'i•tous
ca•lam'i•ty
cal•car'e•ous
cal'ci•fi•ca'tion
cal'ci•fy', -fied',
  -fy'ing
cal'ci•mine',
  -mined', -min'ing
cal'ci•na'tion
cal•cine', -cined',
  -cin'ing
cal'cite'
cal'ci•um

cal'cu·la·bil'i·ty
cal'cu·la·ble
cal'cu·late', -lat'ed,
  -lat'ing
cal'cu·la'tion
cal'cu·la'tor
cal'cu·lus *pl.* -li' *or*
  -lus·es
cal'dron *also*
  caul'dron
cal'en·dar *(time*
  chart)
cal'en·der *(press)*
calf *pl.* calves
calf'skin'
cal'i·ber
cal'i·brate',
  -brat'ed, -brat'ing
cal'i·bra'tion
cal'i·co' *pl.* -coes' *or*
  -cos'
Cal'i·for'nian
cal'i·for'ni·um
cal'i·per *also*
  cal'li·per
ca'liph *also* ca'lif
ca'liph·ate'
cal'is·then'ics
call
cal'la
call'er
cal·lig'ra·pher
cal·lig'ra·phy
call'ing
cal·li'o·pe'
cal·los'i·ty
cal'lous *(having*

  calluses, unfeeling)
  ✓ callus
cal'low
call'-up' *n.*
cal'lus *(hard tissue),*
  pl. -lus·es
  ✓ callous
calm
cal'o·mel'
ca·lor'ic
cal'o·rie
cal'o·rif'ic
cal'o·rim'e·ter
cal'u·met'
ca·lum'ni·ate',
  -at'ed, -at'ing
ca·lum'ni·a'tion
ca·lum'ni·a'tor
ca·lum'ni·ous
cal'um·ny
calve, calved,
  calv'ing
Cal'vin·ism
Cal'vin·ist
Cal'vin·is'tic
Ca·lyp'so *or*
  ca·lyp'so
ca'lyx *pl.* -lyx·es *or*
  -ly·ces'
cal·zo'ne
cam
ca'ma·ra'der·ie
cam'ber
cam'bi·um
Cam'bri·an
Cam·bo'di·an
cam'bric

cam'cord'er
cam'el
ca·mel'lia
cam'el's hair'
Cam'em·bert'
cam'e·o' *pl.* -os'
cam'er·a
cam'er·a·man'
cam'er·a·wom'an
cam'i·sole'
cam'ou·flage',
  -flaged', -flag'ing
camp
cam·paign'
cam·paign'er
cam'pa·ni'le *pl.* -les
  or -li
camp'er
camp'fire'
Camp' Fire' Girl'
camp'ground'
cam'phor
camp'site'
cam'pus *pl.* -pus·es
cam'shaft'
can *aux. v., past tense*
  could
can *(to preserve),*
  canned, can'ning
Ca'naan·ite'
Ca·na'di·an
ca·nal'
ca·nard'
ca·nar'y
can'cel, -celed *also*
  -celled, -cel·ing
  also -cel·ling

can'cel·la'tion
can'cer
can'cer·ous
can·del'a
can·de·la'bra *pl.* -bras
can·de·la'brum *pl.* -bra *or* -brums
can'did
can'di·da·cy
can'di·date'
can'died
can'dle
can'dle·hold'er
can'dle·light'
can'dle·pin'
can'dle·pow'er
can'dle·snuff'er
can'dle·stick'
can'dle·wick'
can'dor
can'dy, -died, -dy·ing
cane, caned, can'ing
cane'brake'
ca'nine
can'is·ter
can'ker
can'ker·ous
can'ker sore'
can'ker·worm'
can'na
can'na·bis
can'ner·y
can'ni·bal
can'ni·bal·ism
can'ni·bal·is'tic

can'ni·bal·ize', -ized', -iz'ing
can'ni·ly
can'non *(gun), pl.* -non
  ✔ *canon*
can'non·ade', -ad'ed, -ad'ing
can'non·ball' *also* can'non ball'
can'non·eer'
can'not
can'ny
ca·noe', -noed', -noe'ing
ca·noe'ist
can'on *(church law, cleric)*
  ✔ *cannon*
ca·non'i·cal *also* ca·non'ic
can'on·i·za'tion
can'on·ize', -ized', -iz'ing
can'o·py, -pied, -py·ing
cant *(slope, jargon)*
can't *contraction*
can'ta·loupe' *also* can'ta·loup'
can·tan'ker·ous
can·ta'ta
can·teen'
can'ter *(gallop)*
  ✔ *cantor*
can'ti·cle
can'ti·le'ver

can'tle
can'to *pl.* -tos
can'ton
Can'ton·ese'
can·ton'ment
can'tor *(singer)*
  ✔ *canter*
can'vas *(cloth)*
  ✔ *canvass*
can'vas·back'
can'vass *(to ask for votes)*
  ✔ *canvas*
can'vass·er
can'yon *also* ca'ñon
caou'tchouc'
cap, capped, cap'ping
ca'pa·bil'i·ty
ca'pa·ble
ca'pa·bly
ca·pa'cious
ca·pac'i·tance
ca·pac'i·tate', -tat'ed, -tat'ing
ca·pac'i·tive
ca·pac'i·tor
ca·pac'i·ty
ca·par'i·son
cape
ca'per
cap·il·lar'y
cap'i·tal *(city, wealth, letter)*
  ✔ *capitol*
cap'i·tal·ism
cap'i·tal·ist

cap'i·tal·is'tic
cap'i·tal·i·za'tion
cap'i·tal·ize', -ized',
  -iz'ing
cap'i·tal
  pun'ish·ment
cap'i·tol *(building)*
  ✓ capital
ca·pit'u·late',
  -lat'ed, -lat'ing
ca·pit'u·la'tion
cap'let
ca'pon'
cap'puc·ci'no *pl.*
  -nos
ca·price'
ca·pri'cious
cap'size', -sized',
  -siz'ing
cap'stan
cap'stone'
cap'su·lar
cap'su·late' *also*
  cap'su·lat'ed
cap'su·la'tion
cap'sule
cap'sul·ize', -ized',
  -iz'ing
cap'tain
cap'tain·cy
cap'tion
cap'tious
cap'ti·vate',
  -vat'ed, -vat'ing
cap'ti·va'tion
cap'ti·va'tor
cap'tive

cap·tiv'i·ty
cap'tor
cap'ture, -tured,
  -tur·ing
cap'u·chin
car
ca·rafe'
car'a·mel
car'a·pace'
car'at *(unit of weight)*
  ✓ caret, carrot, karat
car'a·van'
car'a·van'sa·ry *also*
  car'a·van'se·rai' *pl.*
  -ries *also* -rais
car'a·vel'
car'a·way'
car'bide'
car'bine'
car'bo·hy'drate'
car'bo·lat'ed
car·bol'ic ac'id
car'bon
car'bo·na'ceous
car'bon·ate', -at'ed,
  -at'ing
car'bon·a'tion
car'bon·a'tor
car·bon'ic
car'bon·if'er·ous
  (containing carbon)
Car'bon·if'er·ous
  (geologic period)
car'bon·i·za'tion
car'bon·ize', -ized',
  -iz'ing
car'bon·yl

car·box'yl
car'box·yl'ic
car'bun'cle
car'bu·re'tor
car'cass
car·cin'o·gen
car'cin·o·gen'ic
car·ci·no'ma *pl.*
  -mas *or* -ma·ta
car'da·mom *or*
  car'da·mon
card'board'
car'di·ac'
car'di·gan
car'di·nal
car'di·o·gram'
car'di·o·graph'
car'di·ol'o·gist
car'di·ol'o·gy
car'di·o·pul'mo·
  nar'y
car'di·o·vas'cu·lar
card'sharp' *also*
  card'sharp'er
care, cared, car'ing
ca·reen' *(to swerve,
  to tilt)*
ca·reer' *(to rush)*
ca·reer' *(profession)*
care'free'
care'ful
care'giv'er
care'less
ca·ress'
car'et *(proofreading
  mark)*
  ✓ carat, carrot, karat

care'tak'er
care'worn'
car'fare'
car'go *pl.* -goes *or* -gos
car'hop'
Car'ib *pl.* -ib *or* -ibs
Car'i•ban *pl.* -ban *or* -bans
Car'ib•be'an
car'i•bou' *pl.* -bou' *or* -bous'
car'i•ca•ture', -tured', -tur'ing
car'i•ca•tur'ist
car'ies *pl.* -ies
car'il•lon'
car'jack' *or* car'-jack'
car'load'
Car'mel•ite'
car'mine
car'nage
car'nal
car•nal'i•ty
car•na'tion
car•nel'ian
car'ni•val
car'ni•vore'
car•niv'o•rous
car'ob
car'ol *(song)*, -oled *also* -olled, -ol•ing *or* -ol•ling
✔ *carrel*
car'ol•er *or* car'ol•ler

Car'o•lin'i•an
car'om
car'o•tene'
ca•rot'id
ca•rous'al *(revelry)*
✔ *carousel*
ca•rouse', -roused', -rous'ing
car'ou•sel' *or* car'rou•sel' *(merry-go-round)*
✔ *carousal*
ca•rous'er
carp *(to complain)*
carp *(fish)*, *pl.* carp *or* carps
car'pal *(relating to the carpus)*
car'pel *(flower part)*
car'pen•ter
car'pen•try
car'pet
car'pet•bag'
car'pet•bag'ger
car'pet•ing
car' pool' *n.*
car'-pool' *v.*
car'-pool'er
car'port'
car'pus *pl.* -pi'
car'rel *also* car'rell *(library nook)*
✔ *carol*
car'riage
car'ri•er
car'ri•on
car'rot *(plant)*

✔ *carat, caret, karat*
car'ry, -ried, -ry'ing
car'ry•all'
car'ry•on' *adj. & n.*
car'ry•out' *adj.*
car'ry•o•ver *n.*
car'sick'
cart'age
carte blanche' *pl.* cartes blanches'
car•tel'
Car•te'sian
car'ti•lage
car'ti•lag'i•nous
car•tog'ra•pher
car'to•graph'ic *or* car'to•graph'i•cal
car•tog'ra•phy
car'ton
car•toon'
car•toon'ist
car'tridge
cart'wheel'
carve, carved, carv'ing
carv'er
car' wash'
car'y•at'id *pl.* -ids *or* -i•des'
ca•sa'ba *also* cas•sa'ba
cas•cade', -cad'ed, -cad'ing
cas•car'a
case, cased, cas'ing
ca'sein'
case'load'

case′ment
case′work′
case′work′er
cash *(money)*
  ✔ *cache*
cash′ew
cash·ier′ *(person who receives money)*
ca·shier′ *(to dismiss)*
cash′mere′
ca·si′no *(gambling house), pl.* -nos
ca·si′no *also* cas·si′no *(card game)*
cask *(barrel)*
  ✔ *casque*
cas′ket
casque *(helmet, cask)*
  ✔ *cask*
cas·sa′va
cas′se·role′
cas·sette′
cas′sia
cas′sock
cas′so·war′y
cast *(to throw)*, cast, cast′ing
  ✔ *caste*
cas′ta·nets′
cast′a·way′
caste *(social class)*
  ✔ *cast*
cas′tel·lat′ed
cast′er *(person who casts)*
cast′er *also* cas′tor

(wheel, bottle)
  ✔ *castor*
cas′ti·gate′, -gat′ed, -gat′ing
cas′ti·ga′tion
cas′ti·ga′tor
Cas·tile′ soap′
Cas·til′ian
cast′ i′ron *n.*
cast′-i′ron *adj.*
cas′tle, -tled, -tling
cast′off′ *n.*
cas′tor *(oil)*
  ✔ *caster*
cas′trate′, -trat′ed, -trat′ing
cas·tra′tion
ca′su·al
ca′su·al·ty
ca′su·ist
ca′su·is′tic *or* ca′su·is′ti·cal
ca′su·ist·ry
cat
cat′a·bol′ic
ca·tab′o·lism
cat′a·clysm
cat′a·clys′mic
cat′a·combs′
cat′a·falque′
Cat′a·lan′
cat′a·lep′sy
cat′a·lep′tic
cat′a·log′ *or* cat′a·logue′, -loged′ *or* -logued′, -log′ing *or*

-logu′ing
cat′a·log′er *or* cat′a·logu′er
ca·tal′pa
ca·tal′y·sis *pl.* -ses′
cat′a·lyst
cat′a·lyt′ic
cat′a·lyze′, -lyzed′, -lyz′ing
cat′a·ma·ran′
cat′a·mount′
cat′a·pult′
cat′a·ract′
ca·tarrh′
ca·tas′tro·phe
cat′a·stroph′ic
cat′a·to′ni·a
cat′a·ton′ic
Ca·taw′ba *pl.* -ba *or* -bas
cat′bird′
cat′boat′
cat′call′
catch, caught, catch′ing
catch′all′
catch′er
catch′word′
catch′y
cat′e·chism
cat′e·chist
cat′e·chi·za′tion
cat′e·chize′, -chized′, -chiz′ing
cat′e·chu′men
cat′e·gor′i·cal
cat′e·go·ri·za′tion

cat'e•go•rize',
-rized', -riz'ing

cat'e•go'ry

cat'e•nate', -nat'ed,
-nat'ing

cat'e•na'tion

ca'ter

cat'er-cor'nered
also cat'er-cor'ner
or cat'ty-cor'nered
or cat'ty-cor'ner *or*
kit'ty-cor'nered *or*
kit'ty-cor'ner

ca'ter•er

cat'er•pil'lar

cat'er•waul'

cat'fish' *pl.* -fish' *or*
-fish'es

cat'gut'

ca•thar'sis

ca•thar'tic

ca•the'dral

cath'e•ter

cath'ode'

cath'ode-ray'
tube'

cath'o•lic *(universal)*

Cath'o•lic *(relating
to the Catholic
Church)*

Ca•thol'i•cism

cat'i'on

cat'kin

cat'nap', -napped',
-nap'ping

cat'nip'

cat'-o'-nine'-tails'

pl. cat'-o'-nine'-
tails'

CAT' scan'

cat's'-eye'

cat's'-paw' *also*
cats'paw'

cat'tail'

cat'ti•ness

cat'tle

cat'tle•man

cat'ty

cat'walk'

Cau•ca'sian

Cau•ca•soid'

cau'cus *pl.* -cus•es *or*
-cus•ses

cau'cus, -cused *or*
-cussed, -cus•ing *or*
-cus•sing

cau'dal

cau'li•flow'er

caulk *also* calk

caulk'er

caus'al

cau•sal'i•ty

cau•sa'tion

caus'a•tive

cause, caused,
caus'ing

cause cé•lè'bre *pl.*
causes cé•lè'bres

cause'way'

caus'tic

cau'ter•i•za'tion

cau'ter•ize', -ized',
-iz'ing

cau'tion

cau'tion•ar'y

cau'tious

cav'al•cade'

cav'a•lier'

cav'al•ry

cave, caved, cav'ing

ca've•at'

cave'-in' *n.*

cave'man' *also*
cave' man'

cav'ern

cav'ern•ous

cav'i•ar' *also*
cav'i•are'

cav'il, -iled *also*
-illed, -il'ing *or*
-il'ling

cav'i•ta'tion

cav'i•ty

ca•vort'

ca'vy

caw

cay *(islet)*
✔ key, quay

cay•enne' pep'per

Ca•yu'ga *pl.* -ga *or*
-gas

cay•use'

Cay•use' *pl.* -use' *or*
-us'es

CD/ROM

cease, ceased,
ceas'ing

cease'-fire' *or*
cease'fire'

cease'less

ce'cum *also*

cae′cum *pl.* -ca
ce′dar
ce′dar wax′wing′
cede *(to yield)*,
 ced′ed, ced′ing
 ✔ seed
ce·dil′la
ceil′ing
cel′an·dine′
cel′e·brant
cel′e·brate′,
 -brat′ed, -brat′ing
cel′c·bra′tion
cel′e·bra′tor
cel′e·bra·to′ry
ce·leb′ri·ty
ce·ler′i·ty
cel′er·y
ce·les′ta *also*
 ce·leste′
ce·les′tial
cel′i·ba·cy
cel′i·bate
cell *(room, basic unit*
 of living matter)
 ✔ sell
cel′lar *(storage room)*
 ✔ seller
cell′block′
cel′list
cel′lo *pl.* -los
cel′lo·phane′
cel′lu·lar
cel′lu·lite′
cel′lu·loid′
cel′lu·lose′
Cel′si·us

Celt *also* Kelt
Celt′ic
ce·ment′
cem′e·ter′y
cen′o·bite′
cen′o·taph′
Ce′no·zo′ic
cen′ser *(container for*
 incense)
cen′sor *(examiner)*
cen·so′ri·ous
cen′sor·ship′
cen·sur·a·ble
cen′sure, -sured,
 -sur·ing
cen′sus
cent *(coin)*
 ✔ scent, sent
cen′taur′
cen·ta′vo *pl.* -vos
cen·te·nar′i·an
cen·ten′a·ry
cen·ten′ni·al
cen′ter
cen′ter·board′
cen′ter·fold′
cen′ter·piece′
cen·tes′i·mal
cen′ti·grade′
cen′ti·gram′
cen′ti·li′ter
cen′time′
cen′ti·me′ter
cen′ti·pede′
cen′tral
cen·tral′i·ty
cen′tral·i·za′tion

cen′tral·ize′, -ized′,
 -iz′ing
cen·trif′u·gal
cen·trif′u·ga′tion
cen·tri·fuge′,
 -fuged′, -fug′ing
cen·tri·ole′
cen·trip′e·tal
cen′trist
cen·tro·some′
cen·tu′ri·on
cen′tu·ry
ce·phal′ic
ceph′a·lo·pod′
ceph′a·lo·tho′rax′
Ce′phe·id
ce·ram′ic
ce·ram′ist
ce′re·al *(grain)*
 ✔ serial
cer′e·bel′lum *pl.*
 -bel′lums *or* -bel′la
cer′e·bral
cer′e·bro·spi′nal
cer′e·brum *pl.*
 -brums *or* -bra
ccre′cloth′
cer′e·ment
cer′e·mo′ni·al
cer′e·mo′ni·ous
cer′e·mo′ny
ce·rise′
ce′ri·um
cer′tain
cer′tain·ty
cer′ti·fi′a·ble
cer′ti·fi′a·bly

cer•tif′i•cate

cer′ti•fi•ca′tion

cer′ti•fy′, -fied′,
-fy′ing

cer′ti•tude′

ce•ru′le•an

cer′vi•cal

cer′vix *pl.* -vix•es *or*
-vi•ces′

ce•sar′e•an *also*
cae•sar′e•an

ce′si•um *also*
cae′si•um

ces•sa′tion

ces′sion *(surrender-
ing of territory)*
✔ *session*

cess′pool′

ce•ta′cean

chafe *(to irritate)*,
chafed, chaf′ing

chaff *(husks of grain)*

chaff *(to tease)*

chaff′er *(person who
teases)*

chaf′fer *(to bargain)*

chaf′finch

chaf′ing dish′

cha•grin′

chain

chain′-re•act′

chain′ re•ac′tion

chain′ saw′

chain′-smoke′,
-smoked′,
-smok′ing

chair

chair′ lift′

chair′man

chair′per′son

chair′wom′an

chaise

chaise longue′ *pl.*
chaise longues′ *or*
chaises longues′

chaise lounge′

chal•ced′o•ny

cha•let′

chal′ice *(cup)*
✔ *challis*

chalk

chalk′board′

chalk′i•ness

chalk′y

chal′lah

chal′lenge, -lenged,
-leng•ing

chal′leng•er

chal′lis *(fabric)*
✔ *chalice*

cham′ber

cham′ber•lain

cham′ber•maid′

cham′bray′

cha•me′leon

cham′ois *(antelope)*,
pl. -ois

cham′ois *also*
cham′my *or*
sham′my *(soft
leather)*, *pl.* -ois *also*
-mies

cham′o•mile′ *or*
cam′o•mile′

champ

cham•pagne′

cham′pi•on

cham′pi•on•ship′

chance, chanced,
chanc′ing

chan′cel

chan′cel•ler•y *or*
chan′cel•lor•y

chan′cel•lor

chan′cer•y

chan′cre

chanc′y

chan′de•lier′

chan′dler

change, changed,
chang′ing

change′a•bil′i•ty *or*
change′a•ble•ness

change′a•ble

change′a•bly

change′ling

change′o′ver *n.*

chang′er

chan′nel, -neled
also -nelled,
-nel•ing *also*
-nel•ling

chant

chant′er

chan•teuse′

chan′tey *also*
chan′ty *or* shan′tey
or shan′ty *(song)*,
pl. -teys *also* -ties
✔ *shanty*

chan′ti•cleer′

cha'os'

cha•ot'ic

chap, chapped,
  chap'ping

chap'ar•ral'

cha•peau' *pl.*
  -peaus' *or* -peaux'

chap'el

chap'er•on' *or*
  chap'er•one',
  -oned', -on'ing

chap'lain

chap'let

chaps

chap'ter

char, charred,
  char'ring

char'ac•ter

char'ac•ter•is'tic

char'ac•ter•i•za'-
  tion

char'ac•ter•ize',
  -ized', -iz'ing

cha•rade'

char'coal'

chard *(Swiss chard)*
  ✔ *shard*

char'don•nay' *also*
  Char'don•nay'

charge, charged,
  charg'ing

charge'a•ble

char•gé'
  d'af•faires' *pl.*
  char•gés' d'af•faires'

charg'er

char'i•ness

char'i•ot

char'i•o•teer'

cha•ris'ma

char'is•mat'ic

char'i•ta•ble

char'i•ta•bly

char'i•ty

char'la•tan

Charles'ton

char'ley horse'

charm

charm'er

charm'ing

char'nel house'

chart

char'ter

char'ter•er

char'treuse'

char'wom'an

char'y

chase, chased,
  chas'ing

chas'er

chasm

chas'sis *pl.* -sis

chaste, chast'er,
  chast'est

chas'ten

chas•tise', -tised',
  -tis'ing

chas•tise'ment

chas•tis'er

chas'ti•ty

chas'u•ble

chat, chat'ted,
  chat'ting

cha•teau' *also*

châ•teau' *pl.*
  -teaus' *or* -teaux'

chat'e•laine'

chat'tel

chat'ter

chat'ter•box'

chat'ty

chat'ti•ness

chauf'feur

chau'vin•ism

chau'vin•ist

chau'vin•is'tic

cheap *(inexpensive)*
  ✔ *cheep*

cheap'en

cheap'skate'

cheat

cheat'er

check *(restraint, veri-*
  fication, bank order)
  ✔ *Czech*

check'book'

checked

check'er

check'er•board'

check'ered

check'list'

check'mate',
  -mat'ed, -mat'ing

check'out' *n.*

check'point'

check'rein'

check'room'

check'up' *n.*

Ched'dar

cheek

cheek'bone'

cheek'y
cheep *(chirp)*
  ✔ *cheap*
cheer'ful
cheer'lead'er
cheer'less
cheer'y
cheese'burg'er
cheese'cake'
cheese'cloth'
chees'i·ness
chees'y
chee'tah
chef
chef-d'oeu'vre *pl.*
  chefs-d'oeu'vre
che'la *pl.* -lae
chem'i·cal
che·mise'
chem'ist
chem'is·try
che'mo·syn'the·sis
chem'o·syn·thet'ic
che'mo·ther'a·
  peu'tic
che'mo·ther'a·py
che·nille'
cher'ish
Cher'o·kee' *pl.*
  -kee' *or* -kees'
che·root' *also*
  she·root'
cher'ry
cher'ry·stone'
cher'ub *pl.* -u·bim
  or -ubs
che·ru'bic

chess'board'
chess'man
chest
ches'ter·field'
chest'nut'
chev'a·lier'
Chev'i·ot
chev'ron
chew
chew'i·ness
chew'ing gum'
che·wink'
chew'y
Chey·enne' *pl.*
  -enne' *or* -ennes'
Chi·an'ti
chic *(stylish),* chic'er,
  chic'est
  ✔ *sheik*
Chi·ca'na *pl.* -nas
chi·can'er·y
Chi·ca'no *pl.* -nos
chick
chick'a·dee'
Chick'a·saw' *pl.*
  -saw' *or* -saws'
chick'en
chick'en-heart'ed
chick'en-liv'ered
chick'en·pox' *or*
  chick'en pox'
chick'en wire'
chick'pea'
chick'weed'
chic'le
chic'o·ry
chide, chid'ed *or*

chid, chid'ed *or*
  chid *or* chid'den,
  chid'ing
chief
chief'tain
chif·fon'
chif'fo·nier'
chig'ger
chi·gnon'
chig'oe
Chi·hua'hua
chil'blain'
child *pl.* chil'dren
child'bear'ing
child'birth'
child'hood'
child'ish
child'like'
child'proof'
Chil'e·an
chil'i *(pepper),* pl.
  -ies
  ✔ *chilly*
chil'i con car'ne
chill
chill'i·ness
chill'y *(cold)*
  ✔ *chili*
chime, chimed,
  chim'ing
chi·me'ra *also*
  chi·mae'ra
chi·mer'i·cal
chim'i·chan'ga
chim'ney *pl.* -neys
chimp
chim'pan·zee'

chin, chinned,
  chin'ning
chi'na
chi'na•ber'ry
Chi'na•town'
chi'na•ware'
chinch
chin•chil'la
chine
Chi•nese' *pl.* -nese'
chink
chi'no *pl.* -nos
Chi•nook' *pl.*
  -nook' *or* -nooks'
chin'qua•pin'
chintz
chintz'y
chin'-up' *n.*
chip, chipped,
  chip'ping
Chip'e•wy'an *pl.*
  -an *or* -ans
chip'munk'
chip'per
Chip'pe•wa *pl.* -wa'
  or -was'
chi•rop'o•dist
chi•rop'o•dy
chi'ro•prac'tic
chi'ro•prac'tor
chirp
chir'rup
chis'el, -eled *or*
  -elled, -el'ing *or*
  -el•ling
chis'el•er
chit'chat',

-chat'ted,
  -chat'ting
chi'tin *(horny sub-*
  stance)
  ✔ chiton
chi'tin•ous
chi'ton *(mollusk,*
  tunic)
  ✔ chitin
chit'ter•lings *also*
  chit'lins *or*
  chit'lings
chiv'al•rous
chiv'al•ry
chive
chlo'ral
chlo'rate'
chlor'dane' *also*
  chlor'dan'
chlo'ride'
chlo'ri•nate',
  -nat'ed, -nat'ing
chlo'ri•na'tion
chlo'rine'
chlo'rite'
chlo'ro•fluo'ro•
  car'bon
chlo'ro•form'
chlo'ro•phyll' *also*
  chlo'ro•phyl'
chlo'ro•plast' *also*
  chlo'ro•plas'tid
chock
chock'-full'
choc'o•late
Choc'taw *pl.* -taw
  or -taws

choice, choic'er,
  choic'est
choir *(singers)*
  ✔ quire
choir'boy'
choir'girl'
choke, choked,
  chok'ing
choke'cher'ry
choke'damp'
choke'hold'
chok'er
chol'er *(anger)*
  ✔ collar
chol'er•a
chol'er•ic
cho•les'ter•ol'
chomp
choose, chose,
  cho'sen, choos'ing
choos'er
choos'y *also*
  choos'ey
chop, chopped,
  chop'ping
chop'per
chop'pi•ness
chop'py
chops
chop'sticks'
chop' su'ey
cho'ral *(relating to a*
  chorus)
  ✔ coral
cho•rale' *also*
  cho•ral' *(hymn)*
  ✔ corral

chord *(musical tones, line segment)*
　✔ cord
chord'al
chor'date'
chore
cho•re'a
cho're•o•graph'
cho're•og'ra•pher
cho're•o•graph'ic
cho're•og'ra•phy
cho'ric
cho'ri•on'
cho'ri•on'ic
cho'ris•ter
cho'roid'
chor'tle, -tled, -tling
cho'rus *pl.* -rus•es
cho'rus, -rused *or* -russed, -rus•ing *or* -rus•sing
cho'sen
chow
chow'der
chow' mein'
chrism
chris'ten
Chris'ten•dom
chris'ten•ing
Chris'tian
Chris'ti•an'i•ty
Christ'mas
chro'mate'
chro•mat'ic
chro'ma•tin
chro'ma•tog'ra•

phy
chrome
chro'mic
chro'mite'
chro'mi•um
chro'mo•so'mal
chro'mo•some'
chro'mo•sphere'
chron'ic
chron'i•cle, -cled, -cling
chron'i•cler
chron'o•log'i•cal
chro•nol'o•gy
chro•nom'e•ter
chrys'a•lid
chrys'a•lis *pl.* -lis•es *or* chrys•sal'i•des'
chry•san'the•mum
chub'bi•ness
chub'by
chuck
chuck'le, -led, -ling
chuck'wal'la
chug, chugged, chug'ging
chuk'ka
chum, chummed, chum'ming
chum'my
chump
chunk
chunk'i•ness
chunk'y
church
church'go'er
church'man

church'war'den
church'wom'an
church'yard'
churl
churl'ish
churn
chute *(vertical trough)*
　✔ shoot
chut'ney
chutz'pah
chyle
chyme
ci•ca'da *pl.* -das *or* -dae'
ci'der
ci•gar'
cig'a•rette'
cil'i•a *sing.* -i•um
cil'i•ar'y
cil'i•ate
cinch
cin•cho'na
Cin'co de Ma'yo
cinc'ture
cin'der
cin'der block' *or* cin'der•block'
cin'e•ma
cin'e•mat'ic
cin'e•ma•tog'ra•pher
cin'e•ma•tog'ra•phy
cin'na•bar'
cin'na•mon
ci'pher *also* cy'pher

cir'ca
cir·ca'di·an
cir'cle, -cled, -cling
cir'clet
cir'cuit
cir·cu'i·tous
cir'cuit·ry
cir'cu·lar
cir·cu·lar'i·ty
cir'cu·lar·ize',
 -ized', -iz'ing
cir'cu·late', -lat'ed,
 -lat'ing
cir·cu·la'tion
cir'cu·la·to'ry
cir'cum·cise',
 -cised', -cis'ing
cir'cum·ci'sion
cir·cum'fer·ence
cir'cum·flex'
cir·cum·lo·cu'tion
cir'cum·nav'i·
 gate', -gat'ed,
 -gat'ing
cir·cum·nav'i·ga'-
 tion
cir'cum·scribe',
 -scribed', -scrib'ing
cir'cum·scrip'tion
cir'cum·spect'
cir'cum·spec'tion
cir'cum·stance
cir'cum·stan'tial
cir'cum·stan'ti·ate'
cir'cum·stan'ti·a'-
 tion
cir'cum·vent'

cir'cum·ven'tion
cir'cus
cir·rho'sis
cir'ro·cu'mu·lus
cir'ro·stra'tus
cir'rus *pl.* -ri'
cis'tern
cit'a·del
ci·ta'tion
cite *(to quote)*, cit'ed,
 cit'ing
 ✔ *sight, site*
cit'i·zen
cit'i·zen·ry
cit'i·zen·ship'
cit'rate'
cit'ric ac'id
cit'ron
cit'ro·nel'la
cit'rus *pl.* cit'rus
cit'y
cit'y-state'
cit'y·wide'
civ'et
civ'ic
civ'il
ci·vil'ian
ci·vil'i·ty
civ'i·li·za'tion
civ'i·lize', -lized',
 -liz'ing
clab'ber
clack *(noise)*
 ✔ *claque*
clad, clad, clad'ding
claim
claim'ant

clair·voy'ance
clair·voy'ant
clam, clammed,
 clam'ming
clam'bake'
clam'ber
clam'mi·ness
clam'my
clam'or
clam'or·ous
clamp
clam'shell'
clan
clan·des'tine
clang
clan'gor
clank
clan'nish
clans'man
clans'wom'an
clap, clapped,
 clap'ping
clap'board
clap'per
clap'trap'
claque *(group)*
 ✔ *clack*
clar'et
clar'i·fi·ca'tion
clar'i·fy', -fied',
 -fy'ing
clar'i·net'
clar'i·net'ist *or*
 clar'i·net'tist
clar'i·on
clar'i·ty
clash

clasp
class
clas'sic
clas'si·cal
clas'si·cism
clas'si·cist
clas'si·fi'a·ble
clas'si·fi·ca'tion
clas'si·fi'er
clas'si·fy', -fied',
  -fy'ing
class'mate'
class'room'
class'y
clat'ter
clause
claus'tro·pho'bi·a
clav'i·chord'
clav'i·cle
cla·vier'
claw
clay
clay'ey *or* clay'ish
clean
clean'-cut'
clean'er
clean'li·ness
cleanse, cleansed,
  cleans'ing
cleans'er
clean'-shav'en
clean'up' *n. & adj.*
clear
clear'ance
clear'-cut'
clear'-eyed'
clear'ing

clear'ing-house' *or*
  clear'ing·house'
clear'-sight'ed
cleat
cleav'age
cleave *(to split)*, cleft
  or cleaved *or* clove,
  cleft *or* cleaved *or*
  clo'ven, cleav'ing
cleave *(to adhere)*,
  cleaved, cleav'ing
cleav'er
clef
cleft
clem'a·tis
clem'en·cy
clem'ent
clench
cler'gy
cler'gy·man
cler'gy·wom'an
cler'ic
cler'i·cal
clerk
clev'er
clew *(ball of yarn)*
  ✔ *clue*
clew *also* clue *(corner
  of a sail)*
  ✔ *clue*
cli·ché'
click *(sound)*
  ✔ *clique*
cli'ent
cli'en·tele'
cliff
cliff' dwell'er

cliff'hang'er
cli·mac'ter·ic
cli·mac'tic *also*
  cli·mac'ti·cal (*relat-
  ing to a climax*)
  ✔ *climatic*
cli'mate
cli·mat'ic (*relating
  to climate*)
  ✔ *climactic*
cli'ma·tol'o·gy
cli'max'
climb (*ascent*)
  ✔ *clime*
climb'a·ble
climb'er
clime (*climate*)
  ✔ *climb*
clinch
clinch'er
cling, clung,
  cling'ing
cling'stone'
clin'ic
clin'i·cal
cli·ni'cian
clink
clink'er
clip, clipped,
  clip'ping
clip'board'
clip'per
clique (*group*)
  ✔ *click*
cliqu'ey *or* cliqu'y
  or cliqu'ish
clit'o·ris

clo•a′ca *pl.* -cae′
cloak
cloak′room′
clob′ber
clock
clock′wise′
clock′work′
clod
clod′hop′per
clog, clogged,
 clog′ging
clois′ter
clomp
clone, cloned,
 clon′ing
clop, clopped,
 clop′ping
close, clos′er,
 clos′est
close (*to shut*),
 closed, clos′ing
 ✔ *clothes*
closed′-cap′tioned
closed′ cir′cuit
close′-fist′ed
close′-knit′
close′ly
close′-mouthed′
close′out′
clos′et
close′-up′ *n.*
clo′sure
clot, clot′ted,
 clot′ting
cloth *n.*
clothe, clothed *or*
 clad, cloth′ing

clothes (*garments*)
 ✔ *close*
clothes′horse′
clothes′line′
clothes′pin′
cloth′ier
cloth′ing
clo′ture
cloud
cloud′burst′
cloud′i•ness
cloud′y
clout
clove
clo′ven
clo′ver
clo′ver•leaf′
clown
cloy
club, clubbed,
 club′bing
club′foot′
club′foot′ed
club′house′
cluck
clue (*to give informa-
 tion*), clued,
 clue′ing *or* clu′ing
 ✔ *clew*
clump
clump′y
clum′si•ly
clum′si•ness
clum′sy
clunk′y
clus′ter
clutch

clut′ter
coach
coach′man
co•ag′u•lant
co•ag′u•late′,
 -lat′ed, -lat′ing
co•ag′u•la′tion
coal (*fuel*)
 ✔ *kohl*
co′a•lesce′, -lesced′,
 -lesc′ing
co′a•les′cense
co′a•les′cent
co′a•li′tion
co-an′chor *or*
 co•an′chor *n.*
co-an′chor *v.*
coarse (*rough*),
 coars′er, coars′est
 ✔ *course*
coars′en
coast
coast′al
coast′er
coast′line′
coat (*garment*)
 ✔ *cote*
co•a′ti
co•a′ti•mun′di
coat′ing
coat′room′
coat′tail′
co•au′thor
coax
co•ax′i•al
cob
co′balt′

cob'ble, -bled,
  -bling
cob'bler
cob'ble•stone'
CO'BOL'
co'bra
cob'web'
co'ca
co•caine'
coc'cus *pl.* -ci
coc'cyx *pl.*
  coc•cy'ges
coch'i•neal'
coch'le•a *pl.* -le•ae'
  also -le•as
cock
cock•ade'
cock'a•too' *pl.*
  -toos'
cock'a•trice'
cock'er•el
cock'er span'iel
cock'eyed'
cock'fight'
cock'horse'
cock'i•ness
cock'le
cock'le•bur'
cock'le•shell'
cock'ney *pl.* -neys
cock'pit'
cock'roach'
cocks'comb'
cock'sure'
cock'tail'
cock'y
co'coa

co'coa but'ter
co'co•nut' *also*
  co'coa•nut'
co•coon'
cod *pl.* cod *or* cods
co'da
cod'dle, -dled,
  -dling
code, cod'ed,
  cod'ing
co'de•fen'dant
co'deine'
co'dex' *pl.* -di•ces'
cod'fish'
codg'er
cod'i•cil
cod'i•fi•ca'tion
cod'i•fi'er
cod'i•fy', -fied',
  -fy'ing
cod'-liv'er oil'
co'ed' *or* co'-ed'
co•ed'u•ca'tion
co'ef•fi'cient
coe•la•canth'
coe•len'ter•ate'
co•en'zyme
co•e'qual
co•erce', -erced',
  -erc'ing
co•erc'er
co•erc'i•ble
co•er'cion
co•er'cive
co•e'val
co'ex•ist'
co'ex•is'tence

co'ex•is'tent
co'ex•tend'
co'ex•ten'sive
cof'fee
cof'fee break'
cof'fee•cake'
cof'fee•house'
cof'fee•mak'er *also*
  cof'fee mak'er
cof'fee•pot'
coffee shop'
cof'fer
cof'fin
co•found'
co'func'tion
cog
co'gen•cy
co'gent
cog'i•tate', -tat'ed,
  -tat'ing
cog'i•ta'tion
co'gnac'
cog'nate'
cog•ni'tion
cog'ni•tive
cog'ni•zance
cog'ni•zant
cog•no'men *pl.*
  -no'mens *or*
  -nom'i•na
co'gno•scen'te *pl.*
  -ti
cog'wheel'
co•hab'it
co•hab'i•tant
co•hab'i•ta'tion
co•here' *(to stick to-*

gether), -hered', -her'ing
✔ *adhere*
co•her'ence
co•her'en•cy
co•her'ent
co•he'sion
co•he'sive
co'hort'
coif
coif•feur' *(hairdresser)*
coif•fure' *(hairstyle)*
coil
coin *(money)*
✔ *quoin*
coin'age
co'in•cide', -cid'ed, -cid'ing
co•in'ci•dence
co•in'ci•dent
co•in'ci•den'tal
co'i•tus
coke
co'la
col'an•der
cold
cold'-blood'ed
cold'-call' *or* cold'
call' *v.*
cold'-heart'ed
cole'slaw'
co'le•us
col'ic
col'ick•y
col•i•se'um *also*
col'os•se'um

co•li'tis
col•lab'o•rate', -rat'ed, -rat'ing
col•lab'o•ra'tion
col•lab'o•ra'tor
col•lage'
col'la•gen
col•lapse', -lapsed', -laps'ing
col•laps'i•ble
col'lar *(neck band)*
✔ *choler*
col'lar•bone'
col'lard
col•late', -lat'ed, -lat'ing
col•lat'er•al
col•la'tion
col'league'
col•lect'
col•lect'a•ble *or*
col•lect'i•ble
col•lect'ed
col•lec'tion
col•lec'tive
col•lec'tiv•ism
col•lec'tiv•ist
col•lec'tiv•i•za'-
tion
col•lec'tiv•ize', -ized', -iz'ing
col•lec'tor
col'lege
col•le'gian
col•le'giate
col•lide', -lid'ed, -lid'ing

col'lie
col'lier
col'lier•y
col•lin'e•ar
col•li'sion
col'lo•cate'
col'lo•ca'tion
col'loid'
col•loi'dal
col•lo'qui•al
col•lo'qui•al•ism
col•lo'qui•um *pl.*
-qui'ums *or* -qui•a
col'lo•quy *pl.*
col'lo•quies
col•lude', -lud'ed, -lud'ing
col•lu'sion
col•lu'sive
co•logne'
Co•lom'bi•an *(relating to Colombia)*
✔ *Columbian*
co'lon *(punctuation mark)*, *pl.* -lons
co'lon *(intestine)*, *pl.*
-lons *or* -la
colo'nel *(officer)*
✔ *kernel*
co•lo'ni•al
co•lo'ni•al•ism
col'o•nist
col'o•ni•za'tion
col'o•nize', -nized', -niz'ing
col'o•niz'er
col'on•nade'

col'o•ny
col'o•phon'
col'or
Col'o•ra'dan
col'or•a'tion
col'or•a•tu'ra
col'or•blind' or
  col'or-blind'
col'or-blind'ness
col'or-code',
  -cod'ed, -cod'ing
col'ored
col'or•er
col'or•fast'
col'or•ful
col'or•im'e•ter
col'or•ing
col'or•i•za'tion
col'or•ize', -ized',
  -iz'ing
col'or•less
co•los'sal
co•los'sus pl. -los'si'
  or -los'sus•es
colt
colt'ish
Co•lum'bi•an (re-
  lating to the U. S.)
  ✓ Colombian
col'um•bine'
col'umn
co•lum'nar
col'um•nist
co'ma (state of un-
  consciousness), pl.
  -mas
co'ma (gas cloud), pl.

-mae
Co•man'che pl.
  -che or -ches
co'ma•tose'
comb
com•bat', -bat'ed or
  -bat'ted, -bat'ing or
  -bat'ting
com'bat n.
com•bat'ant
com•bat'ive
comb'er
com'bi•na'tion
com•bine', -bined',
  -bin'ing
com'bine' n.
com'bo pl. -bos
com•bus'ti•bil'i•ty
com•bus'ti•ble
com•bus'ti•bly
com•bus'tion
come, came, come,
  com'ing
come'back' n.
co•me'di•an
co•me'dic
co•me'di•enne'
come'down' n.
com'e•dy
come'li•ness
come'ly
come'-on' n.
com'er
co•mes'ti•ble
com'et
com'fit
come'up'pance

com'fort
com'fort•a•ble
com'fort•a•bly
com'fort•er
com'fy
com'ic
com'i•cal
com'ing
com'ing-out' n.
com'ma
com•mand'
com'man•dant'
com'man•deer'
com•mand'er
com•mand'er in
  chief' pl.
  com•mand'ers in
  chief'
com•mand'ing
com•mand'ment
com•man'do pl.
  -dos or -does
com•mem'o•rate',
  -rat'ed, -rat'ing
com•mem'o•ra'-
  tion
com•mem'o•ra•
  tive
com•mem'o•ra'tor
com•mem'o•ra•
  to'ry
com•mence',
  -menced',
  -menc'ing
com•mence'ment
com•mend'
com•mend'a•ble

com·mend'a·bly
com'men·da'tion
com·men'da·to·ry
com·men'sal
com·men'sal·ism
com·men'su·ra·ble
com·men'su·ra·bly
com·men'su·rate
com'ment
com'men·tar'y
com'men·tate',
  -tat'ed, -tat'ing
com'men·ta'tor
com'merce
com·mer'cial
com·mer'cial·ism
com·mer'cial·i·za'-
  tion
com·mer'cial·ize',
  -ized', -iz'ing
com·min'gle,
  -gled, -gling
com·mis'er·ate',
  -at'ed, -at'ing
com·mis'er·a'tion
com·mis'er·a'tive
com·mis'er·a'tor
com'mis·sar
com'mis·sar'i·at
com'mis·sar'y
com·mis'sion
com·mis'sion·er
com·mit', -mit'ted,
  -mit'ting
com·mit'ta·ble
com·mit'tal
com·mit'ment

com·mit'tee
com·mit'tee·man
com·mit'tee·
  wom'an
com·mix'
com·mix'ture
com·mode'
com·mo'di·ous
com·mod'i·ty
com'mo·dore'
com'mon
com'mon·al'i·ty
com'mon·al·ty
com'mon·er
com'mon-law' *adj.*
com'mon·place'
com'mon sense' *n.*
com'mon·sense'
  adj.
com'mon·sen'si·
  ble
com'mon·weal'
com'mon·wealth'
com·mo'tion
com·mu'nal
com·mu'nal'i·ty
com·mune',
  -muned', -mun'ing
com·mune' *n.*
com·mu'ni·ca·
  bil'i·ty
com·mu'ni·ca·ble
com·mu'ni·ca·bly
com·mu'ni·cant
com·mu'ni·cate',
  -cat'ed, -cat'ing
com·mu'ni·ca'tion

com·mu'ni·ca'tive
com·mu'ni·ca'tor
com·mun'ion
com·mu'ni·qué'
com'mu·nism *also*
  Com'mu·nism
Com'mu·nist *also*
  com'mu·nist
com'mu·nis'tic
com·mu'ni·ty
com·mu'ta'tion
com·mu'ta·tive
com·mu'ta'tor
com·mute',
  -mut'ed, -mut'ing
com·mut'er
com·pact' *adj. & v.*
com'pact' *n.*
com'pact disk' *or*
  com'pact disc'
com·pac'tor *or*
  com·pact'er
com·pan'ion
com·pan'ion·a·
  bil'i·ty
com·pan'ion·a·ble
com·pan'ion·a·bly
com·pan'ion·ship'
com·pan'ion·way'
com'pa·ny
com'pa·ra·ble
com'pa·ra·bly
com·par'a·tive
com·pare', -pared',
  -par'ing
com·par'i·son
com·part'ment

com'part·men'tal·
  ize', -ized', -iz'ing
com'pass
com·pas'sion
com·pas'sion·ate
com·pat'i·bil'i·ty
com·pat'i·ble
com·pat'i·bly
com·pa'tri·ot
com·pel', -pelled',
  -pel'ling
com·pen'di·ous
com·pen'di·um *pl.*
  -di·ums *or* -di·a
com'pen·sate',
  -sat'ed, -sat'ing
com·pen·sa'tion
com·pen'sa'tor
com·pen'sa·to'ry
com·pete', -pet'ed,
  -pet'ing
com'pe·tence
com'pe·ten·cy
com'pe·tent
com·pe·ti'tion
com·pet'i·tive
com·pet'i·tor
com·pi·la'tion
com·pile', -piled',
  -pil'ing
com·pil'er
com·pla'cence
com·pla'cen·cy
com·pla'cent *(self-
  satisfied)*
  ✔ *complaisant*
com·plain'

com·plain'ant
com·plaint'
com·plai'sance
com·plai'sant
  (willing)
  ✔ *complacent*
com'ple·ment
  *(something that
  completes)*
  ✔ *compliment*
com'ple·men'ta·ry
  (completing)
  ✔ *complimentary*
com·plete', -plet'er,
  -plet'est
com·plete',
  -plet'ed, -plet'ing
com·ple'tion
com·plex' *adj.*
com·plex' *n.*
com·plex'ion
com·plex'i·ty
com·pli'ance
com·pli'an·cy
com·pli'ant
com'pli·cate',
  -cat'ed, -cat'ing
com'pli·ca'tion
com·plic'it
com·plic'i·ty
com'pli·ment
  (praise)
  ✔ *complement*
com'pli·men'ta·ry
  (praising)
  ✔ *complementary*
com·ply', -plied',

-ply'ing
com·po'nent
com·port'
com·port'ment
com·pose', -posed',
  -pos'ing
com·pos'ed·ly
com·pos'er
com·pos'ite
com·po·si'tion
com·pos'i·tor
com·post'
com·po'sure
com'pote
com·pound' *v.*
com·pound' *adj.
  & n.*
com·pound'a·ble
com·pound'er
com'pre·hend'
com'pre·hend'i·
  ble
com'pre·hen'si·
  bil'i·ty
com'pre·hen'si·ble
com'pre·hen'si·bly
com'pre·hen'sion
com'pre·hen'sive
com·press'
com·pressed'
com·press'i·bil'i·ty
com·press'i·ble
com·pres'sion
com·pres'sor
com·prise',
  -prised', -pris'ing
com'pro·mise',

-mised', -mis'ing
com·pul'sion
com·pul'sive
com·pul'so·ry
com·punc'tion
com·put'a·ble
com·pu·ta'tion
com·pute', -put'ed,
-put'ing
com·put'er
com·put'er·i·za'-
tion
com·put'er·ize',
-ized', -iz'ing
com'rade
com'rade·ship'
con, conned,
con'ning
con·cat'e·nate',
-nat'ed, -nat'ing
con·cat'e·na'tion
con·cave'
con·cav'i·ty
con·ceal'
con·ceal'a·ble
con·ceal'er
con·ceal'ment
con·cede', -ced'ed,
-ced'ing
con·ceit'
con·ceit'ed
con·ceiv'a·bil'i·ty
con·ceiv'a·ble
con·ceive',
-ceived', -ceiv'ing
con·ceiv'er
con'cen·trate',

-trat'ed, -trat'ing
con'cen·tra'tion
con'cen·tra'tor
con'cen'tric
con'cept'
con·cep'tion
con·cep'tu·al
con·cep'tu·al·ism
con·cep'tu·al·ist
con·cep'tu·al·i·za'-
tion
con·cep'tu·al·ize',
-ized', -iz'ing
con·cern'
con·cerned'
con·cern'ing
con·cert'
con·cert'ed
con·cer·ti'na
con·cer'to pl. -tos
or -ti
con·ces'sion
con·ces'sion·aire'
conch (mollusk), pl.
conchs or conch'es
✔ conk
con·cierge'
con·cil'i·ate',
-at'ed, -at'ing
con·cil'i·a'tion
con·cil'i·a'tor
con·cil'i·a·to'ry
con·cise'
con·cise'ly
con·clave'
con·clude',
-clud'ed, -clud'ing

con·clud'er
con·clu'sion
con·clu'sive
con·clu'sive·ly
con·clu'so·ry
con·coct'
con·coc'tion
con·com'i·tance
con·com'i·tant
con'cord'
con·cor'dance
con'course'
con·cres'cence
con·cres'cent
con·crete' *adj.*
con'crete' *n.*
con·crete'ly
con'cu·bine'
con·cur', -curred',
-cur'ring
con·cur'rence
con·cur'rent
con·cus'sion
con·demn'
con'dem·na'tion
con·dens'a·ble *or*
con·dens'i·ble
con'den·sate'
con'den·sa'tion
con·dense',
-densed', -dens'ing
con·dens'er
con'de·scend'
con'de·scend'ing
con'de·scen'sion
con'di·ment
con·di'tion

con·di'tion·al
con·di'tioned
con·di'tion·er
con·di'tion·ing
con'do *pl.* -dos
con·dole', -doled',
-dol'ing
con·do'lence
con'dom
con·do·min'i·um
con·done',
-doned', -don'ing
con'dor
con·duce', -duced',
-duc'ing
con·du'cive
con·du'cive·ness
con·duct' *v.*
con'duct' *n.*
con·duc'tance
con·duct'i·bil'i·ty
con·duct'i·ble
con·duc'tion
con·duc'tive
con'duc·tiv'i·ty
con·duc'tor
con'du·it
cone
Con·es·to'ga
wag'on
co'ney *also* co'ny *pl.*
-neys *also* -nies
con'fab' *n.*
con'fab', -fabbed',
-fab'bing
con·fab'u·late',
-lat'ed, -lat'ing

con·fab'u·la'tor
con·fec'tion
con·fec'tion·er
con·fec'tion·er'y
con·fed'er·a·cy
con·fed'er·ate',
-at'ed, -at'ing
con·fed'er·a'tion
con·fer', -ferred',
-fer'ring
con'fer·ence
con·fess'
con·fes'sion
con·fes'sion·al
con·fes'sor
con·fet'ti
con'fi·dant' *(friend)*
✔ *confident*
con'fi·dante' *(fe-
male friend)*
✔ *confident*
con·fide', -fid'ed,
-fid'ing
con'fi·dence
con'fi·dent *(certain)*
✔ *confidant, confi-
dante*
con'fi·den'tial
con'fi·den'ti·al'i·
ty
con·fid'er
con·fid'ing
con·fig'u·ra'tion
con·fig'u·ra'tive *or*
con·fig'u·ra'tion·al
con·fig'ure
con·fine', -fined',

-fin'ing
con·fine'ment
con'fines'
con·firm'
con'fir·ma'tion
con·firmed'
con·firm'ed·ly
con'fis·cate',
-cat'ed, -cat'ing
con'fis·ca'tion
con'fis·ca'tor
con'fla·gra'tion
con·flict' *n.*
con·flict' *v.*
con·flic'tive
con'flu·ence
con'flu·ent
con·form'
con·form'a·ble
con'for·ma'tion
con·form'er
con·form'ist
con·form'i·ty
con·found'
con'fra·ter'ni·ty
con·front'
con'fron·ta'tion
Con·fu'cian
Con·fu'cian·ism
con·fuse', -fused',
-fus'ing
con·fus'ed·ly
con·fu'sion
con'fu·ta'tion
con·fute', -fut'ed,
-fut'ing
con·fut'er

con·geal'
con·geal'ment
con·gen'ial
con·ge'ni·al'i·ty
con·gen'i·tal
con'ger
con·gest'
con·ges'tion
con·ges'tive
con·glom'er·ate',
  -at'ed, -at'ing
con·glom'er·a'-
  tion
Con'go·lese' *pl.*
  -lese'
con·grat'u·late',
  -lat'ed, -lat'ing
con·grat'u·la'tion
con·grat'u·la·to'ry
con'gre·gate',
  -gat'ed, -gat'ing
con'gre·ga'tion
con'gre·ga'tion·al
con'gre·ga'tion·al·
  ism *also* Con'gre·
  ga'tion·al·ism
con'gre·ga'tion·al·
  ist *also* Con'gre·
  ga'tion·al·ist
con'gre·ga'tor
con'gress *also*
  Con'gress
con·gres'sion·al
con'gress·man
con'gress·wom'an
con'gru·ence
con'gru·en·cy

con'gru·ent
con·gru'i·ty
con'ic
con'i·cal
con'i·fer
co·nif'er·ous
con·jec'tur·al
con·jec'ture,
  -tured, -tur·ing
con·join'
con·join'er
con·joint'
con'ju·gal
con'ju·gate',
  -gat'ed, -gat'ing
con'ju·ga'tion
con·junc'tion
con·junc·ti'va *pl.*
  -vas *or* -vae
con·junc'tive
con·junc'ti·vi'tis
con·jure, -jured,
  -jur·ing
con'jur·er *also*
  con'jur·or
conk *(hit)*
  ✔ conch
con·nect'
con·nect'er *or*
  con·nec'tor
con·nect'i·ble
con·nec'tion
con·nec'tive
con·niv'ance
con·nive', -nived',
  -niv'ing
con'nois·seur'

con'no·ta'tion
con'no·ta'tive
con·note', -not'ed,
  -not'ing
con·nu'bi·al
con'quer
con'quer·a·ble
con'quer·or *or*
  con'quer·er
con'quest'
con·quis'ta·dor' *pl.*
  -dors' *or* -dor·es
con·san·guin'e·ous
con·san·guin'i·ty
con'science
con'sci·en'tious
con'scious
con'script' *n.*
con·script' *v.*
con·scrip'tion
con'se·crate',
  -crat'ed, -crat'ing
con'se·cra'tion
con'se·cra'tor
con·sec'u·tive
con·sec'u·tive·ly
con·sen'sus
con·sent'
con'se·quence
con'se·quent
con'se·quen'tial
con·serv'a·ble
con'ser·va'tion
con'ser·va'tion·ist
con·ser'va·tism
con·ser'va·tive
con·ser'va·tor

con·ser'va·to'ry
con·serve',
  -served', -serv'ing
con·sid'er
con·sid'er·a·ble
con·sid'er·a·bly
con·sid'er·ate
con·sid'er·ate·ly
con·sid'er·a'tion
con·sid'ered
con·sid'er·ing
con·sign'
con·sign'a·ble
con·sign'ment
con·sist'
con·sis'ten·cy
con·sis'tent
con·sis'to·ry
con·sol'a·ble
con'so·la'tion
con·sole', -soled',
  -sol'ing
con'sole' n.
con·sol'i·date',
  -dat'ed, -dat'ing
con·sol'i·da'tor
con·sol'i·da'tion
con'som·mé'
con'so·nance
con'so·nant
con'so·nan'tal
con'sort' n.
con·sort' v.
con·sor'ti·um pl.
  -ti·a
con·spec'tus
con·spic'u·ous

con·spir'a·cy
con·spir'a·tor
con·spir'a·to'ri·al
con·spire', -spired',
  -spir'ing
con·spir'er
con'sta·ble
con·stab'u·lar'y
con'stan·cy
con'stant
con'stel·la'tion
con'ster·na'tion
con'sti·pate',
  -pat'ed, -pat'ing
con'sti·pa'tion
con·stit'u·en·cy
con·stit'u·ent
con'sti·tute',
  -tut'ed, -tut'ing
con'sti·tu'tion
con'sti·tu'tion·al
con'sti·tu'tion·
  al'i·ty
con'sti·tu'tion·al·
  ize', -ized', -iz'ing
con'sti·tu'tive
con·strain'
con·strain'ed·ly
con·strain'er
con·straint'
con·strict'
con·stric'tion
con·stric'tive
con·stric'tor
con·struct'
con·struc'tion
con·struc'tion·al

con·struc'tive
con·struc'tive·ly
con·struc'tive·ness
con·struc'tor
con·strue', -strued',
  -stru'ing
con'sul
con'su·lar
con'su·late
con·sult'
con·sult'ant
con'sul·ta'tion
con·sul'ta·tive
con·sum'a·ble
con·sume',
  -sumed', -sum'ing
con·sum'er
con·sum'er·ism
con·sum'mate',
  -mat'ed, -mat'ing
con·sum'mate·ly
con'sum·ma'tion
con·sump'tion
con·sump'tive
con'tact'
con·ta'gion
con·ta'gious
con·tain'
con·tain'a·ble
con·tain'er
con·tain'er·ize',
  -ized', -iz'ing
con·tain'ment
con·tam'i·nant
con·tam'i·nate',
  -nat'ed, -nat'ing
con·tam'i·na'tion

con•tam′i•na′tor
con•tem′
con•tem•plate′,
-plat′ed, -plat′ing
con′tem•pla′tion
con•tem′pla•tive
con•tem′pla•tive•ly
con′tem•pla′tor
con•tem′po•ra′ne•
ous
con•tem′po•rar′y
con•tempt′
con•tempt′i•ble
con•tempt′i•bly
con•temp′tu•ous
con•tend′
con•tend′er
con′tent′ *n.*
con•tent′ *adj. & v.*
con•tent′ed
con•ten′tion
con•ten′tious
con•tent′ment
con′test′ *n.*
con•test′ *v.*
con•test′a•ble
con•tes′tant
con′text′
con•tex′tu•al
con•tex′tu•al•i•
za′tion
con•tex′tu•al•ize′,
-ized′, -iz′ing
con•ti•gu′i•ty
con•tig′u•ous
con′ti•nence
con′ti•nent

con′ti•nen′tal
con•tin′gen•cy
con•tin′gent
con•tin′u•al
con•tin′u•ance
con•tin′u•a′tion
con•tin′ue, -ued,
-u•ing
con′ti•nu′i•ty
con•tin′u•ous
con•tin′u•um *pl.*
-u•a *or* -u•ums
con•tort′
con•tor′tion
con•tor′tion•ist
con′tour
con′tra•band′
con′tra•bass′
con′tra•bas•soon′
con′tra•cep′tion
con′tra•cep′tive
con′tract′ *n.*
con•tract′ *v.*
con•tract′i•ble
con•trac′tile′
con•trac′tion
con′trac′tor
con•trac′tu•al
con′tra•dict′
con′tra•dic′tion
con′tra•dic′to•ri•ly
con′tra•dic′tor•i•
ness
con′tra•dic′to•ry
con′tra•dis•tinc′-
tion
con•tral′to *pl.* -tos

con•trap′tion
con′tra•pun′tal
con′tra•pun′tist
con′trar′i•ly
con′trar′i•ness
con′trar′i•wise′
con′trar′y *(com-
pletely different)*
con•trar′y *(willful)*
con•trast′ *v.*
con′trast′ *n.*
con′tra•vene′,
-vened′, -ven′ing
con′tra•ven′tion
con′tre•danse′ *also*
con′tre•dance′ *or*
con′tra•dance′ *or*
con′tra•danse′
con′tre•temps′ *pl.*
-temps′
con•trib′ute′,
-ut′ed, -ut′ing
con′tri•bu′tion
con•trib′u•tive
con•trib′u•tor
con•trib′u•to′ry
con•trite′
con•tri′tion
con•tri′vance
con•trive′, -trived′,
-triv′ing
con•triv′er
con•trol′, -trolled′,
-trol′ling
con•trol′la•ble
con•trol′ler *also*
comp•trol′ler

con'tro•ver'sial
con'tro•ver'sy
con'tro•vert'
con'tro•vert'i•ble
con•tu•ma'cious
con•tu•ma•cy
con•tu•me'li•ous
con•tu•me•ly
con•tuse', -tused',
  -tus'ing
con•tu'sion
co•nun'drum
con•va•lesce',
  -lesced', -lesc'ing
con•va•les'cence
con•va•les'cent
con•vect'
con•vec'tion
con•vene', -vened',
  -ven'ing
con•ven'ience
con•ven'ient
con'vent
con•ven'tion
con•ven'tion•al
con•ven'tion•al'i•
  ty
con•verge',
  -verged', -verg'ing
con•ver'gence
con•ver'gent
con•ver'sant
con'ver•sa'tion
con'ver•sa'tion•al
con'ver•sa'tion•al•
  ist
con•verse',

-versed', -vers'ing
con•verse' *n.*
con•verse'ly
con•ver'sion
con•vert' *v.*
con'vert' *n.*
con•vert'er
con•vert'i•bil'i•ty
con•vert'i•ble
con•vert'i•bly
con'vex'
con•vex'i•ty
con•vey'
con•vey'ance
con•vey'er *also*
  con•vey'or
con•vict' *v.*
con'vict' *n.*
con•vic'tion
con•vince',
  -vinced', -vinc'ing
con•vinc'i•ble
con•viv'i•al
con•viv'i•al'i•ty
con'vo•ca'tion
con•voke', -voked',
  -vok'ing
con'vo•lut'ed
con'vo•lu'tion
con'voy'
con•vulse',
  -vulsed', -vuls'ing
con•vul'sion
con•vul'sive
coo *(to murmur),*
  cooed, coo'ing
  ✔ *coup*

cook
cook'book'
cook'er
cook'er•y
cook'ie *also* cook'y
  pl. -ies
cook'out'
cool
cool'ant
cool'er
cool'-head'ed
cool'ly *(in a cool*
  manner)
  ✔ *coulee*
coon'skin'
coop *(cage)*
  ✔ *coupe*
co'-op' *n.*
coop'er
co•op'er•ate',
  -at'ed, -at'ing
co•op'er•a'tion
co•op'er•a•tive
co•op'er•a•tive•ly
co-opt'
co•or'di•nate *adj.*
co•or'di•nate',
  -nat'ed, -nat'ing
co•or'di•na'tion
co•or'di•na'tor
coot
coo'tie
cop
cope, coped, cop'ing
co'pe•pod'
Co•per'ni•can
cop'i•er

co·pi′lot
cop′ing
co′pi·ous
co·pla′nar
co·pol′y·mer
cop′-out′ *also*
  cop′out′
cop′per
cop′per·as
cop′per·head′
cop′per·plate′
cop′per·smith′
cop′per·y
cop′pice
co′pra
copse
Copt
cop′ter
Cop′tic
cop′u·la
cop′u·late′, -lat′ed,
  -lat′ing
cop′u·la′tion
cop′y, -ied, -y·ing
cop′y·book′
cop′y·cat′
cop′y·ed′it *or*
  cop′y-ed·it
cop′y·ed′i·tor
cop′y·ist
cop′y·right′
cop′y·writ′er
co·quet·ry
co·quette′
co·quet′tish
co·qui′na
cor′a·cle

cor′al *(stony sub-*
  stance)
  ✔ *choral*
cor′bel
cord *(rope)*
  ✔ *chord*
cord′age
cord′ed
cor′dial
cor·dial′i·ty
cor′dil·le′ra
cord′ite′
cord′less
cor′do·ba
cor′don
cor′do·van
cor′du·roy′
cord′wood′
core *(to remove the*
  center), cored,
  cor′ing
  ✔ *corps*
cor′er
co·ri·an′der
Co·rin′thi·an
cork
cork′er
cork′screw′
cork′y
corm
cor′mo·rant
corn
corn′ bread′ *or*
  corn′bread′
corn′cob′
corn′crib′
cor′ne·a

cor′ner
cor′ner·stone′
cor·net′
cor·net′ist *also*
  cor·net′tist
corn′field′
corn′ flakes′
corn′flow′er
corn′husk′
cor′nice
Cor′nish
corn′meal′ *also*
  corn′ meal′
corn′pone′ *or* corn′
  pone′
corn′stalk′
corn′starch′
cor′nu·co′pi·a
corn′y
co·rol′la
cor·ol·lar′y
co·ro′na *pl.* -nas *or*
  -nae
cor′o·nar′y
cor′o·na′tion
cor′o·ner
cor′o·net′
cor′po·ral
cor′po·rate
cor′po·ra′tion
cor·po′re·al
corps *(military unit),*
  pl. corps
  ✔ *core, corpse*
corps′ de bal·let′
corpse *(body)*
  ✔ *corps*

corps'man
cor'pu•lence
cor'pu•lent
cor'pus *pl.* -po•ra
cor'pus•cle
cor•ral' *(enclosed area)*, -ralled', -ral'ling
   ✔ *chorale*
cor•rect'
cor•rec'tion
cor•rec'tive
cor're•late', -lat'ed, -lat'ing
cor're•la'tion
cor•rel'a•tive
cor're•spond'
cor're•spon'dence
cor're•spon'dent
cor're•spond'ing
cor'ri•dor
cor•rob'o•rate', -rat'ed, -rat'ing
cor•rob'o•ra'tion
cor•rob'o•ra'tive
cor•rob'o•ra'tor
cor•rode', -rod'ed, -rod'ing
cor•ro'sion
cor•ro'sive
cor'ru•gate', -gat'ed, -gat'ing
cor'ru•ga'tion
cor•rupt'
cor•rupt'er
cor•rupt'i•ble
cor•rupt'i•bil'i•ty

cor•rupt'i•bly
cor•rup'tion
cor•sage'
cor•sair'
cor'se•let
cor'set
Cor'si•can
cor•tege'
cor'tex' *pl.* -ti•ces' *or* -tex'es
cor'ti•cal
cor'ti•sone'
co•run'dum
cor'us•cate', -cat'ed, -cat'ing
cor'us•ca'tion
cor•vette'
cor'ymb
co•se'cant'
co•sign' *(to sign jointly)*
co'sine' *(mathematical function)*
cos•met'ic
cos'me•tol'o•gist
cos'me•tol'o•gy
cos'mic
cos•mog'o•ny
cos•mog'ra•phy
cos'mo•log'i•cal
cos•mol'o•gist
cos•mol'o•gy
cos'mo•naut'
cos'mo•pol'i•tan
cos'mos
Cos'sack
cos'set

cost
cos'tal
co'star' *also* co'-star'
Cos'ta Ri'can
cost'-ef•fec'tive
cost'li•ness
cost'ly
cos'tume', -tumed', -tum'ing
cos'tum'er
cot
co•tan'gent
cote *(shed)*
   ✔ *coat*
co'ter•ie
co•til'lion *also* co•til'lon
cot'tage
cot'tag•er
cot'ter pin'
cot'ton
cot'ton•mouth'
cot'ton•seed'
cot'ton•tail'
cot'ton•wood'
cot'ton•y
cot'y•le'don
couch
cou'gar
cough
could
could'n't
cou'lee *(ravine)*
   ✔ *coolly*
cou'lomb'
coul'ter
coun'cil *(group)*

✔ *counsel*
coun'cil•man
coun'cil•or *also*
   coun'cil•lor *(member of a council)*
   ✔ *counselor*
coun'cil•wom'an
coun'sel *(to advise),*
   -seled *or* -selled,
   -sel'ing *or* -sel•ling
   ✔ *council*
coun'sel•or *also*
   coun'sel•lor *(adviser)*
   ✔ *councilor*
count
count'a•ble
count'down'
coun'te•nance,
   -nanced, -nanc'ing
coun'ter *(contrary)*
count'er *(flat surface, small object, one that counts)*
coun'ter•act'
coun'ter•at•tack'
coun'ter•bal'ance
   n.
coun'ter•bal'ance,
   -anced, -anc'ing
coun'ter•claim' *n.*
coun'ter•claim' *v.*
coun'ter•clock'-
   wise'
coun'ter•cul'ture
coun'ter•cur'rent
coun'ter•dem'on•

stra'tion
coun'ter•es'pi•o•
   nage'
coun'ter•feit'
coun'ter•feit'er
coun'ter•in•tel'li•
   gence
coun'ter•mand'
coun'ter•march' *n.*
coun'ter•meas'ure
   n.
coun'ter•mine' *v.*
coun'ter•move' *n.*
coun'ter•of•fen'-
   sive
coun'ter•of'fer *n.*
coun'ter•pane'
coun'ter•part'
coun'ter•point'
coun'ter•poise',
   -poised', -pois'ing
coun'ter•pro•duc'-
   tive
coun'ter•rev'o•lu'-
   tion
coun'ter•rev'o•lu'-
   tion•ar'y
coun'ter•sign'
coun'ter•sink',
   -sunk', -sink'ing
coun'ter•spy'
coun'ter•ten'or
coun'ter•weight'
count'ess
count'less
coun'tri•fied'
coun'try

coun'try•man
coun'try•side'
coun'try•wom'an
coun'ty
coup *(stratagem), pl.*
   coups
   ✔ *coo*
coup' d'é•tat' *pl.*
   coups' d'é•tat' *or*
   coup' d'é•tats'
coupe *(dessert)*
   ✔ *coop*
cou•pé' *also* coupe
   (car)
cou'ple, -pled,
   -pling
cou'pler
cou'plet
cou'pling
cou'pon'
cour'age
cou•ra'geous
cou'ri•er
course *(to flow),*
   coursed, cours'ing
   ✔ *coarse*
cours'er
court
cour'te•ous
cour'te•san
cour'te•sy
court'house'
court'i•er
court'li•ness
court'ly
court'-mar'tial *pl.*
   courts'-mar'tial

court'-mar'tial,
  -tialed *also* -tialled,
  -tial•ing *or* -tial•ling
court'room'
court'ship'
court'yard'
cous'in *(relative)*
  ✓ *cozen*
co•va'lence
co•va'lent
cove
cov'en
cov'e•nant
cov'er
cov'er•age
cov'er•alls'
cov'er•ing
cov'er•let
cov'ert
cov'er-up' *or*
  cov'er•up' *n.*
cov'et
cov'et•ous
cov'ey *pl.* -eys
cow
cow'ard
cow'ard•ice
cow'ard•li•ness
cow'ard•ly
cow'bell'
cow'bird'
cow'boy'
cow'catch'er
cow'er
cow'girl'
cow'hand'
cow'herd'

cow'hide'
cowl
cow'lick'
cowl'ing
cow'man
co'work'er
cow'poke'
cow'pox'
cow'punch'er
cow'rie *or* cow'ry *pl.*
  -ries
cow'slip'
cox'comb'
cox'swain
coy
coy•o'te
coy'pu *pl.* -pus
coz'en *(to deceive)*
  ✓ *cousin*
coz'en•er
co'zi•ly
co'zi•ness
co'zy
crab, crabbed,
  crab'bing
crab'bed *adj.*
crab'ber
crab'bi•ly
crab'by
crab'grass' *or* crab'
  grass'
crack
crack'down' *n.*
cracked
crack'er
crack'er•jack'
crack'ing

crack'le, -led, -ling
crack'pot'
crack'up' *or*
  crack'-up' *n.*
cra'dle, -dled, -dling
craft *(skill), pl.* crafts
craft *(boat or plane),*
  pl. craft
craft'i•ly
crafts'man
crafts'man•ship'
crafts'wom'an
craft'y
crag
crag'gi•ness
crag'gy
cram, crammed,
  cram'ming
cramp
cramped
cram'pon'
cran'ber'ry
crane, craned,
  cran'ing
cra'ni•al
cra'ni•um *pl.*
  -ni•ums *or* -ni•a
crank
crank'case'
crank'shaft'
crank'y
cran'ny
crape
crap'pie *pl.* -pies
craps
crash
crash'-land'

crass

crate, crat'ed,
   crat'ing

cra'ter

cra•vat'

crave, craved,
   crav'ing

cra'ven

craw

crawl

crawl'er

cray'fish' *also*
   craw'fish' *pl.* -fish'
   or -fish'es

cray'on'

craze, crazed,
   craz'ing

cra'zi•ly

cra'zi•ness

cra'zy

creak *(squeak)*
   ✔ *creek*

creak'i•ness

creak'y

cream

cream'er

cream'er•y

cream'i•ness

cream'y

crease, creased,
   creas'ing

cre•ate', -at'ed,
   -at'ing

cre•a'tion

cre•a'tion•ism

cre•a'tive

cre•a'tive•ly

cre'a•tiv'i•ty *or*
   cre•a'tive•ness

cre•a'tor

crea'ture

crèche

cre'dence

cre•den'tial

cred'i•bil'i•ty

cred'i•ble

cred'i•bly

cred'it

cred'it•a•bil'i•ty *or*
   cred'it•a•ble•ness

cred'it•a•ble

cred'it•a•bly

cred'i•tor

cre'do *pl.* -dos

cre•du'li•ty

cred'u•lous

Cree *pl.* Cree *or*
   Crees

creed

creek *(stream)*
   ✔ *creak*

Creek *pl.* Creek *or*
   Creeks

creel

creep, crept,
   creep'ing

creep'er

creep'i•ness

creep'y

cre'mate', -mat'ed,
   -mat'ing

cre•ma'tion

cre•ma•to'ri•um *pl.*
   -ri•ums *or* -ri•a

cre'ma•to'ry

Cre'ole'

cre'o•sol'

cre'o•sote', -sot'ed,
   -sot'ing

crepe *also* crêpe

crepe' pap'er

cre•pus'cu•lar

cres•cen'do *pl.* -dos
   or -di

cres'cent

cress

cres'set

crest

crest'fall'en

Cre•ta'ceous

Cre'tan *(relating to
   Crete)*
   ✔ *cretin*

cre'tin *(person with
   cretinism)*
   ✔ *Cretan*

cre'tin•ism

cre•tonne'

cre•vasse' *(chasm)*

crev'ice *(narrow
   crack)*

crew

crew' cut' *or*
   crew'cut'

crew'el *(yarn)*
   ✔ *cruel*

crew'el•work'

crib, cribbed,
   crib'bing

crib'bage

crick

crick'et
crick'et•er
cri'er
crime
Cri•me'an
crim'i•nal
crim'i•nal•ist
crim'i•nal•is'tics
crim'i•no•log'i•cal
crim'i•nol'o•gist
crim'i•nol'o•gy
crimp
crimp'y
crim'son
cringe, cringed,
  cring'ing
cring'er
crin'kle, -kled,
  -kling
crin'kly
cri'noid'
crin'o•line
crip'ple, -pled,
  -pling
crip'pler
cri'sis *pl.* -ses
crisp
crisp'i•ness
crisp'y
criss'cross'
cri•te'ri•on *pl.* -ri•a
  or -ri•ons
crit'ic
crit'i•cal
crit'i•cism
crit'i•cize', -cized',
  -ciz'ing

crit'i•ciz'er
cri•tique', -tiqued',
  -tiqu'ing
crit'ter
croak
Croat
Cro•a'tian
cro•chet'
crock
crock'er•y
croc'o•dile'
cro'cus *pl.* -cus•es
croft
croft'er
crois•sant'
Cro-Mag'non
crone
cro'ny
crook
crook'ed
croon
croon'er
crop, cropped,
  crop'ping
crop'-dust'ing
crop'land'
crop'per
cro•quet' *(game)*
cro•quette' *(small
  cake)*
cro'sier *or* cro'zier
cross
cross'bar'
cross'beam'
cross'bill'
cross'bones'
cross'bow'

cross'breed', -bred',
  -breed'ing
cross'-coun'try
cross'-cul'tur•al
cross'cur'rent
cross'cut', -cut',
  -cut'ting
cross'-ex•am'i•na'-
  tion
cross'-ex•am'ine,
  -ined, -in•ing
cross'-ex•am'in•er
cross'-eyed'
cross'-fer'til•i•za'-
  tion
cross'-fer'til•ize',
  -ized', -iz'ing
cross'fire'
cross'-grained'
cross'hatch'
cross'ing
cross'-leg'ged
cross'o'ver *n.*
cross'piece'
cross'-pol'li•nate',
  -nat'ed, -nat'ing
cross'-pol'li•na'-
  tion
cross'-pur'pose'
cross'-re•fer',
  -ferred', -fer'ring
cross'-ref'er•ence
cross'road'
cross' sec'tion
cross'-stitch'
cross'-town' *or*
  cross'town'

cross'walk'
cross'way'
cross'wise' *also*
   cross'ways'
cross'word' puz'-
   zle
crotch
crotch'et
crotch'et•i•ness
crotch'et•y
crouch
croup
croup'y
crou'ton'
crow
Crow *pl.* Crow *or*
   Crows
crow'bar'
crowd
crown
crown' prince'
crown' prin'cess
crow's'-feet'
crow's'-nest'
cru'cial
cru'ci•ble
cru'ci•fi'er
cru'ci•fix'
cru'ci•fix'ion
cru'ci•form'
cru'ci•fy', -fied',
   -fy'ing
crud'dy
crude, crud'er,
   crud'est
crude'ly
cru'di•ty

cru'el *(merciless)*,
   -el•er *or* -el•ler,
   -el•est *or* -el•lest
   ✓ *crewel*
cru'el•ty
cru'et
cruise *(travel)*,
   cruised, cruis'ing
   ✓ *cruse*
cruise' mis'sile
cruis'er
crul'ler
crumb
crum'ble, -bled,
   -bling
crum'bli•ness
crum'bly
crum'my
crum'pet
crum'ple, -pled,
   -pling
crunch
crunch'y
cru•sade', -sad'ed,
   -sad'ing
cru•sad'er
cruse *(small bottle)*
   ✓ *cruise*
crush
crush'a•ble
crush'er
crust
crus•ta'cean
crust'i•ness
crust'y
crutch
crux *pl.* crux'es *or*

cru'ces
cry, cried, cry'ing
cry'ba'by
cry'o•bank'
cry'o•gen
cry'o•gen'ic
cry'o•gen'ics
cry•on'ics
crypt
cryp'tic
cryp'to•gram'
cryp'to•graph'
cryp•tog'ra•pher
cryp'to•graph'ic
cryp•tog'ra•phy
crys'tal
crys'tal•line
crys'tal•li•za'tion
crys'tal•lize',
   -lized', -liz'ing
crys'tal•log'ra•phy
cub
Cu'ban
cub'by•hole'
cube, cubed,
   cub'ing
cu'bic
cu'bi•cal *(cubic)*
cu'bi•cle *(small
   room)*
cub'ism
cub'ist
cu'bit
Cub' Scout'
cuck'old
cuck'old•ry
cuck'oo *pl.* -oos

cu'cum'ber

cud

cud'dle, -dled,
-dling

cud'dly

cudg'el, -eled or
-elled, -el'ing or
-el'ling

cue (stick, signal)
✔ queue

cue (to strike with a
stick, to signal),
cued, cu'ing
✔ queue

cue' ball'

cuff

cuff' link' or
cuff'link'

cui·rass'

cui·sine'

cul'-de-sac' pl.
culs'-de-sac' or
cul'-de-sacs'

cu'li·nar'y

cull

culm

cul'mi·nate',
-nat'ed, -nat'ing

cul'mi·na'tion

cu'lottes'

cul'pa·bil'i·ty

cul'pa·ble

cul'pa·bly

cul'prit

cult

cul'ti·vate', -vat'ed,
-vat'ing

cul'ti·va'tion

cul'ti·va'tor

cul'tur·al

cul'ture, -tured,
-tur·ing

cul'vert

cum'ber

cum'ber·some

cum'brous

cum'in

cum lau'de

cum'mer·bund'

cu'mu·la'tive

cu'mu·lo·nim'bus
pl. -bus·es or -bi

cu'mu·lus pl. -li'

cu'ne·i·form'

cun'ning

cup, cupped,
cup'ping

cup'board

cup'cake'

cup'ful'

cu'pid

cu·pid'i·ty

cu'po·la

cu'pric

cu'prous

cur

cur·a·bil'i·ty

cur'a·ble

cu·ra're also cu·ra'ri

cu'rate

cu'ra·tive

cu·ra'tor

curb

curb'ing

curb'side' n. & adj.

curb'stone'

curd

cur'dle, -dled,
-dling

cure, cured, cur'ing

cu·ré'

cure'-all'

cu'ret·tage'

cu·rette' also cu·ret'

cur'few

cu'rie

cu'ri·o' pl. -os'

cu'ri·os'i·ty

cu'ri·ous

cu'ri·um

curl

curl'er

cur'lew

curl'i·cue'

curl'i·ness

curl'ing

curl'y

cur·mudg'eon

cur'rant (fruit)
✔ current

cur'ren·cy

cur'rent (present-
day)
✔ currant

cur'rent (electric
charge)
✔ currant

cur·ric'u·lar

cur·ric'u·lum pl. -la
or -lums

cur'ry, -ried, -ry·ing

cur'ry•comb'

curse, cursed *or*
curst, curs'ing

curs'ed *also* curst
adj.

curs'er *(person who
curses)*
✔ cursor

cur'sive

cur'sor *(indicator)*
✔ curser

cur•so'ri•al

cur'so•ri•ly

cur'so•ry

curt

cur•tail'

cur•tail'ment

cur'tain

curt'sy *or* curt'sey
pl. -sies *or* -seys

curt'sy *or* curt'sey,
-sied *or* -seyed,
-sy•ing *or* -sey•ing

cur•va'ceous

cur'va•ture

curve, curved,
curv'ing

curve' ball' *or*
curve'ball'

cur'vi•lin'e•ar

cush'ion

cush'y

cusp

cus'pid

cus'pi•dor'

cuss

cus'tard

cus•to'di•al

cus•to'di•an

cus'to•dy

cus'tom

cus'tom•ar'i•ly

cus'tom•ar'y

cus'tom-built'

cus'tom•er

cus'tom•house'
also cus'toms•
house'

cus'tom•ize', -ized',
-iz'ing

cus'tom-made'

cut, cut, cut'ting

cut'-and-dried'
also cut'-and-dry'

cu•ta'ne•ous

cut'a•way'

cut'back' *n.*

cute, cut'er, cut'est

cu'ti•cle

cut'ie *also* cut'ey

cu'tin

cut'lass *also* cut'las

cut'ler•y

cut'let

cut'off' *n.*

cut'out' *n.*

cut'-rate'

cut'ter

cut'throat'

cut'ting

cut'tle•bone'

cut'tle•fish'

cut'up' *n.*

cut'worm'

cy'an'

cy'a•nide'

cy'a•no'sis

cy'a•not'ic

cy'ber•net'ic

cy'ber•punk'

cy'ber•space'

cy'cad'

cy'cla•mate'

cy'cla•men

cy'cle, -cled, -cling

cy'clic *or* cy'cli•cal

cy'clist

cy'clone'

cy•clon'ic

Cy'clops *pl.*
Cy•clo'pes

cy'clo•ram'a

cy'clo•tron'

cyg'net *(young
swan)*
✔ signet

cyl'in•der

cy•lin'dri•cal *also*
cy•lin'dric

cym'bal *(instru-
ment)*
✔ symbol

cyn'ic

cyn'i•cal

cyn'i•cism

cy'no•sure'

cy'press

Cyp'ri•ot *also*
Cyp'ri•ote'

Cy•ril'lic

cyst

cys'tic
cys'tic fi·bro'sis
cys·ti'tis
cy'to·log'i·cal
cy·tol'o·gist
cy·tol'o·gy
cy'to·plasm
cy'to·plas'mic
cy'to·plast'
cy'to·sine'
czar *also* tsar *or* tzar
czar'e·vitch'
cza·rev'na
cza·ri'na
czar'ist
cza·rit'za
Czech *(relating to the Czech Republic)*
  ✔ *check*
Czech'o·slo'vak *or* Czech'o·slo·va'ki·an

D

dab, dabbed,
  dab'bing
dab'ble, -bled,
  -bling
dab'bler
da ca'po
dace *pl.* dace *or*
  dac'es
dachs'hund'
dac'tyl
dac·tyl'ic

dad'dy
daddy long'legs'
  pl. daddy long'legs'
da'do *pl.* -does
daf'fo·dil
daf'fy
dag'ger
da·guerre'o·type'
dahl'ia
dai'ly
dain'ty
dai'qui·ri *pl.* -ris
dair'y
dair'y·ing
dair'y·maid'
dair'y·man
dair'y·wom'an
da'is
dai'sy
Da·ko'tan
dale
dal'li·ance
dal'ly, -lied, -ly·ing
Dal·ma'tian
dam *(barrier, to re-strain)*, dammed,
  dam'ming
  ✔ *damn*
dam *(female animal)*
  ✔ *damn*
dam'age, -aged,
  -ag·ing
dam'ask
dame
damn *(to condemn)*
  ✔ *dam*
dam'na·ble

dam·na'tion
damned
damp'en
damp'er
dam'sel
dam'sel·fly'
dam'son
dance, danced,
  danc'ing
danc'er
dance'wear'
dan'de·li'on
dan'der
dan'di·fy', -fied',
  -fy'ing
dan'dle, -dled,
  -dling
dan'druff
dan'dy
Dane *(native of Den-mark)*
  ✔ *deign*
dan'ger
dan'ger·ous
dan'gle, -gled,
  -gling
Dan'ish
dap'per
dap'ple, -pled,
  -pling
dare, dared, dar'ing
dare'dev'il
dare'say'
dar'ing
dark'en
dark'ling
dark'room'

dar′ling
darn
Dar•win′i•an
Dar′win•ism
dash′board′
dash′ing
das′tard
da′ta
da′ta•base′
dat′a•ble *or*
 date′a•ble
da′ta proc′ess•ing
date, dat′ed, dat′ing
date′line′
da′tive
da′tum *pl.* -ta *also*
 -tums
daub
daugh′ter
daugh′ter-in-law′
 pl. daugh′ters-in-
 law′
daunt
dau′phin
dav′en•port′
dav′it
daw
daw′dle, -dled,
 -dling
dawn
day′break′
day′care′ *or* day′
 care′
day′dream′,
 -dreamed′ *or*
 -dreamt′,
 -dream′ing

day′light′
day′light-sav′ing
 time′
day′long′
day′school′
day′star′
day′time′
day′-to-day′
daze, dazed, daz′ing
daz′zle, -zled, -zling
dea′con
dea′con•ess
dea′con•ry
de•ac′ti•vate′,
 -vat′ed, -vat′ing
de•ac′ti•va′tion
dead
dead′beat′
dead′en
dead′end′ *n.*
dead′-end′ *adj.*
dead′head′
dead′line′
dead′lock′
dead′pan′
dead′wood′
deaf′en
deal, dealt, deal′ing
deal′er
deal′er•ship′
dean
dean′er•y
dear *(beloved)*
 ✔ *deer*
dearth
death
death′bed′

death′blow′
death′s′-head′
death′trap′
de•ba′cle
de•bar′, -barred′,
 -bar′ring
de•bark′
de•bar•ka′tion
de•base′, -based′,
 -bas′ing
de•base′ment
de•bat′a•ble
de•bate′, -bat′ed,
 -bat′ing
de•bauch′
de•bauch′er•y
de•bil′i•tate′,
 -tat′ed, -tat′ing
de•bil′i•ta′tion
de•bil′i•ta′tive
de•bil′i•ty
de•bone′, -boned′,
 -bon′ing
deb′it
deb′o•nair′ *also*
 deb′o•naire′
de•brief′
de•bris′ *also* dé•bris′
debt
debt′or
de•bug′, -bugged′,
 -bug′ging
de•bunk′
de•but′ *also* dé•but′
deb′u•tante′
dec′ade′
dec′a•dence

dec'a•dent
de•caf'fein•at'ed
dec'a•gon'
dec'a•he'dron *pl.*
  -drons *or* -dra
de'cal'
de•cal'ci•fi•ca'tion
de•cal'ci•fy', -fied',
  -fy'ing
dec'a•li'ter
de•camp'
de•cant'
de•cant'er
de•cap'i•tate',
  -tat'ed, -tat'ing
de•cap'i•ta'tion
de•car'bon•ate',
  -at'ed, -at'ing
de•cath'lon
de•cay'
de•cease', -ceased',
  -ceas'ing
de•ce'dent
de•ceit'
de•ceit'ful
de•ceive', -ceived',
  -ceiv'ing
de•ceiv'er
de•cel'er•ate',
  -at'ed, -at'ing
de•cel'er•a'tion
de•cel'er•a'tor
De•cem'ber
de'cen•cy
de'cent *(proper)*
  ✔ *descent, dissent*
de•cen'tral•i•za'-

tion
de•cen'tral•ize',
  -ized', -iz'ing
de•cep'tion
de•cep'tive
dec'i•bel
de•cide', -cid'ed,
  -cid'ing
de•cid'u•ous
dec'i•gram'
dec'i•li'ter
dec'i•mal
dec'i•mate',
  -mat'ed, -mat'ing
dec'i•ma'tion
dec'i•me'ter
de•ci'pher
de•ci'pher•a•ble
de•ci'sion
de•ci'sive
de•claim'
dec'la•ma'tion
de•clam'a•to'ry
de•clar'a•ble
dec'la•ra'tion
de•clar'a•tive
de•clare', -clared',
  -clar'ing
de•class'i•fi•ca'tion
de•class'i•fy', -fied',
  -fy'ing
de•claw'
de•clen'sion
dec'li•na'tion
de•cline', -clined',
  -clin'ing
de•cliv'i•ty

de•coct'
de•coc'tion
de•code', -cod'ed,
  -cod'ing
de•cod'er
dé'colle•tage'
dé'colle•té'
de'com•mis'sion
de'com•pos'a•ble
de'com•pose',
  -posed', -pos'ing
de'com•po•si'tion
de'com•press'
de'com•pres'sion
de'con•gest'
de'con•ges'tant
de'con•tam'i•nate',
  -nat'ed, -nat'ing
de'con•tam'i•na'-
tion
de'con•trol',
  -trolled', -trol'ling
dé'cor' *or* de'cor'
dec'o•rate', -rat'ed,
  -rat'ing
dec'o•ra'tion
dec'o•ra'tive
dec'o•ra'tor
dec'o•rous
de•co'rum
de'coy'
de•crease',
  -creased',
  -creas'ing
de'crease' *n.*
de•cree', -creed',
  -cree'ing

dec're•ment
de•crep'it
de•crep'i•tude'
de•cre•scen'do *pl.*
  -dos
de•crim'i•nal•i•za'-
  tion
de•crim'i•nal•ize',
  -ized', -iz'ing
de•cry', -cried',
  -cry'ing
ded'i•cate', -cat'ed,
  -cat'ing
ded'i•ca'tion
ded'i•ca•to'ry
de•duce', -duced',
  -duc'ing
de•duc'i•ble
de•duct'
de•duct'i•ble
de•duc'tion
de•duc'tive
deed
dee'jay'
deem
deep
deep'en
deep'-fry', -fried',
  -fry'ing
deep' fry'er
deep'-root'ed
deep'-sea' *adj.*
deep'-seat'ed
deer *(animal)*, pl.
  deer
  ✔ *dear*
deer'skin'

de-es'ca•late',
  -lat'ed, -lat'ing
de-es'ca•la'tion
de•face', -faced',
  -fac'ing
de•face'ment
de fac'to
def'a•ma'tion
de•fam'a•to'ry
de•fame', -famed',
  -fam'ing
de•fault'
de•feat'
de•feat'ism
de•feat'ist
def'e•cate', -cat'ed,
  -cat'ing
def'e•ca'tion
de•fect' *n.*
de•fect' *v.*
de•fec'tion
de•fec'tive
de•fec'tor
de•fend'
de•fen'dant
de•fense'
de•fense'less
de•fen'si•ble
de•fen'sive
de•fer', -ferred',
  -fer'ring
de•fer'ra•ble
def'er•ence *(submis-
  sion)*
  ✔ *difference*
def'er•en'tial
de•fer'ment

de•fi'ance
de•fi'ant
de•fib'ril•late',
  -lat'ed, -lat'ing
de•fi'cien•cy
de•fi'cient
def'i•cit
de•file', -filed',
  -fil'ing
de•file'ment
de•fine', -fined',
  -fin'ing
def'i•nite *(clear)*
  ✔ *definitive*
def'i•ni'tion
de•fin'i•tive *(final)*
  ✔ *definite*
de•flate', -flat'ed,
  -flat'ing
de•fla'tion
de•flect'
de•flec'tion
de•flec'tive
de•flec'tor
de•fog', -fogged',
  -fog'ging
de•fog'ger
de•fo'li•ant
de•fo'li•ate', -at'ed,
  -at'ing
de•fo'li•a'tion
de•for'est
de•for'es•ta'tion
de•form'
de'for•ma'tion
de•formed'
de•for'mi•ty

de·fraud'
de·fray'
de·frost'
de·frost'er
de·funct'
de·fuse', -fused',
　-fus'ing
de·fy', -fied', -fy'ing
de·gen'er·a·cy
de·gen'er·ate *adj.*
de·gen'er·ate',
　-at'ed, -at'ing
de·gen'er·a'tion
de·gen'er·a·tive
de'glu·ti'tion
de·grad'a·ble
deg'ra·da'tion
de·grade', -grad'ed,
　-grad'ing
de·gree'
de·hisce', -hisced',
　-hisc'ing
de·his'cence
de·his'cent
de·hu'man·i·za'-
　tion
de·hu'man·ize',
　-ized', -iz'ing
de'hu·mid'i·fi·ca'-
　tion
de'hu·mid'i·fi'er
de'hu·mid'i·fy',
　-fied', -fy'ing
de·hy'drate',
　-drat'ed, -drat'ing
de'hy·dra'tion
de·ice', -iced',

-ic'ing
de·ic'er
de'i·fi·ca'tion
de'i·fy', -fied',
　-fy'ing
deign *(to condescend)*
　✔ **Dane**
de·i'on·ize', -ized',
　-iz'ing
de'ism
de'ist
de·is'tic
de'i·ty
de·ject'ed
de·jec'tion
de ju're
Del'a·war'e·an
de·lay'
de·lec'ta·ble
del'e·gate', -gat'ed,
　-gat'ing
del'e·ga'tion
de·lete', -let'ed,
　-let'ing
del'e·te'ri·ous
de·le'tion
delft
del'i *pl.* -is
de·lib'er·ate *adj.*
de·lib'er·ate',
　-at'ed, -at'ing
de·lib'er·a'tion
de·lib'er·a'tive
del'i·ca·cy
del'i·cate
del'i·ca·tes'sen
de·li'cious

de·light'
de·light'ed
de·light'ful
de·lim'it
de·lin'e·ate', -at'ed,
　-at'ing
de·lin'e·a'tion
de·lin'e·a'tive
de·lin'e·a'tor
de·lin'quen·cy
de·lin'quent
del'i·quesce',
　-quesced',
　-quesc'ing
del'i·ques'cence
del'i·ques'cent
de·lir'i·ous
de·lir'i·um *pl.*
　-i·ums *or* -i·a
de·liv'er
de·liv'er·a·ble
de·liv'er·ance
de·liv'er·y
dell
de·louse', -loused',
　-lous'ing
Del'phic
del·phin'i·um
del'ta
del'toid'
de·lude', -lud'ed,
　-lud'ing
del'uge, -uged,
　-ug·ing
de·lu'sion
de·lu'sive
de luxe' *also*

de•luxe'
delve, delved,
delv'ing
de•mag'net•ize',
-ized', -iz'ing
dem'a•gog'ic
dem'a•gogue'
dem'a•gogu'er•y
dem'a•gog'y
de•mand'
de•mand'ing
de•mar'cate',
-cat'ed, -cat'ing
de'mar•ca'tion
de•mean'
de•mean'or
de•ment'ed
de•mer'it
de•mesne'
dem'i•god'
dem'i•god'dess
dem'i•john'
de•mil'i•ta•ri•za'-
tion
de•mil'i•ta•rize',
-rized', -riz'ing
de•mise'
dem'i•tasse'
dem'o *pl.* -os
de•mo'bi•li•za'-
tion
de•mo'bil•ize',
-ized', -iz'ing
de•moc'ra•cy
dem'o•crat'
dem'o•crat'ic
de•moc'ra•ti•za'-

tion
de•moc'ra•tize',
-tized', -tiz'ing
de•mog'ra•pher
dem'o•graph'ic
de•mog'ra•phy
de•mol'ish
dem'o•li'tion
de'mon
de•mon'ic
de•mon'stra•ble
dem'on•strate',
-strat'ed, -strat'ing
dem'on•stra'tion
de•mon'stra•tive
dem'on•stra'tor
de•mor'al•i•za'-
tion
de•mor'al•ize',
-ized', -iz'ing
de•mote', -mot'ed,
-mot'ing
de•mo'tion
de•mur' *(to object)*,
-murred',
-mur'ring
de•mure' *(modest)*
de•mur'ral
de•mur'rer
de•mys'ti•fi•ca'-
tion
de•mys'ti•fy',
-fied', -fy'ing
de•na'tur•a'tion
de•na'ture, -tured,
-tur'ing
den'drite'

de•ni'al
de•ni'er
den'i•grate',
-grat'ed, -grat'ing
den'i•gra'tion
den'im
den'i•zen
de•nom'i•nate',
-nat'ed, -nat'ing
de•nom'i•na'tion
de•nom'i•na'tion•
al
de•nom'i•na'tor
de'no•ta'tion
de•no'ta•tive
de•note', -not'ed,
-not'ing
de•noue•ment' *also*
dé'noue•ment'
de•nounce',
-nounced',
-nounc'ing
dense, dens'er,
dens'est
den'si•ty
den'tal
den'ti•frice'
den'tin *or* den'tine'
den'tist
den'tist•ry
den•ti'tion
den'ture
de•nude', -nud'ed,
-nud'ing
de•nun'ci•a'tion
de•ny', -nied',
-ny'ing

de•o'dor•ant
de•o'dor•i•za'tion
de•o'dor•ize',
  -ized', -iz'ing
de•o'dor•iz'er
de•ox'i•dize',
  -dized', -diz'ing
de•ox'i•diz'er
de•ox'y•ri'bo•nu•
  cle'ic ac'id
de•part'
de•part'ed
de•part'ment
de'part•men'tal
de•par'ture
de•pend'
de•pend'a•bil'i•ty
de•pend'a•ble
de•pend'ence
de•pend'en•cy
de•pend'ent
de•pict'
de•pic'tion
de•pil'a•to'ry
de•plane', -planed',
  -plan'ing
de•plet'a•ble
de•plete', -plet'ed,
  -plet'ing
de•ple'tion
de•plor'a•ble
de•plore', -plored',
  -plor'ing
de•ploy'
de•po'nent
de•pop'u•late',
  -lat'ed, -lat'ing

de•pop'u•la'tion
de•port'
de•por•ta'tion
de•port•ee'
de•port'ment
de•pose', -posed',
  -pos'ing
de•pos'it
dep'o•si'tion
de•pos'i•tor
de•pos'i•to'ry
de'pot
dep'ra•va'tion
  (corruption)
  ✔ *deprivation*
de•prave', -praved',
  -prav'ing
de•prav'i•ty
dep're•cate',
  -cat'ed, -cat'ing
dep're•ca'tion
de•pre'ci•ate',
  -at'ed, -at'ing
de•pre'ci•a'tion
de•pre'ci•a'tor
de•pre'ci•a'to'ry
dep're•da'tion
de•press'
de•pres'sant
de•pressed'
de•press'ing
de•pres'sion
de•pres'sive
de•pres'sor
dep'ri•va'tion *(loss)*
  ✔ *depravation*
de•prive', -prived',

-priv'ing
depth
dep'u•ta'tion
de•pute', -put'ed,
  -put'ing
dep'u•tize', -tized',
  -tiz'ing
dep'u•ty
de•rail'
de•rail'leur
de•range', -ranged',
  -rang'ing
der'by
de•reg'u•late',
  -lat'ed, -lat'ing
de•reg'u•la'tion
de•reg'u•la'tor
de•reg'u•la•to'ry
der'e•lict'
der'e•lic'tion
de•ride', -rid'ed,
  -rid'ing
de•ri'sion
de•ri'sive
de•riv'a•ble
der'i•va'tion
de•riv'a•tive
de•rive', -rived',
  -riv'ing
der'ma
der'mal
der'ma•ti'tis
der'ma•tol'o•gist
der'ma•tol'o•gy
der'mis
der'o•gate', -gat'ed,
  -gat'ing

der'o•ga'tion
de•rog'a•tive
de•rog'a•to'ry
der'rick
der'ring-do'
der'rin•ger
der'vish
de•sal'i•nize',
 -nized', -niz'ing
des'cant
de•scend'
de•scen'dant *(off-spring)*
de•scen'dent *also* de•scen'dant *(descending)*
de•scent' *(downward incline, ancestry)*
 ✔ *decent, dissent*
de•scrib'a•ble
de•scribe',
 -scribed', -scrib'ing
de•scrip'tion
de•scrip'tive
de•scry', -scried',
 -scry'ing
des'e•crate',
 -crat'ed, -crat'ing
des'e•cra'tion
de•seg're•gate',
 -gat'ed, -gat'ing
de•seg're•ga'tion
des'ert *(barren region)*
de•sert' *(punishment)*
 ✔ *dessert*

de•sert' *(to abandon)*
 ✔ *dessert*
de•ser'tion
de•serve', -served',
 -serv'ing
de•serv'ed•ly
des'ic•cate', -cat'ed,
 -cat'ing
des'i•ca'tion
de•sign'
des'ig•nate',
 -nat'ed, -nat'ing
des'ig•na'tion
des'ig•na'tive
des'ig•na'tor
des'ig•nee'
de•sign'er
de•sign'ing
de•sir'a•bil'i•ty
de•sir'a•ble
de•sir'a•bly
de•sire', -sired',
 -sir'ing
de•sir'ous
de•sist'
desk'top'
des'o•late *adj.*
des'o•late', -lat'ed,
 -lat'ing
des'o•la'tion
de•spair'
de•spair'ing
des'per•a'do *pl.*
 -does *or* -dos
des'per•ate *(despairing)*
 ✔ *disparate*

des'per•a'tion
des'pi•ca•ble
des'pi•ca•bly
de•spise', -spised',
 -spis'ing
de•spite'
de•spoil'
de•spo'li•a'tion
de•spon'dence *also* de•spon'den•cy
de•spon'dent
des'pot
des•pot'ic
des'pot•ism
des•sert' *(food)*
 ✔ *desert*
des'ti•na'tion
des'tine, -tined,
 -tin'ing
des'ti•ny
des'ti•tute'
des'ti•tu'tion
de•stroy'
de•stroy'er
de•struct'
de•struc'ti•ble
de•struc'tion
de•struc'tive
des'ul•to'ry
de•tach'
de•tach'a•bil'i•ty
de•tach'a•ble
de•tach'a•bly
de•tached'
de•tail'
de•tailed'
de•tain'

de·tect'
de·tect'a·ble *also*
   de·tect'i·ble
de·tec'tion
de·tec'tive
de·tec'tor
dé·tente'
de·ten'tion
de·ter', -terred',
   -ter'ring
de·ter'gent
de·te'ri·o·rate',
   -rat'ed, -rat'ing
de·te'ri·o·ra'tion
de·ter'min·a·ble
de·ter'mi·nant
de·ter'mi·nate',
   -nated', -nat'ing
de·ter'mi·na'tion
de·ter'mine,
   -mined, -min'ing
de·ter'min·er
de·ter'rence
de·ter'rent
de·test'
de·test'a·ble
de·test'a·bly
de·tes·ta'tion
de·throne',
   -throned',
   -thron'ing
de·throne'ment
det'o·nate',
   -nat'ed, -nat'ing
det'o·na'tion
det'o·na'tor
de'tour'

de·tox'i·fi·ca'tion
de·tox'i·fy', -fied',
   -fy'ing
de·tract'
de·trac'tion
de·trac'tor
det'ri·ment
det'ri·men'tal
de·tri'tus *pl.* -tus
deuce
deu·te'ri·um
de·val'u·a'tion
de·val'ue, -ued,
   -u'ing
dev'as·tate', -tat'ed,
   -tat'ing
dev'as·ta'tion
de·vel'op
de·vel'op·er
de·vel'op·ing
de·vel'op·ment
de·vel'op·men'tal
de'vi·ance
de'vi·ant
de'vi·ate', -at'ed,
   -at'ing
de'vi·a'tion
de·vice' *(con-*
   trivance)
   ✔ *devise*
dev'il, -iled *or* -illed,
   -il'ing *or* -il'ling
dev'il·fish'
dev'il·ish
dev'il-may-care'
dev'il·ment
dev'il·try *or*

dev'il·ry
de'vi·ous
de·vise' *(to invent)*,
   -vised', -vis'ing
   ✔ *device*
de·void'
de·volve', -volved',
   -volv'ing
De·vo'ni·an
de·vote', -vot'ed,
   -vot'ing
dev'o·tee'
de·vo'tion
de·vour'
de·vout'
dew *(moisture)*
   ✔ *do, due*
dew'ber'ry
dew'claw'
dew'drop'
dew'lap'
dew'y
dew'i·ness
dex·ter'i·ty
dex'ter·ous *also*
   dex'trous
dex'trose'
di'a·be'tes
di'a·bet'ic
di'a·bol'i·cal *also*
   di'a·bol'ic
di'a·crit'ic
di'a·crit'i·cal
di'a·dem'
di'ag·nose',
   -nosed', -nos'ing
di'ag·no'sis *pl.* -ses

di·ag·nos'tic

di·ag·nos·ti'cian

di·ag'o·nal

di'a·gram',
-grammed' *or*
-gramed',
-gram'ming *or*
-gram'ing

di'a·gram·mat'ic

di'al, -aled *or* -alled,
-al·ing *or* -al·ling

dl'a·lect'

di'a·lec'tal

di'a·lec'tic

di'a·lec'ti·cal

di'a·logue' *or*
di'a·log'

di·al'y·sis *pl.* -ses'

di·am'e·ter

di'a·met'ri·cal *also*
di'a·met'ric

di'a·mond

di'a·mond·back'

di'a·pa'son

di'a·per

di·aph'a·nous

di'a·phragm'

di'ar·rhe'a

di'a·rist

di'a·ry

Di·as'po·ra *also*
di·as'po·ra

di·as'to·le

di'a·stol'ic

di'a·tom'

di'a·tom'ic

di'a·ton'ic scale'

dice *sing.* die

dice, diced, dic'ing

di·chot'o·my

dick'ens

dick'er

dick'ey *pl.* -eys

di'cot'

di'cot'y·le'don

di'cot'y·le'don·ous

dic'tate', -tat'ed,
-tat'ing

dic·ta'tion

dic·ta'tor

dic·ta·to'ri·al

dic·ta'tor·ship'

dic'tion

dic'tion·ar'y

dic'tum *pl.* -ta *or*
-tums

di·dac'tic

did'n't

die *(to become dead),*
died, dy'ing
✔ *dye*

die *(tool for stamp-
lng), pl.* dies
✔ *dye*

die *(small cube), pl.*
dice
✔ *dye*

die'-hard' *also*
die'hard'

di·er'e·sis *or*
di·aer'e·sis *pl.* -ses'

die'sel

di'et

di'et·er

di'e·tar'y

di'e·tet'ic

di'e·ti'tian *or*
di'e·ti'cian

dif'fer

dif'fer·ence *(dissim-
ilarity)*
✔ *deference*

dif'fer·ent

dif'fer·en'tial

dif'fer·en'ti·ate',
-at'ed, -at'ing

dif'fer·en'ti·a'tion

dif'fi·cult'

dif'fi·cul'ty

dif'fi·dence

dif'fi·dent

dif·fract'

dif·frac'tion

dif·fuse', -fused',
-fus'ing

dif·fu'sion

dig, dug, dig'ging

di·gest' *v.*

di'gest' *n.*

di·gest'i·bil'i·ty

di·gest'i·ble

di·ges'tion

di·ges'tive

dig'ger

dig'gings

dig'it

dig'i·tal

dig'i·tal'is

dig'ni·fy', -fied',
-fy'ing

dig'ni•tar'y
dig'ni•ty
di•gress'
di•gres'sion
di•he'dral
dike, diked, dik'ing
di•lap'i•dat'ed
di•lap'i•da'tion
di•lat'a•ble
dil'a•ta'tion
di•late', -lat'ed,
  -lat'ing
di•la'tion
dil'a•to'ry
di•lem'ma
dil'et•tante' *pl.*
  -tantes *also* -tan'ti
dil'et•tan'tism
dil'i•gence
dil'i•gent
dill
dil'ly-dal'ly,
  -dal'lied, -dal'ly•ing
di•lute', -lut'ed,
  -lut'ing
di•lu'tion
dim, dim'mer,
  dim'mest
dim, dimmed,
  dim'ming
dime
di•men'sion
di•men'sion•al
di•min'ish
di•min'ish•ing
di•min'u•en'do
dim'i•nu'tion

di•min'u•tive
dim'i•ty
dim'mer
dim'ple, -pled,
  -pling
dine *(to eat)*, dined,
  din'ing
  ✓ *dyne*
din'er
di•nette'
ding'-dong'
din'ghy *(small*
  boat)
  ✓ *dingy*
din'gle
din'go *pl.* -goes
din'gy *(dirty)*
  ✓ *dinghy*
din'gi•ness
din'ing room'
din'ky
din'ner
din'ner•time'
di'no•flag'el•late
di'no•saur'
dint
di'o•cese
di•ode'
di'o•ram'a
di•ox'ide
dip, dipped,
  dip'ping
diph•the'ri•a
diph'thong'
dip'loid'
di•plo'ma
di•plo'ma•cy

dip'lo•mat'
dip'lo•mat'ic
dip'per
dip'stick'
dip'ter•ous
dip'tych
dire, dir'er, dir'est
di•rect'
di•rec'tion
di•rec'tion•al
di•rec'tive
di•rec'tor
di•rec'tor•ate
di•rec'to'ri•al
di•rec'to•ry
dirge
dir•ham'
dir'i•gi•ble
dirn'dl
dirt
dirt'-cheap'
dirt'y, -ied, -y•ing
dis'a•bil'i•ty
dis•a'ble, -bled,
  -bling
dis'a•buse', -bused',
  -bus'ing
dis'ad•van'tage
dis'ad•van'taged
dis'ad•van•ta'-
  geous
dis'af•fect'
dis'af•fect'ed
dis'af•fec'tion
dis'a•gree', -greed',
  -gree'ing
dis'a•gree'a•ble

dis'a•gree'a•bly
dis'a•gree'ment
dis•al•low'
dis'ap•pear'
dis'ap•pear'ance
dis'ap•point'
dis'ap•point'ed
dis'ap•point'ing
dis'ap•prov'al
dis'ap•prove',
  -proved', -prov'ing
dis•arm'
dis•ar'ma•ment
dis•arm'ing
dis•ar•range',
  -ranged', -rang'ing
dis•ar•ray'
dis•as•sem'ble,
  -bled, -bling
dis•as•so•ci•ate',
  -at'ed, -at'ing
dis•as•so•ci•a'tion
dis•as'ter
dis•as'trous
dis'a•vow'
dis'a•vow'al
dis•band'
dis•bar', -barred',
  -bar'ring
dis'be•lief'
dis'be•lieve',
  -lieved', -liev'ing
dis'be•liev'er
dis•bur'den
dis•burse' *(to pay
  out)*, -bursed',
  -burs'ing

✔ *disperse*
dis•burse'ment
dis•card' *v.*
dis'card' *n.*
disc' brake' *also*
  disk' brake'
dis•cern'
dis•cern'i•ble
dis•cern'i•bly
dis•cern'ing
dis•cern'ment
dis•charge',
  -charged',
  -charg'ing
dis'charge' *n.*
dis•ci'ple
dis'ci•pli•nar'i•an
dis'ci•pli•nar'y
dis'ci•pline,
  -plined, -plin•ing
disc' jock'ey
dis•claim'
dis•claim'er
dis•close', -closed',
  -clos'ing
dis•clo'sure
dis'co *pl.* -cos
dis'co, -coed,
  -co•ing
dis•cog'ra•phy
dis'coid'
dis•col'or
dis•col'or•a'tion
dis'com•bob'u•
  late', -lat'ed,
  -lat'ing
dis'com•bob'u•la'-

tion
dis•com'fit *(to make
  uneasy)*
  ✔ *discomfort*
dis•com'fi•ture'
dis•com'fort *(un-
  easiness)*
  ✔ *discomfit*
dis'com•pose',
  -posed', -pos'ing
dis'com•po'sure
dis'con•cert'
dis'con•nect'
dis'con•nect'ed
dis'con•nec'tion
dis•con'so•late
dis'con•tent'
dis'con•tent'ed
dis'con•tin'u•ance
dis'con•tin'u•a'-
  tion
dis'con•tin'ue,
  -ued, -u'ing
dis'con•tin'u•ous
dis'cord'
dis•cor'dance
dis•cor'dant
dis'co•theque'
dis'count'
dis'count'a•ble
dis•cour'age, -aged,
  -ag'ing
dis'course' *n.*
dis'course',
  -coursed',
  -cours'ing
dis•cour'te•ous

dis•cour'te•sy
dis•cov'er
dis•cov'er•a•ble
dis•cov'er•y
dis•cred'it
dis•cred'it•a•ble
dis•cred'it•a•bly
dis•creet' *(prudent)*
  ✔ *discrete*
dis•crep'an•cy
dis•crep'ant
dis•crete' *(distinct)*
  ✔ *discreet*
dis•cre'tion
dis•cre'tion•ar'y
dis•crim'i•nate',
  -nat'ed, -nat'ing
dis•crim'i•na'tion
dis•crim'i•na'tor
dis•crim'i•na•to'ry
dis•cur'sive
dis'cus *pl.* -cus•es
dis•cuss'
dis•cus'si•ble
dis•cus'sion
dis•dain'
dis•ease'
dis•eased'
dis'em•bark'
dis•em•bar•ka'tion
dis'em•bod'ied
dis'em•bod'i•ment
dis'em•bod'y, -ied,
  -y•ing
dis'em•bow'el,
  -eled *or* -elled,
  -el'ing *or* -el'ling

dis'en•chant'
dis'en•cum'ber
dis'en•fran'chise',
  -chised', -chis'ing
dis'en•gage',
  -gaged', -gag'ing
dis'en•gage'ment
dis'en•tan'gle,
  -gled, -gling
dis'en•tan'gle•
  ment
dis•fa'vor
dis•fig'ure, -ured,
  -ur•ing
dis•fran'chise',
  -chised', -chis'ing
dis•gorge',
  -gorged', -gorg'ing
dis•grace', -graced',
  -grac'ing
dis•grace'ful
dis•grun'tle, -tled,
  -tling
dis•guise', -guised',
  -guis'ing
dis•gust'
dis•gust'ed
dis•gust'ing
dish
dis'ha•bille' *also*
  des'ha•bille'
dis'har•mo'ni•ous
dis•har'mo•ny
dish'cloth'
dis•heart'en
di•shev'eled *or*
  di•shev'elled

dis•hon'est
dis•hon'es•ty
dis•hon'or
dis•hon'or•a•ble
dis•hon'or•a•bly
dish'pan'
dish'rag'
dish'tow'el
dish'wash'er
dish'wa'ter
dis•il•lu'sion
dis'in•cli'na'tion
dis'in•clined'
dis'in•fect'
dis'in•fec'tion
dis'in•fec'tant
dis'in•her'it
dis'in•te•grate',
  -grat'ed, -grat'ing
dis'in•te•gra'tion
dis'in•ter', -terred',
  -ter'ring
dis'in•ter'ment
dis'in•ter•est•ed
dis•joint'
dis•joint'ed
disk *also* disc
disk' drive'
disk•ette'
dis•like', -liked',
  -lik'ing
dis•lo•cate', -cat'ed,
  -cat'ing
dis•lo•ca'tion
dis•lodge',
  -lodged', -lodg'ing
dis•loy'al

dis•loy'al•ty

dis'mal

dis•man'tle, -tled, -tling

dis•may'

dis•mem'ber

dis•miss'

dis•miss'al

dis•mount'

dis'o•be'di•ence

dis'o•be'di•ent

dis'o•bey'

dis'o•blige', -bliged', -blig'ing

dis•or'der

dis•or'der•li•ness

dis•or'der•ly

dis•or'gan•i•za'tion

dis•or'gan•ize', -ized', -iz'ing

dis•o'ri•ent

dis•o'ri•en•ta'tion

dis•own'

dis•par'age, -aged, -ag•ing

dis'pa•rate *(different)*
  ✔ *desperate*

dis•par'i•ty

dis•pas'sion•ate

dis•patch' *also* des•patch'

dis•patch'er

dis•pel', -pelled', -pel'ling

dis•pen'sa•bil'i•ty

dis•pen'sa•ble

dis•pen'sa•ry

dis•pen•sa'tion

dis•pense', -pensed', -pens'ing

dis•pens'er

dis•per'sal

dis•perse' *(to scatter)*, -persed', -pers'ing
  ✔ *disburse*

dis•per'sion

dis•pir'it

dis•pir'it•ed

dis•place', -placed', -plac'ing

dis•place'ment

dis•play'

dis•please', -pleased', -pleas'ing

dis•pleas'ure

dis•port'

dis•pos'a•ble

dis•pos'al

dis•pose', -posed', -pos'ing

dis'po•si'tion

dis'pos•sess'

dis'pos•ses'sion

dis•proof'

dis'pro•por'tion

dis'pro•por'tion•ate

dis•prove', -proved', -prov'ing

dis•put'a•bil'i•ty

dis•put'a•ble

dis•pu'tant

dis'pu•ta'tion

dis•pute', -put'ed, -put'ing

dis•qual'i•fi•ca'tion

dis•qual'i•fy', -fied', -fy'ing

dis•qui'et

dis•qui'e•tude'

dis'qui•si'tion

dis're•gard'

dis're•pair'

dis•rep'u•ta•ble

dis're•pute'

dis're•spect'

dis're•spect'ful

dis•robe', -robed', -rob'ing

dis•rupt'

dis•rup'tion

dis•rup'tive

dis•sat'is•fac'tion

dis•sat'is•fy', -fied', -fy'ing

dis•sect'

dis•sec'tion

dis•sem'ble, -bled, -bling

dis•sem'bler

dis•sem'i•nate', -nat'ed, -nat'ing

dis•sem'i•na'tion

dis•sen'sion

dis•sent' *(disagreement)*
  ✔ *decent, descent*

dis•sent'er
dis'ser•ta'tion
dis•serv'ice
dis•sev'er
dis'si•dence
dis'si•dent
dis•sim'i•lar
dis•sim'i•lar'i•ty
dis•sim'u•late',
 -lat'ed, -lat'ing
dis•sim'u•la'tion
dis'si•pate', -pat'ed,
 -pat'ing
dis'si•pa'tion
dis•so'ci•ate',
 -at'ed, -at'ing
dis•so'ci•a'tion
dis•sol'u•ble
dis'so•lute'
dis'so•lu'tion
dis•solv'a•ble
dis•solve', -solved',
 -solv'ing
dis'so•nance
dis'so•nant
dis•suade',
 -suad'ed, -suad'ing
dis•sua'sion
dis'taff'
dis'tance
dis'tant
dis•taste'
dis•taste'ful
dis•tem'per
dis•tend'
dis•ten'tion *also*
 dis•ten'sion

dis•till' *also* dis•til',
 -tilled', -till'ing
dis'til•late'
dis'til•la'tion
dis•till'er
dis•till'er•y
dis•tinct'
dis•tinc'tion
dis•tinc'tive
dis•tin'guish
dis•tin'guish•a•ble
dis•tin'guished
dis•tort'
dis•tor'tion
dis•tract'
dis•trac'tion
dis•traught'
dis•tress'
dis•trib'ute, -ut•ed,
 -ut'ing
dis'tri•bu'tion
dis•trib'u•tive
dis•trib'u•tor
dis'trict'
dis•trust'
dis•turb'
dis•tur'bance
di•sul'fide'
dis•un'ion
dis'u•nite', -nit'ed,
 -nit'ing
dis•u'ni•ty
dis•use'
ditch
dith'er
dit'to *pl.* -tos
dit'ty

di'u•ret'ic
di•ur'nal
di'va
di•va'lent
di•van'
dive, dived *or* dove,
 dived, div'ing
dive'-bomb'
div'er
di•verge', -verged',
 -verg'ing
di•ver'gence
di•ver'gent
di'vers *(various)*
di•verse' *(different)*
di•ver'si•fi•ca'tion
di•ver'si•fy', -fied',
 -fy'ing
di•ver'sion
di•ver'si•ty
di•vert'
di•ver'ti•men'to *pl.*
 -tos *or* -ti
di•vest'
di•ves'ti•ture
di•vid'a•ble
di•vide', -vid'ed,
 -vid'ing
div'i•dend'
di•vid'er
div'i•na'tion
di•vine', -vined',
 -vin'ing
div'ing board'
div'ing suit'
di•vin'ing rod'
di•vin'i•ty

di•vis'i•bil'i•ty
di•vis'i•ble
di•vis'i•bly
di•vi'sion
di•vi'sive
di•vi'sor
di•vorce', -vorced',
  -vorc'ing
di•vor•cé'
di•vor•cée'
div'ot
di•vulge', -vulged',
  -vulg'ing
div'vy, -vied,
  -vy•ing
Dix'ie•land'
diz'zy, -zied,
  -zy•ing
diz'zi•ness
DNA
do (to perform), did,
  done, do'ing, does
  ✔ dew, due
do (what should be
  done, party), pl. do's
  or dos
  ✔ dew, due
do (musical tone)
  ✔ doe, dough
dob'bin
Do'ber•man
  pin'scher
doc'ile
do•cil'i•ty
dock
dock'et
dock'yard'

doc'tor
doc'tor•al
doc'tor•ate
doc'tri•naire'
doc'tri•nal
doc'trine
doc'u•dra'ma
doc'u•ment
doc'u•men'ta•ry
doc'u•men•ta'tion
dod'der
dod'der•ing
do•dec'a•gon'
do'dec•a•he'dron
  pl. -drons or -dra
dodge, dodged,
  dodg'ing
dodg'er
do'do pl. -does or
  -dos
doe (female deer), pl.
  doe or does
  ✔ do, dough
do'er
doe'skin'
does'n't
doff
dog, dogged,
  dog'ging
dog'cart'
dog'catch'er
doge
dog'-ear'
dog'-eared'
dog'fight'
dog'fish'
dog'ged

dog'ger•el
dog'gy or dog'gie
dog'gy bag'
dog'house'
dog'ma
dog•mat'ic
dog'ma•tism
do'-good'er
dog'sled'
dog'trot'
dog'watch'
dog'wood'
doi'ly
do'lugs
do'-it-your•self'
dol'drums
dole, doled, dol'ing
dole'ful
doll
dol'lar
doll'house'
dol'lop
dol'ly
dol'man (garment)
dol'men (stone
  structure)
dol'o•mite'
do'lor
do'lor•ous
dol'phin
dolt
do•main'
dome, domed,
  dom'ing
do•mes'tic
do•mes'ti•cate',
  -cat'ed, -cat'ing

do•mes'ti•ca'tion
do•mes•tic'i•ty
dom'i•cile', -ciled',
 -cil'ing
dom'i•nance
dom'i•nant
dom'i•nate',
 -nat'ed, -nat'ing
dom'i•na'tion
dom'i•neer'
dom'i•neer'ing
Do•min'i•can
do•min'ion
dom'i•no' *pl.* -noes'
 or -nos'
don, donned,
 don'ning
do'nate', -nat'ed,
 -nat'ing
do•na'tion
done *(finished)*
 ✔ *dun*
don'jon *(tower)*
 ✔ *dungeon*
don'key *pl.* -keys
don'nish
don'ny•brook'
do'nor
do'-no'thing
don't
doo'dad'
doo'dle, -dled,
 -dling
doo'dler
doo'dle•bug'
doom
dooms'day'

door
door'bell'
door'jamb'
door'knob'
door'man
door'mat'
door'nail'
door'sill'
door'step'
door'stop'
door'way'
door'yard'
doo'zy *or* doo'zie
do'pa•mine'
dope, doped,
 dop'ing
dop'ey, dop'i•er,
 dop'i•est
Dop'pler ef•fect'
Dor'ic
dor'man•cy
dor'mant
dor'mer
dor'mi•to'ry
dor'mouse'
dor'sal
do'ry
dos'age
dose, dosed, dos'ing
dos'si•er'
dot, dot'ted, dot'-
 ting
dot'age
do'tard
dote, dot'ed,
 dot'ing
dot'ty

dou'ble, -bled,
 -bling
dou'ble-bar'reled
dou'ble-breast'ed
dou'ble-check' *v.*
dou'ble-cross'
dou'ble-deal'er
dou'ble-deal'ing
dou'ble-deck'er
dou'ble-dig'it
 adj.
dou'ble-edged'
dou'ble-en•ten'-
 dre
dou'ble-head'er
 also dou'ble•head'-
 er
dou'ble-joint'ed
dou'ble knit' *also*
 dou'ble-knit'
dou'ble-park'
dou'ble-quick'
dou'ble-space',
 -spaced', -spac'ing
dou'blet
dou'ble talk' *or*
 dou'ble-talk' *or*
 dou'ble•talk'
dou'ble time' *n.*
dou'ble-time' *v.*
dou•bloon'
dou'bly
doubt
doubt'ful
doubt'less
douche, douched,
 douch'ing

dough *(bread mixture, money)*
  ✔ *do, doe*
dough′i•ness
dough′nut′ *also*
  do′nut′
dough′ti•ness
dough′ty
dough′y
dour
douse *(to immerse, to extinguish)*, doused, dous′ing
  ✔ *dowse*
dove
dove′cotc′ *also*
  dove′cot′
dove′tail′
dow′a•ger
dow′dy
dow′el, -eled *or*
  -elled, -el•ing *or*
  -el•ling
dow′er
down
down′beat′
down′cast′
down′er
down′fall′
down′grade′,
  -grad′ed, -grad′ing
down′heart′ed
down′hill′ *adv.*
down′hill′ *adj.*
down′load′
down′play′
down′pour′

down′right′
down′scale′,
  -scaled′, -scal′ing
down′shift′
down′side′
down′stage′
down′stairs′ *adv.*
down′stairs′ *adj.*
down′stream′ *adj.*
down′stream′ *adv.*
down′swing′
down′time′
down′-to-earth′
down′town′ *adj.*
down′town′ *adv.*
down′trod′den
down′turn′
down′ward
down′wind′
down′y
dow′ry
dowse *(to divine)*,
  dowsed, dows′ing
  ✔ *douse*
dows′er
dox•ol′o•gy
doze, dozcd, doz′ing
doz′en *pl.* doz′en *or*
  doz′ens
doz′enth
drab, drab′ber,
  drab′best
drach′ma *pl.* -mas
  or -mae
draft•ee′
dratts′man
drafts′man•ship′

drafts′per•son
drafts′wom′an
draft′y
drag, dragged,
  drag′ging
drag′gle, -gled,
  -gling
drag′net′
drag′on
drag′on•fly′
dra•goon′
drain
drain′age
drain′pipe′
drake
dram
dra′ma
dra•mat′ic
dram′a•tis
  per•so′nae′
dram′a•tist
dram′a•ti•za′tion
dram′a•tize′,
  -tized′, -tiz′ing
drape, draped,
  drap′ing
drap′er
drap′er•y
dras′tic
Dra•vid′i•an *or*
  Dra•vid′ic
draw, drew, drawn,
  draw′ing
draw′back′
draw′bridge′
draw′cr *(one who draws)*

drawer *(compart-
   ment)*
draw'ing
draw'ing room'
draw'knife'
drawl
draw'string'
dread
dread'ful
dread'locks'
dread'nought'
dream, dreamed *or*
   dreamt, dream'ing
dream'land'
dream'y
drear'i•ness
drear'y
dredge, dredged,
   dredg'ing
dregs
drench
drenched
dress
dres•sage'
dress'er
dress'ing
dress'mak'er
dress'mak'ing
dress'y
drib'ble, -bled,
   -bling
drib'bler
drib'let
dri'er *also* dry'er
   (one that dries)
   ✓ *dryer*
drift'er

drift'wood'
drink, drank, drunk,
   drink'ing
drip, dripped,
   drip'ping
drip'-dry', -dried',
   -dry'ing
drive, drove,
   driv'en, driv'ing
drive'-in' *n.*
driv'el, -eled *or*
   -elled, -el•ing *or*
   -el•ling
driv'el•er *or*
   driv'el•ler
driv'er
drive' shaft'
drive'way'
driz'zle, -zled, -zling
driz'zly
droll
drom'e•dar'y
drone, droned,
   dron'ing
drool
droop *(to sag)*
   ✓ *drupe*
droop'y
drop, dropped,
   drop'ping
drop' cloth'
drop' kick'
drop' leaf'
drop'let
drop'out' *n.*
drop'per
drop'pings

drop'sy
dross
drought
drove
drov'er
drown
drowse, drowsed,
   drows'ing
drows'y
drub, drubbed,
   drub'bing
drudge, drudged,
   drudg'ing
drudg'er•y
drug, drugged,
   drug'ging
drug'gist
drug'store'
dru'id
drum, drummed,
   drum'ming
drum'beat'
drum'lin
drum'mer
drum'stick'
drunk'ard
drunk'en
drupe *(fruit)*
   ✓ *droop*
druth'ers
dry, dri'er *or* dry'er,
   dri'est *or* dry'est
dry, dried, dry'ing
dry'ad
dry'-clean'
dry' clean'er
dry' clean'ing

dry' dock' *n.*

dry'-dock' *v.*

dry'er *(appliance that dries)*
  ✔ drier

dry'ly

dry' wall' *or* dry'wall'

du'al *(double)*
  ✔ duel

du·al'i·ty

dub, dubbed, dub'bing

du'bi·ous

du'cal

duc'at

duch'ess

duch'y

duck'bill'

duck'ling

duck'weed'

duct

duc'tile

duc·til'i·ty

dude

dudg'eon

due *(owed as a debt)*
  ✔ dew, do

du'el *(to fight)*, -eled *or* -elled, -el·ing *or* -el·ling
  ✔ dual

du'el·er *or* du'el·ler *or* du'el·ist *or* du'el·list

du·et'

duf'fel *or* duf'fle

duf'fle bag' *or* duf'fel bag'

dug'out' *n.*

duke

duke'dom

dul'cet

dul'ci·mer

dull

dull'ard

du'ly

dumb

dumb'bell'

dumb'found' *also* dum'found'

dumb'wait'er

dum'my

dump'ling

dump'site'

dump'y

dun *(to ask for payment)*, dunned, dun'ning
  ✔ done

dun *(grayish brown)*
  ✔ done

dunce

dune

dung

dun·ga·ree'

dun'geon *(prison)*
  ✔ donjon

dunk

du'o *pl.* -os

du'o·dec'i·mal

du'o·de'nal

du'o·de'num *pl.* -na *or* -nums

dupe, duped, dup'ing

du'ple

du'plex'

du'pli·cate *adj. & n.*

du'pli·cate', -cat'ed, -cat'ing

du'pli·ca'tion

du'pli·ca'tor

du·plic'i·ty

du'ra·bil'i·ty

du'ra·ble

du'ra·bly

du'rance

du·ra'tion

du·ress'

dur'ing

du'rum

dusk'y

dust' bowl'

dust'er

dust' jack'et

dust'pan'

dust'y

Dutch

Dutch'man

Dutch' ov'en

Dutch' treat'

Dutch'wom'an

du'te·ous

du'ti·a·ble

du'ti·ful

du'ty

dwarf *pl.* dwarfs *or* dwarves

dwell, dwelt *or* dwelled, dwell'ing

dwin'dle, -dled,
  -dling
dye *(to color)*, dyed,
  dye'ing
  ✔ *die*
dyed'-in-the-wool'
dy'er
dye'stuff'
dy•nam'ic
dy'na•mism
dy'na•mite',
  -mit'ed, -mit'ing
dy'na•mo' *pl.* -mos'
dy•nas'tic
dy'nas•ty
dyne *(unit of force)*
  ✔ *dine*
dys'en•ter•y
dys•func'tion
dys•gen'ic
dys•lex'i•a
dys•lex'ic
dys•pep'sia
dys•pep'tic
dys•pro'si•um
dys•troph'ic
dys'tro•phy *also*
  dis•tro'phi•a

E

each
ea'ger
ea'gle
ea'gle-eyed'
ea'glet

ear
ear'ache'
ear'drum'
eared
ear'flap'
earl
earl'dom
ear'lobe'
ear'ly
ear'mark'
ear'muff'
earn *(to gain)*
  ✔ *urn*
earn'er
ear'nest
earn'ings
ear'phone'
ear'piece'
ear'plug'
ear'ring
ear'shot'
ear'split'ting
earth
earth'bound' *also*
  earth'-bound'
earth'en
earth'en•ware'
earth'ling
earth'ly *(relating to
  the earth, not heav-
  enly)*
  ✔ *earthy*
earth'quake'
earth'shak'ing
earth'ward *adv. &
  adj.*
earth'wards *adv.*

earth'work'
earth'worm'
earth'y *(relating to
  the soil, natural)*
  ✔ *earthly*
ear'wax'
ear'wig'
ease, eased, eas'ing
ea'sel
eas'i•ly
eas'i•ness
east
east'bound'
Eas'ter
east'er•ly
east'ern
east'ern•er
east'ern•most'
east'ward *adv. &
  adj.*
east'wards *adv.*
eas'y
eas'y chair'
eas'y•go'ing *also*
  eas•y-go'ing
eat, ate, eat'en,
  eat'ing
eat'a•ble
eat'er
eat'er•y
eats
eau' de co•logne'
  pl. eaux' de
  co•logne'
eaves
eaves'drop',
  -dropped',

-drop'ping
eaves'drop'per
ebb
eb'on·ite'
eb'on·y
e·bul'lience
e·bul'lient
ec·cen'tric
ec·cen·tric'i·ty
ec·cle'si·as'tic
ec·cle'si·as'ti·cal
ech'e·lon'
e·chid'na
e·chi'no·derm'
ech'o *pl.* -oes
ech'o, -oed, -o·ing
ech'o·car'di·o·
    gram'
ech'o·car'di·o·
    graph'
e·cho'ic
ech'o·lo·ca'tion
é·clair'
é·clat'
e·clec'tic
e·clec'ti·cism
e·clipse', e·clipsed',
    e·clips'ing
e·clip'tic
ec'o·cide'
ec'o·log'i·cal
e·col'o·gist
e·col'o·gy
e·con'o·met'rics
ec'o·nom'ic
ec'o·nom'i·cal
ec'o·nom'ics

e·con'o·mist
e·con'o·mize',
    -mized', -miz'ing
e·con'o·my
ec'o·sys'tem
ec'ru
ec'sta·sy
ec·stat'ic
ec'to·derm'
ec'to·plasm
Ec'ua·dor'i·an
ec'u·men'i·cal
ec'ze·ma
E'dam
ed'dy, -died, -dy·ing
e'del·weiss'
e·de'ma
E'den
edge, edged, edg'ing
edge'wise' *also*
    edge'ways'
edg'i·ness
edg'y
ed'i·ble
e'dict'
ed'i·fi·ca'tion
ed'i·fice
ed'i·fy', -fied',
    -fy'ing
ed'it
e·di'tion *(publica-
    tion)*
    ✔ addition
ed'i·tor
ed'i·to'ri·al
ed'i·to'ri·al·ize',
    -ized', -iz'ing

ed'u·ca·ble
ed'u·cate', -cat'ed,
    -cat'ing
ed'u·ca'tion
ed'u·ca'tion·al
ed'u·ca'tor
e·duce', e·duced',
    e·duc'ing
e·duc'i·ble
eel *pl.* eel *or* eels
e'en *(evening)*
e'en *(even)*
e'er *(ever)*
    ✔ air, are, ere, heir
ee'rie *or* ee'ry *(weird)*
    ✔ aerie
ee'ri·ly
ef·face', -faced',
    -fac'ing
ef·face'ment
ef·fac'er
ef·fect' *(result)*
    ✔ affect
ef·fec'tive
ef·fec'tive·ness
ef·fec'tu·al
ef·fec'tu·ate',
    -at'ed, -at'ing
ef·fem'i·na·cy *or*
    ef·fem'i·nate·ness
ef·fem'i·nate
ef'fer·ent
ef'fer·vesce',
    -vesced', -vesc'ing
ef'fer·ves'cence
ef'fer·ves'cent
ef·fete'

ef•fete′ness
ef•fi•ca′cious
ef′fi•ca•cy
ef•fi′cien•cy
ef•fi′cient
ef′fi•gy
ef′flo•resce′
ef′flo•res′cence
ef′flo•res′cent
ef′flu•ence
ef′flu•ent
ef•flu′vi•um *pl.*
  -vi•a *or* -vi•ums
ef′fort
ef•front′er•y
ef•ful′gence
ef•ful′gent
ef•fu′sion
ef•fu′sive
ef•fu′sive•ly
eft
e•gal′i•tar′i•an
e•gal′i•tar′i•an•ism
egg
egg′beat′er
egg′head′
egg′nog′
egg′plant′
egg′shell′
eg′lan•tine′
e′go *pl.* e•gos
e′go•cen′tric
e′go•ism
e′go•ist
e′go•is′tic *or*
  e′go•is′ti•cal
e′go•tism

e′go•tist
e′go•tis′tic *or*
  e′go•tis′ti•cal
e′go trip′ *n.*
e′go-trip′, -tripped′,
  -trip′ping
e•gre′gious
e′gress′
e′gret
E•gyp′tian
E′gyp•tol′o•gist
E′gyp•tol′o•gy
eh
ei′der
ei′der•down′
eight
eight•een′
eight•eenth′
eighth
eight′i•eth
eight′y
ein•stein′i•um
ei′ther
e•jac′u•late′,
  -lat′ed, -lat′ing
e•jac′u•la′tion
e•ject′
e•jec′tion
e•jec′tor
eke, eked, ek′ing
e•lab′o•rate
e•lab′o•rate′,
  -rat′ed, -rat′ing
e•lab′o•rate•ly
e•lab′o•ra′tion
e′land *pl.* e′land
  also e′lands

e•lapse′, e•lapsed′,
  e•laps′ing
e•las′tic
e•las•tic′i•ty
e•las′ti•cized′
e•late′, e•lat′ed,
  e•lat′ing
e•la′tion
el′bow
el′bow•room′
eld′er *(older)*
el′der *(shrub)*
el′der•ber′ry
eld′er•li•ness
eld′er•ly
eld′est
El′ Do•ra′do
e•lect′
e•lec′tion
e•lec′tion•eer′
e•lec′tive
e•lec′tor
e•lec′tor•al
e•lec′tor•ate
e•lec′tric *also*
  e•lec′tri•cal
e•lec•tri′cian
e•lec•tric′i•ty
e•lec′tri•fi•ca′tion
e•lec′tri•fy′, -fied′,
  -fy′ing
e•lec′tro•car′di•o•
  gram′
e•lec′tro•car′di•o•
  graph′
e•lec′tro•chem′i•
  cal

e·lec'tro·chem'is·try

e·lec'tro·con·vul'sive

e·lec'tro·cute', -cut'ed, -cut'ing

e·lec'tro·cu'tion

e·lec'trode'

e·lec'tro·en·ceph'a·lo·gram'

e·lec'tro·en·ceph'a·lo·graph'

c·lec·trol'y·sis

e·lec'tro·lyte'

e·lec'tro·lyt'ic

e·lec'tro·lyze', -lyzed', -lyz'ing

e·lec'tro·mag'net

e·lec'tro·mag'net'ic

e·lec'tro·mag'net·ism

e·lec'tro·mo'tive

e·lec'tron

e·lec·tron'ic

e·lec'tro·plate', -plat'ed, -plat'ing

e·lec'tro·scope'

e·lec'tro·scop'ic

e·lec'tro·shock'

e·lec'tro·stat'ic

e·lec'tro·ther'a·py

e·lec'tro·va'lence

e·lec'tro·va'len·cy

e·lec'tro·va'lent

el'e·gance

el'e·gant

el'e·gi'ac

el'e·gize', -gized', -giz'ing

el'e·gy

el'e·ment

el'e·men'tal

el'e·men'ta·ry

el'e·phant

el'e·phan'tine'

el'e·vate', -vat'ed, -vat'ing

el'e·va'tion

el'e·va'tor

e·lev'en

e·lev'enth

elf *pl.* elves

elf'in

elf'ish

e·lic'it *(to bring out)*
✔ illicit

e·lide', e·lid'ed, e·lid'ing

el'i·gi·bil'i·ty

el'i·gi·ble

e·lim'i·nate', -nat'ed, -nat'ing

e·lim'i·na'tion

e·li'sion

e·lite' *or* é·lite'

e·lit'ism *or* é·lit'ism

e·lit'ist

e·lix'ir

E·liz'a·be'than

elk *pl.* elk *or* elks

elk'hound'

ell

el·lipse'

el·lip'sis *pl.* -ses

el·lip'soid'

el·lip·soi'dal

el·lip'tic *or* el·lip'ti·cal

elm

el'o·cu'tion

e·lon'gate', -gat'ed, -gat'ing

e·lon·ga'tion

e·lope', e·loped', e·lop'ing

e·lope'ment

el'o·quence

el'o·quent

else

else'where'

e·lu'ci·date', -dat'ed, -dat'ing

e·lu'ci·da'tion

e·lude' *(to escape from)*, e·lud'ed, e·lud'ing
✔ allude

e·lu'sive *(tending to escape)*
✔ allusive, illusive

el'ver

el'y·tron' *pl.* -tra

e·ma'ci·ate', -at'ed, -at'ing

e·ma'ci·a'tion

E'-mail' *or* e'·mail'

em'a·nate', -nat'ed, -nat'ing

em'a·na'tion

em'a·na'tive

e•man'ci•pate',
   -pat'ed, -pat'ing
e•man'ci•pa'tion
e•man'ci•pa'tor
e•mas'cu•late',
   -lat'ed, -lat'ing
e•mas'cu•la'tion
em•balm'
em•balm'er
em•bank'ment
em•bar'go pl. -goes
em•bar'go, -goed,
   -go•ing
em•bark'
em'bar•ka'tion
em•bar'rass
em•bar'rass•ment
em'bas•sy
em•bat'tled
em•bed' also
   im•bed', -bed'ded,
   -bed'ding
em•bel'lish
em'ber
em•bez'zle, -zled,
   -zling
em•bez'zle•ment
em•bez'zler
em•bit'ter
em•bla'zon
em'blem
em'blem•at'ic or
   em'blem•at'i•cal
em•bod'i•ment
em•bod'y, -bod'ied,
   -bod'y•ing
em•bold'en

em•bo•lism
em'bo•lus pl. -li'
em•boss'
em•brace', -braced',
   -brac'ing
em•bra'sure
em•broi'der
em•broi'der•y
em•broil'
em'bry•o' pl. -os'
em'bry•o•log'i•cal
   or em'bry•o•log'ic
em'bry•ol'o•gist
em'bry•ol'o•gy
em'bry•on'ic
em•cee', -ceed',
   -cee'ing
e•mend' (to correct
   by editing)
   ✔ amend
e'men•da'tion
e'men•da'tor
e•men'da•to'ry
em'er•ald
e•merge',
   e•merged',
   e•merg'ing
e•mer'gence
e•mer'gen•cy
e•mer'gent
e•mer'i•ta
e•mer'i•tus
em'er•y
e•met'ic
em'i•grant (one who
   leaves one's native
   land)

   ✔ immigrant
em'i•grate' (to leave
   one's native land),
   -grat'ed, -grat'ing
   ✔ immigrate
em'i•gra'tion (leav-
   ing one's native
   land)
   ✔ immigration
é'mi•gré'
em'i•nence
em'i•nent (promi-
   nent)
   ✔ immanent, immi-
   nent
e•mir'
e•mir'ate
em'is•sar'y
e•mis'sion
e•mis'sive
e•mit', e•mit'ted,
   e•mit'ting
e•mit'ter
e•mol'lient
e•mol'u•ment
e•mote', e•mot'ed,
   e•mot'ing
e•mo'tion
e•mo'tion•al
e•mo'tive
em'pa•thet'ic
em•path'ic
em'pa•thize',
   -thized', -thiz'ing
em'pa•thy
em'per•or
em'pha•sis pl. -ses'

em'pha·size',
-sized', -siz'ing
em·phat'ic
em'phy·se'ma
em'pire
em·pir'i·cal
em·pir'i·cism
em·pir'i·cist
em·place'ment
em·ploy'
em·ploy'ee *also*
em·ploy'e
em·ploy'er
em·ploy'ment
em·po'ri·um *pl.*
-ri·ums *or* -ri·a
em·pow'er
em'press
emp'ti·ness
emp'ty, -tied,
-ty·ing
emp'ty-hand'ed
em·py·re'al
em·py·re'an
e'mu
em'u·late', -lat'ed,
-lat'ing
em'u·la'tion
em'u·la'tor
em'u·lous
e·mul'si·fi·ca'tion
e·mul'si·fy', -fied',
-fy'ing
e·mul'sion
en·a'ble, -bled,
-bling
en·act'

en·ac'tor
en·act'ment
e·nam'el, -eled *or*
-elled, -el·ing *or*
-el·ling
e·nam'el·ware'
en·am'or, -ored,
-or·ing
en·camp'
en·camp'ment
en·cap'su·late' *also*
in·cap'su·late',
-lat'ed, -lat'ing
en·cap'su·la'tion
en·case', -cased',
-cas'ing
en·ce·phal'ic
en·ceph'a·li'tis
en·ceph'a·lo·gram'
en·ceph'a·lo·
graph'
en·ceph'a·log'ra·
phy
en·ceph'a·lon'
en·chant'
en·chant'er
en·chant'ing
en·chant'ment
en·chi·la'da
en·ci'pher
en·cir'cle, -cled,
-cling
en·cir'cle·ment
en'clave'
en·close' *also*
in·close', -closed',
-clos'ing

en·clo'sure
en·code', -cod'ed,
-cod'ing
en·cod'er
en·co'mi·um *pl.*
-mi·ums *or* -mi·a
en·com'pass
en·core', -cored',
-cor'ing
en·coun'ter
en·cour'age, -aged,
-ag·ing
en·cour'age·ment
en·croach'
en·crust' *also*
in·crust'
en'crus·ta'tion
en·cum'ber
en·cum'brance
en·cyc'li·cal
en·cy'clo·pe'di·a
en·cy'clo·pe'dic
end
en·dan'ger
en·dan'gered
en·dear'
en·deav'or
en·dem'ic
end'game' *also*
end' game'
end'ing
end'dive'
end'less
end'most'
end'note'
en'do·car'di·um
pl. -di·a

en'do·carp'
en'do·crine
en'do·cri·nol'o·gist
en'do·cri·nol'o·gy
en'do·derm' *also* en'to·derm'
en'do·don'tia
en'do·don'tics
en'do·me'tri·o'sis
en'do·me'tri·um
en'do·morph'
en'do·mor'phic
en'do·plasm
en·dor'phin
en·dorse', -dorsed', -dors'ing
en·dorse'ment
en·dors'er
en'do·scope'
en'do·skel'e·ton
en'do·sperm'
en'do·ther'mic
en·dow'
en·dow'ment
end'pa'per *also* end' pa'per
end' plate'
end'play'
end'point' *or* end' point' *also* end'-point'
en·due' *also* in·due', -dued', -du'ing
en·dur'a·ble
en·dur'a·bly

en·dur'ance
en·dure', -dured', -dur'ing
end'wise' *also* end'ways'
en·e'ma *pl.* -mas
en'e·my
en'er·get'ic
en'er·gize', -gized', -giz'ing
en'er·giz'er
en'er·gy
en'er·vate', -vat'ed, -vat'ing
en'er·va'tion
en·fee'ble, -bled, -bling
en·fee'ble·ment
en'fi·lade', -lad'ed, -lad'ing
en·fold'
en·force', -forced', -forc'ing
en·force'a·ble
en·force'ment
en·forc'er
en·fran'chise', -chised', -chis'ing
en·fran'chise·ment
en·gage', -gaged', -gag'ing
en·gage'ment
en·gag'ing
en·gen'der
en'gine
en'gi·neer'
en'gi·neer'ing

Eng'lish
Eng'lish·man
Eng'lish·wom'an
en·gorge', -gorged', -gorg'ing
en·gorge'ment
en·graft'
en·grave', -graved', -grav'ing
en·grav'er
en·gross'
en·gross'ing
en·gulf'
en·hance', -hanced', -hanc'ing
en·hance'ment
e·nig'ma
en·ig·mat'ic *or* en·ig·mat'i·cal
en·join'
en·joy'
en·joy'a·ble
en·joy'ment
en·kin'dle, -dled, -dling
en·large', -larged', -larg'ing
en·large'ment
en·larg'er
en·light'en
en·light'en·ment
en·list'
en·list'ment
en·liv'en
en masse'
en·mesh'

en'mi·ty
en·no'ble, -bled,
  -bling
en·nui'
e·nor'mi·ty
e·nor'mous
e·nough'
en·plane' *also*
  em'plane'
en·rage', -raged',
  -rag'ing
en·rap'ture, -tured,
  -tur·ing
en·rich'
en·rich'ment
en·roll' *also* en·rol',
  -rolled', -roll'ing
en·roll'ment *also*
  en·rol'ment
en route'
en·sconce',
  -sconced',
  -sconc'ing
en·sem'ble
en·shrine' *also*
  in·shrine',
  -shrined',
  -shrin'ing
en·shrine'ment
en·shroud'
en'sign
en'si·lage
en·slave', -slaved',
  -slav'ing
en·slave'ment
en·snare', -snared',
  -snar'ing

en·snarl'
en·sue', -sued',
  -su'ing
en·sure' *(to make*
  sure), -sured',
  -sur'ing
  ✔ assure, insure
en·tab'la·ture'
en·tail'
en·tan'gle, -gled,
  -gling
en·tan'gle·ment
en'ter
en·ter'ic
en·ter·i'tis
en'ter·prise'
en'ter·pris'ing
en'ter·tain'
en'ter·tain'er
en'ter·tain'ment
en·thrall'
en·throne',
  -throned',
  -thron'ing
en·throne'ment
en·thuse', -thused',
  -thus'ing
en·thu'si·asm
en·thu'si·ast
en·thu'si·as'tic
en·tice', -ticed',
  -tic'ing
en·tice'ment
en·tire'
en·tire'ly
en·tire'ty
en·ti'tle, -tled,

  -tling
en·ti'tle·ment
en'ti·ty
en·tomb'
en·tomb'ment
en'to·mo·log'ic *or*
  en'to·mo·log'i·cal
en'to·mol'o·gist
en'to·mol'o·gy
en·tou'rage'
en'trails
en·train'
en'trance *n.*
en·trance',
  -tranced',
  -tranc'ing
en'trant
en·trap', -trapped',
  -trap'ping
en·trap'ment
en·treat' *also*
  in·treat'
en·treat'y
en·trée *or* en'tree
en·trench' *also*
  in·trench'
en'tre·pre·neur'
en'tro·py
en·trust' *also*
  in·trust'
en'try
en'try·way'
en·twine' *also*
  in·twine',
  -twined', -twin'ing
e·nu'mer·ate',
  -at'ed, -at'ing

e·nu′mer·a′tion
e·nu′mer·a′tive
e·nu′mer·a′tor
e·nun′ci·ate′ *(to articulate)*, -at′ed,
-at′ing
✔ annunciate
e·nun′ci·a′tion
e·nun′ci·a′tor
en·vel′op *v.*
en′ve·lope′ *n.*
en·vel′op·ment
en·ven′om
en′vi·a·ble
en′vi·a·bly
en′vi·ous
en·vi′ron·ment
en·vi′ron·men′tal
en·vi′rons
en·vis′age, -aged,
-ag·ing
en·vi′sion
en′voy′
en′vy, -vied, -vy·ing
en·wrap′,
-wrapped′,
-wrap′ping
en′zy·mat′ic
en′zyme
E′o·cene′
e′o·hip′pus
E′o·lith′ic
e′on′
ep′au·let′ *also*
ep′au·lette′
e·phed′rine
e·phem′er·al

E·phe′sian
ep′ic *(poem)*
✔ epoch
ep′i·cen′ter
ep′i·cure′
ep′i·cu·re′an
ep′i·dem′ic
ep′i·de′mi·o·log′ic
or ep′i·de′mi·o·
log′i·cal
ep′i·de′mi·ol′o·gist
ep′i·de′mi·ol′o·gy
ep′i·der′mis
ep′i·glot′tis *pl.*
-glot′tis·es *or*
-glot′ti·des′
ep′i·gram′
ep′i·gram·mat′ic
ep′i·graph′
ep′i·lep′sy
ep′i·lep′tic
ep′i·logue′ *also*
ep′i·log′
ep′i·neph′rine *also*
ep′i·neph′rin
e·piph′a·ny
ep′i·phyte′
ep′i·phyt′ic
e·pis′co·pa·cy
e·pis′co·pal
E·pis′co·pa′lian
e·pis′co·pate
ep′i·sode′
ep′i·sod′ic
e·pis′te·mol′o·gy
e·pis′tle
e·pis′to·lar′y

ep′i·taph′
ep′i·the′li·al
ep′i·the′li·um *pl.*
-li·ums *or* -li·a
ep′i·thet′
e·pit′o·me
e·pit′o·mize′,
-mized′, -miz′ing
ep′och *(period of
time)*
✔ epic
ep′och·al
ep′o·nym′
e·pon′y·mous
ep·ox′y
ep′si·lon′
Ep′som salts′
eq′ua·bil′i·ty
eq′ua·ble
eq′ua·bly
e′qual, e′qualed *or*
e′qualled,
e′qual·ing *or*
e′qual·ling
e·qual′i·ty
e′qual·i·za′tion
e′qual·ize′, -ized′,
-iz′ing
e′qual·ize′
e′qua·nim′i·ty
e·quate′, e·quat′ed,
e·quat′ing
e·qua′tion
e·qua′tor
e′qua·to′ri·al
eq′uer·ry
e·ques′tri·an

e'qui·an'gu·lar
e'qui·dis'tant
e'qui·lat'er·al
e'qui·lib'ri·um
e'quine'
e'qui·noc'tial
e'qui·nox'
e·quip', e·quipped',
  e·quip'ping
eq'ui·page
e·quip'ment
e'qui·poise'
eq'ui·ta·ble
eq'ui·ta·bly
eq'ui·ty
e·quiv'a·lence
e·quiv'a·lent
e·quiv'o·cal
e·quiv'o·cate',
  -cat'ed, -cat'ing
e·quiv'o·ca'tion
e·quiv'o·ca'tor
e'ra
e·rad'i·ca·ble
e·rad'i·cate',
  -cat'ed, -cat'ing
e·rad'i·ca'tion
e·ras'a·ble
e·rase', e·rased',
  e·ras'ing
e·ras'er
e·ra'sure
er'bi·um
ere *(before)*
  ✔ air, are, e'er, heir
e·rect'
e·rec'tion

e·rec'tor
erg
er'go
er'go·nom'ics
er'got
er'got·ism
E'rie *pl.* E'rie *or*
  E'ries
er'mine
e·rode', e·rod'ed,
  e·rod'ing
e·rog'e·nous
e·ro'sion
e·ro'sive
e·rot'ic
e·rot'i·cism
err
er'rand
er'rant
er·rat'ic
er·ra'tum *pl.* -ta
er·ro'ne·ous
er'ror
er'satz'
erst'while'
e·ruct'
e·ruc·ta'tion
er'u·dite'
er'u·di'tion
e·rupt' *(to explode)*
  ✔ irrupt
e·rup'tion
e·rup'tive
e·ryth'ro·blast'
e·ryth'ro·cyte'
es'ca·late', -lat'ed,
  -lat'ing

es'ca·la'tion
es'ca·la'tor
es·cap'a·ble
es'ca·pade'
es·cape', -caped',
  -cap'ing
es·cap'ee'
es·cape'ment
es·cap'ism
es·cap'ist
es'car·got'
es'ca·role'
es·carp'ment
es·chew'
es'cort' *n.*
es·cort' *v.*
es'crow'
es·cutch'eon
es'ker
Es'ki·mo' *pl.* -mo'
  or -mos'
e·soph'a·ge'al
e·soph'a·gus *also*
  oe·soph'a·gus *pl.*
  -gi'
es'o·ter'ic
es'pa·drille'
es·pe'cial
es·pe'cial·ly
es'pi·o·nage'
es'pla·nade'
es·pous'al
es·pouse', -poused',
  -pous'ing
es·pres'so *pl.* -sos
es·prit'
es·prit' de corps'

es•py', -pied',
-py'ing
es'quire'
es'say' n.
es•say' (to attempt)
  ✔ assay
es'say•ist
es'sence
es•sen'tial
es•tab'lish
es•tab'lish•ment
es•tate'
es•teem'
es'ter
es'ti•ma•ble
es'ti•ma•bly
es'ti•mate',
  -mat'ed, -mat'ing
es'ti•ma'tion
es'ti•vate', -vat'ed,
  -vat'ing
Es•to'ni•an
es•trange',
  -tranged',
  -trang'ing
es•trange'ment
es'tro•gen
es'trous adj.
es'trus n.
es'tu•ar'y
e'ta
et cet'er•a
etch
etch'ing
e•ter'nal
e•ter'ni•ty
eth'ane'

eth'a•nol'
e'ther
e•the're•al
eth'ic
eth'i•cal
eth'i•cist
eth'ics
E'thi•o'pi•an
eth'nic
eth•nic'i•ty
eth'no•cen'tric
eth'no•cen'trism
eth•nog'ra•pher
eth'no•graph'ic or
  eth'no•graph'i•cal
eth•nog'ra•phy
eth'no•log'ic or
  eth'no•log'i•cal
eth•nol'o•gist
eth•nol'o•gy
e'thos'
eth'yl
eth'yl•ene'
e'ti•o•log'ic or
  e'ti•o•log'i•cal
e'ti•ol'o•gist
e'ti•ol'o•gy also
  ae'ti•ol'o•gy
et'i•quette'
E•trus'can
e'tude'
et'y•mo•log'i•cal
et'y•mol'o•gist
et'y•mol'o•gy
eu'ca•lyp'tus pl.
  -tus•es or -ti'
Eu'cha•rist

Eu•clid'e•an or
  Eu•clid'i•an
eu•gen'ics
eu•gle'na
eu'lo•gist
eu'lo•gize', -gized',
  -giz'ing
eu'lo•gy
eu'nuch
eu'phe•mism
eu'phe•mis'tic
eu•pho'ni•ous
eu•pho'ni•um
eu'pho•ny
eu•pho'ri•a
eu•phor'ic
Eur•a'sian
eu•re'ka
Eu'ro-A•mer'i•can
Eu'ro•pe'an
eu•ro'pi•um
eu•sta'chian tube'
  or Eu•sta'chian
  tube'
eu'tha•na'sia
e•vac'u•ate', -at'ed,
  -at'ing
e•vac'u•a'tion
e•vac'u•ee'
e•vade', e•vad'ed,
  e•vad'ing
e•val'u•ate', -at'ed,
  -at'ing
e•val'u•a'tion
ev'a•nes'cence
ev'a•nes'cent
e'van•gel'i•cal also

e'van•gel'ic
e•van'gel•ism
e•van'gel•ist
e•van'gel•ize',
  -ized', -iz'ing
e•vap'o•rate',
  -rat'ed, -rat'ing
e•vap'o•ra'tion
e•va'sion
e•va'sive
eve
e'ven
e'ven•hand'ed
eve'ning
e'ven•ly
e'ven•ness
e'ven•song'
e•vent'
e•vent'ful
e'ven•tide'
e•ven'tu•al
e•ven'tu•al'i•ty
e•ven'tu•al•ly
e•ven'tu•ate',
  -at'ed, -at'ing
ev'er
ev'er•glade'
ev'er•green'
ev'er•last'ing
ev'er•more'
e•ver'sion
e•vert'
eve'ry
eve'ry•bod'y
eve'ry•day'
eve'ry•one'
eve'ry•place'

eve'ry•thing'
eve'ry•where'
e•vict'
e•vic'tion
ev'i•dence,
  -denced, -denc•ing
ev'i•dent
e'vil
e'vil•do'er
e'vil•mind'ed
e•vince', e•vinced',
  e•vinc'ing
e•vinc'i•ble
e•vis'cer•ate',
  -at'ed, -at'ing
e•vis'cer•a'tion
ev'o•ca'tion
e•voc'a•tive
e•voke', e•voked',
  e•vok'ing
ev'o•lu'tion
ev'o•lu'tion•ar'y
ev'o•lu'tion•ism
ev'o•lu'tion•ist
e•volve', e•volved',
  e•volv'ing
ewe *(female sheep)*
  ✔ yew, you
ew'er
ex•ac'er•bate',
  -bat'ed, -bat'ing
ex•ac'er•ba'tion
ex•act'
ex•act'ing
ex•ac'tion
ex•ac'ti•tude'
ex•act'ly

ex•ac'tor
ex•ag'ger•ate',
  -at'ed, -at'ing
ex•ag'ger•a'tion
ex•ag'ger•a'tor
ex•alt'
ex'al•ta'tion
ex•alt'ed
ex•am'
ex•am'i•na'tion
ex•am'ine, -ined,
  -in'ing
ex•am'in•er
cx•am'ple
ex•as'per•ate',
  -at'ed, -at'ing
ex•as'per•a'tion
ex•ca'vate', -vat'ed,
  -vat'ing
ex'ca•va'tion
ex'ca•va'tor
ex•ceed' *(to surpass)*
  ✔ accede
ex•ceed'ing
ex•cel', -celled',
  -cel'ling
ex'cel•lence
Ex'cel•len•cy
ex'cel•lent
ex•cept' *(to leave out)*
  ✔ accept
ex•cept'ing
ex•cep'tion
ex•cep'tion•a•ble
ex•cep'tion•al
ex'cerpt' *n.*

ex·cerpt′ *v.*

ex·cess′ *(surplus)*
  ✔ access

ex·ces′sive

ex·change′,
  -changed′,
  -chang′ing

ex·change′a·ble

ex·chang′er

ex·cheq′uer

ex′cise′ *(tax)*

ex·cise′ *(to cut)*,
  -cised′, -cis′ing

ex·ci′sion

ex·cit′a·bil′i·ty *or*
  ex·cit′a·ble·ness

ex·cit′a·ble

ex·cit′a·bly

ex′ci·ta′tion

ex·ci′ta·tive *or*
  ex·ci′ta·to′ry

ex·cite′, -cit′ed,
  -cit′ing

ex·cite′ment

ex·claim′

ex′cla·ma′tion

ex·clam′a·to′ry

ex·clud′a·ble *or*
  ex·clud′i·ble

ex·clude′, -clud′ed,
  -clud′ing

ex·clu′sion

ex·clu′sion·ar′y

ex·clu′sive

ex′com·mu′ni·
  cate′, -cat′ed,
  -cat′ing

ex′com·mu′ni·ca′-
  tion

ex·co′ri·ate′, -at′ed,
  -at′ing

ex·co′ri·a′tion

ex′cre·ment

ex·cres′cence

ex·cres′cent

ex·cre′ta

ex·crete′, -cret′ed,
  -cret′ing

ex·cre′tion

ex′cre·to′ry

ex·cru′ci·at′ing

ex′cul·pate′

ex′cul·pa′tion

ex·cul′pa·to′ry

ex·cur′sion

ex·cus′a·ble

ex·cus′a·bly

ex·cuse′, -cused′,
  -cus′ing

ex·cus′er

ex·e′cra·ble

ex′e·crate′, -crat′ed,
  -crat′ing

ex′e·cra′tion

ex′e·cute′, -cut′ed,
  -cut′ing

ex′e·cu′tion

ex′e·cu′tion·er

ex·ec′u·tive

ex·ec′u·tor

ex·ec′u·trix′

ex′e·ge′sis *pl.* -ses

ex·em′plar

ex·em′plar′i·ly

ex·em′pla·ry

ex·em′pli·fi·ca′-
  tion

ex·em′pli·fy′,
  -fied′, -fy′ing

ex·empt′

ex·empt′i·ble

ex·emp′tion

ex′er·cise′ *(to make
  use of)*, -cised′,
  -cis′ing
  ✔ exorcise

ex′er·cis′er

ex·ert′

ex·er′tion

ex·fo′li·ate′

ex·fo′li·a′tion

ex′ha·la′tion

ex·hale′, -haled′,
  -hal′ing

ex·haust′

ex·haust′i·ble

ex·haus′tion

ex·haus′tive

ex·hib′it

ex′hi·bi′tion

ex′hi·bi′tion·ism

ex′hi·bi′tion·ist

ex·hib′i·tor *or*
  ex·hib′it·er

ex·hil′a·rate′,
  -rat′ed, -rat′ing

ex·hil′a·ra′tion

ex·hort′

ex′hor·ta′tion

ex·hor′ta·tive *also*
  ex·hor′ta·to′ry

ex'hu•ma'tion
ex•hume',
-humed', -hum'ing
ex'i•gence
ex'i•gen•cy
ex'i•gent
ex•ile', -iled', -il'ing
ex•ist'
ex•is'tence
ex•is'tent
ex'is•ten'tial
ex'is•ten'tial•ism
ex'is•ten'tial•ist
ex'it
cx'o•bi•ol'o•gy
ex'o•bi•ol'o•gist
ex'o•crine
ex'o•dus
ex' of•fi'ci•o'
ex•on'er•ate',
-at'ed, -at'ing
ex•on'er•a'tion
ex•or'bi•tance
ex•or'bi•tant
ex•or'cise' *(to drive away)*, -cised',
-cis'ing
✔ *exercise*
ex'or•cism
ex'or•cist
ex'o•skel'e•ton
ex'o•sphere'
ex'o•spher'ic
ex'o•ther'mic *also*
ex'o•ther'mal
ex•ot'ic
ex•ot'i•ca

ex•pand'
ex•pand'a•ble
ex•panse'
ex•pan'sion
ex•pan'sion•ism
ex•pan'sion•ist
ex•pan'sive
ex•pa'ti•ate', -at'ed,
-at'ing
ex•pa'ti•a'tion
ex•pa'tri•ate',
-at'ed, -at'ing
ex•pa'tri•a'tion
ex•pect'
ex•pec'tan•cy
ex•pec'tant
ex•pec•ta'tion
ex•pec'to•rant
ex•pec'to•rate',
-rat'ed, -rat'ing
ex•pec'to•ra'tion
ex•pe'di•ence
ex•pe'di•en•cy
ex•pe'di•ent
ex•pe•dite', -dit'ed,
-dit'ing
ex'pe•dit'er *or*
ex'pe•di'tor
ex'pe•di'tion
ex'pe•di'tion•ar'y
ex'pe•di'tious
ex•pel', -pelled',
-pel'ling
ex•pend'
ex•pend'a•ble
ex•pen'di•ture
ex•pense'

ex•pen'sive
ex•pen'sive•ly
ex•pe'ri•ence,
-enced, -enc'ing
ex•per'i•ment
ex•per'i•men'tal
ex•per'i•men•ta'-
tion
ex•per'i•men'er
ex•pert'
ex'per•tise'
ex'pi•ate', -at'ed,
-at'ing
ex'pi•a'tion
ex'pi•a'tor
ex'pi•ra'tion
ex•pire', -pired',
-pir'ing
ex•plain'
ex•plain'a•ble
ex•plain'er
ex'pla•na'tion
ex•plan'a•to'ry
ex•ple'tive
ex'pli•ca•ble
ex'pli•cate', -cat'ed,
-cat'ing
ex'pli•ca'tion
ex'pli•ca'tor
ex•plic'it
ex•plode', -plod'ed,
-plod'ing
ex•plod'er
ex'ploit' *n.*
ex•ploit' *v.*
ex•ploit'a•ble
ex'ploi•ta'tion

ex·ploit'er
ex·plo·ra'tion
ex·plor'a·to'ry
ex·plore', -plored',
  -plor'ing
ex·plor'er
ex·plo'sion
ex·plo'sive
ex·plo'sive·ly
ex·po'nent
ex·po·nen'tial
ex·port' *v.*
ex'port' *n.*
ex'port'a·ble
ex'por·ta'tion
ex·port'er
ex·pose', -posed',
  -pos'ing
ex'po·sé'
ex·pos'er
ex'po·si'tion
ex·pos'i·tor
ex' post fac'to
ex·pos'tu·late',
  -lat'ed, -lat'ing
ex·pos'tu·la'tion
ex·po'sure
ex·pound'
ex·pound'er
ex·press'
ex·press'i·ble
ex·pres'sion
ex·pres'sion·ism
ex·pres'sion·ist
ex·pres'sive
ex·press'ive·ly
ex·press'way'

ex·pro'pri·ate',
  -at'ed, -at'ing
ex·pro'pri·a'tion
ex·pro'pri·a'tor
ex·pul'sion
ex·punge',
  -punged',
  -pung'ing
ex'pur·gate',
  -gat'ed, -gat'ing
ex'pur·ga'tion
ex'pur·ga'tor
ex'qui·site
ex'tant *(existing)*
  ✔ *extent*
ex·tem'po·ra'ne·
  ous
ex·tem'po·rar'i·ly
ex·tem'po·rar'y
ex·tem'po·re
ex·tem'po·rize',
  -rized', -riz'ing
ex·tend'
ex·tend'ed
ex·tend'i·ble
ex·ten'si·ble
ex·ten'sion
ex·ten'sive
ex·ten'sor
ex·tent' *(size)*
  ✔ *extant*
ex·ten'u·ate',
  -at'ed, -at'ing
ex·ten'u·a'tion
ex·ten'u·a'tor
ex·ten'u·a·to'ry
ex·te'ri·or

ex·ter'mi·nate',
  -nat'ed, -nat'ing
ex·ter'mi·na'tion
ex·ter'mi·na'tor
ex·ter'nal
ex·ter'nal·i·za'-
  tion
ex·ter'nal·ize'
ex·tinct'
ex·tinc'tion
ex·tin'guish
ex·tin'guish·a·ble
ex·tin'guish·er
ex'tir·pate', -pat'ed,
  -pat'ing
ex'tir·pa'tion
ex·tol' *also* ex·toll',
  -tolled', -tol·ling
ex·tol'ler
ex·tort'
ex·tort'er
ex·tor'tion
ex·tor'tion·ate
ex·tor'tion·ist
ex'tra
ex·tract' *v.*
ex'tract' *n.*
ex·trac'tion
ex·trac'tor
ex'tra·cur·ric'u·lar
ex'tra·dite', -dit'ed,
  -dit'ing
ex'tra·di'tion
ex'tra·mar'i·tal
ex'tra·ne·ous
ex·traor'di·naire'
ex·traor'di·nar'i·ly

ex·traor′di·nar′y
ex·trap′o·late′,
    -lat′ed, -lat′ing
ex·trap′o·la′tion
ex′tra·sen′so·ry
ex′tra·ter·res′tri·al
ex·trav′a·gance
ex·trav′a·gant
ex·trav′a·gan′za
ex·treme′
ex·trem′ism
ex·trem′ist
ex·trem′l·ty
ex′tri·cate′, -cat′ed,
    -cat′ing
ex′tri·ca′tion
ex·trin′sic
ex′tra·ver′sion
ex′tro·vert′
ex·trude′, -trud′ed,
    -trud′ing
ex·tru′sion
ex·u′ber·ance
ex·u′ber·ant
ex′u·da′tion
ex·ude′, -ud′ed,
    -ud′ing
ex·ult′
ex·ul′tant
ex′ul·ta′tion
eye *(organ or sight)*,
    eyed, eye′ing *or*
    ey′ing
    ✔ *aye, I*
eye′ball′
eye′brow′
eye′cup′

eye′drop′per
eye′glass′
eye′lash′
eye′let *(small hole)*
    ✔ *islet*
eye′lid′
eye′lin′er
eye′ o′pen·er
eye′piece′
eye′ shad′ow
eye′sight′
eye′ sock′et
eye′sore′
eye′spot′
eye′stalk′
eye′strain′
eye′tooth′
eye′wash′
eye′wit′ness

F

fa′ble
fa′bled
fab′ric
fab′ri·cate′, -cat′ed,
    -cat′ing
fab′ri·ca′tion
fab′u·list
fab′u·lous
fa·çade′ *also*
    fa·cade′
face, faced, fac′ing
face′down′ *n.*
face′down′ *adv.*
face′less

face′-lift′
face′mask′
face′-off′ *n.*
fac′et
fa·ce′tious
face′up′ *adv.*
fa′cial
fac′ile
fa·cil′i·tate′,
    -tat′ed, -tat′ing
fa·cil′i·ta′tion
fa·cil′i·ty
fac·sim′i·le
fact
fact′find′ing
fac′tion
fac′tion·al·ism
fac′tious
fac·ti′tious *(artifi-cial)*
    ✔ *fictitious*
fac′toid
fac′tor
fac·to′ri·al
fac′to·ry
fac·to′tum
fac′tu·al
fac′ul·ty
fad
fad′dish
fade, fad′ed, fad′ing
fade′-in′ *or* fade′in′
    n.
fade′-out′ *or*
    fade′out′ *n.*
fa′er·ie *also* fa′er·y
    pl. -ies

fag, fagged, fag'ging
fag'ot *also* fag'got
Fahr'en•heit'
fail *(to be unsuccess-*
  ful)
  ✔ *faille*
fail'ing
faille *(silk)*
  ✔ *fail, file*
fail'-safe'
fail'ure
fain *(willingly)*
  ✔ *feign*
faint *(pass out)*
  ✔ *feint*
faint'-heart'ed
fair *(just, lovely, light)*
  ✔ *fare*
fair *(market)*
  ✔ *fare*
fair'ground'
fair'-haired'
fair'-mind'ed
fair'way'
fair'-weath'er *adj.*
fair'y
fair'y•land'
fait' ac•com•pli' *pl.*
  faits' ac•com•plis'
faith
faith'ful
faith'less
fa•ji'ta
fake, faked, fak'ing
fak'er *(impostor)*
  ✔ *fakir*
fak'er•y

fa•kir' *(beggar)*
  ✔ *faker*
fal'con
fal'con•er
fal'con•ry
fall, fell, fall'en,
  fall'ing
fal•la'cious
fal'la•cy
fal•li•bil'i•ty
fal'li•ble
fal'li•bly
fall'ing-out' *pl.*
  fall'ings-out' *or*
  fall'ing-outs'
fal•lo'pi•an
fall'out' *n.*
fal'low
false, fals'er, fals'est
false'hood'
false'ly
fal•set'to *pl.* -tos
fal'si•fi•ca'tion
fal'si•fi'er
fal'si•fy', -fied',
  -fy'ing
fal'si•ty
fal'ter
fal'ter•ing•ly
fame
famed
fa•mil'ial
fa•mil'iar
fa•mil•iar'i•ty
fa•mil'iar•ize',
  -ized', -iz'ing
fam'i•ly

fam'ine
fam'ished
fa'mous
fan, fanned,
  fan'ning
fa•nat'ic
fa•nat'i•cal
fa•nat'i•cism
fan'ci•er
fan'ci•ful
fan'cy, -cied, -cy•ing
fan'cy-free'
fan'cy•work'
fan•dan'go *pl.* -gos
fan'fare'
fang
fan'tail'
fan•ta'sia
fan'ta•size', -sized',
  -siz'ing
fan•tas'tic
fan•tas'ti•cal•ly
fan'ta•sy
far, far'ther *or*
  fur'ther, far'thest
  or fur'thest
far'ad
far'a•day'
far'a•way'
farce
far'ci•cal
fare *(to get along),*
  fared, far'ing
  ✔ *fair*
fare *(money charged)*
  ✔ *fair*
fare•well'

far'-fetched'
far'-flung'
fa•ri'na
far'i•na'ceous
farm
farm'er
farm' hand'
farm'house'
farm'land'
farm'stead'
farm' team'
farm'yard'
far'-off'
far'-out'
far•ra'go pl. -goes
far'-reach'ing
far'ri•er
far'row
far'see'ing
Far'si
far'sight'ed or
  far'-sight'ed
far'ther (to a greater
  distance)
  ✔ further
far'ther•most'
far'thest (to the most
  distant point)
  ✔ furthest
far'thing
far'thin•gale'
fas'ci•a pl. -ci•ae'
fas'ci•cle
fas'ci•nate',
  -nat'ed, -nat'ing
fas'ci•na'tion
fas'cism

fas'cist
fash'ion
fash'ion•a•ble
fash'ion•a•bly
fast
fast'ball'
fas'ten
fas'ten•er
fas'ten•ing
fast' food' n.
fast'-food' adj.
fas•tid'i•ous
fat, fat'ter, fat'test
fa'tal
fa'tal•ism
fa'tal•ist
fa'tal•is'tic
fa•tal'i•ty
fa'tal•ly
fat'back'
fat'ed
fate'ful
fa'ther
fa'ther•hood'
fa'ther-in-law' pl.
  fa'thers-in-law'
fa'ther•land'
fa'ther•less
fa'ther•li•ness
fa'ther•ly
fath'om pl. -om or
  -oms
fath'om•a•ble
fa•tigue', -tigued',
  -tigu'ing

fat'ten
fat'ti•ness
fat'ty
fa•tu'i•ty
fat'u•ous
fau'cet
fault
fault'find'er
fault'find'ing
fault'i•ness
fault'y
faun (deity)
  ✔ fawn
fau'na pl. -nas or
  -nae'
faux pas' pl. faux
  pas'
fa'vor
fa'vor•a•ble
fa'vor•a•bly
fa'vor•ite
fa'vor•it•ism
fawn (to flatter)
  ✔ faun
fawn (young deer)
  ✔ faun
fax
fax' ma•chine'
fay
faze (to upset), fazed,
  faz'ing
  ✔ phase
fe'al•ty
fear
fear'ful
fear'less
fear'some

fea·si·bil'i·ty
fea'si·ble
fea'si·bly
feast
feat *(exploit)*
  ✔ *feet*
feath'er
feath'er bed'
feath'er·bed'ding
feath'er·brain'
feath'er·brained'
feath'ered
feath'er·weight'
feath'er·y
fea'ture
feb'rile
Feb'ru·ar'y
fe'cal
fe'ces
feck'less
fe'cund
fe·cun'di·ty
fed'er·al
fed'er·al·ism
fed'er·al·ist
fed'er·ate', -at'ed,
  -at'ing
fed'er·a'tion
fe·do'ra
fee
fee'ble, -bler, -blest
fee'ble-mind'ed
fee'bly
feed, fed, feed'ing
feed'back'
feed'bag'
feed'er

feel, felt, feel'ing
feel'er
feel'ing·ly
feet *sing.* foot
  ✔ *feat*
feign *(to pretend)*
  ✔ *fain*
feint *(deceptive action)*
  ✔ *faint*
feist'y
feld'spar *also*
  fel'spar
fe·lic'i·tate',
  -tat'ed, -tat'ing
fe·lic'i·ta'tion
fe·lic'i·tous
fe·lic'i·ty
fe'line'
fell
fel'lah *pl.* fel'la·hin'
  or fel'la·heen'
fel'low
fel'low·ship'
fel'on
fe·lo'ni·ous
fel'o·ny
felt
fe'male'
fem'i·nine
fem'i·nin'i·ty
fem'i·nism
fem'i·nist
femme' fa·tale' *pl.*
  femmes' fa·tales'
fem'o·ral
fe'mur *pl.* -murs *or*
  fem'o·ra

fen
fence, fenced,
  fenc'ing
fenc'er
fend
fend'er
fend'er-bend'er *or*
  fend'er bend'er
fen'nel
fe'ral
fer'-de-lance' *pl.*
  fer'-de-lance'
fer'ment' *n.*
fer'ment' *v.*
fer'men·ta'tion
fer'mi·um
fern
fe·ro'cious
fe·roc'i·ty
fer'ret *(animal, to*
  hunt)
fer'ret *also*
  fer'ret·ing *(tape)*
fer'ric
Fer'ris wheel' *also*
  fer'ris wheel'
fer'rous
fer'rule *(metal ring)*
  ✔ *ferule*
fer'ry, -ried, -ry·ing
fer'ry·boat'
fer'tile
fer·til'i·ty
fer'til·i·za'tion
fer'til·ize', -ized',
  -iz'ing
fer'til·iz'er

fer'ule *(stick)*
  ✔ ferrule
fer'ven·cy
fer'vent
fer'vid
fer'vor
fes'tal
fes'ter
fes'ti·val
fes'tive
fes·tiv'i·ty
fes·toon'
fet'a
fe'tal *also* foe'tal
fetch
fete *also* fête *(festival)*
  ✔ fate
fete *also* fête *(to honor)*, fet'ed *also* fêt'ed, fet'ing *or* fêt'ing
  ✔ fate
fet'id
fet'ish
fet'ish·ism
fet'ish·ist
fet'lock'
fet'ter
fet'tle
fet'tuc·ci·ne
fe'tus *also* foe'tus *pl.* -tus·es
feud
feu'dal
feu'dal·ism
feu'dal·is'tic
fe'ver

fe'ver·ish
few
fez *pl.* fez'zes
fi'an·cé' *(male)*
fi'an·cée' *(female)*
fi·as'co *pl.* -coes *or* -cos
fi'at'
fib, fibbed, fib'bing
fib'ber
fi'ber
fi'ber·board'
fi'ber·glass'
fib'ril·la'tion
fi'brin
fi·brin'o·gen
fi'broid'
fi'brous
fib'u·la *pl.* -lae' *or* -las
fick'le
fic'tion
fic'tion·al
fic'tion·al·ize', -ized', -iz'ing
fic·ti'tious *(imaginary)*
  ✔ factitious
fic'tive
fid·dle, -dled, -dling
fid'dler
fid'dle·sticks'
fi·del'i·ty
fidg'et
fidg'et·y
fie
fief

fief'dom
field
field'er
field'stone'
field' test' *n.*
field'-test' *v.*
field' trip'
field'work'
fiend
fiend'ish
fierce, fierc'er, fierc'est
fier'i·ness
fier'y
fi·es'ta
fife
fif·teen'
fif·teenth'
fifth
fif'ti·eth
fif'ty
fif'ty-fif'ty
fig
fight, fought, fight'ing
fight'er
fig'ment
fig'u·ra·tive
fig'ur·a·tive·ly
fig'ure, -ured, -ur·ing
fig'ure·head'
fig'u·rine'
Fi'ji·an
fil'a·ment
fil'bert
filch

filch'er
file *(folder, tool)*
  ✔ faille
file *(to put in order, to*
  smooth), filed,
  fil'ing
  ✔ faille
fi·let' *(lace)*
  ✔ fillet
fi·let' mi·gnon' *pl.*
  fi·lets' mi·gnons'
fil'i·al
fil'i·bus'ter
fil'i·gree', -greed',
  -gree'ing
fil'ing
Fil·i·pi'no *pl.* -nos
fill'er
fil'let *(ribbon)*
fil·let' *also* fi·let'
  (piece of meat or
  fish)
  ✔ filet
fil·let' *also* fi·let' *(to*
  slice), fil·let'ed *also*
  fi·let'ed, fil·let'ing
  or fi·let'ing
  ✔ filet
fill'-in'
fill'ing
fil'lip
fil'ly
film
film'mak'er
film'mak'ing
film'strip'
film'y

fil'ter *(strainer)*
  ✔ philter
fil'ter·a·ble *also*
  fil'tra·ble
filth
filth'i·ness
filth'y
fil'trate', -trat'ed,
  -trat'ing
fil·tra'tion
fin
fi·na'gle, -gled,
  -gling
fi·na'gler
fi'nal
fi·nal'e
fi'nal·ist
fi·nal'i·ty
fi'nal·i·za'tion
fi'nal·ize', -ized',
  -iz'ing
fi'nal·iz'er
fi'nal·ly
fi·nance', -nanced',
  -nanc'ing
fi·nan'cial
fin·an·cier'
finch
find, found, find'ing
find'er
fine, fin'er, fin'est
fine, fined, fin'ing
fine'-drawn'
fine'-grained'
fin'er·y
fi·nesse', -nessed',
  -ness'ing

fin'ger
fin'ger·board'
fin'ger hole'
fin'ger·ing
fin'ger·nail'
fin'ger-paint'
fin'ger paint'ing
fin'ger·print'
fin'ger·spell'
fin'ger·spell'ing
fin'ger·tip'
fin'i·cal
fin'ick·y
fin'is
fin'ish
fin'ished
fin'ish·er
fi'nite'
Finn
fin'nan had'die
finned
Finn'ish
fin'ny
fir *(tree)*
  ✔ fur
fire, fired, fir'ing
fire'arm'
fire'ball'
fire'boat'
fire'bomb'
fire'box'
fire'brand'
fire'break'
fire'bug'
fire'crack'er
fire'damp'
fire'dog'

fire′ drill′
fire′fight′er *also* fire′ fight′er
fire′fight′ing
fire′fly′
fire′house′
fire′ hy′drant
fire′light′
fire′man
fire′place′
fire′plug′
fire′pow′er
fire′proof′
fire′ screen′
fire′side′
fire′ sta′tion
fire′storm′
fire′ tow′er
fire′trap′
fire′ truck′
fire′wall′
fire′wood′
fire′work′
firm
fir′ma•ment
first
first′ aid′ *n.*
first′-aid′ *adj.*
first′ base′
first′ base′man
first′-born′
first′ class′ *n.*
first′-class′ *adj.*
first′-de•gree′ burn′
first′hand′
first′-rate′ *adj.*

first′-string′ *adj.*
firth
fis′cal
fish *pl.* fish *or* fish′es
fish′bowl′
fish′er *(one that fishes)*
  ✔ *fissure*
fish′er•man
fish′er•y
fish′hook′
fish′i•ness
fish′ing
fish′ing rod′
fish′meal′
fish′mon′ger
fish′net′
fish′pond′
fish′ stick′
fish′tail′
fish′wife′
fish′y
fis′sion
fis′sure *(crack)*
  ✔ *fisher*
fist′fight′
fist′ful′
fist′i•cuffs′
fis′tu•la *pl.* -las *or* -lae′
fit, fit′ted *or* fit, fit′ted, fit′ting
fit, fit′ter, fit′test
fitch
fit′ful
fit′ness
five

five′-and-dime′
five′-and-ten′
five′fold′
fix
fix′a•ble
fix′ate′, -at′ed, -at′ing
fix•a′tion
fix′a•tive
fixed
fix′ed•ly
fix′er
fix′ings
fix′ture
fizz
fiz′zle, -zled, -zling
fizz′y
fjord *or* fiord
flab
flab′ber•gast′
flab′bi•ness
flab′by
flac′cid
flac•cid′i•ty *or* flac′cid•ness
flack *(press agent)*
  ✔ *flak*
flac′on
flag, flagged, flag′ging
flag′el•late′, -lat′ed, -lat′ing
flag′el•la′tion
fla•gel′lum *pl.* -gel′la
flag′eo•let′
flag′man

flag'on
flag'pole'
fla'grance *or* fla'gran•cy
fla'grant
flag'ship'
flag'staff'
flag'stone'
flail
flair *(knack)*
   ✔ *flare*
flak *(artillery, criticism)*
   ✔ *flack*
flake, flaked, flak'ing
flak'i•ness
flak'y
flam•boy'ance *or* flam•boy'an•cy
flam•boy'ant
flame, flamed, flam'ing
fla•men'co *pl.* -cos
flame'throw'er
fla•min'go *pl.* -gos *or* -goes
flam'ma•bil'i•ty
flam'ma•ble *(easily ignited)*
   ✔ *inflammable, nonflammable*
flange
flank
flank'er
flan'nel
flan'nel•ette'

flap, flapped, flap'ping
flap'jack'
flap'per
flare *(to flame up)*, flared, flar'ing
   ✔ *flair*
flare'-up' *n.*
flash'back' *n.*
flash'bulb' *or* flash'bulb'
flash'er
flash'i•ness
flash'light'
flash'y
flask
flat, flat'ter, flat'test
flat'bed'
flat'boat'
flat'car'
flat'fish' *pl.* -fish' *or* -fish'es
flat'foot' *(fallen arch)*, *pl.* -feet'
flat'foot' *(police officer)*, *pl.* -foots
flat'-foot'ed
Flat'head' *pl.* -head' *or* -heads'
flat'i'ron
flat'land'
flat'ten
flat'ter
flat'ter•er
flat'ter•y
flat'top'
flat'u•lence

flat'u•lent
flat'ware'
flat'worm'
flaunt *(to show off)*
   ✔ *flout*
flau'tist
fla'vor
fla'vor•ful *or* fla'vor•some
flaw
flax
flax'en
flax'seed'
flay
flea *(insect)*
   ✔ *flee*
flea'bag'
flea'-bit'ten
fleck
fledge, fledged, fledg'ing
fledg'ling *also* fledge'ling
flee *(to run away)*, fled, flee'ing
   ✔ *flea*
fleece, fleeced, fleec'ing
fleec'i•ness
fleec'y
fleet
fleet'ing
Flem'ing
Flem'ish
flesh'ly *(physical)*
flesh'y *(plump)*
fleur'-de-lis' *or*

fleur'-de-lys' *pl.*
fleurs'-de-lis' *or*
fleurs'-de-lys'

flew *past tense of*
fly
  ✔ *flu, flue*

flex'i·bil'i·ty

flex'i·ble

flex'i·bly

flex'ion

flex'or *(muscle)*
  ✔ *flexure*

flex'time'

flex'ure *(bend)*
  ✔ *flexor*

flick'er

fli'er *also* fly'er

flight

flight'i·ness

fight'-test' *v.*

flight'wor'thy

flight'y

flim'si·ly

flim'si·ness

flim'sy

flinch

fling, flung,
fling'ing

flint'lock'

flint'y

flip, flipped,
flip'ping

flip, flip'per,
flip'pest

flip'-flop'

flip'pan·cy

flip'pant

flip'per

flirt

flir·ta'tion

flir·ta'tious

flit, flit'ted, flit'ting

float

float'er

flock

floe *(floating ice)*
  ✔ *flow*

flog, flogged,
flog'ging

flog'ger

flood

flood'gate'

flood'light',
  -light'ed *or* -lit',
  -light'ing

flood'plain'

flood'wa'ter

floor

floor'board'

floor'ing

floor'show'

floor'walk'er

flop, flopped,
flop'ping

flop'pi·ness

flop'py

flop'py disk'

flo'ra *pl.* -ras *or*
-rae'

flo'ral

Flor'en·tine'

flo·res'cence
(flowering)
  ✔ *fluorescence*

flo'ret

flor'id

flor'in

flo'rist

floss

floss'y

flo·til'la

flot'sam

flounce, flounced,
flounc'ing

floun'der *v.*

floun'der *pl.* -der *or*
-ders

flour *(powdery meal)*
  ✔ *flower*

flour'ish

flout *(to scorn)*
  ✔ *flaunt*

flout'er

flow *(stream)*
  ✔ *floe*

flow' chart' *also*
flow'chart'

flow'er *(blossom)*
  ✔ *flour*

flow'er·i·ness

flow'er·pot'

flow'er·y

flu *(influenza)*
  ✔ *flew, flue*

flub, flubbed,
flub'bing

fluc'tu·ate', -at'ed,
-at'ing

fluc'tu·a'tion

flue *(pipe)*
  ✔ *flew, flu*

flu'en·cy
flu'ent
fluff
fluff'i·ness
fluff'y
flu'id
flu·id'i·ty
fluke
flume
flum'mox
flunk
flun'ky *also*
 flun'key *pl.* -kies
 also -keys
fluo·resce',
 -resced', -resc'ing
fluo·res'cence *(giv-
 ing off of light)*
 ✔ *florescence*
fluo·res'cent
fluor'i·date',
 -dat'ed, -dat'ing
fluor'i·da'tion
fluor'ide'
fluor'ine'
fluor'o·car'bon
fluor'o·scope'
fluor'o·scop'ic
fluo·ros'co·py
flur'ry, -ried, -ry·ing
flush
flus'ter
flute, flut'ed,
 flut'ing
flut'ist
flut'ter
flux

fly *(to move through
 the air)*, flew, flown,
 fly'ing
fly *(to hit a baseball)*,
 flied, fly'ing
fly *(insect)*
fly' ball'
fly'-by-night'
fly'catch'er
fly'er
fly'-fish'ing
fly'leaf'
fly'pa'per
fly'speck'
fly' swat'ter
fly'way'
fly'weight'
fly'wheel'
f'-num'ber
foal
foam
foam'y
fob, fobbed,
 fob'bing
fo'cal
fo'cus *pl.* -cus·es *or*
 -ci'
fo'cus, -cused *or*
 -cussed, -cus·ing *or*
 -cus·sing
fod'der
foe
fog, fogged, fog'ging
fog'gi·ness
fog'gy
fog'horn'
fo'gy *also* fo'gey *pl.*

-gies *also* -geys
foi'ble
foil
foist
fold
fold'er
fo'li·age
fo'lic
fo'li·o' *pl.* -os'
folk *pl.* folk *or* folks
folk' dance'
folk' danc'ing
folk'lore'
folk'lor'ist
folk'-rock'
folk'sing'er
folk' sing'ing
folk'song'
folk'sy
folk'tale'
fol'li·cle
fol'low
fol'low·er
fol'low·ing
fol'low-up' *or*
 fol'low·up' *n.*
fol'ly
fo·ment'
fond
fon'dle, -dled,
 -dling
fon·due' *also*
 fon·du'
font
food
food'stuff'
fool

fool'er•y
fool'har'di•ness
fool'har'dy
fool'ish
fool'proof'
foot *pl.* feet
foot'age
foot'-and-mouth' dis•ease'
foot'ball'
foot'board'
foot'bridge'
foot'-can'dle
foot'ed
foot'fall'
foot'hill'
foot'hold'
foot'ing
foot'lights'
foot'lock'er
foot'loose'
foot'man
foot'note'
foot'path'
foot'-pound'
foot'print'
foot'race' *or* foot'race'
foot'rest'
foot'sore'
foot'step'
foot'stool'
foot'wear'
foot'work'
fop
fop'per•y
fop'pish

for *prep. & conj.*
✔ fore, four
for'age, -aged, -ag•ing
for'ag•er
for•as•much' as
for•ay'
for•bear' (to resist), -bore', -borne', -bear'ing
✔ forebear
for•bear'ance
for•bid', -bade' *or* -bad', bid'den *or* -bid', -bid'ding
force, forced, forc'ing
force'a•ble (able to be forced, forcible)
✔ forcible
force'ful
for'ceps *pl.* -ceps
forc'er
forc'i•ble (accomplished by force)
✔ forceable
for'ci•bly
ford
ford'a•ble
fore (forward)
✔ for, four
fore'-and-aft' *adj.*
fore•arm' *v.*
fore'arm' *n.*
fore'bear' *also* for'bear' (ancestor)
✔ forbear

fore•bode', -bod'ed, -bod'ing
fore•bod'er
fore'brain'
fore'cast', -cast' *or* -cast'ed, -cast'ing
fore'cast'er
fore'cas'tle *also* fo'c's'le
fore•close', -closed', -clos'ing
fore•clo'sure
fore'court'
fore•doom'
fore'fa'ther
fore'fin'ger
fore'foot'
fore'front'
fore•go' (to precede), -went', -gone', -go'ing
✔ forgo
fore'ground'
fore'hand'
fore'head'
for'eign
for'eign•er
fore•know', -knew', -known', -know'ing
fore•knowl'edge
fore'leg'
fore'limb'
fore'lock'
fore'man
fore'mast
fore'most'

fore'named'
fore'noon'
fo·ren'sic
fore·or·dain'
fore'part'
fore'paw'
fore'quar'ter
fore'run'ner
fore'sail
fore·see', -saw',
  -seen', -see'ing
fore·see'a·ble
fore·se'er
fore·shad'ow
fore·short'en
fore'sight'
fore'sight'ed
fore'skin'
for'est
fore·stall'
fore·stall'er
for'es·ta'tion
for'est·er
for'est·ry
fore'taste'
fore·tell', -told',
  -tell'ing
fore'thought'
for·ev'er
for·ev'er·more'
fore·warn'
fore'wing'
fore·wom'an
fore'word' *(preface)*
  ✔ *forward*
for'feit

for·fei'ture'
for·gath'er *also*
  fore·gath'er
forge, forged,
  forg'ing
forg'er
for'ger·y
for·get', -got',
  -got'ten *or* -got',
  -get'ting
for·get'ful
for·get'-me-not'
for·get'ta·ble
for·get'ter
for·giv'a·ble
for·give', -gave',
  -giv'en, -giv'ing
for·giv'er
for·give'ness
for·go' *also* fore·go'
  (to do without),
  -went', -gone',
  -go'ing
  ✔ *forego*
fork
forked
fork'lift'
for·lorn'
form
for'mal
for'mal'de·hyde'
for'mal·ism
for·mal'i·ty
for'mal·ize', -ized',
  -iz'ing
for'mal·iz'er

for'mal·ly *(in a for-*
  mal manner)
  ✔ *formerly*
for'mat', -mat'ted,
  -mat'ting
for·ma'tion
for'ma·tive
form'er *(one that*
  forms)
for'mer *(earlier)*
for'mer·ly *(once)*
  ✔ *formally*
form'fit'ting
for'mi·da·bil'i·ty
for'mi·da·ble
for'mi·da·bly
for'mu·la *pl.* -las *or*
  -lae'
for'mu·la'ic
for'mu·late',
  -lat'ed, -lat'ing
for'mu·la'tion
for·ni·cate', -cat'ed,
  -cat'ing
for·ni·ca'tion
for·sake', -sook',
  -sak'en, -sak'ing
for·sooth'
for·swear', -swore',
  -sworn', -swear'ing
for·syth'i·a
fort *(fortified place)*
forte *(strong point)*
for'te' *(musical direc-*
  tion)
forth *(forward)*

✔ fourth
forth•com'ing
forth'right'
forth•with'
for'ti•eth
for'ti•fi•ca'tion
for'ti•fi'er
for'ti•fy', -fied',
  -fy'ing
for•tis'si•mo'
for'ti•tude'
fort'night'
FOR'TRAN'
for'tress
for•tu'i•tous
for'tu•nate
for'tune
for'tune•tell'er
for'tune•tell'ing
for'ty
for'ty-nin'er
fo'rum pl. -rums
for'ward (at or near
  the front)
  ✔ foreword
for'wards
fos'sil
fos'sil•i•za'tion
fos'sil•ize', -ized',
  -iz'ing
fos'ter
foul (rotten)
  ✔ fowl
fou•lard'
foul'-mouthed'
foul'-up' n.

found
foun•da'tion
foun'der (to sink)
found'er (person
  who founds)
found'ling
foun'dry
fount
foun'tain
foun'tain•head'
four (number)
  ✔ for, fore
Four'-H' Club'
four'-leaf' clo'ver
four'-post'er
four'score'
four'some
four'square'
four•teen'
four•teenth'
fourth (number)
  ✔ forth
four'-wheel' drive'
fowl (bird), pl. fowl
  or fowls
  ✔ foul
fox pl. fox'es also
  fox
fox'glove'
fox'hole'
fox'hound'
fox' ter'ri•er
fox'trot', -trot'ted,
  -trot'ting
fox' trot' n.
fox'y

foy'er
fra'cas
frac'tion
frac'tion•al
frac'tious
frac'ture, -tured,
  -tur•ing
frag'ile
frag'ile•ly
fra•gil'i•ty
frag'ment
frag'men•tar'y
frag'men•ta'tion
fra'grance
fra'grant
frail
frail'ty
frame, framed,
  fram'ing
fram'er
frame'-up' n.
frame'work'
franc (money)
  ✔ frank
fran'chise'
Fran•cis'can
fran'ci•um
fran'gi•ble
frank (sincere)
  ✔ franc
frank (frankfurter)
  ✔ franc
frank'furt•er
frank'in•cense'
Frank'ish
fran'tic

fran′ti·cal·ly
frap·pé′ *also* frappe
fra·ter′nal
fra·ter′ni·ty
frat′er·ni·za′tion
frat′er·nize′,
  -nized′, -niz′ing
frat′ri·cid′al
frat′ri·cide′
Frau *pl.* Frau′en
fraud
fraud′u·lence
fraud′u·lent
fraught
Fräu′lein′ *pl.* -lein′
fray
fraz′zle, -zled, -zling
freak
freak′ish
freck′le, -led, -ling
free, fre′er, fre′est
free, freed, free′ing
free′bie *also* free′bee
free′boot′er
free′born′
freed′man
free′dom
freed′wom·an
free′ fall′ *or*
  free′-fall′
free′-for-all′
free′form′ *adj.*
free′hand′
free′hand′ed
free′lance′,
  -lanced′, -lanc′ing
free′lanc′er

free′load′
free′load′er
free′man
Free′ma′son
Free′ma′son·ry
free′stand′ing
free′stone′
free′style′
free′think′er
free′think′ing
free′ throw′ *n.*
free′way′
free′wheel′ing
free′will′ *adj.*
free′ will′ *n.*
freeze (*to form ice*),
  froze, fro′zen,
  freez′ing
  ✔ *frieze*
freeze′-dry′, -dried′,
  -dry′ing
freez′er
freight
freight′er
French
French′-
  Ca·na′di·an *also*
  French′
  Ca·na′di·an
French′ fry′ *n.*
French′-fry′ *v.*
French′man
French′wom·an
fre·net′ic
fre·net′i·cal·ly
fren′zied
fren′zy

fre′quen·cy
fre′quent *adj.*
fre·quent′ *v.*
fres′co *pl.* -coes *or*
  -cos
fresh′en
fresh′et
fresh′man
fresh′wa′ter *adj.*
fret, fret′ted,
  fret′ting
fret′ful
fret′work′
Freud′i·an
fri′a·bil′i·ty *or*
  fri′a·ble·ness
fri′a·ble
fri′ar (*member of a
  religious order*)
  ✔ *fryer*
fric′as·see′, -seed′,
  -see′ing
fric′tion
Fri′day
friend
friend′li·ness
friend′ly
friend′ship′
frieze (*horizontal
  band*)
  ✔ *freeze*
frig′ate
fright
fright′en
fright′en·ing
fright′ful
frig′id

fri•gid′i•ty *or*
  frig′id•ness
fri•jol′ *also* fri•jo′le
  pl. fri•jo′les
frill
frill′y
fringe, fringed,
  fring′ing
frip′per•y
Fri′sian
frisk
frisk′i•ly
frisk′y
frit′ter
fri•vol′i•ty
friv′o•lous
frizz
friz′zle, -zled, -zling
friz′zly
friz′zy
fro
frock
frog′man′
frol•ic, -icked,
  -ick•ing
frol′ic•some
from
frond
front
front′age
fron′tal
fron•tier′
fron′tiers′man
fron′tiers′wom′an
fron′tis•piece′
front′line′
front′-run′ner *also*

front′run′ner
frost′bite′, -bit′,
  -bit′ten, -bit′ing
frost′ing
frost′y
froth
froth′y
frown
frow′zi•ness
frow′zy *also* frow′sy
fruc′tose′
fru′gal
fru•gal′i•ty
fruit *pl.* fruit *or* fruits
fruit′cake′
fruit′ful
fruit′i•ness
fru•i′tion
fruit′less
fruit′y
frump′ish
frump′y
frus′trate′, -trat′ed,
  -trat′ing
frus•tra′tion
frus′tum *pl.* -tums
  or -ta
fry, fried, fry′ing
fry′er *also* fri′er
  (young chicken, one
  that fries)
  ✓ *friar*
fry′ing pan′
f′-stop′
fuch′sia
fud′dle, -dled,
  -dling

fudge
fu′el, -eled *also*
  -elled, -el•ing *or*
  -el•ling
fu′gi•tive
fugue
ful′crum *pl.* -crums
  or -cra
ful•fill′ *also* ful•fil′,
  -filled′, -fill′ing
ful•fill′ment
full′back′
full′-blood′ed
full′-blown′
full′-bod′ied
ful′ler•ene′
full′-fledged′
full′-length′
full′ness
full′-scale′
full′-size′
full′-time′
ful′ly
ful′mi•nate′,
  -nat′ed, -nat′ing
ful′mi•na′tion
ful′some
fum′ble, -bled,
  -bling
fume, fumed,
  fum′ing
fu′mi•gant
fu′mi•gate′, -gat′ed,
  -gat′ing
fu′mi•ga′tion
fu′mi•ga′tor
fun

func'tion
func'tion•al
func'tion•ar'y
fund
fun'da•men'tal
fun'da•men'tal•ism
fun'da•men'tal•ist
fu'ner•al
fu'ner•ar'y
fu•ne're•al
fun'gal *also*
  fun'gous
fun'gi•cide'
fun'gus *pl.* -gi *or*
  -gus•es
funk'y
fun'nel, -neled *or*
  -nelled, -nel•ing *or*
  -nel•ling
fun'nies
fun'ny
fur *(pelt)*
  ✔ *fir*
fur'bish
fur'bish•er
fu'ri•ous
furl
fur'long'
fur'lough
fur'nace
fur'nish
fur'nish•er
fur'nish•ing
fur'ni•ture
fu'ror'
furred

fur'ri•er
fur'ri•ness
fur'row
fur'ry *(having fur)*
  ✔ *fury*
fur'ther *(to a greater
  extent)*
  ✔ *farther*
fur'ther•ance
fur'ther•more'
fur'ther•most'
fur'thest *(to the
  greatest extent)*
  ✔ *farthest*
fur'tive
fu'ry *(rage)*
  ✔ *furry*
furze
fuse *also* fuze *(light-
  ing device)*
fuse *(to melt)*, fused,
  fus'ing
fu'se•lage'
fu'si•bil'i•ty
fu'si•ble
fu'sil•lade'
fu'sion
fuss'i•ness
fuss'y
fus'ti•ness
fus'ty
fu'tile
fu'tile•ly
fu•til'i•ty
fu'ton *pl.* -ton *or*
  -tons
fu'ture

fu•tur•is'tic
fu•tu'ri•ty
fuzz'i•ly
fuzz'i•ness
fuzz'y

G

gab, gabbed,
  gab'bing
gab'ar•dine'
gab'ber
gab'bi•ness
gab'by
ga'ble
ga'bled
gad, gad'ded,
  gad'ding
gad'a•bout'
gad'fly'
gadg'et
gad'o•lin'i•um
Gael *(Celt)*
  ✔ *gale*
Gael'ic
gaff *(hook)*
gaffe *(error)*
gaf'fer
gag, gagged,
  gag'ging
gage *(pledge)*
  ✔ *gauge*
gag'gle
gai'e•ty *also*
  gay'e•ty
gai'ly *also* gay'ly

gain
gain'er
gain'ful
gain•say', -said',
  -say'ing
gait *(way of walking)*
  ✔ gate
gai'ter
ga'la
ga•lac'tic
Ga•la'tians
gal'ax•y
gale *(wind)*
  ✔ Gael
ga•le'na
Gal'i•le'an
gall
gal'lant
gal'lant•ry
gall'blad'der *also*
  gall' blad'der
gal'le•on
gal'ler•y
gal'ley *pl.* -leys
gall'fly'
Gal'lic
gall'ing
gal'li•um
gal'li•vant'
gal'lon
gal'lop
gal'lows *pl.* -lows *or*
  -lows•es
gall'stone'
ga•lore'
ga•losh'
gal•van'ic

gal'va•nism
gal'va•ni•za'tion
gal'va•nize',
  -nized', -niz'ing
gal'va•nom'e•ter
gam'bit
gam'ble *(bet)*, -bled,
  -bling
  ✔ gambol
gam'bler
gam'bol *(frolic)*,
  -boled *or* -bolled,
  -bol•ing *or*
  -bol•ling
  ✔ gamble
game, gamed,
  gam'ing
game, gam'er,
  gam'est
game'cock'
game'keep'er
game'ster
gam'ete'
gam'in
gam'ma
gam'ut
gam'y
gan'der
gang
gang'gling
gang'gli•on *pl.* -gli•a
  or -gli•ons
gang'plank'
gan'grene',
  -grened', -gren'ing
gan'gre•nous
gang'ster

gang'way'
gan'net
gant'let *(track)*
  ✔ gauntlet
gap, gapped,
  gap'ping
gape, gaped, gap'ing
gar
ga•rage', -raged',
  -rag'ing
garb
gar'bage
gar•ban'zo *pl.* -zos
gar'ble, -bled,
  -bling
gar'den
gar'den•er
gar•de'nia
gar'fish' *pl.* -fish' *or*
  -fish'es
gar•gan'tu•an
gar'gle, -gled,
  -gling
gar'goyle'
gar'ish
gar'land
gar'lic
gar'lick•y
gar'ment
gar'ner
gar'net
gar'nish
gar'nish•ee', -eed',
  -ee'ing
gar'ni•ture
gar'ret
gar'ri•son

gar•rote′ *or*
  gar•rotte′, -rot′ed
  or -rot′ted, -rot′ing
  or -rot′ting
gar•ru′li•ty
gar′ru•lous
gar′ter
gas *pl.* gas′es *or*
  gas′ses
gas, gassed, gas′sing
gas′e•ous
gas′-guz′zler
gash
gas′ket
gas′light′
gas′o•hol′
gas′o•line′
gasp
gas′sy
gas′tric
gas′tro•in•tes′ti•nal
gas′tro•nom′ic *also*
  gas′tro•nom′i•cal
gas•tron′o•my
gas′tro•pod′
gas•tru′la *pl.* -las *or*
  -lae′
gate *(entrance)*
  ✔ *gait*
gate′crash′er
gate′house′
gate′keep′er
gate′post′
gate′way′
gath′er
gath′er•ing
Gat′ling gun′

gauche
gau′cho *pl.* -chos
gaud′i•ly
gaud′y
gauge *also* gage *(to
  measure),* gauged
  also gaged,
  gaug′ing *also*
  gag′ing
  ✔ *gage*
gauge′a•ble
Gaul
Gaul′ish
gaunt
gaunt′let *also*
  gant′let *(glove,
  punishment)*
  ✔ *gantlet*
gauze
gauz′i•ness
gauz′y
gav′el
ga•votte′
gawk′y
gay
gaze, gazed, gaz′ing
ga•ze′bo *pl.* -bos *or*
  -boes
ga•zelle′
ga•zette′
gaz′et•teer′
gaz•pa′cho
gear
gear′ing
gear′shift′
gear′wheel′ *also*
  gear′ wheel′

geck′o *pl.* -os *or*
  -oes
gee
gee′zer
ge•fil′te fish′
Gei′ger count′er
gei′sha *pl.* -sha *or*
  -shas
gel *(jellylike mixture),*
  gelled, gel′ling
  ✔ *jell*
gel′a•tin *also*
  gel′a•tine
ge•lat′i•nous
ge•la′to *pl.* -ti
geld′ing
gel′id
gem, gemmed,
  gem′ming
gem′stone′
gen′darme′
gen′der
gene
ge′ne•a•log′i•cal
ge′ne•al′o•gist
ge′ne•al′o•gy
gen′er•al
gen′er•al•ist
gen′er•al′i•ty
gen′er•al•i•za′tion
gen′er•al•ize′,
  -ized′, -iz′ing
gen′er•al•ly
gen′er•al•ship′
gen′er•ate′, -at′ed,
  -at′ing
gen′er•a′tion

gen'er•a•tive
gen'er•a'tor
ge•ner'ic
gen'er•os'i•ty
gen'er•ous
gen'e•sis *pl.* -ses'
gene'-splic'ing
ge•net'ic
ge•net'i•cist
ge•net'ics
gen'ial
ge'ni•al'i•ty
ge'nie
gen'i•tal
gen'i•ta'li•a
gen'i•tals
gen'i•tive
gen'ius *(gifted person),* *pl.* -ius•es
gen'ius *(guardian spirit),* *pl.* ge'ni•i'
gen'o•cid'al
gen'o•cide'
Gen'o•ese'
ge'nome
gen'o•type'
gen're
gent
gen•teel'
gen'tian
gen'tile' *also* Gen'tile'
gen•til'i•ty
gen'tle, -tler, -tlest
gen'tle•folk'
gen'tle•man
gen'tle•wom'an

gen'tly
gen'tri•fi•ca'tion
gen'tri•fy', -fied', -fy'ing
gen'try
gen'u•flect'
gen'u•flec'tion
gen'u•ine
ge'nus *pl.* gen'er•a
ge'o•cen'tric
ge'o•chem'is•try
ge'ode
ge'o•des'ic
ge•od'e•sy
ge'o•det'ic
ge•og'ra•pher
ge'o•graph'ic *also* ge'o•graph'i•cal
ge•og'ra•phy
ge'o•log'ic *or* ge'o•log'i•cal
ge•ol'o•gist
ge•ol'o•gy
ge'o•mag•net'ic
ge'o•mag'ne•tism
ge'o•met'ric *also* ge'o•met'ri•cal
ge•om'e•try
ge'o•mor'phic
ge'o•mor'pho•log'ic *or* ge'o•mor'-pho•log'i•cal
ge'o•mor•phol'o•gy
ge'o•phys'i•cal
ge'o•phys'i•cist
ge'o•phys'ics

ge'o•po•lit'i•cal
ge'o•pol'i•tics
Geor'gian
ge'o•tac'tic
ge'o•tax'is
ge'o•ther'mal
ge'o•trop'ic
ge•ot'ro•pism
ge•ra'ni•um
ger'bil
ger'i•at'ric
germ
Ger'man
ger•mane'
Ger•man'ic
ger•ma'ni•um
ger'mi•cid'al
ger'mi•cide'
ger'mi•nal
ger'mi•nate', -nat'ed, -nat'ing
ger'mi•na'tion
ger'mi•na'tor
ger'ry•man'der
ger'und
Ge•sta'po
ges•ta'tion
ges•tic'u•late', -lat'ed, -lat'ing
ges•tic'u•la'tion
ges'ture, -tured, -tur'ing
get, got, got'ten *or* got, get'ting
get'a•way' *n.*
get'-to•geth'er *n.*
get'up' *n.*

get'-up'-and-go' *n.*
gew'gaw'
gey'ser
ghast'li•ness
ghast'ly
gher'kin
ghet'to *pl.* -tos *or*
-toes
ghost
ghost'li•ness
ghost'ly
ghost' town'
ghost'write',
-wrote', -writ'ten,
-writ'ing
ghost'writ'er
ghoul
ghoul'ish
GI *pl.* GIs *or* GI's
gi'ant
gib'ber
gib'ber•ish
gib'bet, -bet•ed *or*
-bet•ted, -bet•ing *or*
-bet•ting
gib'bon
gib'bous
gibe *also* jibe *(tease),*
gibed *also* jibed,
gib'ing *also* jib'ing
✔ *jibe*
gib'lets
gid'di•ness
gid'dy
gift
gift'ed
gift'-wrap',

-wrapped',
-wrap'ping
gig, gigged, gig'ging
gig'a•bit'
gig'a•byte'
gig'a•hertz'
gi•gan'tic
gi•gan'tism
gig'a•watt'
gig'gle, -gled, -gling
gig'gler
gig'gly
Gi'la mon'ster
gild *(to cover with*
gold), gild'ed *or*
gilt, gild'ing
✔ *guild*
gill
gill' net'
gil'ly•flow'er
gilt *(gold)*
✔ *guilt*
gim'crack'
gim'let
gim'mick
gim'mick•ry
gim'mick•y
gimp'y
gin, ginned, gin'ning
gin'ger
gin'ger ale'
gin'ger•bread'
gin'ger•ly
gin'ger•snap'
ging'ham
gin'gi•val
gin'gi•vi'tis

gink'go *also* ging'ko
pl. -goes *also* -koes
gin'seng'
gi•raffe' *pl.* -raffes'
or -raffe'
gird, gird'ed *or* girt,
gird'ing
gird'er
gir'dle, -dled, -dling
girl
girl'friend' *also* girl'
friend'
Girl' Guide'
girl'hood'
girl'ish
Girl' Scout'
girth
gist
give, gave, giv'en,
giv'ing
give'-and-take'
also give' and take'
give'a•way'
giv'er
giz'mo *also* gis'mo
pl. -mos
giz'zard
gla'cial
gla'cier *(ice mass)*
✔ *glazier*
gla'ci•ol'o•gy
glad, glad'der,
glad'dest
glad'den
glade
glad'-hand' *v.*
glad'i•a'tor

glad'i•o'lus *also*
glad'i•o'la *pl.* -li *or*
-lus•es *also* -las
glad'some
glam'or•ize' *also*
glam'our•ize',
-ized', -iz'ing
glam'or•ous *also*
glam'our•ous
glam'our *also*
glam'or
glance, glanced,
glanc'ing
glan'du•lar
glare, glared,
glar'ing
glar'y
glass
glass'ful'
glass'ware'
glass'y
glau•co'ma
glaze, glazed,
glaz'ing
glaz'er *(one that glazes)*
gla'zier *(one that cuts glass)*
✓ glacier
gleam
glean
glean'er
glee
glen
glib, glib'ber,
glib'best
glide, glid'ed,

glid'ing
glid'er
glim'mer
glimpse, glimpsed,
glimps'ing
glint
glis•sade', -sad'ed,
-sad'ing
glis•san'do *pl.* -di *or*
-dos
glis'ten
glis'ter
glitch
glit'ter
glit'te•ra'ti
glit'ter•y
gloam'ing
gloat
glob
glob'al
globe
globe'fish' *pl.* -fish'
or -fish'es
globe'trot'ter
glob'u•lar
glob'ule
glob'u•lin
glock'en•spiel'
gloom'i•ly
gloom'i•ness
gloom'y
glo'ri•fi•ca'tion
glo'ri•fi'er
glo'ri•fy', -fied',
-fy'ing
glo'ri•ous
glo'ry, -ried, -ry•ing

gloss
glos'sa•ry
gloss'i•ness
gloss'y
glot'tal
glot'tis *pl.* -tis•es *or*
-ti•des'
glove, gloved,
glov'ing
glow
glow'er
glow'ing
glow'worm'
glu'cose'
glue, glued, glu'ing
glum, glum'mer,
glum'mest
glut, glut'ted, glut'-
ting
glu'ten
glu'ten•ous *(relating to gluten)*
glu'ti•nous *(sticky)*
glut'ton
glut'ton•ous
glut'ton•y
glyc'er•in *also*
glyc'er•ine
glyc'er•ol
gly'co•gen
gly'col'
glyph
G'-man'
gnarl
gnarled
gnash
gnat

gnaw

gneiss *(rock)*
  ✔ *nice*

gnoc'chi

gnome

gnu *(antelope)*
  ✔ *knew, new*

go, went, gone,
  go'ing, goes

go *pl.* goes

goad

go'-a•head'

goal

goal'ie

goal'keep'er

goal' post'

goat

goat•ee'

goat'skin'

gob

gob'ble, -bled,
  -bling

gob'ble•dy•gook'
  also gob'ble•de•
  gook'

gob'bler

go'-be•tween'

gob'let

gob'lin

go'-cart'

god'child'

god'daugh'ter

god'dess

god'fa'ther

god'for•sak'en *also*
  God'for•sak'en

god'head'

god'hood'

god'less

god'like'

god'li•ness

god'ly

god'moth'er

god'par'ent

god'send'

god'son'

God'speed'

go'fer *also* go'-fer
  (employee)
  ✔ *gopher*

go'-get'ter

gog'gle, -gled,
  -gling

gog'gle-eyed'

gog'gles

go'ing

goi'ter

gold'brick'

gold'brick'er

gold'en

gold'en•rod'

gold'-filled'

gold'finch'

gold'fish' *pl.*
  -fish' *or* -fish'es

gold'smith'

golf

golf'er

go'nad'

gon'do•la

gon'do•lier'

gon'er

gong

gon'or•rhe'a

goo

goo'ber

good, bet'ter, best

good-bye' *or*
  good•bye' *also*
  good-by' *pl.* -byes
  also -bys

good'-for-
  noth'ing

good'heart'ed

good'-hu'mored

good'-look'ing

good'-na'tured

good'ness

Good' Sa•mar'i•tan

good'-sized'

good'-tem'pered

good'will' *also*
  good' will'

good'y *also* good'ie

goo'ey, -i•er, -i•est

goof'ball' *or* goof'
  ball'

goof'i•ness

goof'off' *n.*

goof'y

goo'gol'

goo'gol•plex'

goon

goose *pl.* geese

goose'ber'ry

goose'neck'

goose'-step',
  -stepped',
  -step'ping

go'pher *(animal)*
  ✔ *gofer*

gore, gored, gor'ing

gorge, gorged,
    gorg'ing

gor'geous

go•ril'la *(animal)*
    ✔ guerrilla

gorse

gor'y

gosh

gos'hawk'

gos'ling

gos'pel

gos'sa•mer

gos'sip

gos'sip•er

Goth

Goth'ic

gouache

gouge, gouged,
    goug'ing

goug'er

gou'lash

gourd

gour•mand'

gour•met'

gout

gout'i•ness

gout'y

gov'ern

gov'ern•a•ble

gov'er•ness

gov'ern•ment

gov'ern•men'tal

gov'er•nor

gown

grab, grabbed,
    grab'bing

grace, graced,
    grac'ing

grace'ful

grace'less

gra'cious

grack'le

gra'date', -dat'ed,
    -dat'ing

gra•da'tion

grade, grad'ed,
    grad'ing

grad'er

gra'di•ent

grad'u•al

grad'u•ate', -at'ed,
    -at'ing

grad'u•a'tion

graf•fi'ti

graft

gra'ham

grail *or* Grail

grain

grain'y

gram

gram'mar

gram•mar'i•an

gram•mat'i•cal

gram'o•phone'

gram'pus

gran'a•ry

grand'aunt'

grand'child'

grand'dad'

grand'dad'dy

grand'daugh'ter

gran•dee'

gran'deur

grand'fa'ther

gran•dil'o•quence

gran•dil'o•quent

gran'di•ose'

gran'di•os'i•ty *or*
    gran'di•ose'ness

grand'ma'

grand'moth'er

grand'neph'ew

grand'niece'

grand'pa'

grand'par'ent

grand'son'

grand'stand'

grand'un'cle

gran'ite

gran'ny *or* gran'nie

gra•no'la

grant•ee'

gran'tor

gran'u•lar

gran'u•late',
    -lat'ed, -lat'ing

gran'u•la'tion

gran'ule

grape

grape'fruit'

grape'shot'

grape'vine'

graph

graph'eme'

graph'ic *also*
    graph'i•cal

graph'ite'

grap'nel

grap'ple, -pled,
    -pling

grasp
grasp'ing
grass
grass'hop'per
grass'land'
grass'roots'
grass'y
grate *(to shred)*,
  grat'ed, grat'ing
  ✔ great
grate *(framework)*
  ✔ great
grate'ful
grat'er
grat'i•fi•ca'tion
grat'i•fi'er
grat'i•fy', -fied',
  -fy'ing
grat'is
grat'i•tude'
gra•tu'i•tous
gra•tu'i•ty
grave, grav'er,
  grav'est
grave, graved,
  grav'en *or* graved,
  grav'ing
grave'dig'ger
grav'el, -eled *or*
  -elled, -el•ing *or*
  -el•ling
grave'side'
grave'site'
grave'stone'
grave'yard'
grav'id

grav'i•tate', -tat'ed,
  -tat'ing
grav'i•ta'tion
grav'i•ty
gra•vure'
gra'vy
gray *also* grey
gray'beard'
gray'ish
gray'ling *pl.* -ling *or*
  -lings
graze, grazed,
  graz'ing
grease, greased,
  greas'ing
grease'paint' *also*
  grease' paint'
greas'i•ness
greas'y
great *(large)*
  ✔ grate
great'-aunt' *or*
  great' aunt'
great'coat'
Great' Dane'
great'-grand'child'
great'-
  grand'daugh'ter
great'-grand'fa'ther
great'-
  grand'moth'er
great'-
  grand'par'ent
great'-grand'son
great'heart'ed
great'neph'ew

great'niece'
great'-un'cle *or*
  great' un'cle
greave
grebe
Gre'cian
Grec'o-Ro'man
greed'i•ly
greed'i•ness
greed'y
Greek
green'back'
green'er•y
green'-eyed'
green'gage'
green'gro'cer
green'horn'
green'house'
green'ish
green'mail'
green'room'
green'sward'
green'wood'
greet
greet'ing
gre•gar'i•ous
Gre•go'ri•an
grem'lin
gre•nade'
gren'a•dier'
gren'a•dine'
grey'hound'
grid
grid'dle
grid'dle•cake'
grid'i'ron

grid'lock'
grief
griev'ance
grieve, grieved,
 griev'ing
griev'ous
grif'fin *also* grif'fon
 or gryph'on
grill *(cooking utensil)*
grille *also* grill *(grating)*
grill'work'
grim, grim'mer,
 grim'mest
grim'ace, -aced,
 -ac•ing
grime
grim'i•ness
grim'y
grin, grinned,
 grin'ning
grind, ground,
 grind'ing
grind'er
grind'stone'
grip *(to grasp)*,
 gripped, grip'ping
 ✔ grippe
gripe *(to complain)*,
 griped, grip'ing
grippe *also* grip
 (influenza)
 ✔ grip
gris'ly *(gruesome)*
 ✔ grizzly
grist

gris'tle
gris'tly
grist'mill'
grit, grit'ted,
 grit'ting
grits
grit'ti•ness
grit'ty
griz'zled
griz'zly *(flecked with
 gray, bear)*
 ✔ grisly
groan
groan'er
groats
gro'cer
gro'cer•y
grog
grog'gi•ness
grog'gy
groin
grom'met
groom
grooms'man
groove
groov'y
grope, groped,
 grop'ing
gros'beak'
gros'grain'
gross *pl.* gross
gro•tesque'
grot'to *pl.* -toes *or*
 -tos
grouch
grouch'i•ly

grouch'i•ness
grouch'y
ground
ground' ball'
ground'break'ing
ground'er
ground'hog'
ground'less
ground'nut'
ground' out' *n.*
grounds'keep'er
ground' speed'
 also ground'speed'
ground'swell'
ground' wa'ter *also*
 ground'wa'ter
ground'work'
group
grou'per *pl.* -per *or*
 -pers
group'ie
group'ing
grouse *pl.* grouse *or*
 grous'es
grouse, groused,
 grous'ing
grout
grove
grov'el, -eled *also*
 -elled, -el•ing *or*
 -el•ling
grov'el•er *or*
 grov'el•ler
grow, grew, grown,
 grow'ing
grow'er

growl
grown'up' *also*
  grown'-up' *n.*
grown'-up' *adj.*
growth
grub, grubbed,
  grub'bing
grub'bi•ly
grub'bi•ness
grub'by
grub'stake',
  -staked', -stak'ing
grudge, grudged,
  grudg'ing
gru'el
gru'el•ing *also*
  gru'el•ling
grue'some
gruff
grum'ble, -bled,
  -bling
grum'bler
grump'i•ly
grump'i•ness
grump'y
grunt
gua'ca•mo'le
gua•na'co *pl.* -cos *or*
  -co
gua'nine'
gua'no *pl.* -nos
gua'no•sine'
Gua'ra•ni' *pl.* -ni' *or*
  -nis'
guar'an•tee', -teed',
  -tee'ing
guar'an•tor'

guar'an•ty, -tied,
  -ty•ing
guard
guard'ed
guard'house'
guard'i•an
guard'rail'
guard'room'
guards'man
Gua'te•ma'lan
gua'va
gu'ber•na•to'ri•al
gudg'eon
Guern'sey *pl.* -seys
guer•ril'la *or*
  gue•ril'la *(soldier)*
  ✔ *gorilla*
guess
guess'er
guess'ti•mate
guess'work'
guest
guf•faw'
guid'a•ble
guid'ance
guide, guid'ed,
  guid'ing
guide'book'
guide'line'
guide'post'
guid'er
guide'word'
guild *(association)*
  ✔ *gild*
guild'hall'
guile
guile'ful

guile'less
guil'lo•tine',
  -tined', -tin'ing
guilt *(remorse)*
  ✔ *gilt*
guilt'i•ly
guilt'i•ness
guilt'y
guin'ea
guin'ea fowl'
guin'ea pig'
guise
gui•tar'
gui•tar'ist
gu'lag'
gulch
gulf
gull
gul'let
gul'li•bil'i•ty
gul'li•ble
gul'ly
gulp
gum, gummed,
  gum'ming
gum' ar'a•bic
gum'ball'
gum'bo *pl.* -bos
gum'drop'
gum'mi•ness
gum'my
gump'tion
gum'shoe'
gun, gunned,
  gun'ning
gun'boat'
gun'cot'ton

gun'fight'
gun'fire'
gung' ho'
gun'lock'
gun'man
gun'ner
gun'ner•y
gun'ny
gun'ny•sack'
gun'pow'der
gun'shot'
gun'-shy'
gun'sling'er
gun'smith'
gun'wale *also*
gun'nel
gup'py
gur'gle, -gled, -gling
gu'ru *pl.* -rus
gush
gush'er
gush'i•ness
gush'y
gus'set
gust
gus'ta•to'ry
gust'i•ness
gus'to *pl.* -toes
gust'y
gut, gut'ted, gut'ting
guts'y
gut'ter
gut'tur•al
guy
guz'zle, -zled, -zling
guz'zler
gym

gym•na'si•um *pl.*
-si•ums *or* -si•a
gym'nast
gym•nas'tics
gym'no•sperm'
gy'ne•co•log'i•cal
or gy'ne•co•log'ic
gy'ne•col'o•gist
gy'ne•col'o•gy
gyp *also* gip, gypped
or gipped, gyp'ping
or gip'ping
gyp'sum
Gyp'sy *also* Gip'sy
gy'rate', -rat'ed,
-rat'ing
gy•ra'tion
gyr'fal'con *also*
ger'fal'con
gy'ro *pl.*-ros
gy'ro•com'pass
gy'ro•scope'
gy'ro•scop'ic

H

ha *also* hah
ha'be•as cor'pus
hab'er•dash'er
hab'er•dash'er•y
ha•bil'i•ment
hab'it
hab'it•a•bil'i•ty
hab'it•a•ble
hab'i•tat'
hab'i•ta'tion

hab'it-form'ing
ha•bit'u•al
ha•bit'u•ate',
-at'ed, -at'ing
ha•bit'u•a'tion
hab'i•tude'
ha•bit'u•é'
ha'ci•en'da
hack
hack'er
hack'le
hack'ney *pl.* -neys
hack'neyed
hack'saw'
had'dock *pl.* -dock
or -docks
haf'ni•um
haft
hag
hag'gard
hag'gle, -gled,
-gling
hag'gler
hag'i•og'ra•pher
hag'i•o•graph'ic *or*
hag'i•o•graph'i•cal
hag'i•og'ra•phy
hah'ni•um
Hai'da *pl.* -da *or* -das
Hai'dan
hai'ku *pl.* -ku *also*
-kus
hail (*ice pellets, to*
greet)
✓ hale
hail'er
hail'stone'

hail′storm′

hair *(threadlike growth)*
  ✔ hare

hair′brush′

hair′cloth′

hair′cut′

hair′do′ *pl.* -dos′

hair′dress′er

hair′i•ness

hair′line′

hair′piece′

hair′pin′

hair′-rais′ing

hairs′breadth′ *or* hair′s′-breadth′ *also* hair′breadth′

hair′split′ter

hair′split′ting

hair′ spray′

hair′spring′

hair′style′

hair′-trig′ger *adj.*

hair′y

Hai′tian

hake *pl.* hake *or* hakes

hal′berd

hal′cy•on

hale *(healthy)*, hal′er, hal′est
  ✔ hail

hale *(to force)*, haled, hal′ing
  ✔ hail

half *pl.* halves

half′-and-half′

half′back′

half′-baked′

half′-cocked′

half′-dol′lar

half′heart′ed

half′-hour′

half′-life′

half′-mast′

half′-moon′

half′pen•ny *pl.* -pence *or* -pen•nies

half′-slip′

half′-staff′

half′-tim′bered *also* half′-tim′ber

half′time′

half′tone′ *(value between light and dark)*

half′ tone′ *(semitone)*

half′-track′

half′-truth′

half′way′

half′-wit′ted

hal′i•but *pl.* -but *or* -buts

hal′ite

hal′i•to′sis

hall *(corridor)*
  ✔ haul

hal′le•lu′jah

hall′mark′

hal•loo′, -looed′, -loo′ing

hal′low

hal′lowed

Hal′low•een′ *also* Hal′low•e′en′

hal•lu′ci•nate′, -nat′ed, -nat′ing

hal•lu′ci•na′tion

hal•lu′ci•na•to′ry

hal•lu′cin•o•gen

hal•lu′cin•o•gen′ic

hall′way′

ha′lo *pl.* -los *or* -loes

hal′o•gen

halt

hal′ter

halt′ing

halve *(to divide)*, halved, halv′ing
  ✔ have

hal′yard

ham, hammed, ham′ming

ham′burg′er *also* ham′burg′

ham′let

ham′mer

ham′mer•head′

ham′mer•lock′

ham′mock

ham′per

ham′ster

ham′string′, -strung′, -string′ing

hand′bag′

hand′ball′

hand′bill′

hand′book′

hand′cart′

hand′craft′

hand'cuff'
hand'ful'
hand'gun'
hand'i•cap', -capped', -cap'ping
hand'i•craft' *also* hand'craft'
hand'i•ly
hand'i•work'
hand'ker•chief *pl.* -chiefs *also* -chieves
han'dle, -dled, -dling
han'dle•bar'
han'dler
hand'made'
hand'maid' *also* hand'maid'en
hand'-me-down'
hand'-off' *n.*
hand'out' *n.*
hand'pick'
hand'rail'
hand'saw'
hand'shake'
hand'some *(good-looking)*, -som•er, -som•est
✔ hansom
hands'-on'
hand'spike'
hand'spring'
hand'stand'
hand'-to-hand' *adj.*
hand'-to-mouth' *adj.*

hand'work'
hand'writ'ing
hand'y
hand'y•man' *also* hand'y man'
hang *(to fasten from above)*, hung, hang'ing
hang *(to execute)*, hanged, hang'ing
han'gar *(building)*
✔ hanger
hang'dog'
hang'er *(one that hangs something)*
✔ hangar
hang'er-on' *pl.* hang'ers-on'
hang' glid'er
hang' glid'ing
hang'man
hang'nail'
hang'out' *n.*
hang'o'ver
hang'-up' *n.*
hank
han'ker
han'som *(carriage)*
✔ handsome
Ha'nuk•kah *or* Ha'nu•kah *also* Cha'nu•kah
hap, happed, hap'ping
hap•haz'ard
hap'less
hap'loid'

hap'ly *(by chance)*
✔ happily
hap'pen
hap'pen•ing
hap'pen•stance'
hap'pi•ly *(in a happy way)*
✔ haply
hap'pi•ness
hap'py
hap'py-go-luck'y
ha'ra-ki'ri *pl.* -ris
ha•rangue', -rangued', -rangu'ing
ha•rass'
ha•rass'ment
har'bin•ger
har'bor
hard'back'
hard'ball'
hard'-bit'ten
hard'-boiled'
hard'bound'
hard'-core' *also* hard'core' *adj.*
hard'cov'er
hard' disk'
hard'en
hard'hat' *or* hard'-hat'
hard'head'ed
hard'heart'ed
har'di•hood'
hard'-line' *also* hard'line' *adj.*
hard'lin'er

hard'ly

hard'pan'

hard'-shell' *also*
  hard'-shelled' *adj.*

hard'ship'

hard'tack'

hard'top'

hard'ware'

hard'wood'

har'dy

hare *(animal)*
  ✔ hair

hare'bell'

hare'brained'

hare'lip'

hare'lipped'

har'em

hark

har'le•quin

har'lot

harm'ful

harm'less

har•mon'ic

har•mon'i•ca

har•mo'ni•ous

har•mo'ni•um

har'mo•ni•za'tion

har'mo•nize',
  -nized', -niz'ing

har'mo•ny

har'ness

harp

harp'ist

har•poon'

harp'si•chord'

Har'py *also* har'py

har'que•bus *also*

ar'que•bus

har'ri•dan

har'ri•er

har'row

har'row•er

har'row•ing

har'ry, -ried, -ry•ing

harsh

hart *(male deer)*, pl.
  harts or hart
  ✔ heart

har'te•beest' pl.
  -beests' or -beest'

har'um-scar'um

har'vest

har'vest•er

has'-been' n.

hash

hash'ish' *also*
  hash'eesh'

Ha'sid *or* Has'sid
  also Chas'sid pl.
  Ha•si'dim *or*
  Has•si'dim *also*
  Chas•si'dim

has'n't

hasp

has'sle, -sled, -sling

has'sock

haste

has'ten

hast'i•ly

hast'y

hat'band'

hat'box'

hatch

hatch'back'

hatch'er•y

hatch'et

hatch'way'

hate, hat'ed, hat'ing

hate'ful

hat'er

hat'pin'

ha'tred

hat'ter

hau'berk

haugh'ti•ly

haugh'ty

haul *(to tug)*
  ✔ hall

haul'er

haunch

haunt

haunt'ed

haunt'ing

Hau'sa pl. -sa or -sas

haut'boy' pl. -boys'

hau•teur'

have *(to own)*, had,
  hav'ing, has
  ✔ halve

ha'ven

have'-not' n.

have'n't

hav'er•sack'

hav'oc

haw

Ha•wai'ian

hawk

hawk'er

hawk'-eyed'

haw'ser

haw'thorn'

hay *(grass)*
  ✔ hey
hay'cock'
hay' fe'ver
hay'fork'
hay'loft'
hay'mow'
hay'rack'
hay'rick'
hay'ride'
hay'seed'
hay'stack'
hay'wire'
haz'ard
haz'ard•ous
haze *(air)*
haze *(to humiliate)*,
  hazed, haz'ing
ha'zel
ha'zel•nut'
haz'i•ly
haz'y
H'-bomb'
he
head
head'ache'
head'band'
head'board'
head'cheese'
head'dress'
head'ed
head'first'
head'gear'
head'hunt'er
head'hunt'ing
head'ing
head'land

head'light'
head'line', -lined',
  -lin'ing
head'lin'er
head'lock'
head'long'
head'man
head'mas'ter
head'mis'tress
head'-on'
head'phone'
head'piece'
head'quar'ters
head'rest'
head'room'
head'set'
head'stand'
head'stone'
head'strong'
head'wait'er
head'wa'ters
head'way'
head'wind'
head'word'
head'work'
head'y
heal *(to cure)*
  ✔ heel
heal'er
health
health'i•ly
health'y
heap
hear *(to perceive
  sound)*, heard,
  hear'ing
  ✔ here

hear'er
hear'ing-
  im•paired'
hear'ken *also*
  har'ken
hear'say'
hearse
heart *(organ)*
  ✔ hart
heart'ache'
heart'beat'
heart'break'
heart'break'ing
heart'bro'ken
heart'burn'
heart'en
heart'felt'
hearth
hearth'stone'
heart'i•ly
heart'land'
heart'less
heart'-rend'ing *or*
  heart'rend'ing
hearts'ease' *also*
  heart's'-ease'
heart'sick'
heart'strings'
heart'-to-heart'
heart'wood'
heart'y
heat
heat'ed
heat'er
heath
hea'then *pl.* -thens
  or -then

heath'er
heave, heaved *or* hove, heav'ing
heave'-ho'
heav'en
heav'en·li·ness
heav'en·ly
heav'en·ward
heav'i·ly
heav'y
heav'y-dut'y
heav'y-hand'ed
heav'y-heart'ed
heav'y·set'
heav'y·weight'
He·bra'ic
He'brew
heck'le, -led, -ling
heck'ler
hec'tare'
hec'tic
hec'to·me·ter
hec'tor
hedge, hedged, hedg'ing
hedge'hog'
hedge'row'
he'don·ism
he'don·ist
he'don·is'tic
heed
heed'less
hee'haw'
heel *(part of a foot, to tilt)*
✔ *heal*
heft

heft'y
he·gem'o·ny
he·gi'ra *also* he·ji'ra
heif'er
heigh'-ho'
height
height'en
Heim'lich' ma·neu'ver
hei'nous
heir *(person who inherits)*
✔ *air, are, e'er, ere*
heir' ap·par'ent *pl.* heirs' ap·par'ent
heir'ess
heir'loom'
heir' pre·sump'tive *pl.* heirs' pre·sump'tive
heist
hel'i·cal
hel'i·con'
hel'i·cop'ter
he'li·o·cen'tric
he'li·o·trope'
he'li·ot'ro·pism
hel'i·pad'
hel'i·port'
he'li·um
he'lix *pl.* -lix·es *or* hel'i·ces'
hell
hell'-bent' *or* hell'bent'
hell'cat'
hel'le·bore'

Hel'lene'
Hel·len'ic
Hel'le·nism
Hel'le·nis'tic
hell'-for-leath'er
hell'hole'
hell'ion
hell'ish
hel·lo' *also* hul·lo' *pl.* -los'
helm
hel'met
helms'man
hel'ot
help'er
help'ful
help'ing
help'less
help'mate'
hel'ter-skel'ter
helve
hem, hemmed, hem'ming
he'ma·tite'
he'ma·to·log'ic *or* he'ma·to·log'i·cal
he'ma·tol'o·gist
he'ma·tol'o·gy
hem'i·sphere'
hem'i·spher'ic *or* hem'i·spher'i·cal
hem'lock'
he'mo·di·al'y·sis *pl.* -ses'
he'mo·glo'bin
he'mo·phil'i·a
he'mo·phil'i·ac'

hem′or•rhage,
  -rhaged, -rhag′ing
hem′or•rhag′ic
hem′or•rhoid′
hemp
hemp′en
hem′stitch′
hen
hen′bane′
hence
hence′forth′
hence•for′ward
hench′man
hen′na, -naed,
  -na•ing
hen′ry *pl.* -ries or
  -rys
hep′a•rin
he•pat′i•ca
hep′a•ti′tis *pl.*
  -tit′i•des′
hep′ta•gon′
hep•tag′o•nal
hep•tath′lon
her
her′ald
he•ral′dic
her′ald•ry
herb
her•ba′ceous
herb′age
herb′al
herb′al•ist
her•bar′i•um *pl.*
  -i•ums or -i•a
her′bi•cid′al
her′bi•cide′

her′bi•vore′
her•biv′o•rous
Her′cu•le′an
herd *(group)*
  ✔ *heard*
herd′er
herds′man
here *(at this place)*
  ✔ *hear*
here′a•bout′ *also*
  here′a•bouts′
here•af′ter
here•by′
he•red′i•tar′y
he•red′i•ty
Here′ford
here•in′
here•of′
here•on′
her′e•sy
her′e•tic
he•ret′i•cal
here•to′
here′to•fore′
here•un′to
here•up•on′
here•with′
her′i•ta•bil′i•ty
her′i•ta•ble
her′i•tage
her•maph′ro•dite′
her•maph′ro•dit′ic
her•met′ic *also*
  her•met′i•cal
her′mit
her′mit•age
her′ni•a *pl.* -ni•as *or*

  -ni•ae′
he′ro *pl.* -roes
he•ro′ic *also*
  he•ro′i•cal
her′o•in *(narcotic)*
her′o•ine *(female*
  character)
her′o•ism
her′on
her′pes
her′pe•tol′o•gist
her′pe•tol′o•gy
her′ring *pl.* -ring *or*
  -rings
her′ring•bone′
hers
her•self′
hertz *pl.* hertz
hes′i•tan•cy
hes′i•tant
hes′i•tate′, -tat′ed,
  -tat′ing
hes′i•tat′er
hes′i•ta′tion
Hes′sian
het′er•o•dox′
het′er•o•dox′y
het′er•o′ge•ne′i•ty
het′er•o•ge′ne•ous
  also het′er•og′e•
  nous
het′er•ol′o•gous
het′er•o•sex′ism
het′er•o•sex′u•al
het′er•o•sex′u•al′-
  i•ty
het′er•o•zy′gous

heu•ris'tic

hew *(to cut)*, hewed,
hewn *or* hewed,
hew'ing
✔ *hue*

hex

hex'a•dec'i•mal

hex'a•gon'

hex•ag'o•nal

hex'a•he'dron *pl.*
-drons *or* -dra

hex•am'e•ter

hey *interj.*
✔ *hay*

hey'day'

hi *interj.*
✔ *hie, high*

hi•a'tus *pl.* -tus•es *or*
-tus

hi•ba'chi *pl.* -chis

hi'ber•nate',
-nat'ed, -nat'ing

hi'ber•na'tion

hi•bis'cus

hic'cup *also*
hic'cough, -cupped
also -coughed,
-cup•ping *also*
-cough•ing

hick

hick'o•ry

hide, hid, hid'den *or*
hid, hid'ing

hide'-and-seek'

hide'a•way'

hide'bound'

hid'e•ous

hide'out' *n.*

hie *(hurry)*, hied,
hie'ing *or* hy'ing
✔ *hi, high*

hi'er•ar'chi•cal *or*
hi'er•ar'chic

hi'er•ar'chy

hi'er•o•glyph' *also*
hi'er•o•glyph'ic *n.*

hi'er•o•glyph'ic
also hi'er•o•glyph'-
i•cal *adj.*

hi'-fi' *pl.* -fis'

hig'gle•dy-
pig'gle•dy

high *(tall)*
✔ *hi, hie*

high'ball'

high'born'

high'boy'

high'bred'

high'brow'

high'chair'

high'-class' *adj.*

high'-den'si•ty *adj.*

high'-end' *adj.*

high'er-up' *n.*

high'fa•lu'tin *or*
hi'fa•lu'tin

high'-five' *n.*

high'fli'er *also*
high'-fli'er

high'-flown'

high'-fly'ing *adj.*

high'-grade'

high'hand'ed

high'-hat',

-hat'ted, -hat'ting

high' jinks' *or*
hi'jinks'

high'land

high'land•er

high'light',
-light'ed, -light'ing

high'ly

high'-mind'ed

high'-pitched'

high'-pres'sure

high'-rise'

high' school' *n.*

high'-school' *adj.*

high'-speed' *adj.*

high'-spir'it•ed

high'-strung'

high'-tail' *v.*

high'-ten'sion

high'-wa'ter
mark'

high'way'

high'way'man

hi'jack'

hi'jack'er

hike, hiked, hik'ing

hik'er

hi•lar'i•ous

hi•lar'i•ty

hill'bil'ly

hill'i•ness

hill'ock

hill'side'

hill'top'

hill'y

hilt

hi'lum *pl.* -la

him *pron.*
  ✔ *hymn*
him•self'
hind
hin'der
Hin'di
hind'most'
hind'quar'ter
hin'drance
hind'sight'
Hin'du
Hin'du•ism
Hin'du•sta'ni
hinge, hinged,
  hing'ing
hint
hint'er
hin'ter•land'
hip, hip'per,
  hip'pest
hip'bone'
hip' joint'
hip'pie *also* hip'py
  pl. -pies
hip'po *pl.* -pos
Hip'po•crat'ic
  oath'
hip'po•drome'
hip'po•pot'a•mus
  pl. -mus•es *or* -mi'
hire, hired, hir'ing
hire'ling
hir'sute'
his
His•pan'ic
hiss
his'ta•mine'

his'ta•min'ic
his'to•log'i•cal *or*
  his'to•log'ic
his'tol'o•gy
his•to'ri•an
his•tor'ic *(important
  in history)*
his•tor'i•cal *(relat-
  ing to history)*
his•tor'i•cize',
  -cized', -ciz'ing
his'to•ried'
his•to'ri•og'ra•
  pher
his•to'ri•og'ra•phy
his'to•ry
his'tri•on'ic *also*
  his'tri•on'i•cal
hit, hit, hit'ting
hit'-and-run'
hitch
hitch'hike',
  -hiked', -hik'ing
hitch'hik'er
hith'er
hith'er•to'
hit'-or-miss' *adj.*
hit'ter
Hit'tite'
hive, hived, hiv'ing
hives
ho *interj.*
  ✔ *hoe*
hoar *(white or gray)*
  ✔ *whore*
hoard *(cache)*
  ✔ *horde*

hoard'er
hoar'frost'
hoar'i•ness
hoarse *(grating)*,
  hoars'er, hoars'est
  ✔ *horse*
hoar'y
hoax
hoax'er
hob
hob'ble, -bled,
  -bling
hob'by
hob'by•horse'
hob'by•ist
hob'gob'lin
hob'nail'
hob'nob',
  -nobbed',
  -nob'bing
ho'bo *pl.* -boes *or*
  -bos
hock
hock'ey
ho'cus-po'cus
hod
hodge'podge'
hoe *(to weed)*, hoed,
  hoe'ing
  ✔ *ho*
hoe'cake'
hoe'down'
hog, hogged,
  hog'ging
ho'gan'
hog'gish
hogs'head'

hog'-tie' *also*
  hog'tie', -tied',
  -tie'ing *or* -ty'ing
hog'wash'
hog'-wild'
hoi' pol•loi'
hoist
hold, held, hold'ing
hold'er
hold'out' *n.*
hold'o•ver *n.*
hold'up' *n.*
hole *(opening)*,
  holed, hol'ing
  ✔ whole
hol'ey *(having holes)*
  ✔ holy, wholly
hol'i•day'
ho'li•er-than-
  thou' *adj.*
ho'li•ness
ho•lis'tic
hol'lan•daise'
  sauce'
hol'ler
hol'low
hol'ly
hol'ly•hock'
hol'mi•um
hol'o•caust' *also*
  Hol'o•caust'
Hol'o•cene'
hol'o•gram'
hol'o•graph'
hol'o•graph'ic *also*
  hol'o•graph'i•cal
ho•log'raph•y

Hol'stein'
hol'ster
ho'ly *(sacred)*
  ✔ holey, wholly
hom'age
hom'bre
home, homed,
  hom'ing
home' base'
home'bod'y
home'-brew'
home'-brewed'
home'buy'er
home'com'ing
home'grown'
home'land'
home'less
home'li•ness
home'ly
home'made'
home'mak'er
home'mak'ing
ho'me•o•path' *or*
  ho'me•op'a•thist
ho'me•o•path'ic
ho'me•op'a•thy
ho'me•o•sta'sis
home'own'er
home' plate'
hom'er
Ho•mer'ic
home'room'
home'sick'
home'spun'
home'stead'
home'stead'er
home'stretch'

home'ward
home'wards
home'work'
hom'ey *also* hom'y,
  -i•er, -i•est
hom'i•cid'al
hom'i•cide'
hom'i•let'ic *also*
  hom'i•let'i•cal
hom'i•ly
hom'i•nid
hom'i•noid'
hom'i•ny
ho'mo•ge•ne'i•ty
ho'mo•ge'ne•ous
ho•mog'e•ni•za'-
  tion
ho•mog'e•nize',
  -nized', -niz'ing
hom'o•graph'
ho•mol'o•gous
hom'o•nym'
ho•mon'y•mous
hom'o•phone'
hom'o•phon'ic
ho•moph'o•nous
ho•moph'o•ny
ho•mop'ter•ous
Ho'mo sa'pi•ens
ho'mo•sex'u•al
ho'mo•sex'u•al'i•ty
ho'mo•zy'gous
hon'cho *pl.* -chos
Hon•du'ran
hone, honed,
  hon'ing
hon'est

hon'es•ty
hon'ey *pl.* -eys
hon'ey, -eyed *or*
  -ied, -ey•ing
hon'ey•bee'
hon'ey•comb'
hon'ey•dew'
hon'ey•moon'
hon'ey•moon'er
hon'ey•suck'le
honk
honk'er
hon'or
hon'or•a•ble
hon'or•a•bly
hon'o•rar'i•um *pl.*
  -i•ums *or* -i•a
hon'or•ar'y
hon'or•if'ic
hood
hood'ed
hood'lum
hood'wink'
hoo'ey
hoof *pl.* hoofs *or*
  hooves
hook
hook'ah
hook'up' *n.*
hook'worm'
hook'y
hoo'li•gan
hoop *(circle)*
  ✔ whoop
hoop'la
hoo•ray'
hoot

hoot'en•an'ny
hop, hopped,
  hop'ping
hope, hoped,
  hop'ing
hope'ful
hope'less
Ho'pi *pl.* -pi *or* -pis
hop'per
hop'scotch'
ho'ra
horde *(group)*
  ✔ hoard
hore'hound'
ho•ri'zon
hor'i•zon'tal
hor•mon'al
hor'mone'
horn'bill'
horn'book'
horned
hor'net
horn'pipe'
horn'y
hor'o•scope'
hor•ren'dous
hor'ri•ble
hor'ri•bly
hor'rid
hor•rif'ic
hor'ri•fy', -fied',
  -fy'ing
hor'ror
hors d'oeuvre' *pl.*
  hors d'oeuvres' *or*
  hors d'oeuvre'
horse *(animal)*

✔ hoarse
horse'back'
horse'fly'
horse'hair'
horse'hide'
horse'man
horse'man•ship'
horse'play'
horse'pow'er
horse'rad'ish
horse'shoe'
horse'whip',
  -whipped',
  -whip'ping
horse'wom'an
hors'y *also* hors'ey,
  -i•er, -i•est
hor'ta•tive
hor'ta•to'ry
hor'ti•cul'tur•al
hor'ti•cul'ture
hor'ti•cul'tur•ist
ho•san'na
hose *pl.* hose *or*
  hos'es
hose, hosed, hos'ing
ho'sier•y
hos'pice
hos'pi•ta•ble
hos'pi•ta•bly
hos'pi•tal
hos'pi•tal'i•ty
hos'pi•tal•i•za'tion
hos'pi•tal•ize',
  -ized', -iz'ing
host
hos'tage

hos'tel *(lodging)*
✔ hostile
hos'tel·ry
host'ess
hos'tile *(showing enmity)*
✔ hostel
hos·til'i·ty
hos'tler *also* os'tler
hot, hot'ter, hot'test
hot'bed'
hot'-blood'ed
hot'cake'
hot' dog' *or* hot'dog'
ho·tel'
hot'foot' *v.*
hot'head'ed
hot'house'
hot' line' *or* hot'line'
hot' plate'
hot'shot'
hound
hour *(time)*
✔ our
hour'glass'
hour'long' *or* hour'-long' *adj.*
house, housed, hous'ing
house'boat'
house'break', -broke', -bro'ken, -break'ing
house'clean'ing

house'fly'
house'guest'
house'hold'
house'hold'er
house'hus'band
house'keep'er
house'keep'ing
house'maid'
house'moth'er
house'plant'
house'top'
house'wares'
house'warm'ing
house'wife'
house'work'
hous'ing
hov'el
hov'er
hov'er·craft'
how
how'dah
how'dy
how·ev'er
how'it·zer
howl'er
how'so·ev'er
hoy'den
hub'bub'
hub'cap'
hu'bris
huck'le·ber'ry
huck'ster
hud'dle, -dled, -dling
hue *(color, clamor)*
✔ hew

huff'i·ly
huff'y
hug, hugged, hug'ging
huge, hug'er, hug'est
Hu'gue·not'
hu'la
hulk'ing
hull
hul'la·ba·loo' *pl.* -loos'
hum, hummed, hum'ming
hu'man
hu·mane'
hu'man·ism
hu'man·ist
hu·man'i·tar'i·an
hu·man'i·tar'i·an·ism
hu·man'i·ty
hu'man·i·za'tion
hu'man·ize', -ized', -iz'ing
hu'man·kind'
hu'man·oid'
hum'ble, -bled, -bling
hum'bly
hum'bug', -bugged', -bug'ging
hum'drum'
hu'mer·us *(bone)*, *pl.* -mer·i'
✔ humorous

hu'mid
hu·mid'i·fi'er
hu·mid'i·fy', -fied', -fy'ing
hu·mid'i·ty
hu·mil'i·ate', -at'ed, -at'ing
hu·mil'i·a'tion
hu·mil'i·ty
hum'ming·bird'
hum'mock
hum'mus *also* hum'us *or* hom'-mos (*mashed chick-peas*)
  ✔ *humus*
hu'mor
hu'mor·ist
hu'mor·ous (*funny*)
  ✔ *humerus*
hump'back'
hump'backed'
humph
hu'mus (*decayed matter*)
  ✔ *hummus*
Hun
hunch'back'
hunch'backed'
hun'dred *pl.* -dred *or* -dreds
hun'dredth
hun'dred·weight' *pl.* -weight' *or* -weights'
Hun·gar'i·an

hun'ger
hun'gri·ly
hun'gri·ness
hun'gry
hunk
Hunk'pa'pa *pl.* -pa *or* -pas
Hun'nish
hunt
hunt'er
hunt'ing
hunts'man
hur'dle (*to leap over*), -dled, -dling
  ✔ *hurtle*
hur'dler
hur'dy-gur'dy
hurl
hurl'er
hur'ly-bur'ly
Hu'ron *pl.* -ron *or* -rons
hur·rah' *also* hoo·ray' *or* hur'ray'
hur'ri·cane'
hur'ry, -ried, -ry·ing
hurt, hurt, hurt'ing
hurt'ful
hur'tle (*to hurl*), -tled, -tling
  ✔ *hurdle*
hus'band
hus'band·ry
husk'y (*hoarse, burly*)

hus'ky *also* hus'kie (*dog*)
hus·sar'
hus'sy
hus'tle, -tled, -tling
hut
hutch
hy'a·cinth'
hy'brid
hy'brid·i·za'tion
hy'brid·ize', -ized', iz'ing
hy'dra
hy·dran'gea
hy'drant
hy'drate', -drat'ed, -drat'ing
hy·dra'tion
hy·drau'lic
hy'dra·zine'
hy'dride'
hy'dro·car'bon
hy'dro·ce·phal'ic *or* hy'dro·ceph'-a·loid' *or* hy'dro·ceph'a·lous
hy'dro·ceph'a·lus
hy'dro·ceph'a·ly
hy'dro·chlo'ric ac'id
hy'dro·cor'ti·sone'
hy'dro·cy·an'ic ac'id
hy'dro·dy·nam'ic
hy'dro·e·lec'tric

hy′dro•e•lec•tric′-
  i•ty
hy′dro•fluor′ic
  ac′id
hy′dro•foil′
hy′dro•gen
hy′dro•gen•ate′,
  -at′ed, -at′ing
hy′dro•gen•a′tion
hy•drog′e•nous
hy′dro•graph′ic
hy•drog′ra•phy
hy•drol′o•gy
hy•drol′y•sis
hy′dro•lyze′,
  -lyzed′, -lyz′ing
hy•drom′e•ter
hy′dro•pho′bi•a
hy′dro•plane′
hy′dro•pon′ics
hy′dro•pow′er
hy′dro•sphere′
hy′dro•stat′ic *also*
  hy′dro•stat′i•cal
hy′dro•ther′a•py
hy′drot′ro•pism
hy′drous
hy•drox′ide
hy•drox′yl
hy′dro•zo′an
hy•e′na *also*
  hy•ae′na
hy′giene′
hy′gi•en′ic
hy′gien′ist
hy′grom′e•ter
hy′gro•met′ric

hy•grom′e•try
hy′gro•scope′
hy′gro•scop′ic
hy′men
hy′me•ne′al
hymn *(song)*
  ✔ *him*
hym′nal
hype, hyped,
  hyp′ing
hy′per•ac′id
hy′per•a•cid′i•ty
hy′per•ac′tive
hy•per′bo•la *pl.* -las
  or -lae
hy•per′bo•le
hy′per•bol′ic
hy′per•crit′i•cal
  (overcritical)
  ✔ *hypocritical*
hy′per•gly•ce′mi•a
hy′per•sen′si•tive
hy′per•sen′si•tiv′i•
  ty
hy′per•son′ic
hy′per•ten′sion
hy′per•text′
hy′per•thy′roid′
hy′per•thy′roid•
  ism
hy•per′tro•phy
hy′per•ven′ti•late′,
  -lat′ed, -lat′ing
hy′per•ven′ti•la′-
  tion
hy′pha *pl.* -phae
hy′phen

hy′phen•ate′,
  -at′ed, -at′ing
hy′phen•a′tion
hyp•no′sis *pl.* -ses
hyp′no•ther′a•py
hyp•not′ic
hyp′no•tism
hyp′no•tist
hyp′no•tize′,
  -tized′, -tiz′ing
hyp′no•tiz′er
hy′po *pl.* -pos
hy′po•chon′dri•a
hy′po•chon′dri•
  ac′
hy•poc′ri•sy
hyp′o•crite′
hyp′o•crit′i•cal
  (insincere)
  ✔ *hypercritical*
hy′po•der′mic
hy′po•gly•ce′mi•a
hy′po•sul′fite′
hy′po•sul•fu′rous
  ac′id
hy•pot′e•nuse′
hy′•po•thal′a•mus
hy•poth′e•sis *pl.*
  -ses′
hy•poth′e•size′,
  -sized′, -siz′ing
hy′po•thet′i•cal
  also hy′po•thet′ic
hy′po•thy′roid•ism
hy′rax′ *pl.* -rax′es *or*
  -ra•ces′
hys′sop

hys·ter·ec′to·my
hys·ter′i·a
hys·ter′ic
hys·ter′i·cal

I

I *pron.*
  ✓ *aye, eye*
i′amb′
i·am′bic
l·be′ri·an
i′bex′ *pl.* i′bex′ *or*
  i′bex·es
i′bis *pl.* i′bis *or*
  i′bis·es
ice, iced, ic′ing
ice′berg′
ice′boat′
ice′bound′
ice′box′
ice′break′er
ice′cap′ *or* ice′ cap′
ice′-cold′
ice′ cream′
ice′-cream′ cone′
Ice′land·er
Ice·land′ic
ice′man
ice′ skate′ *n.*
ice′-skate′, -skat′ed,
  -skat′ing
ice′ skat′er
ich·neu′mon
ich′thy·ol′o·gist

ich′thy·ol′o·gy
ich′thy·o·saur′
i′ci·cle
i′ci·ly
i′ci·ness
ic′ing
i′con′
i·con′o·clast′
i·con′o·clas′tic
ic′y
i·de′a
i·de′al
i·de′al·ism
i·de′al·ist
i·de′al·is′tic
i·de′al·i·za′tion
i·de′al·ize′, -ized′,
  -iz′ing
i·den′ti·cal
i·den′ti·fi′a·ble
i·den′ti·fi·ca′tion
i·den′ti·fy′, -fied′,
  fy′ing
i·den′ti·ty
id′e·o·gram′
id′e·o·graph′
l′de·o·log′i·cal
i′de·ol′o·gy
ides
id′i·o·cy
id′i·om
id′i·o·mat′ic
id′i·o·syn′cra·sy
id′i·o·syn·crat′ic
id′i·ot
id′i·ot′ic
id′i·ot′i·cal·ly

i′dle *(to pass time
  lazily)*, i′dled,
  i′dling
  ✓ *idol, idyll*
i′dly
i′dler
i′dol *(image)*
  ✓ *idle, idyll*
i·dol′a·ter *or*
  i·dol′a·tor
i·dol′a·trous
i·dol′a·try
i′dol·ize′, -ized′,
  -iz′ing
i′dyll *also* i′dyl
  (poem)
  ✓ *idle, idol*
i·dyl′lic
i·dyl′li·cal·ly
if
if′fy
ig′loo *pl.* -loos
ig′ne·ous
ig·nite′, -nit′ed,
  -nit′ing
ig·ni′tion
ig·no′ble
ig·no′bly
ig′no·min′i·ous
ig′no·min′y
ig′no·ra′mus *pl.*
  -mus·es
ig′no·rance
ig′no·rant
ig·nore′, -nored′,
  -nor′ing
i·gua′na

il′e•ac′
il′e•i′tis
il′e•um (*intestine*),
  pl. -e•a
il′i•um (*bone*), pl.
  -i•a
ilk
ill, worse, worst
ill′-ad•vised′
ill′-bred′
il•le′gal
il′le•gal′i•ty
il′leg′i•ble
il′le•git′i•ma•cy
il′le•git′i•mate
ill′-fat′ed
ill′-fa′vored
ill′-got′ten
ill′-hu′mored
il•lib′er•al
il•lic′it (*unlawful*)
  ✔ elicit
il•lim′it•a•ble
il•lit′er•a•cy
il•lit′er•ate
ill′-man′nered
ill′-na′tured
ill′ness
il•log′i•cal
ill′-starred′
ill′-tem′pered
ill′-timed′
ill′-treat′
ill′-treat′ment
il•lu′mi•nate′,
  -nat′ed, -nat′ing
il•lu′mi•na′tion

il•lu′mine, -mined,
  -min•ing
ill′-us′age
ill′-use′, -used′,
  -us′ing
ill′-use′ n.
il•lu′sion (*miscon-
  ception*)
  ✔ allusion
il•lu′sive (*deceptive*)
  ✔ allusive, elusive
il•lu′so•ry
il′lus•trate′,
  -trat′ed, -trat′ing
il′lus•tra′tion
il′lus•tra′tive
il′lus•tra′tor
il•lus′tri•ous
im′age
im′age•ry
i•mag′i•na•ble
i•mag′i•nar′y
i•mag′i•na′tion
i•mag′i•na•tive
i•mag′ine, -ined,
  -in′ing
i•ma′go pl. -goes or
  -gi•nes′
i•mam′
im•bal′ance
im•be•cile
im•bibe′, -bibed′,
  -bib′ing
im•bro′glio pl.
  -glios
im•bue′, -bued′,
  -bu′ing

im′i•ta•ble
im′i•tate′, -tat′ed,
  -tat′ing
im′i•ta′tion
im′i•ta′tive
im′i•ta′tor
im•mac′u•late
im•ma′nent
  (*inherent*)
  ✔ eminent, immi-
  nent
im•ma•te′ri•al
im•ma•ture′
im•ma•tur′i•ty
im•meas′ur•a•ble
im•me′di•a•cy
im•me′di•ate
im•me•mo′ri•al
im•mense′
im•men′si•ty
im•merse′,
  -mersed′, -mers′ing
im•mer′sion
im′mi•grant (*one
  who settles in a for-
  eign country*)
  ✔ emigrant
im′mi•grate′ (*to set-
  tle in a foreign coun-
  try*), -grat′ed,
  -grat′ing
  ✔ emigrate
im′mi•gra′tion
  (*settling in a foreign
  country*)
  ✔ emigration
im′mi•nence

im'mi·nent *(about to happen)*
✔ eminent, immanent
im·mo'bile
im·mo·bil'i·ty
im·mo'bi·li·za'tion
im·mo'bi·lize', -lized', -liz'ing
im·mod'er·ate
im·mod'est
im·mod'es·ty
im'mo·late', -lat'ed, -lat'ing
im·mo·la'tion
im·mor'al
im·mor·al'i·ty
im·mor'tal
im·mor·tal'i·ty
im·mor'tal·ize', -ized', -iz'ing
im·mov'a·ble
im·mune'
im·mu'ni·ty
im·mu'ni·za'tion
im'mu·nize', -nized', -niz'ing
im'mu·nol'o·gy
im·mure', -mured', -mur'ing
im·mu'ta·bil'i·ty
or im·mu'ta·ble·ness
im·mu'ta·bly
imp
im'pact' *n.*
im·pact' *v.*

im·pair'
im·pair'ment
im·pa'la
im·pale', -paled', -pal'ing
im·pal'pa·ble
im·pal'pa·bly
im·pan'el, -eled or -elled, -el'ing or -el'ling
im·part'
im·par'tial
im'par·ti·al'i·ty
im·pass'a·bil'i·ty
im·pass'a·ble *(impossible to cross)*
✔ impassible
im·pass'a·bly
im'passe'
im·pass'i·ble *(unfeeling)*
✔ impassable
im·pas'sioned
im·pas'sive
im'pas·siv'i·ty
im·pa'tience
im·pa'tient
im·peach'
im·pec'ca·ble
im·pec'ca·bly
im'pe·cu'ni·ous
im·pede', -ped'ed, -ped'ing
im·ped'i·ment
im·pel', -pelled', -pel'ling
im·pend'

im·pen'e·tra·bil'i·ty
im·pen'e·tra·ble
im·pen'e·tra·bly
im·pen'i·tent
im·per'a·tive
im'per·cep'ti·bil'i·ty
im'per·cep'ti·ble
im'per·cep'ti·bly
im·per'fect
im·per·fec'tion
im·per'fo·rate
im·pe'ri·al
im·pe'ri·al·ism
im·pe'ri·al·ist
im·pe'ri·al·is'tic
im·per'il, -iled or -illed, -il'ing or -il'ling
im·pe'ri·ous
im·per'ish·a·ble
im·per'ma·nence
im·per'ma·nent
im·per'me·a·ble
im·per'son·al
im·per'son·al'i·ty
im·per'son·ate', -at'ed, -at'ing
im·per'son·a'tion
im·per'son·a'tor
im·per'ti·nence
im·per'ti·nent
im'per·turb'a·bil'i·ty
im'per·turb'a·ble
im'per·turb'a·bly

im·per'vi·ous
im·pe·ti'go *pl.* -gos
im·pet'u·os'i·ty
im·pet'u·ous
im·pe'tus *pl.* -tus·es
im·pi'e·ty
im·pinge',
  -pinged', -ping'ing
im'pi·ous
imp'ish
im·plac'a·bil'i·ty
im·plac'a·ble
im·plac'a·bly
im·plant' *v.*
im'plant' *n.*
im'plan·ta'tion
im·plau'si·bil'i·ty
im·plau'si·ble
im·plau'si·bly
im'ple·ment
im'ple·men·ta'tion
im'pli·cate',
  -cat·ed, -cat·ing
im'pli·ca'tion
im·plic'it
im·plode',
  -plod·ed, -plod·ing
im·plore', -plored',
  -plor'ing
im·plo'sion
im·plo'sive
im·ply', -plied',
  -ply'ing
im'po·lite'
im·pol'i·tic
im·pon'der·a·ble
im·port' *v.*

im·port' *n.*
im·por'tance
im·por'tant
im'por·ta'tion
im·port'er
im·por'tu·nate
im'por·tune',
  -tuned', -tun'ing
im'por·tu'ni·ty
im·pose', -posed',
  -pos'ing
im'po·si'tion
im·pos'si·bil'i·ty
im·pos'si·ble
im·pos'si·bly
im·post'
im·pos'tor
im·pos'ture
im·po'tence
im·po'tent
im·pound'
im·pov'er·ish
im·prac'ti·ca·ble
im·prac'ti·ca·bly
im·prac'ti·cal
im·prac'ti·cal'i·ty
im'pre·cate',
  -cat·ed, -cat·ing
im'pre·ca'tion
im'pre·ca·to'ry
im'pre·cise'
im'pre·ci'sion
im·preg'na·ble
im·preg'na·bly
im·preg'nate',
  -nat·ed, -nat·ing
im'preg·na'tion

im'pre·sa'ri·o' *pl.*
  -os'
im·press' *v.*
im'press' *n.*
im·pres'sion
im·pres'sion·a·bil'-
  i·ty
im·pres'sion·a·ble
im·pres'sion·ism
im·pres'sion·ist
im·pres'sion·is'tic
im·pres'sive
im·print' *v.*
im'print' *n.*
im·pris'on
im·pris'on·ment
im·prob'a·bil'i·ty
im·prob'a·ble
im·prob'a·bly
im·promp'tu
im·prop'er
im'pro·pri'e·ty
im·prove',
  -proved', -prov'ing
im·prove'ment
im·prov'i·dence
im·prov'i·dent
im·prov'i·sa'tion
im'pro·vise',
  -vised', -vis'ing
im'pro·vis'er
im·pru'dence
im·pru'dent
im·pu'dence
im·pu'dent
im·pugn'
im'pulse

im·pul'sion
im·pul'sive
im·pu'ni·ty
im·pure', -pur'er,
  -pur'est
im·pu'ri·ty
im·put'a·ble
im·pu·ta'tion
im·pute', -put'ed,
  -put'ing
in (within)
  ✓ inn
in'a·bil'i·ty
in'ac·ces'si·ble
in'ac·ces'si·bly
in·ac'cu·ra·cy
in·ac'cu·rate
in·ac'tion
in·ac'tive
in·ac·tiv'i·ty
in·ad'e·qua·cy
in·ad'e·quate
in'ad·mis'si·bil'i·ty
in'ad·mis'si·ble
in'ad·ver'tence
in'ad·ver'tent
in'ad·vis'a·bil'i·ty
in'ad·vis'a·ble
in·al'ien·a·ble
in·ane'
in·an'i·mate
in·an'i·ty
in·ap'pli·ca·bil'i·ty
in·ap'pli·ca·ble
in'ap·pre'cia·ble
in'ap·pre'cia·bly
in'ap·pro'pri·ate

in·apt'
in·ap'ti·tude'
in'ar·tic'u·late
in'ar·tis'tic
in'as·much' as'
in'at·ten'tion
in'at·ten'tive
in·au'di·ble
in·au'di·bly
in·au'gu·ral
in·au'gu·rate',
  -rat'ed, -rat'ing
in·au'gu·ra'tion
in'aus·pi'cious
in'board'
in'born'
in'bound'
in'bred'
in'breed', -bred',
  -breed'ing
in'breed'ing
In'ca pl. -ca or -cas
in·cal'cu·la·bil'i·ty
in·cal'cu·la·ble
In'can
in'can·des'cence
in'can·des'cent
in'can·ta'tion
in·ca'pa·bil'i·ty
in·ca'pa·ble
in'ca·pac'i·tate',
  -tat'ed, -tat'ing
in'ca·pac'i·ta'tion
in'ca·pac'i·ty
in·car'cer·ate',
  -at'ed, -at'ing
in·car'cer·a'tion

in·car'nate',
  -nat'ed, -nat'ing
in'car·na'tion
in·cau'tious
in·cen'di·ar'y
in·cense' (to infuri-
  ate), -censed',
  -cens'ing
in'cense' (aromatic
  substance)
in·cen'tive
in·cep'tion
in·cer'ti·tude'
in·ces'sant
in'cest'
in·ces'tu·ous
in·cho'ate
inch'worm'
in'ci·dence
in'ci·dent
in'ci·den'tal
in·cin'er·ate',
  -at'ed, -at'ing
in·cin'er·a'tion
in·cin'er·a'tor
in·cip'i·en·cy or
  in·cip'i·ence
in·cip'i·ent
in·cise', -cised',
  -cis'ing
in·ci'sion
in·ci'sive
in·ci'sor
in·cite' (to provoke),
  -cit'ed, -cit'ing
  ✓ insight
in·cite'ment

in·clem'en·cy
in·clem'ent
in'cli·na'tion
in·cline', -clined',
-clin'ing
in·clude', -clud·ed,
-clud'ing
in·clu'sion
in·clu'sive
in'cog·ni'to
in'co·her'ence *also*
in'co·her'en·cy
in'co·her'ent
in'com·bus'ti·ble
in'come'
in'com'ing
in'com·men'su·
rate
in'com·mode',
-mod'ed, -mod'ing
in'com·mo'di·ous
in'com·mu'ni·ca·
ble
in'com·mu'ni·
ca'do
in'com·mu'ni·ca·
tive
in·com'pa·ra·ble
in·com'pa·ra·bly
in'com·pat'i·bil'-
i·ty
in'com·pat'i·ble
in'com·pat'i·bly
in·com'pe·tence *or*
in·com'pe·ten·cy
in·com'pe·tent
in'com·plete'

in'com·pre·hen'-
si·bil'i·ty
in'com·pre·hen'-
si·ble
in'com·pre·hen'-
si·bly
in'com·pre·hen'-
sion
in'com·press'i·ble
in'con·ceiv'a·bil'-
i·ty
in'con·ceiv'a·ble
in'con·ceiv'a·bly
in'con·clu'sive
in·con'gru·ent
in'con·gru'i·ty
in·con'gru·ous
in·con'se·quen'-
tial
in'con·sid'er·a·ble
in'con·sid'er·a·bly
in'con·sid'er·ate
in'con·sis'ten·cy
in'con·sis'tent
in'con·sol'a·ble
in'con·sol'a·bly
in'con·spic'u·ous
in·con'stan·cy
in·con'stant
in'con·test'a·ble
in·con'ti·nence
in·con'ti·nent
in'con·tro·vert'i·
ble
in'con·tro·vert'i·
bly
in'con·ven'ience,

-ienced, -ienc·ing
in'con·ven'ient
in·cor'po·rate',
-rat'ed, -rat'ing
in'cor·po're·al
in'cor·rect'
in'cor·ri·gi·bil'i·ty
in·cor'ri·gi·ble
in·cor'ri·gi·bly
in'cor·rupt'i·bil'-
i·ty
in'cor·rupt'i·ble
in·crease',
-creased',
-creas'ing
in'crease' *n.*
in·cred'i·ble *(unbe-
lievable)*
✔ *incredulous*
in·cred'i·bly
in'cre·du'li·ty
in·cred'u·lous
(skeptical)
✔ *incredible*
in'cre·ment
in·crim'i·nate',
-nat'ed, -nat'ing
in·crim'i·na'tion
in·crim'i·na'tor
in·crim'i·na·to'ry
in·crust'
in'cu·bate', -bat'ed,
-bat'ing
in'cu·ba'tion
in'cu·ba'tor
in'cul·cate',
-cat'ed, -cat'ing

in·cul·ca'tion
in·cum'ben·cy
in·cum'bent
in·cur', -curred',
　-cur'ring
in·cur'a·ble
in·cur'a·bly
in·cu'ri·ous
in·cur'sion
in'cus *pl.* in·cu'des
in·debt'ed
in·de·cen·cy
in·de·cent
in'de·ci'pher·
　a·ble
in·de·ci'sion
in·de·ci'sive
in·dec'o·rous
in·deed'
in'de·fat'i·ga·ble
in'de·fat'i·ga·bly
in'de·fen'si·ble
in'de·fen'si·bly
in'de·fin'a·ble
in'de·fin'a·bly
in·def'i·nite
in·del'i·bil'i·ty *or*
　in·del'i·ble·ness
in·del'i·ble
in·del'i·bly
in·del'i·ca·cy
in·del'i·cate
in·dem'ni·fi·ca'-
　tion
in·dem'ni·fy',
　-fied', -fy'ing
in·dem'ni·ty

in·dent'
in·den·ta'tion
in·den'ture, -tured,
　-tur·ing
in'de·pend'ence
in'de·pend'ent
in'-depth'
in'de·scrib'a·ble
in'de·scrib'a·bly
in'de·struc'ti·ble
in'de·struc'ti·bly
in'de·ter'mi·nate
in'dex' *pl.* -dex'es *or*
　-di·ces'
In'di·an
In'di·an'an *or*
　In'di·an'i·an
In'dic
in'di·cate', -cat'ed,
　-cat'ing
in'di·ca'tion
in·dic'a·tive
in'di·ca'tor
in·dict' *(to accuse)*
　✔ indite
in·dict'a·ble
in·dict'er *or*
　in·dic'tor
in·dict'ment
in'dif'fer·ence
in'dif'fer·ent
in'di·gence
in·dig'e·nous
in'di·gent
in'di·gest'i·ble
in'di·ges'tion
in·dig'nant

in'dig·na'tion
in·dig'ni·ty
in'di·go' *pl.* -gos' *or*
　-goes'
in'di·rect'
in'di·rec'tion
in'dis·creet' *(lack-*
　ing discretion)
in'dis·crete' *(not*
　divided)
in'dis·cre'tion
in'dis·crim'i·nate
in'dis·pen'sa·ble
in'dis·pen'sa·bly
in'dis·posed'
in'dis·po·si'tion
in'dis·put'a·ble
in'dis·put'a·bly
in'dis·sol'u·ble
in'dis·sol'u·bly
in'dis·tinct'
in'dis·tin'guish·
　a·ble
in·dite' *(to write)*
　✔ indict
in'di·um
in'di·vid'u·al
in'di·vid'u·al·ism
in'di·vid'u·al·ist
in'di·vid'u·al·is'tic
in'di·vid'u·al'i·ty
in'di·vid'u·al·ize',
　-ized', -iz'ing
in'di·vis'i·bil'i·ty
in'di·vis'i·ble
in'di·vis'i·bly
In'do·chi·nese'

in·doc'tri·nate',
  -nat'ed, -nat'ing
in·doc'tri·na'tion
In'do-Eu·ro·pe'an
In'do-I·ra'ni·an
in'do·lence
in'do·lent
in·dom'i·ta·ble
in·dom'i·ta·bly
In'do·ne'sian
in'door' *adj.*
in'doors' *adv.*
in·du'bi·ta·ble
in·du'bi·ta·bly
in·duce', -duced',
  -duc'ing
in·duce'ment
in·duct'
in·duc'tance
in·duct·ee'
in·duc'tion
in·duc'tive
in·duc'tor
in·dulge', -dulged',
  -dulg'ing
in·dul'gence
in·dul'gent
in·dus'tri·al
in·dus'tri·al·ist
in·dus'tri·al·i·za'-
  tion
in·dus'tri·al·ize',
  -ized', -iz'ing
in·dus'tri·ous
in'dus·try
in·e'bri·ate', -at'ed,
  -at'ing

in·e'bri·a'tion
in·ed'i·ble
in·ef'fa·ble
in·ef'fa·bly
in·ef·fec'tive
in·ef·fec'tu·al
in·ef·fi'cien·cy
in·ef·fi'cient
in·e·las'tic
in·e·las·tic'i·ty
in·el'e·gance
in·el'e·gant
in·el'i·gi·bil'i·ty
in·el'i·gi·ble
in·el'i·gi·bly
in·ept'
in·ep'ti·tude'
in·e·qual'i·ty
in·eq'ui·ta·ble
in·eq'ui·ta·bly
in·eq'ui·ty *(unfair-
  ness)*
  ✔ *iniquity*
in·ert'
in·er'tia
in·es·cap'a·ble
in·es·cap'a·bly
in·es'ti·ma·ble
in·es'ti·ma·bly
in·ev'i·ta·bil'i·ty
in·ev'i·ta·ble
in·ev'i·ta·bly
in·ex·act'
in·ex·cus'a·ble
in·ex·cus'a·bly
in·ex·haust'i·ble
in·ex·haust'i·bly

in·ex'o·ra·ble
in·ex'o·ra·bly
in·ex·pe'di·ent
in·ex·pen'sive
in·ex·pe'ri·ence
in·ex·pe'ri·enced
in·ex'pert'
in·ex'pli·ca·ble
in·ex'pli·ca·bly
in·ex·press'i·ble
in·ex·press'i·bly
in·ex·tin'guish·
  a·ble
in·ex'tri·ca·ble
in·fal'li·bil'i·ty
in·fal'li·ble
in'fa·mous
in'fa·my
in'fan·cy
in'fant
in·fan'ti·cide'
in'fan·tile'
in'fan·try
in'fan·try·man
in·fat'u·ate', -at'ed,
  -at'ing
in·fat'u·a'tion
in·fect'
in·fec'tion
in·fec'tious
in·fe·lic'i·tous
in·fe·lic'i·ty
in·fer', -ferred',
  -fer'ring
in·fer'a·ble
in'fer·ence
in'fer·en'tial

in•fe′ri•or
in•fe′ri•or′i•ty
in•fer′nal
in•fer′no *pl.* -nos
in•fer′tile
in′fer•til′i•ty
in•fest′
in′fes•ta′tion
in′fi•del
in′fi•del′i•ty
in′field′
in′field′er
in′fight′ing
in′fil•trate′,
  -trat′ed, -trat′ing
in′fil•tra′tion
in′fi•nite
in•fin•i•tes′i•mal
in•fin′i•tive
in•fin′i•ty
in•firm′
in•fir′ma•ry
in•fir′mi•ty
in•flame′, -flamed′,
  -flam′ing
in•flam′ma•ble
  (easily ignited)
  ✔ *flammable,*
  nonflammable
in′flam•ma′tion
in•flam′ma•to′ry
in•flat′a•ble
in•flate′, -flat′ed,
  -flat′ing
in•flat′er *or* in•fla′tor
in•fla′tion
in•fla′tion•ar′y

in•flect′
in•flec′tion
in•flex′i•bil′i•ty
in•flex′i•ble
in•flict′
in•flic′tion
in′flo•res′cence
in′flow′
in′flu•ence, -enced,
  -enc•ing
in′flu•en′tial
in′flu•en′za
in′flux′
in′fo
in•form′
in•for′mal
in′for•mal′i•ty
in•form′ant
in′for•ma′tion
in•form′a•tive
in•formed′
in•form′er
in•frac′tion
in′fra•red′
in′fra•son′ic
in′fra•struc′ture
in•fre′quen•cy *or*
  in•fre′quence
in•fre′quent
in•fringe′,
  -fringed′, -fring′ing
in•fringe′ment
in•fu′ri•ate′, -at′ed,
  -at′ing
in•fuse′, -fused′,
  -fus′ing
in•fus′i•ble

in•fu′sion
in•gen′ious *(clever)*
  ✔ *ingenuous*
in•gé′nue′
in′ge•nu′i•ty
in•gen′u•ous
  (candid)
  ✔ *ingenious*
in•gest′
in•ges′tion
in•glo′ri•ous
in′got
in•grain′
in•grained′
in′grate′
in•gra′ti•ate′,
  -at′ed, -at′ing
in•gra′ti•a′tion
in•grat′i•tude′
in•gre′di•ent
in′gress′
in′grown′
in•hab′it
in•hab′it•a•ble
in•hab′i•tant
in•ha′lant
in′ha•la′tion
in′ha•la′tor
in•hale′, -haled′,
  -hal′ing
in•hal′er
in′har•mo′ni•ous
in•her′ent
in•her′it
in•her′it•a•ble
in•her′i•tance
in•her′i•tor

in·hib′it
in′hi·bi′tion
in·hib′i·tor
in·hib′i·to′ry
in·hos′pi·ta·ble
in·hos′pi·ta·bly
in′-house′ *adj.* &
  adv.
in·hu′man
in·hu′mane′
in′hu·man′i·ty
in·im′i·cal
in·im′i·ta·bil′i·ty
in·im′i·ta·ble
in·im′i·ta·bly
in·iq′ui·tous
in ✔ iq′ui·ty *(sin)*
  ✔ *inequity*
in·i′tial, -tialed *also*
  -tialled, -tial·ing
  also -tial·ling
in·i′ti·ate′, -at′ed,
  -at′ing
in·i′ti·a′tion
in·i′ti·a·tive
in·i′ti·a′tor
in·ject′
in·jec′tion
in·jec′tor
in′ju·di′cious
in·junc′tion
in′jure, -jured,
  -jur·ing
in′ju′ri·ous
in′ju·ry
in·jus′tice
ink′blot′

ink′horn′
in′kling
ink′stand′
ink′well′
ink′y
in′laid′
in′land
in′-law′
in′lay′, -laid′,
  -lay·ing
in′let′
in′mate′
in′most′
inn *(hotel)*
  ✔ *in*
in′nards
in′nate′
in′ner
in′ner-cit′y *adj.*
in′ner·most′
in′ner·vate′,
  -vat′ed, -vat′ing
in′ning
inn′keep′er
in′no·cence
in′no·cent
in·noc′u·ous
in′no·vate′, -vat′ed,
  -vat′ing
in′no·va′tion
in′no·va′tive
in′no·va′tor
in′nu·en′do *pl.*
  -does
in·nu′mer·a·ble
in·nu′mer·a·bly
in·nu′mer·ate

in·oc′u·late′,
  -lat′ed, -lat′ing
in·oc′u·la′tion
in′of·fen′sive
in·op′er·a·ble
in·op′er·a·tive
in′op·por·tune′
in·or′di·nate
in′or·gan′ic
in·pa′tient
in′put′, -put′ted *or*
  -put′, -put′ting
in′quest′
in·qui′e·tude′
in·quire′ *also*
  en·quire′, -quired′,
  -quir′ing
in·quir′y *also*
  en·quir′y
in′qui·si′tion
in·quis′i·tive
in·quis′i·tor
in·quis′i·to′ri·al
in′road′
in′rush′
in′sa·lu′bri·ous
in·sane′
in·san′i·tar′y
in·san′i·ty
in·sa′tia·ble
in·sa′tia·bly
in·sa′ti·ate
in·scribe′, -scribed′,
  -scrib′ing
in·scrip′tion
in·scru′ta·bil′i·ty
in·scru′ta·ble

in•scru'ta•bly
in'seam'
in'sect'
in•sec'ti•cide'
in•sec'ti•vore'
in'sec•tiv'o•rous
in•se•cure'
in•se•cu'ri•ty
in•sem'i•nate',
  -nat'ed, -nat'ing
in•sem'i•na'tion
in•sen'sate'
in•sen'si•bil'i•ty
in•sen'si•ble
in•sen'si•bly
in•sen'si•tive
in•sen'si•tiv'i•ty
in•sep'a•ra•bil'i•ty
in•sep'a•ra•ble
in•sep'a•ra•bly
in•sert' *v.*
in'sert' *n.*
in•ser'tion
in•set', -set',
  -set'ting
in'shore'
in•side'
in•sid'er
in•sid'i•ous
in'sight' *(under-*
  standing)
  ✔ incite
in•sight'ful
in•sig'ni•a *pl.* -ni•a
  or -ni•as
in'sig•nif'i•cance
in'sig•nif'i•cant

in'sin•cere'
in'sin•cer'i•ty
in•sin'u•ate',
  -at'ed, -at'ing
in•sin'u•a'tion
in•sip'id
in•sist'
in•sis'tence *or*
  in•sis'ten•cy
in•sis'tent
in'so•far' as
in'sole'
in'so•lence
in'so•lent
in•sol'u•bil'i•ty
in•sol'u•ble
in•sol'u•bly
in•sol'ven•cy
in•sol'vent
in•som'ni•a
in•som'ni•ac'
in'so•much' as
in•sou'ci•ance
in•sou'ci•ant
in•spect'
in•spec'tion
in•spec'tor
in'spi•ra'tion
in'spi•ra'tion•al
in•spire', -spired',
  -spir'ing
in•spir'it
in'sta•bil'i•ty
in•stall' *also*
  in'stal', -stalled',
  -stall'ing
in'stal•la'tion

in•stall'ment
in'stance
in'stant
in'stan•ta'ne•ous
in•stead'
in'step'
in'sti•gate', -gat'ed,
  -gat'ing
in'sti•ga'tion
in'sti•ga'tor
in•still'
in'stinct
in•stinc'tive
in•stinc'tu•al
in'sti•tute', -tut'ed,
  -tut'ing
in'sti•tu'tion
in'sti•tu'tion•al
in'sti•tu'tion•al•
  ize', -ized', -iz'ing
in•struct'
in•struc'tion
in•struc'tive
in•struc'tor
in'stru•ment
in'stru•men'tal
in'stru•men'tal•ist
in'stru•men•tal'i•ty
in'stru•men•ta'-
  tion
in•sub•or'di•nate
in•sub•or'di•na'-
  tion
in'sub•stan'tial
in'sub•stan'ti•al'-
  i•ty
in•suf'fer•a•ble

in·suf'fer·a·bly
in'suf·fi'cien·cy
in'suf·fi'cient
in·su'lar
in·su·lar'i·ty
in'su·late', -lat'ed,
  -lat'ing
in'su·la'tion
in'su·la'tor
in'su·lin *v.*
in·sult' *v.*
in'sult' *n.*
in·su'per·a·ble
in·su'per·a·bly
in'sup·port'a·ble
in·sur'a·ble
in·sur'ance
in·sure' *(to cover*
  with insurance, to
  make sure), -sured',
  -sur'ing
  ✔ assure, ensure
in·sur'er
in·sur'gence
in·sur'gen·cy
in·sur'gent
in'sur·mount'a·ble
in'sur·rec'tion
in·tact'
in'take'
in·tan'gi·ble
in·tan'gi·bly
in'te·ger
in'te·gral
in'te·grate',
  -grat'ed, -grat'ing
in'te·gra'tion

in·teg'ri·ty
in·teg'u·ment
in'tel·lect'
in'tel·lec'tu·al
in·tel'li·gence
in·tel'li·gent
in·tel'li·gent'si·a
in·tel'li·gi·bil'i·ty
in·tel'li·gi·ble
in·tel'li·gi·bly
in·tem'per·ance
in·tem'per·ate
in·tend'
in·tend'ed
in·tense'
in·ten'si·fi·ca'tion
in·ten'si·fi'er
in·ten'si·fy', -fied',
  -fy'ing
in·ten'si·ty
in·ten'sive
in·tent'
in·ten'tion
in·ten'tion·al
in·ter', -terred',
  -ter'ring
in'ter·act'
in'ter·ac'tion
in'ter·ac'tive
in'ter·breed',
  -bred', -breed'ing
in'ter·cede',
  -ced'ed, -ced'ing
in'ter·cel'lu·lar
in'ter·cept'
in'ter·cep'tion
in'ter·cep'tor *also*

in'ter·cept'er
in'ter·ces'sion
in'ter·ces'sor
in'ter·change',
  -changed',
  -chang'ing
in'ter·change' *n.*
in'ter·change'a·ble
in'ter·change'-
  a·bly
in'ter·col·le'giate
in'ter·com'
in'ter·com·mu'ni·
  cate', -cat'ed,
  -cat'ing
in'ter·com·mu'ni·
  ca'tion
in'ter·con·nect'
in'ter·con·nec'tion
in'ter·con·ti·nen'-
  tal
in'ter·course'
in'ter·de·nom'i·
  na'tion·al
in'ter·de·part·
  men'tal
in'ter·de·pend'-
  ence
in'ter·de·pend'ent
in'ter·dict'
in'ter·dic'tion
in'ter·dis·ci·pli·
  nar'y
in'ter·est
in'ter·face', -faced',
  -fac'ing
in'ter·faith'

in'ter·fere', -fered',
  -fer'ing
in'ter·fer'ence
in'ter·fer·on'
in'ter·ga·lac'tic
in'ter·im
in·te'ri·or
in'ter·ject'
in'ter·jec'tion
in'ter·lace', -laced',
  -lac'ing
in'ter·lard'
in'ter·lock'
in'ter·loc'u·tor
in'ter·lop'er
in'ter·lude'
in'ter·mar'riage
in'ter·mar'ry, -ried,
  -ry·ing
in'ter·me'di·ar'y
in'ter·me'di·ate
in·ter'ment
in'ter·mez'zo *pl.*
  -zos *or* -zi
in·ter'mi·na·ble
in·ter'mi·na·bly
in'ter·min'gle,
  -gled, -gling
in'ter·mis'sion
in'ter·mit'tent
in'ter·mix'
in'tern' *also*
  in'terne'
in·ter'nal
in·ter'nal·ize',
  -ized', -iz'ing
in'ter·na'tion·al

in'ter·na'tion·al·
  ism
in'ter·na'tion·al·
  ize', -ized', -iz'ing
in'ter·nec'ine'
in'tern·ee'
In'ter·net'
in'ter·nist'
in·tern'ment
in'tern·ship'
in'ter·per'son·al
in'ter·phase'
in'ter·plan'e·tar'y
in'ter·play'
in·ter'po·late',
  -lat'ed, -lat'ing
in·ter'po·la'tion
in·ter'po·la'tor
in'ter·pose',
  -posed', -pos'ing
in'ter·po·si'tion
in·ter'pret
in·ter'pret·a·ble
in·ter'pre·ta'tion
in·ter'pret·er
in·ter'pre·tive *also*
  in·ter'pre·ta'tive
in'ter·ra'cial
in'ter·reg'num *pl.*
  -nums *or* -na
in'ter·re·late',
  -lat'ed, -lat'ing
in'ter·re·la'tion
in'ter·re·la'tion·
  ship'
in·ter'ro·gate',
  -gat'ed, -gat'ing

in·ter'ro·ga'tion
in·ter'rog·a'tive
in·ter'ro·ga'tor
in·ter'rog·a·to'ry
in'ter·rupt'
in'ter·rup'tion
in'ter·scho·las'tic
in'ter·sect'
in'ter·sec'tion
in'ter·sperse',
  -spersed',
  -spers'ing
in'ter·sper'sion
in'ter·state' *(be-*
  tween states)
  ✔ intrastate
in'ter·stel'lar
in·ter'stice *pl.*
  -sti·ces'
in'ter·sti'tial
in'ter·twine',
  -twined',
  -twin'ing
in'ter·val
in'ter·vene',
  -vened', -ven'ing
in'ter·ven'tion
in'ter·view'
in'ter·view'er
in'ter·weave',
  -wove', -wo'ven,
  -weav'ing
in·tes'tate'
in·tes'ti·nal
in·tes'tine
in'ti·ma·cy
in'ti·mate *adj. & n.*

in'ti·mate',
  -mat'ed, -mat'ing
in'ti·ma'tion
in·tim'i·date',
  -dat'ed, -dat'ing
in·tim'i·da'tion
in·tim'i·da'tor
in'to
in·tol'er·a·ble
in·tol'er·a·bly
in·tol'er·ance
in·tol'er·ant
in'to·na'tion
in·tone', -toned',
  -ton'ing
in·tox'i·cant
in·tox'i·cate',
  -cat'ed, -cat'ing
in·tox'i·ca'tion
in·tox'i·ca'tor
in'tra·cel'lu·lar
in·trac'ta·bil'i·ty
in·trac'ta·ble
in·trac'ta·bly
in'tra·mu'ral
in·tran'si·gence
in·tran'si·gent
in·tran'si·tive
in'tra·state' *(within a state)*
  ✔ interstate
in'tra·u'ter·ine
in'tra·ve'nous
in·trep'id
in'tre·pid'i·ty
in'tri·ca·cy
in'tri·cate

in'trigue' *n.*
in·trigue', -trigued',
  -trigu'ing
in·trin'sic
in'tro' *pl.* -tros'
in'tro·duce',
  -duced', -duc'ing
in'tro·duc'tion
in'tro·duc'to·ry
in'tro·spec'tion
in'tro·spec'tive
in'tro·ver'sion
in'tro·vert'
in·trude', -trud'ed,
  -trud'ing
in·trud'er
in·tru'sion
in·tru'sive
in·tu'i·tion
in·tu'i·tive
In'u·it *pl.* -it *or* -its
in·un'date',
  -dat'ed, -dat'ing
in'un·da'tion
in·ure', -ured',
  -ur'ing
in·vade', -vad'ed,
  -vad'ing
in·vad'er
in'va·lid *(ill)*
in·val'id *(without authority)*
  -dat'ed, -dat'ing
in·val'i·da'tion
in·val'u·a·ble
in·var'i·a·bil'i·ty

in·var'i·a·ble
in·var'i·a·bly
in·var'i·ance
in·var'i·ant
in·va'sion
in·va'sive
in·vec'tive
in·veigh'
in·vei'gle, -gled,
  -gling
in·vent'
in·ven'tion
in·ven'tive
in·ven'tor
in'ven·to'ry, -ried,
  -ry·ing
in·verse' *adj.*
in'verse' *n.*
in·ver'sion
in·vert'
in·ver'te·brate
in·vest'
in·ves'ti·gate',
  -gat'ed, -gat'ing
in·ves'ti·ga'tion
in·ves'ti·ga'tive
  also in·ves'ti·ga'·
  to'ry
in·ves'ti·ga'tor
in·ves'ti·ture'
in·vest'ment
in·ves'tor
in·vet'er·ate
in·vid'i·ous
in·vig'or·ate',
  -at'ed, -at'ing
in·vig'or·a'tion

in•vin′ci•bil′i•ty
in•vin′ci•ble
in•vin′ci•bly
in•vi′o•la•ble
in•vi′o•late
in•vis′i•bil′i•ty
in•vis′i•ble
in•vis′i•bly
in′vi•ta′tion
in•vite′, -vit′ed,
 -vit′ing
in vi′tro
in vi′vo
in′vo•ca′tion
in′voice′, -voiced′,
 -voic′ing
in•voke′, -voked′,
 -vok′ing
in•vol′un•tar′i•ly
in•vol′un•tar′y
in′vo•lu′tion
in•volve′, -volved′,
 -volv′ing
in•volve′ment
in•vul′ner•a•bil′i•ty
in•vul′ner•a•ble
in•vul′ner•a•bly
in′ward adj. & adv.
in′wards adv.
i′o•dide′
i′o•dine′
i′o•dize′, -dized′,
 -diz′ing
i′on
I•o′ni•an
i•on′ic (relating to
 ions)

I•on′ic (relating to
 Ionia)
i′on•i•za′tion
i′on•ize′, -ized′,
 -iz′ing
i•on′o•sphere′
i•o′ta
IOU pl. IOU's or
 IOUs
I′o•wa pl. -wa or
 -was
I′o•wan
ip′e•cac′
I•ra′ni•an
I•ra′qi pl. -quis
i•ras′ci•bil′i•ty
i•ras′ci•ble
i•ras′ci•bly
i•rate′
ire
ir′i•des′cence
ir′i•des′cent
i•rid′i•um
i′ris pl. i′ris•es or
 i′ri•des′
I′rish
I′rish•man
I′rish•wom′an
irk
irk′some
i′ron
i′ron•clad′
i•ron′ic also
 i•ron′i•cal
i′ron•wood′
i′ron•work′
i′ron•work′er

i′ron•works′
i′ro•ny
Ir′o•quoi′an
Ir′o•quois′ pl.
 -quois′
ir•ra′di•ate′, -at′ed,
 -at′ing
ir•ra′di•a′tion
ir•ra′di•a′tor
ir•ra′tion•al
ir•ra′tion•al′i•ty
ir′re•claim′a•ble
ir′re•con•cil′a•ble
ir′re•cov′er•a•ble
ir′re•deem′a•ble
ir•re•duc′i•ble
ir•re•duc′i•bly
ir•ref′u•ta•ble
ir•ref′u•ta•bly
ir•reg′u•lar
ir•reg′u•lar′i•ty
ir•rel′e•vance
ir•rel′e•vant
ir′re•lig′ious
ir′re•me′di•a•ble
ir′re•me′di•a•bly
ir•rep′a•ra•ble
ir•rep′a•ra•bly
ir′re•place′a•ble
ir′re•press′i•ble
ir′re•press′i•bly
ir′re•proach′a•ble
ir′re•proach′a•bly
ir′re•sist′i•bil′i•ty
ir′re•sis′ti•ble
ir′re•sis′ti•bly
ir•res′o•lute′

ir•res′o•lute′ness *or*
  ir•res′o•lu′tion
ir′re•spec′tive of
ir′re•spon′si•bil′i•ty
ir′re•spon′si•ble
ir′re•spon′si•bly
ir′re•triev′a•ble
ir′re•triev′a•bly
ir•rev′er•ence
ir•rev′er•ent
ir′re•vers′i•bil′i•ty
ir′re•vers′i•ble
ir′re•vers′i•bly
ir•rev′o•ca•bil′i•ty
ir•rev′o•ca•ble
ir•rev′o•ca•bly
ir′ri•gate′, -gat′ed,
  -gat′ing
ir′ri•ga′tion
ir′ri•ta•bil′i•ty
ir′ri•ta•ble
ir′ri•ta•bly
ir′ri•tant
ir′ri•tate′, -tat′ed,
  -tat′ing
ir′ri•ta′tion
ir′ri•ta′tor
ir•rupt′ *(to burst in,*
  to increase)
  ✔ *erupt*
ir•rup′tion
ir•rup′tive
is
is•chi•um *pl.* -chi•a
i′sin•glass′
Is′lam
Is•lam′ic

is′land
is′land•er
isle *(island)*
  ✔ *aisle*
is′let *(small island)*
  ✔ *eyelet*
is′n′t
i′so•bar′
i′so•bar′ic
i′so•late′, -lat′ed,
  -lat′ing
i′so•la′tion
i′so•la′tion•ism
i′so•la′tion•ist
i′so•mer
i′so•mer′ic
i•som′er•ism
i′so•met′ric *also*
  i′so•met′ri•cal
i′so•pro′pyl
  al′co•hol′
i•sos′ce•les′
i′so•therm′
i′so•ther′mal
i′so•tope′
i′so•top′ic
i′so•trop′ic
i•sot′ro•py *or*
  i•sot′ro•pism
Is•rae′li *pl.* -lis
Is′ra•el•ite′
is′su•ance
is′sue, -sued, -su•ing
is′su•er
isth′mus *pl.* -mus•es
  or -mi′
I•tal′ian

i•tal′ic
i•tal′i•cize′, -cized′,
  -ciz′ing
itch′y
i′tem
i′tem•i•za′tion
i′tem•ize′, -ized′,
  -iz′ing
it′er•ate′, -at′ed,
  -at′ing
it′er•a′tion
it′er•a′tive
i•tin′er•ant
i•tin′er•ar′y
its *pron.*
it′s *contraction*
it•self′
i′vo•ry
i′vy

J

jab, jabbed, jab′bing
jab′ber
ja•bot′
jac′a•ran′da
jack′al
jack′a•napes′
jack′ass′
jack′boot′
jack′daw′
jack′et
jack′ham′mer
jack′-in-the-box′
  pl. jack′-in-the-
  box′es *or* jacks′-in-

the-box'

jack'-in-the-
   pul'pit pl. jack'-
   in-the-pul'pits
jack'knife',
   -knifed', -knif'ing
jack'-of-all'-
   trades' pl. jacks'-
   of-all'-trades'
jack'-o'-lan'tern pl.
   jack'-o'-lan'terns
jack'pot'
jack'rab'bit or jack'
   rab'bit
jack'stone'
jack'straw'
jade
jad'ed
jag, jagged, jag'ging
jag'ged adj.
jag'uar
jai' a•lai'
jail
jail'bird'
jail'break'
jail'er also jail'or
jal'a•pe'ño pl. -ños
ja•lop'y
jal'ou•sie
jam (to wedge in),
   jammed, jam'ming
   ✔ jamb
jam (fruit preserve)
   ✔ jamb
Ja•mai'can
jamb (door post)
   ✔ jam

jam'bo•ree'
jan'gle, -gled, -gling
jan'i•tor
Jan'u•ar'y
Jap'a•nese' pl. -nese'
jar, jarred, jar'ring
jar'gon
jas'mine also
   jes'sa•mine
jas'per
jaun'dice, -diced,
   -dic•ing
jaunt
jaun'ty
ja'va
Jav'a•nese' pl. -nese'
jave'lin
jaw'bone'
jay'walk'
jazz'y
jeal'ous
jeal'ous•y
jeans
jeep
jeer
Je•ho'vah's
   Wit'ness
je•june'
je•ju'num pl. -na
jell (to congeal)
   ✔ gel
jel'ly, -lied, -ly•ing
jel'ly•bean'
jel'ly•fish' pl. -fish'
   or -fish'es
jel'ly•roll'
jen'net

jen'ny
jeop'ard•ize',
   -ized', -iz'ing
jeop'ard•y
jer•bo'a
jer'e•mi'ad
jerk
jerk'i•ly
jer'kin
jerk'y
jer'ry•build',
   -built', -build'ing
jer'sey pl. -seys
jest
jest'er
Jes'u•it
jet, jet'ted, jet'ting
jet'-pro•pelled'
jet'sam
jet'ti•son
jet'ty
Jew
jew'el, -eled or
   -elled, -el•ing or
   -el•ling
jew'el•er
jew'el•ry
Jew'ish
Jew'ry
jew's'-harp'
jib
jibe (to shift a sail, to
   agree), jibed, jib'ing
   ✔ gibe
jif'fy
jig, jigged, jig'ging
jig'ger

jig′gle, -gled, -gling
jig′saw′
ji•had′
jilt
Jim′ Crow′ *or* jim′ crow′
jim′my, -mied, -my•ing
jim′son•weed′
jin′gle, -gled, -gling
jin′go *pl.* -goes
jin′go•ism
jin′go•is′tic
jin′ni *pl.* jinn
jin•rik′sha′ *or* jin•rick′sha *also* jin•riki′sha
jinx
jit′ney *pl.* -neys
jit′ter•bug′, -bugged′, -bug′ging
jit′ters
jit′ter•y
jive
job
job′ber
jock
jock′ey *pl.* -eys
jock′strap′
jo•cose′
jo•cose′ness *or* jo•cos′i•ty
joc′u•lar
joc′u•lar′i•ty
joc′und
jo•cun′di•ty
jodh′purs

jog, jogged, jog′ging
jog′ger
jog′gle, -gled, -gling
john′ny•cake′
John′ny-come-late′ly *pl.* John′ny-come-late′lies *or* John′nies-come-late′ly
joie′ de vi′vre
join
join′er
join′er•y
joint
join′ture
joist
joke, joked, jok′ing
jok′er
joke′ster
jol′li•ty
jol′ly
jolt
jon′quil
Jor•da′ni•an
josh
jos′tle, -tled, -tling
jos′tler
jot, jot′ted, jot′ting
joule
jounce, jounced, jounc′ing
jour′nal
jour′nal•ism
jour′nal•ist
jour′nal•is′tic
jour′ney *pl.* -neys
jour′ney•man

joust
jo′vi•al
jo′vi•al′i•ty
jowl
joy′ful
joy′ous
ju′bi•lance
ju′bi•lant
ju′bi•la′tion
ju′bi•lee′
Ju•da′ic *also* Ju•da′i•cal
Ju′da•ism
Ju′das
judge, judged, judg′ing
judge′ship′
judg′ment *also* judge′ment
judg•men′tal
ju′di•ca•ble
ju′di•ca•to′ry
ju•di′cial *(relating to the law)*
✔ *judicious*
ju•di′ci•ar′y
ju•di′cious *(prudent)*
✔ *judicial*
ju′do
jug
jug′ger•naut′
jug′gle, -gled, -gling
jug′gler
jug′u•lar
juice
juic′er

juic′i•ness
juic′y
ju•jit′su *also*
    ju•jut′su
juke′box′
ju′lep
Jul′ian cal′en•dar
ju′li•enne′
Ju•ly′
jum′ble, -bled,
    -bling
jum′bo *pl.* -bos
jump
jump′er
jump′-start′
jump′ suit′ *also*
    jump′suit′
jump′y
jun′co *pl.* -cos *or*
    -coes
junc′tion
junc′ture
June
June′ bug′
jun′gle
jun′ior
ju′ni•per
junk
jun′ket
junk′ie *also* junk′y
junk′yard′
jun′ta
Ju•ras′sic
ju•rid′i•cal
ju′ris•dic′tion
ju′ris•pru′dence
ju′rist

ju′ror
ju′ry
just
jus′tice
jus′ti•fi′a•bil′i•ty
jus′ti•fi′a•ble
jus′ti•fi′a•bly
jus′ti•fi•ca′tion
jus′ti•fy′, -fied′,
    -fy′ing
jut, jut′ted, jut′ting
jute *(fiber)*
Jute *(Germanic people)*
ju′ve•nile′
jux′ta•pose′,
    -posed′, -pos′ing
jux′ta•po•si′tion

K

ka•bu′ki
Kai′ser
kale
ka•lei′do•scope′
ka•lei′do•scop′ic
ka′mi•ka′ze
kan′ga•roo′ *pl.*
    -roo′ *or* -roos′
Kan′san
ka′o•lin *also*
    ka′o•line
ka′pok
kap′pa
ka•put′
kar′a•kul
kar′a•o′ke

kar′at *also* car′at
    (unit of measure)
    ✔ carat, caret, carrot
ka•ra′te
kar′ma
ka′ty•did′
kay′ak′
kay•o′, -oed′,
    -o′ing
ka•zoo′ *pl.* -zoos′
ke•bab′ *or* ke•bob′
    also ka•bob′
keel
keel′haul′
keen
keep, kept, keep′ing
keep′er
keep′sake′
keg
kelp
kel′vin
ken, kenned *or* kent,
    ken′ning
ken′nel, -neled *or*
    -nelled, -nel•ing *or*
    -nel•ling
ke′no
Ken•tuck′i•an
ke′pi *pl.* -pis
ker′a•tin
ker′chief *pl.* -chiefs
    also -chieves
ker′nel *(grain)*
    ✔ colonel
ker′o•sene′
kes′trel
ketch

ketch'up *also*
  cat'sup
ket'tle
ket'tle·drum'
key *(implement,
  island), pl.* keys
  ✔ cay, quay
key'board'
key'board'er
key'hole'
key'note'
key'pad'
key'punch'
key'stone'
key'stroke'
khak'i
khan
Khmer *pl.* Khmer *or*
  Khmers
kib'ble, -bled, -bling
kib·butz' *pl.*
  kib'but·zim'
kib'itz
kib'itz·er
ki'bosh'
kick
Kick'a·poo' *pl.*
  -poo' *or* -poos'
kick'back' *n.*
kick'ball'
kick'box'ing
kick'er
kick'off'
kick'stand'
kid, kid'ded,
  kid'ding
kid'der

kid'nap', -napped'
  or -naped',
  -nap'ping *or*
  -nap'ing
kid'nap'per *or*
  kid'nap'er
kid'ney *pl.* -neys
kid'skin'
kill
kill'deer' *pl.* -deer'
  or -deers'
kill'er
kill'joy'
kiln
ki'lo *pl.* -los
kil'o·byte'
kil'o·cal'o·rie
kil'o·cy'cle
kil'o·gram'
kil'o·hertz'
kil'o·me'ter
kil'o·met'ric
kil'o·ton'
kil'o·watt'
kil'o·watt-hour'
kilt
kil'ter
ki·mo'no *pl.* -nos
kin
kind
kin'der·gar'ten
kind'heart'ed
kin'dle, -dled,
  -dling
kind'li·ness
kin'dling
kind'ly

kind'ness
kin'dred
kin'e·mat'ics
kin'e·scope'
ki·ne'sics
ki·net'ic
kin'folk' *also*
  kins'folk' *or*
  kin'folks'
king
king'bird'
king'bolt'
king'dom
king'fish'er
king'li·ness
king'ly
king'pin'
king'-size' *or*
  king'-sized'
kink
kink'a·jou'
kink'i·ness
kink'y
kin'ship'
kins'man
kins'wom'an
ki'osk'
Ki'o·wa' *pl.* -wa' *or*
  -was'
kip'per
kis'met
kiss
kiss'er
kit
kitch'en
kitch'en·ette'
kite

kith' and kin'

kitsch

kit'ten

kit'ty

kit'ty-cor'nered *or*
kit'ty-cor'ner

ki'wi *pl.* -wis

Klans'man

klep'to•ma'ni•a

klep'to•ma'ni•ac'

klieg' light'

klutz

knack

knack'wurst' *or*
knock'wurst'

knap'sack'

knave *(scoundrel)*
✔ *nave*

knav'er•y

knav'ish

knead *(to press with
the hands)*
✔ *need*

knee, kneed,
knee'ing

knee'cap'

knee'-deep'

knee'-high'

kneel, knelt *or*
kneeled, kneel'ing

knee'pad'

knell

knew *past tense of*
know
✔ *gnu, new*

knick'er•bock'ers

knick'ers

knick'knack' *also*
nick'nack'

knife *pl.* knives

knife, knifed,
knif'ing

knife'-edge'

knight *(soldier)*
✔ *night*

knight'-er'rant *pl.*
knights'-er'rant

knight'hood'

knish

knit *(to loop yarn)*,
knit *or* knit'ted,
knit'ting
✔ *nit*

knit'ter

knit'wear'

knob

knob'by

knock

knock'a•bout'

knock'down' *n. &
adj.*

knock'er

knock'-knee'

knock'-kneed'

knock'out' *n.*

knoll

knot *(to tie)*,
knot'ted, knot'ting
✔ *not*

knot'hole'

knot'ty

know *(to have knowl-
edge)*, knew,
known, know'ing

✔ *no*

know'-how'

know'-it-all'

knowl'edge

knowl'edge•a•ble

knuck'le, -led, -ling

knuck'le•bone'

knuck'le•head'

KO, KO'd, KO'ing,
KO's

KO *pl.* KO's

ko•a'la

kohl *(cosmetic)*
✔ *coal*

kohl•ra'bi *pl.* -bies

Ko•mo'do drag'on

kook

kook'a•bur'ra

kook'i•ness

kook'y

ko'peck

Ko•ran' *or* Qur•'an'

Ko•re'an

ko'sher

kow•tow'

krill *pl.* krill

Krish'na

kro'na *(monetary
unit of Iceland)*, *pl.*
-nur

kro'na *(monetary
unit of Sweden)*, *pl.*
-nor

kro'ne *(monetary
unit of Norway and
Denmark)*, *pl.* -ner

kryp'ton

ku′dos′
kud′zu
Ku′ Klux Klan′
kum′quat′
kung′ fu′
kur′cha•tov′i•um
Kwan′zaa

L

la′bel, -beled or
 -belled, -bel•ing or
 -bel•ling
la′bi•al
la′bi•um *pl.* -bi•a
la′bor
lab′o•ra•to′ry
la′bored
la′bor•er
la′bor-in•ten′sive
la•bo′ri•ous
la′bor•sav′ing
Lab′ra•dor
 re•triev′er
la•bur′num
lab′y•rinth′
lab′y•rin′thine
lac *(resin)*
 ✔ lack
lace, laced, lac′ing
lac′er•ate, -at′ed,
 -at′ing
lac′er•a′tion
lace′wing′
lach′ry•mal
lach′ry•mose′

lack *(shortage)*
 ✔ lac
lack′a•dai′si•cal
lack′ey *pl.* -eys
lack′lus′ter
la•con′ic
lac′quer
la•crosse′
lac′tase′
lac′tate′, -tat′ed,
 -tat′ing
lac•ta′tion
lac′te•al
lac′tic
lac′tose′
la•cu′na *pl.* -nae or
 -nas
lac′y
lad
lad′der
lad′die
lade, lad′ed, lad′en
 or lad′ed, lad′ing
la′dle, -dled, -dling
la′dy
la′dy•bird′
la′dy•bug′
la′dy•fin′ger *also*
 la′dys•fin′ger
la′dy in wait′ing
 pl. la′dies in
 wait′ing
la′dy•like′
la′dy•ship′
la′dy's slip′per *pl.*
 la′dy's slip′pers
lag, lagged, lag′ging

la′ger
lag′gard
la•goon′
laid′-back′
lair
lais′sez faire′
la′i•ty
lake
La•ko′ta *pl.* -ta
lam *(to thrash, to
 escape)*, lammed,
 lam′ming
 ✔ lamb
la′ma *(monk)*
 ✔ llama
lamb *(young sheep)*
 ✔ lam
lam•baste′,
 -bast′ed, -bast′ing
lamb′da
lam′bent
lamb′skin′
lame, lam′er,
 lam′est
lame, lamed,
 lam′ing
la•mé′
la•ment′
la•men′ta•ble
lam′en•ta•bly
lam′en•ta′tion
lam′i•na *pl.* -nae′ or
 -nas
lam′i•nate′,
 -nat′ed, -nat′ing
lam′i•na′tion
lam′i•na′tor

lamp'black'
lamp'light'
lam·poon'
lamp'post'
lam'prey' *pl.* -preys'
lamp'shade'
la·nai'
lance, lanced,
  lanc'ing
lanc'er
lan'cet
lan'dau'
land'ed
land'fall'
land'fill'
land'form'
land'hold'er
land'ing
land'la'dy
land'locked'
land'lord'
land'lub'ber
land'mark'
land'mass'
land' mine'
land'own'er
land'scape',
  -scaped', -scap'ing
land'slide'
land'ward *adv. &*
  adj.
land'wards *adv.*
lane
lan'guage
lan'guid
lan'guish
lan'guor

lan'guor·ous
lank'i·ness
lank'ly
lank'y
lan'o·lin
lan'tern
lan'tha·nide'
lan'tha·num
lan'yard
Lao *pl.* Lao *or* Laos
La·o'tian
lap (*to fold over*),
  lapped, lap'ping
  ✔ *Lapp*
la·pel'
lap'i·dar'y
lap'is laz'u·li
Lapp (*native of*
  Lapland)
  ✔ *lap*
lapse, lapsed,
  laps'ing
lap'top'
lap'wing'
lar'board
lar'ce·nous
lar'ce·ny
larch
lard
lar'der
large, larg'er,
  larg'est
large'-heart'ed
large'ly
large'-scale'
lar·gess' *also*
  lar·gesse'

lar'go
lar'i·at
lark
lark'spur'
lar'va *pl.* -vae *or* -vas
lar'val
la·ryn'ge·al *also*
  la·ryn'gal
lar'yn·gi'tis
lar'ynx *pl.*
  la·ryn'ges *or*
  lar'ynx·es
la·sa'gna
las·civ'i·ous
la'ser
lash
lass
las'sie
las'si·tude'
las'so *pl.* -sos *or*
  -soes
last'ing
last'-min'ute *adj.*
latch
latch'key'
late, lat'er, lat'est
late'com'er
la·teen'
late'ly
la'ten·cy
late'ness
la'tent
lat'er·al
la'tex' *pl.* la'ti·ces'
  or la'tex·es
lath (*narrow strip*)
lathe (*machine*)

lathe *(to cut on a lathe)*, lathed, lath'ing
lath'er
Lat'in
La•ti'na *pl.* -nas
Lat'in A•mer'i•can
  or Lat'in-
  A•mer'i•can
La•ti'no *pl.* -nos
lat'i•tude'
lat'i•tu'di•nal
la•trine'
lat'te
lat'ter
Lat'ter-day' Saint'
lat'ter•ly
lat'tice, -ticed, -tic•ing
lat'tice•work'
Lat'vi•an
laud
laud'a•ble
laud'a•bly
lau'da•num
laud'a•to'ry
laugh
laugh'a•ble
laugh'a•bly
laugh'ing•stock'
laugh'ter
launch
launch'er
laun'der
laun'dress
laun'dry
lau're•ate

lau'rel
la'va
lav'a•to'ry
lave, laved, lav'ing
lav'en•der
lav'ish
law'-a•bid'ing
law'break'er
law'ful
law'giv'er
law'less
law'mak'er
law'mak'ing
lawn
lawn' mow'er *also* lawn'mow'er
law•ren'ci•um
law'suit'
law'yer
lax
lax'a•tive
lax'i•ty
lay *(put)*, laid, lay'ing
  ✔ *lei*
lay *(relating to lay-people)*
  ✔ *lei*
lay *(ballad)*
  ✔ *lei*
lay'a•way'
lay'er
lay•ette'
lay'man
lay'off' *n.*
lay'out' *n.*
lay'o'ver *n.*

lay'peo'ple *or* lay' peo'ple
lay'per'son
lay'-up' *n.*
lay'wom'an
laze, lazed, laz'ing
la'zi•ly
la'zi•ness
la'zy
lea *(meadow)*
  ✔ *lee*
leach *(to dissolve)*
  ✔ *leech*
lead *(to guide)*, led, lead'ing
  ✔ *lied*
lead *(element)*
  ✔ *led*
lead'en
lead'er
lead'er•ship'
lead'-in' *n.*
lead'ing
lead'off' *n. & adj.*
leaf *(plant part)*, *pl.* leaves
  ✔ *lief*
leaf'let
leaf'stalk'
leaf'y
league, leagued, leagu'ing
leagu'er
leak *(escape)*
  ✔ *leek*
leak'age
leak'i•ness

leak'y
lean *(to bend)*
  ✔ lien
lean *(thin)*
  ✔ lien
lean'ing
lean'-to' *pl.* -tos'
leap, leaped *or* leapt,
  leap'ing
leap'frog',
  -frogged',
  -frog'ging
learn, learned *also*
  learnt, learn'ing
learn'ed *adj.*
lease, leased,
  leas'ing
leash
least
least'wise'
leath'er
leath'er•ette'
leath'ern
leath'er•y
leave, left, leav'ing
leav'en
leav'en•ing
leave'-tak'ing
leav'ings
Leb'a•nese' *pl.*
  -nese'
lech'er•ous
lech'er•y
lec'i•thin
lec'tern
lec'tor
lec'ture, -tured,

-tur•ing
lec'tur•er
ledge
ledg'er
lee *(shelter)*
  ✔ lea
leech *(worm)*
  ✔ leach
leek *(plant)*
  ✔ leak
leer
leer'y
lees
lee'ward
lee'way'
left'-hand' *adj.*
left'-hand'ed
left'-hand'er
left'ist
left'o'ver *adj.*
left'-wing' *adj.*
left'wing'er
left'y
leg
leg'a•cy
le'gal
le•gal'i•ty
le'gal•i•za'tion
le'gal•ize', -ized',
  -iz'ing
leg'ate
leg'a•tee'
le•ga'tion
le•ga'to
leg'end
leg'en•dar'y
leg'er•de•main'

leg'ged
leg'ging
leg'gy
leg'horn'
leg'i•bil'i•ty *or*
  leg'i•ble•ness
leg'i•ble
leg'i•bly
le'gion
le'gion•ar'y
le'gion•naire'
leg'is•late', -lat'ed,
  -lat'ing
leg'is•la'tion
leg'is•la'tive
leg'is•la'tor
leg'is•la'ture
le•git'i•ma•cy
le•git'i•mate
le•git'i•mize',
  -mized', -miz'ing
leg•ume'
le•gu'mi•nous
leg'work'
lei *(garland), pl.* leis
  ✔ lay
lei'sure
lem'ma *pl.* -mas *or*
  lem'a•ta
lem'ming
lem'on
lem'on•ade'
le'mur
Len'a•pe *pl.* -pe *or*
  -pes
lend, lent, lend'ing
lend'er

length
length'en
length'wise'
length'y
le'ni•ence *or*
  le'ni•en•cy
le'ni•ent
Len'ni Len'a•pe
lens *pl.* lens'es
Lent
Lent'en
len'til
le'o•nine'
leop'ard
le'o•tard'
lep'er
lep're•chaun'
lep'ro•sy
lep'rous
les'bi•an
le'sion
less
les•see'
less'en (to make less)
  ✔ lesson
less'er *a comparative*
  of little
  ✔ lessor
les'son (instruction)
  ✔ lessen
les'sor (landlord)
  ✔ lesser
lest
let (to permit, to
  lease), let, let'ting
  ✔ Lett
let'down' *n.*

le'thal
le•thar'gic
leth'ar•gy
le'the
Lett (Baltic people)
  ✔ let
let'ter
let'ter•head'
let'ter•ing
let'ter-per'fect
Let'tish
let'tuce
let'up' *n.*
leu•ke'mi•a
leu'ko•cyte' *also*
  leu'co•cyte'
lev•ee' (embankment)
  ✔ levy
lev'el, -eled *or*
  -elled, -el•ing *or*
  -el•ling
lev'el•er *or* lev'el•ler
lev'el•head'ed
lev'er
lev'er•age
le•vi'a•than
lev'i•tate', -tat'ed,
  -tat'ing
lev'i•ta'tion
lev'i•ta'tor
Le'vite'
lev'i•ty
lev'y (collect), -ied,
  -y'ing
  ✔ levee
lewd
lex'i•cog'ra•pher

lex'i•co•graph'ic *or*
  lex'i•co•graph'i•cal
lex'i•cog'ra•phy
lex'i•con'
Lha'sa ap'so
li'a•bil'i•ty
li'a•ble (likely)
  ✔ libel
li•ai'son
li'ar (one who lies)
  ✔ lyre
li•ba'tion
li'bel (to defame),
  -beled *or* -belled,
  -bel'ing *or* -bel•ling
  ✔ liable
li'bel•er
li'bel•ous *also*
  li'bel•lous
lib'er•al
lib'er•al•ism
lib'er•al'i•ty
lib'er•al•i•za'tion
lib'er•al•ize', -ized',
  -iz'ing
lib'er•ate', -at'ed,
  -at'ing
lib'er•a'tion
lib'er•a'tor
Li•be'ri•an
lib'er•tar'i•an
lib'er•tine'
lib'er•ty
li•bid'i•nal
li•bid'i•nous
li•bi'do *pl.* -dos
li•brar'i•an

li'brar•'y
li•bret'tist
li•bret'to *pl.* -tos *or* -ti
Lib'y•an
lice *sing.* louse
li'cens•a•ble
li'cense, -censed, -cens•ing
li'cens•ee'
li'cens•er *or* li'cen•sor
li'cen•sure
li•cen'ti•ate
li•cen'tious
li'chen *(plant)*
  ✔ liken
lic'it
lick
lic'o•rice
lid
lie *(to recline)*, lay, lain, ly'ing
  ✔ lye
lie *(to deceive)*, lied, ly'ing
  ✔ lye
lied *(song)*, *pl.* lie'der
  ✔ lead
lief *(willingly)*
  ✔ leaf
liege
liege'man
lien *(claim)*
  ✔ lean
lieu
lieu•ten'an•cy

lieu•ten'ant
life *pl.* lives
life'blood'
life'boat'
life'guard'
life'less
life'like'
life'line'
life'long'
life'sav'er
life'sav'ing
life'-size' *also* life'-sized'
life'style' *also* life'-style' *or* life' style'
life'-sup•port'
life'time'
life'work'
lift
lift'off' *n.*
lig'a•ment
lig'a•ture
light, light'ed *or* lit, light'ing
light'en
light'er
light'face'
light'-faced'
light'-fin'gered
light'-foot'ed
light'head'ed
light'heart'ed
light'house'
light'ing
light'ning
light'ship'

light'weight'
light'-year'
lig'nite'
lik'a•ble *also* like'a•ble
like, liked, lik'ing
like'li•hood'
like'ly
like'-mind'ed
lik'en *(to compare)*
  ✔ lichen
like'ness
like'wise'
li'lac
Lil'li•pu'tian *also* lil'li•pu'tian
lilt
lil'y
lil'y of the val'ley
  pl. lil'ies of the val'ley
lily'-white'
li'ma bean'
limb *(body part)*
  ✔ limn
lim'ber
lim'bo *pl.* -bos
Lim'burg'er
lime
lime•ade'
lime'light'
lim'er•ick
lime'stone'
lime'wa'ter
lim'it
lim'i•ta'tion
lim'it•ed

limn *(to draw)*
  ✔ *limb*
lim'ou·sine'
limp
lim'pet
lim'pid
lim'y
lin'age *also* line'age
  (number of lines)
  ✔ *lineage*
linch'pin'
lin'den
line, lined, lin'ing
lin'e·age *(ancestry)*
  ✔ *linage*
lin'e·al
lin'e·a·ment
lin'e·ar
line'back'er
line'man
lin'en
lin'er
lines'man
line'up' *also*
  line'-up' *n.*
lin'ger
lin'ge·rie'
lin'go *pl.* -goes
lin'gua fran'ca *pl.*
  lin'gua fran'cas
lin'gual
lin·gui'ça
lin·gui'ne *also*
  lin·gui'ni
lin'guist
lin·guis'tic
lin'i·ment

lin'ing
link
link'age
links *(golf course)*
  ✔ *lynx*
lin'net
li·no'le·um
lin'seed'
lin'sey-wool'sey
  pl. -seys
lint
lin'tel
li'on
li'on·ess
li'on·heart'ed
li'on·i·za'tion
li'on·ize', -ized',
  -iz'ing
lip
lip'ase'
lip'id *also* lip'ide'
lip'oid'
lip'-read', -read',
  -read'ing
lip' read'ing *n.*
lip'stick'
liq'ue·fac'tion
liq'ue·fi'er
liq'ue·fy', -fied',
  -fy'ing
li·queur'
liq'uid
liq'ui·date',
  -dat'ed, -dat'ing
liq'ui·da'tion
li·quid'i·ty
liq'uor

li'ra *pl.* -re *or* -ras
lisle
lisp
lis'some *also*
  lis'som
list
lis'ten
lis'ten·er
list'ing
list'less
lit'a·ny
li'tchi *also* li'chee *or*
  ly'chee
li'ter
lit'er·a·cy
lit'er·al *(verbatim)*
  ✔ *littoral*
lit'er·ar'y
lit'er·ate
lit'er·a·ture
lithe, lith'er, lith'est
lith'i·um
lith'o·graph'
li·thog'ra·pher
lith'o·graph'ic *or*
  lith'o·graph'i·cal
li·thog'ra·phy
lith'o·sphere'
Lith·u·a'ni·an
lit'i·gant
lit'i·gate', -gat'ed,
  -gat'ing
lit'i·ga'tion
lit'i·ga'tor
li·ti'gious
lit'mus
lit'ter

lit'ter•bug'
lit'ter•mate'
lit'tle, lit'tler *or* less,
  lit'tlest *or* least
lit'tle•neck'
littoral *(coastal region)*
  ✔ literal
li•tur'gi•cal
lit'ur•gy
liv'a•ble *also* live'a•ble
live, lived, liv'ing
live *adj.*
live'-in' *adj.*
live'li•hood'
live'li•ness
live'long'
live'ly
li'ven
liv'er
liv'er•ied
liv'er•wort'
liv'er•wurst'
liv'er•y
live'stock'
liv'id
liv'ing room'
liz'ard
lla'ma *(animal)*
  ✔ lama
lla'no *pl.* -nos
lo *interj.*
  ✔ low
load *(weight)*
  ✔ lode
load'ed

load'er
loaf *pl.* loaves
loaf *v.*
loaf'er
loam
loam'y
loan *(something lent)*
  ✔ lone
loan' word' *or* loan'word'
loath *(not willing)*
loathe *(to detest)*,
  loathed, loath'ing
loath'some
lob, lobbed, lob'bing
lo'bar
lob'by, -bied, -by•ing
lob'by•ist
lobe
lobed
lo•be'li•a
lob'lol'ly pine'
lob'ster
lo'cal
lo•cale'
lo•cal'i•ty
lo'cal•i•za'tion
lo'cal•ize', -ized', -iz'ing
lo'cate', -cat'ed, -cat'ing
lo•ca'tion
lo'ca'tor
loch *(lake)*
lock *(security device,*

  hair)
lock'er
lock'et
lock'jaw'
lock'out' *n.*
lock'smith'
lock'up' *n.*
lo'co•mo'tion
lo'co•mo'tive
lo'co•weed'
lo'cus *pl.* -ci'
lo'cust
lo•cu'tion
lode *(ore deposit)*
  ✔ load
lode'star' *also* load'star'
lode'stone' *also* load'stone'
lodge, lodged, lodg'ing
lodg'er
lodg'ment *also* lodge'ment
lo'ess
loft
loft'y
log, logged, log'ging
lo'gan•ber'ry
log'a•rithm
log'a•rith'mic *or* log'a•rith'mi•cal
log'book'
log'ger
log'ger•head'
log'gi•a
log'ic

log'i•cal
lo•gi'cian
lo•gis'tic *also*
  lo•gis'ti•cal
lo•gis'tics
log'jam'
lo'go *(symbol), pl.*
  -gos
LO'GO *(computer*
  language)
log'roll'ing
lo'gy
loin
loin'cloth'
loi'ter
loi'ter•er
loll
lol'la•pa•loo'za
  also lal'a•pa•loo'za
  or lal'la•pa•loo'za
lol'li•pop' *also*
  lol'ly•pop'
lone *(solitary)*
  ✔ *loan*
lone'li•ness
lone'ly
lon'er
lone'some
long
long'boat'
long'bow'
long'-dis'tance
  adj.
lon•gev'i•ty
long'hair' *or*
  long'haired'

long'hand'
long'horn'
long'house' *or*
  long' house'
long'ing
lon'gi•tude'
lon'gi•tu'di•nal
long'-lived'
long'-play'ing
long'-range'
long'shore'man
long'-stand'ing
long'-suf'fer•ing
long'-term'
long'-time' *also*
  long'time'
long'-wind'ed
loo'fa *or* loo'fah *also*
  luf'fa
look
look'er
look'ing glass'
look'out' *n.*
look'-up' *n.*
loom
loon'y
loop *(circular path)*
  ✔ *loupe*
loop'hole'
loose, loos'er,
  loos'est
loose, loosed,
  loos'ing
loose'-leaf'
loos'en
loot *(stolen goods)*

✔ *lute*
loot'er
lop, lopped,
  lop'ping
lope, loped, lop'ing
lop'-eared'
lop'sid•ed
lo•qua'cious
lo•quac'i•ty
lord
lord'li•ness
lord'ly
lord'ship'
lore
lor•gnette'
lor'ry
lose, lost, los'ing
los'er
loss
lot
lo'tion
lot'ter•y
lot'to
lo'tus
loud
loud'mouth'
loud'mouthed'
loud'speak'er
lounge, lounged,
  loung'ing
loupe *(magnifying*
  glass)
  ✔ *loup*
lour
louse *(insect), pl.* lice
louse *(contemptible*

person), pl. lous'es
lous'y
lout
lou'ver
lou'vered
lov'a·ble *also*
  love'a·ble
lov'a·bly
love, loved, lov'ing
love'bird'
love'less
love'li·ness
love'lorn'
love'ly
lov'er
love' seat' *or*
  love'seat'
love'sick'
low *(not high)*
  ✔ lo
low *(to bellow)*
  ✔ lo
low'boy'
low'brow'
low'down' *n.*
low'-down' *adj.*
low'er *(to scowl)*
low'er *(below)*
low'er·case' *or*
  low'er-case'
low'er-class' *adj.*
low'er·most'
low'-key' *also*
  low-keyed
low'land
low'li·ness

low'ly
low'-pitched'
low'-pres'sure *adj.*
low'-rise'
low'-spir'it·ed
lox *pl.* lox *or* lox'es
loy'al
loy'al·ist
loy'al·ty
loz'enge
LP *pl.* LP's *or* LPs
lu'au'
lub'ber
lu'bri·cant
lu'bri·cate', -cat'ed,
  -cat'ing
lu'bri·ca'tion
lu'bri·ca'tor
lu'cent
lu'cid
lu·cid'i·ty
luck'i·ly
luck'y
lu'cra·tive
lu'cre
lu'di·crous
luff
lug, lugged, lug'ging
lug'gage
lug'sail
lu·gu'bri·ous
lug'worm'
luke'warm'
lull
lull'a·by'
lum·ba'go

lum'bar *(relating to*
  the lower back)
lum'ber *(wood)*
lum'ber *(to move*
  clumsily)
lum'ber·jack'
lum'ber·yard'
lu'men *pl.*
  -mens *or* -mi·na
lu'mi·nar'y
lu'mi·nes'cence
lu'mi·nes'cent
lu'mi·nos'i·ty
lu'mi·nous
lump'i·ness
lump'y
lu'na·cy
lu'nar
lu·na·tic
lunch
lunch'eon
lunch'eon·ette'
lunch'room'
lung
lunge, lunged,
  lung'ing
lung'fish' *pl.* -fish'
  or -fish'es
lu'pine *also* lu'pin
lu'pus
lurch
lure, lured, lur'ing
lu'rid
lurk
lurk'er
lus'cious

lush
lust
lust'er *(person who lusts)*
lus'ter *(sheen)*
lust'ful
lus'trous
lust'y
lute *(musical instrument)*
  ✔ loot
lu·te'ti·um *also* lu·te'ci·um
Lu'ther·an
lux·u'ri·ance
lux·u'ri·ant
lux·u'ri·ate', -at'ed, -at'ing
lux·u'ri·ous
lux'u·ry
ly·ce'um
lye *(alkaline solution)*
  ✔ lie
Lyme' dis·ease'
lymph
lym·phat'ic
lym'pho·cyte'
lym'phoid'
lynch
lynch'er
lynx *(animal)*, pl. lynx *or* lynx'es
  ✔ links
lyre *(musical instrument)*
  ✔ liar
lyr'ic

lyr'i·cal
lyr'i·cism
lyr'i·cist
ly'sin
ly'sine'
ly'sis *pl.* -ses

M

ma'am
ma·ca'bre
mac·ad'am
mac·ad'am·ize', -ized', -iz'ing
ma·caque'
mac'a·ro'ni *pl.* -ni
mac'a·roon'
ma·caw'
mace
Mac'e·do'ni·an
mac'er·ate', -at'ed, -at'ing
mac'er·a'tion
mac'er·a'tor *also* mac'er·a'ter
ma·chet'e
Mach'i·a·vel'li·an
mach'i·na'tion
ma·chine', -chined', -chin'ing
ma·chine' gun' *n.*
ma·chine'-gun', -gunned', -gun'ning
ma·chine'-read'a·ble

ma·chin'er·y
ma·chin'ist
ma·chis'mo
ma'cho *pl.* -chos
mack'er·el *pl.* -el *or* -els
mack'i·naw'
mack'in·tosh' *also* mac·in·tosh' *(raincoat)*
  ✔ McIntosh
mac'ra·mé'
mac'ro' *pl.* -ros'
mac'ro·bi·ot'ics
mac'ro·cosm
mac'ro·cos'mic
mac'ro·ec'o·nom'·ics
ma·crog'ra·phy
mac'ro·mol'e·cule
ma'cron'
mac'ro·nu'cle·us *pl.* -cle·i'
mac'ro·scop'ic *also* mac'ro·scop'i·cal
mac'u·la *pl.* -lae'
mac'u·lar
mac'u·late', -lat'ed, -lat'ing
mac'u·la'tion
mad, mad'der, mad'dest
Mad'am *pl.* Mad'ams *or* Mes·dames'
Ma·dame' *pl.* Mes·dames'

mad'cap'
mad'den
mad'den·ing
made (created)
  ✓ maid
Mad'e·moi·selle'
  pl. Mad'e·moi·
  selles' or Mes·de·
  moi·selles'
made'-to-or'der
made'-up' adj.
mad'house'
mad'man'
Ma·don'na
mad'ras
mad'ri·gal
mael'strom
mae'nad'
maes'tro pl. -tros or
  -tri
Ma·fi·a
Ma·fi·o'so' pl. -si'
mag'a·zine'
ma·gen'ta
mag'got
Ma'gi'
mag'ic
mag'i·cal
ma·gi'cian
mag·is·te'ri·al
mag'is·tra·cy
mag'is·trate'
mag'ma pl.
  mag·ma'ta or
  mag'mas
Mag'na Car'ta or
  Mag'na Char'ta

mag'na cum
  lau'de
mag'na·nim'i·ty
mag·nan'i·mous
mag'nate'
mag·ne'sia
mag·ne'si·um
mag'net
mag·net'ic
mag'net·ism
mag'net·ite'
mag'net·i·za'tion
mag'net·ize', -ized',
  -iz'ing
mag'net·iz'er
mag·ne'to pl. -tos
mag'ne·tom'e·ter
mag·ne'to·sphere'
mag'ne·tron'
mag·nif·i·ca'tion
mag·nif'i·cence
mag·nif'i·cent
  (splendid)
  ✓ munificent
mag·nif'i·er
mag'ni·fy', -fied',
  -fy'ing
mag·nil'o·quence
mag·nil'o·quent
mag'ni·tude'
mag·no'lia
mag'num
mag'pie
ma·guey' pl.
  -gueys'
Mag'yar'
ma·ha·ra'jah or

ma·ha·ra'ja
ma·ha·ra'ni or
  ma·ha·ra'nee
ma·hat'ma
Ma·hi'can also
  Mo·hi'can pl. -can
  or -cans
mah'jong' also
  mah'jongg'
ma·hog'a·ny
maid (girl, servant)
  ✓ made
maid'en
maid'en·hair'
maid'en·hood'
maid' of hon'or
  pl. maids' of
  hon'or
maid'ser'vant
mail (postal material,
  armor)
  ✓ male
mail'bag'
mail'boat'
mail'box'
mail'man'
mail'-or'der
  house'
mail'room'
maim
main (principal)
  ✓ mane
main'frame'
main'land'
main'line', -lined',
  -lin'ing
main'mast

main'sail'
main'sheet'
main'spring'
main'stay'
main'stream'
main•tain'
main'te•nance
main'top'
maî'tre d'hô•tel'
  pl. maî'tres
  d'hô•tel'
maize *(grain)*
  ✔ *maze*
ma•jes'tic
ma•jes'ti•cal
maj'es•ty
ma•jol'i•ca
ma'jor
ma'jor-do'mo *pl.*
  -mos
ma'jor•ette'
ma'jor•i•ty
ma'jor-league' *adj.*
ma'jor-lea'guer
ma'jor-med'i•cal
  adj.
ma•jus'cule
make, made,
  mak'ing
make'-be•lieve' *n.*
  & *adj.*
make'-do' *adj.* & *n.*
make'-or-break'
  adj.
make'o'ver *n.*
mak'er
make'-read'y *n.*

make'shift'
make'up *or*
  make'-up *n.*
mal'a•chite'
mal'ad•just'ed
mal'a•droit'
mal'a•dy
Mal'a•gas'y *pl.*
  -gas'y *or* -gas'ies
mal•aise'
mal'a•mute' *or*
  mal'e•mute'
mal'a•prop'
mal'a•prop•ism
mal'a•pro•pos'
ma•lar'i•a
ma•lar'i•al *or*
  ma•lar'i•an *or*
  ma•lar'i•ous
ma•lar'key *also*
  ma•lar'ky
Ma•lay'
Ma•lay'an
Mal'a•ya'lam
mal'con•tent' *adj.*
  & *n.*
male *(masculine)*
  ✔ *mail*
mal'e•dic'tion
mal'e•fac'tion
mal'e•fac'tor
ma•lef'ic
ma•lef'i•cent
ma•lev'o•lence
ma•lev'o•lent
mal•fea'sance
mal•fea'sant

mal'for•ma'tion
mal•formed'
mal•func'tion
mal'ice
ma•li'cious
ma•lign'
ma•lig'nan•cy
ma•lig'nant
ma•lig'ni•ty
ma•lin'ger
ma•lin'ger•er
mall *(promenade)*
  ✔ *maul*
mal'lard *pl.* -lard *or*
  -lards
mal'le•a•bil'i•ty
mal'le•a•ble
mal'let
mal'le•us *pl.* -le•i'
mal'low
malm'sey *pl.* -seys
mal•nour'ished
mal'nu•tri'tion
mal'oc•clu'sion
mal•o'dor
mal•o'dor•ous
mal•prac'tice
mal'prac•ti'tion•er
mal'tase'
Mal•tese' *pl.* -tese'
mal'tose'
mal'treat'
ma'ma *or* mam'ma
mam'ba *(snake)*
mam'bo *(dance), pl.*
  -bos
mam'mal

mam·ma′li·an
mam′ma·ry
mam′mo·gram′
mam·mog′ra·phy
mam′moth
man *pl.* men
man, manned,
  man′ning
man′a·cle, -cled,
  -cling
man′age, -aged,
  -ag·ing
man′age·a·bil′i·ty
man′age·a·ble
man′age·ment
man′ag·er
man′a·ge′ri·al
ma·ña′na
man′-at-arms′ *pl.*
  men′-at-arms′
man′a·tee′
Man′chu *pl.* -chu *or*
  -chus
Man·chur′i·an
man′da·la
Man′dan′ *pl.* -dan
  or -dans
man′da·rin
man′date′, -dat′ed,
  -dat′ing
man′da·to′ry
man′di·ble
man′do·lin′
man′drake′
man′drel *or* man′-
  dril *(spindle)*
man′drill *(baboon)*

mane *(hair)*
  ✓ main
man′-eat′er
man′-eat′ing
ma·neu′ver
ma·neu′ver·a·bil′i·
  ty
ma·neu′ver·a·ble
man′ga·nese′
mange
man′ger
man′gi·ness
man′gle, -gled,
  -gling
man′go *pl.* -goes *or*
  -gos
man′grove′
mang′y
man·han′dle,
  -dled, -dling
Man·hat′tan *also*
  man·hat′tan
  (cocktail)
Man·hat′tan
  (people)
man′hole′
man′hood′
man′-hour′
man′hunt′
ma′ni·a
ma′ni·ac′
ma·ni′a·cal
man′ic
man′ic-
  de·pres′sive
man′i·cot′ti
man′i·cure′,

  -cured′, -cur′ing
man′i·cur′ist
man′i·fest′
man′i·fes·ta′tion
man′i·fes′to *pl.*
  -toes *or* -tos
man′i·fold
man′i·kin *or*
  man′ni·kin *(dwarf)*
  ✓ mannequin
ma·nil′a *or*
  ma·nil′la
man′i·oc′ *also*
  man′i·o′ca
man′i·ple
ma·nip′u·la·ble
ma·nip′u·late′,
  -lat′ed, -lat′ing
ma·nip′u·la′tion
ma·nip′u·la′tive
ma·nip′u·la′tor
man′i·tou′ *pl.*
  -tous′
man′kind′
man′li·ness
man′ly
man′-made′
man′na
manned
man′ne·quin
  (model)
  ✓ manikin
man′ner *(behavior)*
  ✓ manor
man′nered
man′ner·ism
man′nish

man'-of-war' pl.
  men'-of-war'
ma·nom'e·ter
man'or (estate)
  ✔ manner
ma·no'ri·al
man'pow'er
man·qué'
man'sard
manse
man'ser'vant pl.
  men'ser'vants
man'sion
man'-sized' also
  man'-size'
man'slaugh'ter
man'ta
man'-tai'lored
man'tel also
  man'tle (shelf)
  ✔ mantle
man'tel·piece' also
  man'tle·piece'
man'tic
man·til'la
man'tis pl. -tis·es or
  -tes
man·tis'sa
man'tle (to cloak),
  -tled, -tling
  ✔ mantel
man'tra
man'trap'
man'u·al
man'u·fac'to·ry
man'u·fac'ture,
  -tured, -tur·ing

man'u·fac'tur·er
man'u·mis'sion
man'u·mit',
  -mit'ted, -mit'ting
ma·nure', -nured',
  -nur'ing
man'u·script'
Manx pl. Manx
man'y, more, most
Mao'ism
Mao'ist
Mao'ri pl. -ri or -ris
map, mapped,
  map'ping
ma'ple
mar, marred,
  mar'ring
mar'a·bou'
ma·ra'ca
mar'a·schi'no
mar'a·thon'
mar'a·thon'er
ma·raud'
mar'ble, -bled,
  -bling
march (journey)
March (month)
mar'chio·ness
Mar'di gras'
mare (female horse)
ma're (region of the
  moon), pl. -ri·a
mar'ga·rine
mar'ga·ri'ta
mar'gin
mar'gin·al
mar'gue·rite'

mar'i·gold'
mar'i·jua'na or
  mar'i·hua'na
ma·rim'ba
ma·ri'na
mar'i·nade'
mar'i·nate',
  -nat'ed, -nat'ing
ma·rine'
mar'i·ner
mar'i·o·nette'
mar'i·po'sa
mar'i·tal
mar'i·time'
mar'jo·ram
mark'down'
marked
mark'ed·ly
mark'er
mar'ket
mar'ket·a·bil'i·ty
mar'ket·a·ble
mar'ket·er
mar'ket·ing
mar'ket·place'
mark'ing
marks'man
marks'man·ship'
marks'wom'an
mark'up'
marl
mar'lin (fish)
mar'line (rope)
mar'line·spike'
mar'ma·lade'
mar·mo're·al
mar'mo·set'

mar'mot
ma•roon'
mar•quee' *(tent, entrance)*
mar'quis or mar'quess *(nobleman)*, pl. -quis•es or mar•quis' or -quess•es
mar•quise' *(marchioness)*
mar'qui•sette'
mar'riage
mar'riage•a•ble
mar'ried
mar'row
mar'ry, -ried, -ry•ing
mar•sa'la
marsh
mar'shal *(to organize)*, -shaled or -shalled, -shal•ing or -shal•ling
✔ *martial*
marsh'i•ness
marsh'land'
marsh'mal'low
marsh'y
mar•su'pi•al
mar'ten *(animal)*, pl. -ten or -tens
✔ *martin*
mar'tial *(warlike)*
✔ *marshal*
Mar'tian
mar'tin *(bird)*

✔ *marten*
mar'ti•net'
mar'tin•gale'
mar•ti'ni pl. -nis
mar'tyr
mar'tyr•dom
mar'vel -veled or -velled, -vel•ing or -vel•ling
mar'vel•ous also mar'vel•lous
Marx'i•an
Marx'ism
Marx'ist
mar'zi•pan'
mas•car'a
mas'cot
mas'cu•line
mas'cu•lin'i•ty
ma'ser
mash'er
mask *(covering)*
✔ *masque*
masked
mask'ing tape'
mas'och•ism
mas'o•chist
mas'o•chis'tic
ma'son
Ma•son'ic
Ma'son jar'
ma'son•ry
masque *(drama)*
✔ *mask*
mas'quer•ade', -ad'ed, -ad'ing
mas'quer•ad'er

mass *(matter)*
Mass also mass *(Eucharist ceremony)*
Mas'sa•chu'sett also Mas'sa•chu'set pl. -sett or -setts also -set or -sets
mas'sa•cre, -cred, -cring
mas•sage', -saged', -sag'ing
mas•seur'
mas•seuse'
mas•sif' *(mountain)*
mas'sive *(large)*
mass'-pro•duce', -duced', -duc'ing
mas•tec'to•my
mas'ter
mas'ter-at-arms' pl. mas'ters-at-arms'
mas'ter•ful
mas'ter•li•ness
mas'ter•ly
mas'ter•mind'
mas'ter•piece'
mas'ter•stroke'
mas'ter•work'
mas'ter•y
mast'head'
mas'ti•cate', -cat'ed, -cat'ing
mas'ti•ca'tion
mas'ti•ca'tor
mas'tiff
mas'to•don

mas'toid'

mas'tur·bate',
-bat'ed, -bat'ing

mas'tur·ba'tion

mat, mat'ted,
mat'ting

mat'a·dor'

match'book'

match'box'

match'mak'er

match'mak'ing

match'stick

match'up' *n.*

mate, mat'ed,
mat'ing

ma'té *or* ma'te

ma·te'ri·al *(sub-
stance)*
✓ materiel

ma·te'ri·al·ism

ma·te'ri·al·ist

ma·te'ri·al·is'tic

ma·te'ri·al·i·za'-
tion

ma·te'ri·al·ize',
-ized', -iz'ing

ma·te'ri·el' *or*
ma·té'ri·el' *(equip-
ment)*
✓ material

ma·ter'nal

ma·ter'ni·ty

math'e·mat'i·cal

math'e·ma·ti'cian

math'e·mat'ics

mat'i·nee' *or*
mat'i·née'

mat'ins

ma'tri·arch'

ma'tri·ar'chal

ma'tri·ar'chy

mat'ri·cid'al

mat'ri·cide'

ma·tric'u·late',
-lat'ed, -lat'ing

ma·tric'u·la'tion

mat'ri·lin'e·age

mat'ri·lin'e·al

mat'ri·mo'ni·al

mat'ri·mo'ny

ma'trix *pl.* -tri·ces'
or -trix·es'

ma'tron

ma'tron of hon'or
pl. ma'trons of
hon'or

mat'ted

mat'ter

mat'ter-of-fact'

mat'ting

mat'tock

mat'tress

mat'u·rate', -rat'ed,
-rat'ing

mat'u·ra'tion

mat'u·ra'tive

ma·ture', -tured',
-tur'ing

ma·ture', -tur'er,
-tur'est

ma·tur'i·ty

mat'zo *pl.* -zos *or*
-zot' *or* -zoth'

maud'lin

maul *(hammer)*
✓ mall

maun'der

Mau·ri·ta'ni·an

Mau·ri'ti·an

mau·so·le'um *pl.*
-le'ums *or* -le'a

mauve

mav'er·ick

maw

mawk'ish

max·il'la *pl.* -lae *or*
-las

max'i·lar

max'il·lar'y

max'im

max'i·mize',
-mized', -miz'ing

max'i·mum *pl.*
-mums *or* -ma

may, *aux. v., past
tense* might

May *(month)*

Ma'ya *pl.* -ya *or* -yas

Ma'yan

may'be

may'day' *(signal)*

may'flow·'er

may'fly'

may'hem'

may·on·naise'

may'or

may'or·al

may'or·al·ty

May'pole' *also*
may'pole'

maze *(labyrinth)*

✔ *maize*
ma•zur'ka *also*
  ma•zour'ka
Mc'In•tosh' *(apple)*
  ✔ *mackintosh*
me *pron.*
  ✔ *mi*
mead *(beverage,*
  meadow)
  ✔ *meed*
mead'ow
mead'ow•lark'
mea'ger *also*
  mea'gre
meal
meal'i•ness
meal'time'
meal'y
meal'y-mouthed'
mean *(to signify),*
  meant, mean'ing
  ✔ *mien*
mean *(unkind)*
  ✔ *mien*
mean *(midpoint)*
  ✔ *mien*
me•an'der
mean'ing
mean'time'
mean'while'
mea'sles
mea'sly
meas'ur•a•ble
meas'ur•a•bly
meas'ure, -ured,
  -ur•ing
meas'ured *adj.*

meas'ure•ment
meat *(food)*
  ✔ *meet, mete*
meat'ball'
meat'i•ness
meat'pack'ing
meat'y
mec'ca
me•chan'ic
me•chan'i•cal
me•chan'ics
mech'a•nism
mech'a•nis'tic
mech'a•ni•za'tion
mech'a•nize',
  -nized', -niz'ing
med'al *(award)*
  ✔ *meddle*
med'al•ist
me•dal'lion
med'dle *(to interfere),*
  -dled, -dling
  ✔ *medal*
med'dler
med'dle•some
me'di•a
me'di•al
me'di•an
me'di•ate', -at'ed,
  -at'ing
me'di•a'tion
me'di•a'tor
med'ic
Med'i•caid' *also*
  med'i•caid'
med'i•cal
me•dic'a•ment

Med'i•care' *also*
  med'i•care'
med'i•cate', -cat'ed,
  -cat'ing
med'i•ca'tion
me•dic'i•nal
med'i•cine
med'i•co' *pl.* -cos'
me'di•e'val *also*
  me'di•ae'val
me'di•o'cre
me'di•oc'ri•ty
med'i•tate', -tat'ed,
  -tat'ing
med'i•ta'tion
med'i•ta'tive
med'i•ta'tor
me'di•um *pl.* -di•a
  or -di•ums
med'ley *pl.* -leys
me•dul'la *pl.*
  -dul'las *or* -dul'lae
me•dul'la
  ob'lon•ga'ta *pl.*
  me•dul'la
  ob'lon•ga'tas *or*
  me•dul'lae
  ob'lon•ga'tae
meed *(reward)*
  ✔ *mead*
meek'ly
meer'schaum
meet *(to come upon),*
  met, meet'ing
  ✔ *meat, mete*
meet *(fitting)*
  ✔ *meat, mete*

meet'ing
meet'ing•house'
meg'a•bit'
meg'a•buck'
meg'a•byte'
meg'a•cy'cle
meg'a•hertz' *pl.*
  -hertz'
meg'a•lith'
meg'a•lith'ic
meg'a•lo•ma'ni•a
meg'a•lo•ma'ni•ac'
meg'a•lop'o•lis
meg'a•phone'
meg'a•ton'
meg'a•watt'
mei•o'sis *pl.* -ses'
mei•ot'ic
mel'a•mine'
mel'an•cho'li•a
mel'an•chol'ic
mel'an•chol'y
Mel'a•ne'sian
mé•lange' *also*
  me•lange'
mel'a•nin
mel'a•no'ma *pl.*
  -mas *or* -ma•ta
Mel'ba toast'
meld
me'lee' *also* mê•lée'
mel'io•rate', -rat'ed,
  -rat'ing
mel'io•ra'tion
mel•lif'lu•ous
mel'low
mel•lo'de•on

me•lod'ic
me•lo'di•ous
mel'o•dra'ma
mel'o•dra•mat'ic
mel'o•dy
mel'on
melt'down'
melt'er
melt'ing point'
mem'ber
mem'ber•ship'
mem'brane'
mem'bra•nous
me•men'to *pl.* -tos
  or -toes
mem'o *pl.* -os
mem'oir'
mem'o•ra•bil'i•a
mem'o•ra•ble
mem'o•ra•bly
mem'o•ran'dum
  pl. -dums *or* -da
me•mo'ri•al
me•mo'ri•al•i•za'-
  tion
me•mo'ri•al•ize',
  -ized', -iz'ing
mem'o•ri•za'tion
mem'o•rize',
  -rized', -riz'ing
mem'o•riz'er
mem'o•ry
men'ace, -aced,
  -ac•ing
mé•nage'
me•nag'er•ie
men•da'cious

men•dac'i•ty
men•de•le'vi•um
mend'er
men'di•can•cy
men'di•cant
men'folk' *or*
  men'folks'
men•ha'den *pl.*
  -den *or* -dens
me'ni•al
men•in•gi'tis
me•ninx *pl.*
  me•nin'ges
me•nis'cal *also*
  me•nis'cate' *also*
  me•nis'coid' *also*
  men'is•coi'dal
me•nis'cus *pl.* -ci'
  or -cus•es
Men'non•ite'
Me•nom'i•nee *pl.*
  -nee *or* -nees
men'o•paus'al
men'o•pause'
me•no'rah
men'sal
men'ses
men'stru•al
men'stru•ate',
  -at'ed, -at'ing
men'stru•a'tion
men'su•ra•bil'i•ty
men'su•ra•ble
men'su•ra'tion
men'su•ra'tive
men'tal
men•tal'i•ty

men'thol'
men'tho•lat'ed
men'tion
men'tor
men'u
me•ow'
me•phit'ic *also*
  me•phit'i•cal
me•phi'tis
mer'can•tile'
mer'can•til•ism
mer'can•til•ist
mer'ce•nar'y
mer'cer•ize', -ized',
  -iz'ing
mer'chan•dise',
  -dised', -dis'ing
mer'chan•dis'er
mer'chant
mer'ci•ful
mer'ci•less
mer•cu'ri•al
mer•cu'ri•al•ism
mer•cu'ric
mer•cu'rous
mer•cu'ry
mer'cy
mere *superl.* mer'est
mer'e•tri'cious
mer•gan'ser
merge, merged,
  merg'ing
merg'er
me•rid'i•an
me•ringue'
me•ri'no *pl.* -nos
mer'it

mer'i•toc'ra•cy
mer'it•o•crat'
mer'i•to'ri•ous
merle *also* merl
mer'lot'
mer'maid'
mer'man'
mer'ri•ly
mer'ri•ment
mer'ry
mer'ry-go-round'
mer'ry•mak'er
mer'ry•mak'ing
me'sa
mes•cal'
mes'ca•line'
mes•en•ter'ic
mes•en•ter'y *also*
  mes'en•ter'i•um *pl.*
  -i•a
mes'mer•ism
mes'mer•ize', -ized',
  -iz'ing
mes'o•derm'
Mes•o•lith'ic
mes'on'
Mes'o•po•ta'mi•an
mes'o•sphere'
Mes'o•zo'ic
mes•quite'
mess
mes'sage
mes'sen•ger
Mes•si'ah
mes'si•an'ic
mess'i•ly
mess'i•ness

mess'mate'
mess'y
mes•ti'za
mes•ti'zo *pl.* -zos *or*
  -zoes
met'a•bol'ic
me•tab'o•lism
me•tab'o•lize'
  -lized', -liz'ing
met'a•car'pal
met'a•car'pus *pl.*
  -pi
met'al *(element)*
  ✔ mettle
me•tal'lic
met'al•loid'
met'al•lur'gi•cal
met'al•lur'gist
met'al•lur'gy
met'al•work'
met'al•work'ing
met'a•mor'phic
met'a•mor'phism
met'a•mor'phose',
  -phosed', -phos'ing
met'a•mor'pho•sis
  pl. -ses'
met'a•phase'
met'a•phor'
met'a•phor'i•cal *or*
  met'a•phor'ic
met'a•phor'i•cal•ly
met'a•phys'i•cal
met'a•phy•si'cian
met'a•phys'ics
me•tas'ta•sis *pl.*
  -ses'

me•tas′ta•size′,
 -sized′, -siz′ing
met′a•tar′sal
met′a•tar′sus *pl.* -si
met′a•zo′an
mete (*to distribute*),
 met′ed, met′ing
 ✔ *meat, meet*
me′te•or
me′te•or′ic
me′te•or•ite′
me′te•or•oid′
me′te•or•o•log′-
 i•cal
me′te•or•ol′o•gist
me′te•or•ol′o•gy
me′ter
meth′ane′
meth′a•no′
me•thinks′ *past*
 tense me•thought′
meth′od
me•thod′i•cal *also*
 me•thod′ic
Meth′od•ist
meth′od•o•log′i•cal
meth′od•ol′o•gy
meth′yl
me•tic′u•lous
mé•tier′
met′o•nym′
me•ton′y•my
met′ric
met′ri•cal
met′ri•ca′tion
met′ro *pl.* -ros
me•trol′o•gy

met′ro•nome′
met′ro•nom′ic
me•trop′o•lis
met′ro•pol′i•tan
met′tle (*spirit*)
 ✔ *metal*
met′tle•some
mew
mewl (*to cry*)
 ✔ *mule*
mews (*street*)
 ✔ *muse*
Mex′i•can
me•zu′zah *also*
 me•zu′za *pl.* -zahs
 also -zas *or*
 me•zu•zot′
mez′za•nine′
mez′zo for′te′
mez′zo-so•pran′o
 pl. -os
mez′zo-tint′
mho (*electrical unit*),
 pl. mhos
 ✔ *mow*
mi (*musical tone*)
 ✔ *me*
Mi•am′i *pl.* -am′i *or*
 -am′is
mi•as′ma *pl.* -mas *or*
 -ma•ta
mi•as′mal *also*
 mi•as′mat′ic *also*
 mi•as′mic
mi′ca
mice
Mic′mac′ *pl.* -mac′

 or -macs′
mi′crobe′
mi′cro•bi•o•log′i•
 cal
mi′cro•bi•ol′o•gist
mi′cro•bi•ol′o•gy
mi′cro•chip′
mi′cro•cir′cuit
mi′cro•coc′cus *pl.*
 -coc′ci′
mi′cro•com•put′er
mi′cro•cosm′
mi′cro•cos′mic
 also mi′cro•cos′-
 mi•cal
mi′cro•ec′o•nom′-
 ics
mi′cro•fiche′
mi′cro•film′
mi•crom′e•ter
 (*measuring device*)
mi′cro•me′ter (*unit*
 of measurement)
mi•crom′e•try
mi′cron′ *also*
 mi′kron′ *pl.* -crons′
 or -cra *also* -krons′
 or -kra
Mi′cro•ne′sian
mi′cro•nu′cle•us
 pl. -cle′i′ *or*
 -cle•us•es
mi′cro•or′gan•ism
mi′cro•phone′
mi′cro•proc′es•sor
mi′cro•scope′
mi′cro•scop′ic *also*

mi′cro•scop′i•cal
mi•cros′co•pist
mi•cros′co•py
mi′cro•sec′ond
mi′cro•sur′ger•y
mi′cro•wave′,
 -waved′, -wav′ing
mid′air′
mid′brain′
mid′course′
mid′day′
mid′dle
mid′dle-aged′
mid′dle-class′
mid′dle•man′
mid′dle•weight′
mid′dling
mid′dy *(blouse)*
 ✔ *midi*
midge
midg′et
mid′i *(skirt)*
 ✔ *middy*
mid′land
mid′lev′el
mid′life′
mid′morn′ing
mid′most′
mid′night′
mid′point′
mid′range′
mid′rib′
mid′riff′
mid′sec′tion
mid′ship′
mid′ship′man
midst

mid′stream′
mid′sum′mer
mid′term′
mid′town′
mid′way′
mid′week′
mid′wife′ *pl.*
 -wives′
mid′wife′ry
mid′win′ter
mid′year′
mien *(bearing)*
 ✔ *mean*
miff
might *past tense of*
 may
 ✔ *mite*
might′y
mi′gnon•ette′
mi′graine′
mi′grant
mi′grate′, -grat′ed,
 -grat′ing
mi•gra′tion
mi′gra•to′ry
mi•ka′do *pl.* -dos
mike
mil *(unit of length)*
 ✔ *mill*
mi•la′dy
milch
mild
mil′dew′
mild′ly
mile′age
mile′post′
mile′stone′

mi•lieu′ *pl.* -lieus′ *or*
 -lieux′
mil′i•tan•cy
mil′i•tant
mil′i•tar′i•ly
mil′i•ta•rism
mil′i•ta•rist
mil′i•ta•ris′tic
mil′i•ta•ri•za′tion
mil′i•ta•rize′,
 -rized′, -riz′ing
mil′i•tar′y
mil′i•tate′, -tat′ed,
 -tat′ing
mi•li′tia
mi•li′tia•man
milk′er
milk′i•ness
milk′maid′
milk′man′
milk′ shake′
milk′ snake′
milk′sop′
milk′ tooth′
milk′weed′
milk′y
mill *(grinder)*
 ✔ *mil*
mill *(money)*
 ✔ *mil*
mill′age
mill′dam′
mil′le•nar′i•an
mil′le•nar′y
 (thousand)
 ✔ *millinery*
mil′len′ni•al

mil·len'ni·um *pl.*
  -ni·ums *or* -ni·a
mill'er
mil'let
mil'li·bar'
mil'li·gram'
mil'li·li·ter
mil'li·me·ter
mil'li·ner
mil'li·ner'y *(hats)*
  ✔ *millenary*
mill'ing
mil'lion *pl.* -lion *or*
  -lions
mil'lion·aire'
mil'lionth
mil'li·pede' *or*
  mil'le·pede'
mill'pond'
mill'race'
mill'stone'
mill'stream'
mill' wheel'
mi·lord'
milque'toast'
mime, mimed,
  mim'ing
mim'e·o·graph'
mim'er
mi·me'sis
mi·met'ic
mim'ic, -icked,
  -ick·ing
mim'ick·er
mim'ic·ry
mi·mo'sa
min'a·ret'

min'a·to'ry
mince, minced,
  minc'ing
mince'meat'
mind
mind'-al'ter·ing
mind'-bog'gling
mind'ed
mind'ful
mind'less
mind' read'er
mind'set' *or*
  mind'-set'
mine, mined,
  min'ing
mine *pron.*
min'er *(one that
  mines)*
  ✔ *minor*
min'er·al
min'er·a·log'i·cal
min'er·al'o·gist
min'er·al'o·gy
min'e·stro'ne
min'gle, -gled,
  -gling
min'i *pl.* -is
min'i·a·ture
min'i·a·tur·ize',
  -ized', -iz'ing
min'i·bar'
min'i·bike'
min'i·bus'
min'i·com·put'er
min'im
min'i·mal'
min'i·mal·ism

min'i·mal·ist
min'i·mal·ize',
  -ized', -iz'ing
min'i·mi·za'tion
min'i·mize',
  -mized', -miz'ing
min'i·miz'er
min'i·mum *pl.*
  -mums *or* -ma
min'ing
min'ion
min'i·se'ries
min'i·skirt'
min'is·ter
min'is·te'ri·al
min'is·tra'tion
min'is·try
min'i·van'
mink *pl.* mink *or*
  minks
Min'ne·so'tan
min'now *pl.* -now
  or -nows
Mi·no'an
mi'nor *(lesser or
  smaller)*
  ✔ *miner*
mi·nor'i·ty
mi'nor-league' *adj.*
min'strel
mint'age
min'u·end'
min'u·et'
mi'nus
min'us·cule' *also*
  min'is·cule'
min'ute *(unit of*

mi·nute' *(small)*

min·ute·ly *(once a minute)*

mi·nute'ly *(on a small scale)*

min'ute·man'

mi·nu'ti·a *pl.* -ti·ae'

minx

Mi'o·cene'

mir'a·cle

mi·rac'u·lous

mi·rage'

mire, mired, mir'ing

mir'ror

mirth

mir'y

mis'ad·ven'ture

mis'al·li'ance

mis·al'lo·cate', -cat'ed, -cat'ing

mis·an·thrope' *also* mis·an'thro·pist

mis·an·throp'ic *also* mis'an·throp'i·cal

mis·an'thro·py

mis'ap·pli·ca'tion

mis'ap·ply', -plied', -ply'ing

mis'ap·pre·hend'

mis·ap're·hen'sion

mis'ap·pro'pri·ate', -at'ed, -at'ing

mis'ap·pro'pri·a'- tion

mis'be·got'ten

mis'be·have', -haved', -hav'ing

mis'be·hav'ior

mis·cal'cu·late', -lat'ed, -lat'ing

mis'cal·cu·la'tion

mis·call'

mis·car'riage

mis'car'ry, -ried, -ry·ing

mis·cast', -cast', -cast'ing

mis'ceg·e·na'tion

mis'cel·la'ne·ous

mis'cel·la'ny

mis·chance'

mis'chief

mis'chie·vous

mis'ci·bil'i·ty

mis'ci·ble

mis'con·ceive', -ceived', -ceiv'ing

mis'con·cep'tion

mis·con'duct

mis'con·strue', -strued', -stru'ing

mis·count' *n.*

mis·count' *v.*

mis·cre·ant

mis·deal', -dealt', -deal'ing

mis·deal' *n.*

mis·deed'

mis·de·mean'or

mis'di·rect'

mis'di·rec'tion

mis·do'ing

mi'ser

mis'er·a·ble

mis'er·a·bly

mi'ser·li·ness

mi'ser·ly

mis'er·y

mis·fire', -fired', -fir'ing

mis'fire' *n.*

mis'fit'

mis·for'tune

mis·giv'ing

mis·gov'ern

mis·gov'ern·ment

mis·guid'ance

mis·guide', -guid'ed, -guid'ing

mis·han'dle, -dled, -dling

mis'hap'

mis·hear', -heard', -hear'ing

mish'mash'

mis'in·form'

mis'in·for·ma'tion

mis'in·ter'pret

mis'in·ter'pre·ta'- tion

mis·judge', -judged', -judg'ing

mis·judg'ment

mis·lay', -laid', -lay'ing

mis·lead', -led', -lead'ing

mis·man'age, -aged, -ag·ing

mis·man'age·ment

mis·match'

mis·name',
-named', -nam'ing

mis·no'mer

mi·sog'a·my

mi·sog'y·nist

mi·sog'y·nous

mi·sog'y·ny

mis·place', -placed',
-plac'ing

mis·play'

mis·print' *v.*

mis·print' *n.*

mis·pro·nounce',
-nounced',
-nounc'ing

mis·pro·nun'ci·a'-
tion

mis·quo·ta'tion

mis·quote',
-quot'ed, -quot'ing

mis·read', -read',
-read'ing

mis·rep're·sent'

mis·rep're·sen·ta'-
tion

mis·rule', -ruled',
-rul'ing

miss

mis·sal *(prayer book)*
✔ *missile*

mis·shape',
-shaped, -shaped' *or*
-shap'en, -shap'ing

mis·sile *(weapon)*
✔ *missal*

miss'ing

mis'sion

mis'sion·ar'y

Mis·sis·sip'pi·an

mis'sive

Mis·sou'ri *pl.* -ri *or*
-ris

mis·speak', -spoke',
-spo'ken,
-speak'ing

mis·spell', -spelled'
or -spelt', -spell'ing

mis·spend', -spent',
-spend'ing

mis·state', -stat'ed,
-stat'ing

mis·state'ment

mis·step'

miss'y

mist

mis·tak'a·ble

mis·take', -took',
-tak'en, -tak'ing

Mis'ter

mist'i·ness

mis'tle·toe'

mis'tral

mis·treat'

mis·treat'ment

mis'tress

mis·tri'al

mis·trust'

mist'y

mis·un·der·stand',
-stood', -stand'ing

mis·use', -used',
-us'ing

mite *(organism,
small amount)*
✔ *might*

mi'ter

mit'i·gate', -gat'ed,
-gat'ing

mit'i·ga'tion

mi·to·chon'dri·on
pl. -dri·a

mi·to'sis *pl.* -ses

mi·tot'ic

mitt

mit'ten

mix

mixed

mix'er

mix'ture

mix'-up' *also*
mix'up'

miz'zen *or* miz'en

miz'zen·mast *or*
miz'en·mast

mne·mon'ic

mo'a

moan

moat *(ditch)*
✔ *mote*

mob, mobbed,
mob'bing

mo'bile

mo·bil'i·ty

mo'bi·li·za'tion

mo'bi·lize', -lized',
-liz'ing

Mö'bi·us strip'

mob'ster

moc'ca·sin

mo'cha
mock
mock'er
mock'er•y
mock'-he•ro'ic
mock'ing•bird'
mock'up' *also*
  mock'-up' *n.*
mod
mod'al
mo•dal'i•ty
mode
mod'el, -eled *also*
  -elled, -el'ing *or*
  -el•ling
mo'dem'
mod'er•ate', -at'ed,
  -at'ing
mod'er•a'tion
mod'er•a'to *pl.* -tos
mod'er•a'tor
mod'ern
mod'ern•ism
mod'ern•ist
mod'ern•is'tic
mo•der'ni•ty
mod'ern•i•za'tion
mod'ern•ize', -ized',
  -iz'ing
mod'est
mod'es•ty
mod'i•cum *pl.*
  -cums *or* -ca
mod'i•fi•ca'tion
mod'i•fi'er
mod'i•fy', -fied',
  -fy'ing

mod'ish
mod'u•lar
mod'u•late', -lat'ed,
  -lat'ing
mod'u•la'tion
mod'u•la'tor
mod'ule
mo'gul *(magnate)*
Mo'gul *(Indian
  Moslem)*
mo'hair'
Mo•ha've *also*
  Mo•ja've *pl.* -ve *or*
  -ves
Mo'hawk' *pl.*
  -hawk' *or* -hawks'
Mo•he'gan *pl.*
  -gan *or* -gans
Mohs' scale'
moi'e•ty
moi•ré'
moist
mois'ten
mois'ture
mo'lar
mo•las'ses
mold'a•ble
mold'i•ness
mold'ing
mold'y
mole
mo•lec'u•lar
mol'e•cule'
mole'hill'
mole'skin'
mo•lest'
mo•les•ta'tion

mo•lest'er
moll
mol'li•fi'a•ble
mol'li•fi•ca'tion
mol'li•fy', -fied',
  -fy'ing
mol'lusk *also*
  mol'lusc
mol'ly•cod'dle,
  -dled, -dling
molt
mol'ten
mol'to
mo•lyb'de•num
mom
mom'-and-pop'
  adj.
mo'ment
mo'men•tar'i•ly
mo'men•tar'y
mo•men'tous
mo•men'tum *pl.*
  -ta *or* -tums
mom'my
mo'nad
mon'arch
mo•nar'chic
mo•nar'chi•cal
mon'ar•chism
mon'ar•chist
mon'ar•chy
mon'as•te'ri•al
mon'as•ter'y
mo•nas'tic
mon'a•tom'ic
mon•au'ral
Mon'day

mo·ne′ran
mon′e·tar′i·ly
mon′e·tar·ism
mon′e·tar′y
mon′ey *pl.* -eys *or*
 -ies
mon′ey·bag′
mon′ey·chang′er
mon′eyed *also*
 mon′ied
mon′ey·lend′er
mon′ey·mak′er
mon′ey·mak′ing
mon′ger
Mon′gol
Mon·go′li·an
mon′goose′ *pl.*
 -goos′es
mon′grel
mon′i·ker *or*
 mon′ick·er
mo′nism
mo·ni′tion
mon′i·tor
mon′i·to′ry
monk
mon′key *pl.* -keys
mon′key·shine′
monk′ish
monks′hood
mon′o
mon′o·chro·mat′ic
mon′o·chro′ma·
 tism
mon′o·chrome′
mon′o·cle
mon′o·cot

mon′o·cot′y·le′-
 don
mon′o·cot′y·le′-
 don·ous
mo·noc′u·lar
mon′o·cul′ture
mon′o·dy
mo·nog′a·mist
mo·nog′a·mous
mo·nog′a·my
mon′o·gram′,
 -grammed′ *also*
 -gramed′,
 -gram′ming *or*
 -gram′ing
mon′o·graph′
mon′o·lith′
mon′o·lith′ic
mon′o·logue′
mon′o·ma′ni·a
mon′o·ma′ni·ac′
mon′o·ma·ni′a·cal
mon′no·mer
mo·no′mi·al
mon′o·nu′cle·
 o′sis
mon′o·phon′ic
mon′o·plane′
mo·nop′o·lis′tic
mo·nop′o·li·za′-
 tion
mo·nop′o·lize′,
 -lized′, -liz′ing
mo·nop′o·liz′er
mo·nop′o·ly
mon′o·rail′
mon′o·so′di·um

glu′ta·mate′
mon′o·syl·lab′ic
mon′o·syl′la·ble
mon′o·the′ism
mon′o·the′ist
mon′o·the·is′tic
mon′o·tone′
mo·not′o·nous
mo·not′o·ny
mon·ox′ide′
Mon·sei·gneur′ *pl.*
 Mes·sei·gneurs′
Mon·sieur′ *pl.*
 Mes·sieurs′
Mon·si′gnor *also*
 mon·si′gnor
mon·soon′
mon′ster
mon·stros′i·ty
mon′strous
mon·tage′
Mon·tan′an
month
mon′u·ment
mon′u·men′tal
moo *pl.* moos
moo, mooed,
 moo′ing
mooch′er
mood′i·ly
mood′i·ness
mood′y
moon′beam′
moon′calf′
moon′light′
moon′light′er
moon′lit′

moon'scape'
moon'shine'
moon'stone'
moon'struck'
moon'walk'
moor *(to secure)*
moor *(open land)*
Moor *(North African)*
moor'ing
Moor'ish
moose *(animal)*, pl.
  moose
  ✔ *mousse*
moot
mop, mopped,
  mop'ping
mope, moped,
  mop'ing
mo'ped'
mop'pet
mo·raine'
mor'al
mo·rale'
mor'al·ist
mor'al·is'tic
mo·ral'i·ty
mor'al·i·za'tion
mor'al·ize', -ized',
  -iz'ing
mo·rass'
mor'a·to'ri·um *pl.*
  -ri·ums *or* -ri·a
Mo·ra'vi·an
mo'ray
mor'bid
mor·bid'i·ty
mor·da'cious

mor·dac'i·ty
mor'dan·cy
mor'dant *(caustic)*
mor'dent *(melodic ornament)*
mo·rel'
more·o'ver
mo'res'
mor'ga·nat'ic
morgue
mor'i·bund'
Mor'mon
morn *(morning)*
  ✔ *mourn*
morn'ing *(dawn)*
  ✔ *mourning*
Mo'ro *pl.* -ro *or* -ros
Mo·roc'can
mo·roc'co *pl.* -cos
mo'ron'
mo·ron'ic
mo·rose'
mor'pheme'
mor'phine'
mor'pho·log'i·cal *or* mor'pho·log'ic
mor·phol'o·gy
mor'row
Morse' code'
mor'sel
mor'tal
mor·tal'i·ty
mor'tar
mor'tar·board'
mort'gage, -gaged,
  -gag·ing

mort'ga·gee'
mort'ga·gor' *also* mort'gag·er
mor·ti'cian
mor'ti·fi·ca'tion
mor'ti·fi'er
mor'ti·fy', -fied',
  -fy'ing
mor'tise *also*
  mor'tice, -tised *also*
  -ticed, -tis·ing *or*
  -tic·ing
mor'tu·ar'y
mo·sa'ic
mo'sey, -seyed,
  -sey·ing
mosque
mos·qui'to *pl.* -toes *or* -tos
moss
moss'back'
moss'y
most'ly
mote *(speck)*
  ✔ *moat*
mo·tel'
moth
moth'ball'
moth'-eat'en
moth'er
moth'er·hood'
moth'er-in-law' *pl.*
  moth'ers-in-law'
moth'er·land'
moth'er·li·ness
moth'er·ly
moth'er-of-pearl'

moth'er su•pe'ri•or
  pl. moth'ers
  su•pe'ri•or *or*
  moth'er su•pe'ri•ors

mo•tif' *(design)*
  ✔ *motive*

mo'tile

mo•til'i•ty

mo'tion

mo'ti•vate', -vat'ed,
  -vat'ing

mo'ti•va'tion

mo'tive *(reason, im-*
  pulse)
  ✔ *motif*

mot'ley *pl.* -leys

mo'tor

mo'tor•bike'

mo'tor•boat'

mo'tor•cade'

mo'tor•car'

mo'tor•cy'cle,
  -cled, -cling

mo'tor•cy'clist

mo'tor•ist

mo'tor•i•za'tion

mo'tor•ize', -ized',
  -iz'ing

mot'tle, -tled, -tling

mot'to *pl.* -toes *or*
  -tos

mound

mount

moun'tain

moun'tain•eer'

moun'tain•ous

moun'tain•side'

moun'tain•top'

moun'te•bank'

Mount'ie *also*
  Mount'y *pl.* -ies

mount'ing

mourn *(to grieve)*
  ✔ *morn*

mourn'er

mourn'ing *(grief)*
  ✔ *morning*

mouse *(animal), pl.*
  mice

mouse *(device), pl.*
  mice *or* mous'es

mouse, moused,
  mous'ing

mous'er

mouse'trap'

mousse *(dessert)*
  ✔ *moose*

mous'y *also*
  mous'ey

mouth

mouth'ful'

mouth'part'

mouth'piece'

mouth'wash'

mouth'wa•ter•ing

mou'ton' *(sheep-*
  skin)
  ✔ *mutton*

mov'a•ble *also*
  move'a•ble

move, moved,
  mov'ing

move'ment

mov'er

mov'ie

mov'ie•mak'er

mov'ing

mow *(to cut down),*
  mowed, mowed *or*
  mown, mow'ing
  ✔ *mho*

mow'er

moz'za•rel'la

mu

much, more, most

mu'ci•lage

mu'ci•lag'i•nous

muck

muck'rake',
  -raked', -rak'ing

muck'rak'er

mu'cous *(like*
  mucus)

mu'cus *(gland secre-*
  tion)

mud'dle, -dled,
  -dling

mud'dle-head'ed

mud'dy, -died,
  -dy'ing

mud'guard'

mud'sling'er

mud'sling'ing

mu•ez'zin

muff

muf'fin

muf'fle, -fled, -fling

muf'fler

muf'ti

mug, mugged,

mug'ging

mug'ger

mug'gi•ness

mug'gy

mug'wump'

muk'luk'

mu•lat'to *pl.* -tos or
-toes

mul'ber'ry

mulch *(covering)*

mulct *(penalty)*

mule *(animal,
slipper)*
✔ *mewl*

mul'ish

mull

mul'lein

mul'let *pl.* -let or
-lets

mul'li•gan

mul'li•ga•taw'ny

mul'lion

mul'ti•cel'lu•lar

mul'ti•col'ored

mul'ti•cul'tur•al

mul'ti•cul'tur•al•
ism

mul'ti•di•men'-
sion•al

mul'ti•eth'nic

mul'ti•far'i•ous

mul'ti•form'

mul'ti•gen'er•a'-
tion•al

mul'ti•lat'er•al

mul'ti•me'di•a

mul'ti•mil'lion•

aire'

mul'ti•na'tion•al

mul'ti•pack'

mul'ti•ple

mul'ti•ple-choice'

mul'ti•plex'

mul'ti•pli•cand'

mul'ti•pli•ca'tion

mul'ti•plic'a•tive

mul'ti•plic'i•ty

mul'ti•pli'er

mul'ti•ply', -plied',
-ply'ing

mul'ti•pronged'

mul'ti•pur'pose'

mul'ti•ra'cial

mul'ti•stage'

mul'ti•tude'

mul'ti•tu'di•nous

mul'ti•va'lent

mum'ble, -bled,
-bling

mum'bler

mum'ble•ty-peg'
also mum'ble-the-
peg'

mum'bo jum'bo
or mum'bo-jum'bo

mum'mer

mum'mer•y

mum'mi•fi•ca'tion

mum'mi•fy', -fied',
-fy'ing

mum'my

numps

munch

mun•dane'

mu•nic'i•pal

mu•nic'i•pal'i•ty

mu•nif'i•cence

mu•nif'i•cent
(generous)
✔ *magnificent*

mu•ni'tions

mu'ral

mu'ral•ist

mur'der

mur'der•er

mur'der•ous

mu'rex *pl.* -ri•ces' or
-rex•es

murk *also* mirk

murk'i•ness

murk'y

mur'mur

mus'ca•tel'

mus'cle *(to force),*
-cled, -cling
✔ *mussel, muzzle*

mus'cle•bound'
also mus'cle-
bound'

mus'co•vite' *(mica)*

Mus'co•vite'
(people)

mus'cu•lar

mus'cu•lar'i•ty

mus'cu•la•ture'

muse *(to ponder),*
mused, mus'ing
✔ *mews*

mu•se'um

mu•se'um•go'er

mush'i•ly

mush'i•ness
mush'room'
mush'y
mu'sic
mu'si•cal *(of music)*
mu'si•cale' *(concert)*
mu'si•cal'i•ty
mu•si'cian
mu•si'cian•ship'
musk
mus'kel•lunge' *or*
  mus'ke•lunge' *pl.*
  -lunge' *or* -lung'es
mus'ket
mus'ket•eer'
mus'ket•ry
musk'i•ness
musk'mel'on
Mus•ko'ge•an *also*
  Mus•kho'ge•an
musk'rat' *pl.* -rat' *or*
  -rats'
musk'y
Mus'lim *or*
  Mos'lem
mus'lin
muss
mus'sel *(shellfish)*
  ✔ *muscle, muzzle*
must
mus'tache' *also*
  mous'tache'
mus•ta'chio *pl.*
  -chios
mus'tang'
mus'tard
mus'ter

must'i•ness
must'y
mu•ta•bil'i•ty
mu'ta•ble
mu'tant
mu'tate, -tat•ed,
  -tat•ing
mu•ta'tion
mute, mut'er,
  mut'est
mute, mut'ed
  mut'ing
mu'ti•late', -lat'ed,
  -lat'ing
mu'ti•la'tion
mu'ti•la'tor
mu'ti•neer'
mu'ti•nous
mu'ti•ny, -nied,
  -ny'ing
mutt
mut'ter
mut'ton *(sheep)*
  ✔ *mouton*
mu'tu•al
mu'tu•al'i•ty
muu'muu'
muz'zle *(to restrain)*,
  -zled, -zling
  ✔ *muscle, mussel*
muz'zle•load'er
my
my'as•the'ni•a
my•ce'li•um *pl.* -li•a
my'co•log'i•cal
  also my'co•log'ic
my•col'o•gist

my•col'o•gy
my•co'sis *pl.* -ses'
my'e•lin *also*
  my'e•line
my'na *or* my'nah
  also mi'na
my'o•car'di•al
my'o•car'di•um
my•o'pi•a
my•op'ic
myr'i•ad
myrrh
myr'tle
my•self'
mys•te'ri•ous
mys'ter•y
mys'tic
mys'ti•cal
mys'ti•cism
mys'ti•fi•ca'tion
mys'ti•fy', -fied',
  -fy'ing
mys•tique'
myth
myth'i•cal *also*
  myth'ic
myth'o•log'i•cal
  also myth'o•log'ic
my•thol'o•gist
my•thol'o•gy

N

nab, nabbed,
  nab'bing
na'bob'

na•celle'
na'cho' *pl.* -chos'
na'cre
na'dir
nag, nagged,
  nag'ging
nag'ger
Na'hua'tl *pl.* -tl *or*
  -tls
nai'ad' *pl.* -a•des' *or*
  -ads'
nail
na•ive' *or* na•ïve'
  also na•if' *or* na•ïf'
na'ive•té' *or*
  na'ïve•té'
na'ked
nam'by-pam'by
name, named,
  nam'ing
name'less
name'ly
name'sake'
name'tag'
name'tape'
nan•keen'
nan'ny
nan'o•sec'ond
nan'o•tech•nol'-
  o•gy
nap, napped,
  nap'ping
na'palm'
nape
naph'tha
naph'tha•lene'
nap'kin

na•po'le•on
nap'time'
nar'cis•sism
nar'cis•sist
nar'cis•sis'tic
nar•cis'sus *pl.*
  -cis'sus•es *or* -cis'si'
nar'co•dol'lar
nar•co'sis
nar•cot'ic
Nar'ra•gan'sett *pl.*
  -sett *or* -setts
nar'rate', -rat'ed,
  -rat'ing
nar•ra'tion
nar'ra•tive
nar'ra'tor *also*
  nar'ra'ter
nar'row
nar'row•cast',
  -cast', -cast'ing
nar'row•gauge'
  also nar'row•
  gauged'
nar'row-mind'ed
nar'whal *also*
  nar'wal *or*
  nar'whale'
nar'y
na'sal
na'sal•i•za'tion
na'sal•ize', -ized',
  -iz'ing
nas'cent
nas•tur'tium
nas'ti•ly
nas'ti•ness

nas'ty
na'tal
Natch'ez *pl.* -ez
na'tion
na'tion•al
na'tion•al•ism
na'tion•al•ist
na'tion•al•is'tic
na'tion•al•i•ty
na'tion•al•i•za'tion
na'tion•al•ize',
  -ized', -iz'ing
na'tion•wide'
na'tive
Na'tive
  A•mer'i•can
na'tive-born'
na•tiv'i•ty
nat'ti•ly
nat'ty
nat'u•ral
nat'ur•al•ism
nat'ur•al•ist
nat'u•ral•is'tic
nat'u•ral•i•za'tion
nat'u•ral•ize',
  -ized', -iz'ing
na'ture
na'tured
naught *also* nought
naugh'ti•ly
naugh'ti•ness
naugh'ty
nau'se•a
nau'se•ate', -at'ed,
  -at'ing
nau'seous

nau'ti·cal
nau'ti·lus pl. -lus·es
  or -li'
Nav'a·jo' also
  Nav'a·ho' pl. -jo' or
  -jos' also -ho' or
  -hos'
na'val (nautical)
  ✔ navel
nave (part of a
  church)
  ✔ knave
na'vel (bellybutton)
  ✔ naval
nav'i·ga·bil'i·ty
nav'i·ga·ble
nav'i·gate', -gat'ed,
  -gat'ing
nav'i·ga'tion
nav'i·ga'tion·al
nav'i·ga'tor
na'vy
nay (no)
  ✔ née, neigh
nay'say', -said,
  -say'ing
nay'say'er
Naz'a·rene'
Na'zi pl. -zis
Na'zism also
  Na'zi·ism
Ne·an'der·thal'
Ne'a·pol'i·tan
neap' tide'
near
near'by'
near'sight'ed

neat
neat's'-foot' oil'
neb'bish
neb'u·la pl. -lae' or
  -las
neb'u·lar
neb'u·lous
nec'es·sar'i·ly
nec'es·sar'y
ne·ces'si·tate',
  -tat'ed, -tat'ing
ne·ces'si·ta'tion
ne·ces'si·ty
neck
neck'band'
neck'er·chief
neck'lace
neck'line'
neck'tie'
neck'wear'
ne·crol'o·gy
nec'ro·man'cer
nec'ro·man'cy
nec'ro·man'tic
ne·crop'o·lis pl.
  -lis·es or -leis'
nec'tar
nec'tar·ine'
née also nee (born)
  ✔ nay, neigh
need (requirement)
  ✔ knead
need'ful
nee'dle, -dled, -dling
nee'dle·fish' pl.
  -fish' or -fish·es
nee'dle·point'

need'less
nee'dle·work'
need'n't
need'y
ne'er
ne'er'-do-well'
ne·far'i·ous
ne·gate', -gat'ed,
  -gat'ing
ne·ga'tion
neg'a·tive
neg'a·tiv·ism
neg'a·tiv·ist
ne·glect'
ne·glect'ful
neg'li·gee' also
  neg'li·gée' or
  neg'li·gé'
neg'li·gence
neg'li·gent
neg'li·gi·bil'i·ty
neg'li·gi·ble
ne·go'tia·bil'i·ty
ne·go'tia·ble
ne·go'ti·ate', -at'ed,
  -at'ing
ne·go'ti·a'tion
ne·go'ti·a'tor
Ne·gri'to pl. -tos or
  -toes
Ne'gro pl. -groes
Ne'groid'
neigh (horse's cry)
  ✔ nay, née
neigh'bor
neigh'bor·hood'
neigh'bor·li·ness

nei'ther *(not either)*
✔ nether

nek'ton

nek·ton'ic

nel'son

nem'a·to·cyst'

nem'a·tode'

nem'e·sis *pl.* -ses'

ne'o·clas'sic *also*
ne'o·clas'si·cal

ne'o·clas'si·cism

ne'o·clas'si·cist

ne'o·co·lo'ni·al·ist

ne'o·con·ser'va·
tism

ne'o·dym'i·um

ne·ol'o·gism

ne'on'

ne'o·na'tal

ne'o·nate'

Ne'o-Na'zi

ne'o·phyte'

ne'o·plasm'

ne'o·prene'

Nep'al·ese' *pl.* -ese'

neph'ew

neph'rite'

ne·phri'tis *pl.*
-phrit'i·des' *or*
-phri'tis·es'

neph'ron

nep'o·tism

nep·tu'ni·um

ner·va'tion

nerve

nerve'-rack'ing *or*
nerve'-wrack'ing

nerv'i·ness

nerv'ous

nerv'y

nest

nes'tle, -tled, -tling

nest'ling *(young
bird)*

net, net'ted, net'ting

neth'er *(below)*
✔ neither

neth'er·most'

net'su·ke'

net'ting

net'tle, -tled, -tling

net'tle·some

net'work'

net'work'ing

Neuf·châ·tel'

neu'ral

neu·ral'gia

neu·ral'gic

neu·ras·the'ni·a

neu·ri'tis

neu'ro·bi·ol'o·gy

neu'ro·chem'is·try

neu'ro·log'i·cal

neu·rol'o·gist

neu·rol'o·gy

neu'ron'

neu'ro·pa·thol'-
o·gy

neu·ro'sis *pl.* -ses'

neu·rot'ic

neu'ro·trans·mit·
ter

neu'ter

neu'tral

neu·tral'i·ty

neu'tral·i·za'tion

neu'tral·ize', -ized',
-iz'ing

neu'tral·iz'er

neu·tri'no *pl.* -nos

neu'tron'

Ne·vad'an

nev'er

nev'er·more'

nev'er·the·less'

ne'vus

new *(recent)*
✔ gnu, knew

new'born'

new'com'er

new'el

New Eng'land·er

new'fan'gled

New'found·land

New Hamp'-
shir·ite'

New Jer'sey·ite'

new'ly·wed'

New Mex'i·can

news'boy'

news'cast'

news'cast'er

news'gath'er·ing

news'girl'

news'let'ter

news'mak'er

news'man'

news'pa'per

news'pa'per·man'

news'pa'per·
wom'an

news'print'
news'reel'
news'stand'
news'wom'an
news'wor'thy
news'y
newt
new'ton
New York'er
next
nex'us pl. -us or
   -us•es
Nez' Perce' also
   Nez' Per•cé' pl.
   Nez' Perce' or Nez'
   Per•ces also Nez'
   Per•cé' or Nez'
   Per•cés'
ni'a•cin
nib
nib'ble -bled, -bling
Nic'a•ra'guan
nice (pleasing),
   nic'er, nic'est
   ✔ gneiss
Ni'cene' Creed'
ni'ce•ty
niche (recess)
nick (notch)
nick'el
nick'el•o'de•on
nick'name',
   -named', -nam'ing
nic'o•tine'
nic'o•tin'ic
niece
niels•bohr'i•um

nif'ty
Ni•ger'i•an
nig'gard•ly
nig'gling
nigh
night (darkness)
   ✔ knight
night'cap'
night'clothes'
night'club'
night'fall'
night'gown'
night'hawk'
night'in•gale'
night'-light'
night'mare'
night'mar'ish
night'ri'der
night'shade'
night'shirt'
night'spot'
night'stick'
night'time'
ni'hil•ism
ni'hil•ist
ni'hil•is'tic
nil
nim'ble, -bler, -blest
nim'bly
nim'bo•stra'tus pl.
   -stra'ti
nim'bus pl. -bi' or
   -bus•es
nin'com•poop'
nine'pin'
nine•teen'
nine•teenth'

nine'ti•eth
nine'ty
nin'ja
nin'ny
ninth
ni•o'bi•um
nip, nipped, nip'ing
nip'per
nip'ple
nip'py
nir•va'na
Ni•sei' pl. -sei' or
   -seis'
nit (insect egg)
   ✔ knit
ni'ter
nit'-pick'
ni'trate', -trat'ed,
   -trat'ing
ni•tra'tion
ni'tric
ni'tride'
ni'tri•fi•ca'tion
ni'tri•fy' -fied',
   -fy'ing
ni'trite'
ni'tro•bac•te'ri•um
   pl. -ri•a
ni'tro•ben'zene'
ni'tro•cel'lu•lose'
ni'tro•gen
ni•trog'e•nous
ni'tro•glyc'er•in
   also ni'tro•glyc'er•
   ine
ni'trous
nit'ty-grit'ty

nit'wit'

nix

no (refusal), pl. noes
✔ know

no•bel'i•um

No•bel' Prize'

no•bil'i•ty

no'ble, -bler, -blest

no'ble•man

no•blesse' o•blige'

no'ble•wom'an

no'bly

no'bod'y

noc•tur'nal

noc'turne'

nod, nod'ded,
  nod'ding

nod'al

nod'der

node

nod'u•lar

nod'ule

No•ël' or No•el'

no'-fault'

nog'gin

no'-good'

no'-hit'ter

noise, noised,
  nois'ing

noise'mak'er

nois'i•ly

noi'some

nois'y

no'mad'

no•mad'ic

nom' de plume'
  pl. noms' de

plume'

no'men•cla'ture

nom'i•nal

nom'i•nate',
  -nat'ed, -nat'ing

nom'i•na'tion

nom'i•na'tive

nom'i•nee'

non'age

non'a•ge•nar'i•an

non'ag•gres'sion

non'a•gon'

non'al•co•hol'ic

non'a•ligned'

nonce

non'cha•lance'

non'cha•lant'

non'com'

non'com•bat'ant

non'com•mis'-
  sioned of'ficer

non'com•mit'tal

non'com•pet'i•tive

non'com•pli'ance

non com'pos
  men'tis

non'con•duc'tor

non'con•form'ist

non'con•form'i•ty

non'de•nom'i•na'-
  tion•al

non'de•script'

none (not one)
  ✔ nun

non•en'ti•ty

non'es•sen'tial

none'such'

none'the•less'

non'-Eu•clid'e•an

non'ex•ist'ence

non'ex•ist'ent

non'fat'

non•fea'sance

non•fer'rous

non•fic'tion

non•fic'tion•al

non'flam'ma•bil'-
  i•ty

non•flam'ma•ble
  (not easily ignited)
  ✔ flammable, in
  flammable

non•flow'er•ing

no•nil'lion

no•nil'lionth'

non'in•ter•ven'-
  tion

non'judg•men'tal

non•ju'ror

non•mem'ber

non•met'al

non'me•tal'lic

non'ne•go'tia•ble

no'-no' pl. -noes'

non•ob•jec'tive

no-non'sense'

non'pa•reil'

non•par'ti•san

non•plus', -plused'
  or -plussed',
  -plus'ing or
  -plus'sing

non'pre•scrip'tion

non'pro•duc'tive

non·prof'it
non'pro·lif'er·a'-
  tion
non're·cov'er·a·ble
non'rep·re·sen·ta'-
  tion·al
non·res'i·dent
non're·sis'tant
non're·stric'tive
non·sched'uled
non'sec·tar'i·an
non·sense'
non·sen'si·cal
non se'qui·tur
non·skid'
non·smok'er
non·smok'ing
non·stan'dard
non·stop'
non·sup·port'
non·un'ion
non·ver'bal
non·vi'o·lence
non·vi'o·lent
non·white'
noo'dle
nook
noon
noon'day'
no' one'
noon'tide'
noon'time'
noose
Noot'ka *pl.* -ka *or*
  -kas
no'par'
nor

Nor'dic
norm
nor'mal
nor'mal·cy
nor·mal'i·ty
nor'mal·i·za'tion
nor'mal·ize', -ized',
  -iz'ing
nor'ma·tive
Nor'man
Norse
Norse'man
north
North' A·mer'i·
  can
north'bound'
north·east'
North' Car'o·lin'-
  i·an
North' Da·ko'tan
north·east'er
north·east'er·ly
north·east'ern
north·east'ward
  adv. & adj.
north·east'wards
  adv.
north'er
north'er·ly
north'ern
north'ern·er
north'ern·most'
north'ing
north'land'
north'-north·east'
north'-north·
  west'

north'ward *adv. &*
  adj.
north'wards *adv.*
north·west'
north·west'er
north·west'ern
north·west'er·ly
north·west'ward
  adv. & adj.
north·west'wards
  adv.
Nor·we'gian
nose, nosed, nos'ing
nose'bleed'
nose'-dive' -dived'
  or -dove', -div'ing
nose'gay'
nose'piece'
nose' ring'
no'-show'
nos·tal'gi·a
nos·tal'gic
nos'tril
nos'trum
nos'y *or* nos'ey
not *(in no way)*
  ✔ *knot*
no'ta be'ne
no'ta·bil'i·ty
no'ta·ble
no'ta·bly
no'ta·ri·za'tion
no'ta·rize', -rized',
  -riz'ing
no'ta·ry
no'ta·ry pub'lic *pl.*
  no'ta·ries pub'lic

no'tate, -tat•ed,
    -tat•ing
no•ta'tion
notch
note, not'ed, not'ing
note'book'
note'wor'thy
noth'ing
no'tice, -ticed,
    -tic•ing
no'tice•a•ble
no'tice•a•bly
no'ti•fi•ca'tion
no'ti•fi'er
no'ti•fy', -fied',
    -fy'ing
no'tion
no'to•chord'
no'to•ri'e•ty
no•to'ri•ous
no'-trump'
not'with•stand'ing
nou'gat
noun
nour'ish
nour'ish•ment
nou'veau riche' *pl.*
    nou'veaux riches'
no'va *pl.* -vae *or* -vas
No'va Sco'tian
nov'el
nov'el•ette'
nov'el•ist
no•vel'la *pl.* -las *or*
    -le
nov'el•ty
No•vem'ber

no•ve'na *pl.* -nas *or*
    -nae
nov'ice
no•vi'ti•ate
now'a•days'
no'way' *also*
    no'ways'
no'where'
no'-win'
no'wise'
nox'ious
noz'zle
nu
nu'ance'
nub'bin
nub'ble
nub'by
nu'bile
nu'cle•ar
nu'cle•ase'
nu'cle•ate', -at'ed,
    -at'ing
nu'cle•a'tion
nu•cle'ic ac'id
nu•cle'o•lar
nu•cle'o•lus *pl.* -li'
nu'cle•on'
nu'cle•on'ic
nu'cle•o•pro'tein
nu'cle•o•side'
nu'cle•o•tide'
nu'cle•us *pl.* -cle•i'
    or -cle•us•es
nude, nud'er,
    nud'est
nudge, nudged,
    nudg'ing

nud'ism
nud'ist
nu'di•ty
nug'get
nui'sance
nuke, nuked,
    nuk'ing
null
nul'li•fi•ca'tion
nul'li•fi'er
nul'li•fy', -fied',
    -fy'ing
nul'li•ty
numb, numb'er,
    numb'est
num'ber
nu'mer•a•ble
nu'mer•al
nu'mer•ate', -at'ed,
    -at'ing
nu'mer•a'tion
nu'mer•a'tor
nu•mer'i•cal *also*
    nu•mer'ic
nu'mer•o•log'i•cal
nu'mer•ol'o•gist
nu'mer•ol'o•gy
nu'mer•ous
nu'mis•mat'ic
nu•mis'ma•tist
num'skull' *also*
    numb'(skull')
nun *(religious sister)*
    ✔ none
nun'ci•o' *pl.* -os'
nun'ner•y
nup'tial

nurse, nursed,
  nurs'ing
nurse'maid'
nurs'er•y
nurs'ling
nur'ture, -tured,
  -tur•ing
nut'crack'er
nut'hatch'
nut'meat'
nut'meg'
nu'tri•ent
nu'tri•ment
nu•tri'tion
nu•tri'tion•al
nu•tri'tion•ist
nu•tri'tious
nu'tri•tive
nut'shell'
nut'ti•ness
nut'ty
nuz'zle -zled, -zling
ny'lon'
nymph
nym•phet'
nym'pho•ma'ni•a
nym'pho•ma'ni•
  ac'

O

oaf
oak'en
oa'kum
oar *(paddle)*
  ✔ o'er, or, ore

oar'lock'
oars'man
oars'wom'an
o•a'sis *pl.* -ses
oat
oat'en
oath
oat'meal'
ob'bli•ga'to
ob'du•ra•cy
ob'du•rate
o•be'di•ence
o•be'di•ent
o•bei'sance
o•bei'sant
ob'e•lisk
o•bese'
o•be'si•ty
o•bey'
ob'fus•cate',
  -cat'ed, -cat'ing
ob'fus•ca'tion
ob•fus'ca•to'ry
o'bi
o•bit'u•ar'y
ob•ject' *n.*
ob•ject' *v.*
ob•jec'tion
ob•jec'tion•a•ble
ob•jec'tion•a•bly
ob•jec'tive
ob•jec•tiv'i•ty
ob•jec'tor
ob'jet d'art' *pl.* ob'-
  jets d'art'
ob•la'tion
ob'li•gate', -gat'ed,

-gat'ing
ob'li•ga'tion
o•blig'a•to'ri•ly
o•blig'a•to'ry
o•blige', o•bliged',
  o•blig'ing
o•blique'
o•bliq'ui•ty
o•blit'er•ate',
  -at'ed, -at'ing
o•blit'er•a'tion
o•blit'er•a'tor
o•bliv'i•on
o•bliv'i•ous
ob'long'
ob'lo•quy *pl.* -quies
ob•nox'ious
o'boe
o'bo•ist
ob•scene'
ob•scen'i•ty
ob•scure', -scur'er,
  -scur'est
ob•scure', -scured',
  -scur'ing
ob•scu'ri•ty
ob•se'qui•ous
ob'se•quy *pl.* -quies
ob•serv'a•ble
ob•serv'a•bly
ob•ser'vance
ob•ser'vant
ob'ser•va'tion
ob•ser'va•to'ry
ob•serve', -served',
  -serv'ing
ob•serv'er

ob•sess'
ob•ses'sion
ob•ses'sive
ob•sid'i•an
ob'so•les'cence
ob'so•les'cent
ob'so•lete'
ob'sta•cle
ob•stet'ric *also*
  ob•stet'ri•cal
ob'ste•tri'cian
ob'sti•na•cy
ob'sti•nate
ob•strep'er•ous
ob•struct'
ob•struc'tion
ob•struc'tion•ism
ob•struc'tion•ist
ob•struc'tive
ob•struct'er *or*
  ob•struc'tor
ob•tain'
ob•tain'a•ble
ob•trude', -trud'ed,
  -trud'ing
ob•tru'sion
ob•tru'sive
ob•tuse', -tus'er,
  -tus'est
ob•verse' *adj.*
ob'verse' *n.*
ob•ver'sion
ob•vert'
ob'vi•ate', -at'ed,
  -at'ing
ob'vi•a'tion
ob'vi•a'tor

ob'vi•ous
oc'a•ri'na
oc•ca'sion
oc•ca'sion•al
oc'ci•dent *or*
  Oc'ci•dent
oc'ci•den'tal *or*
  Oc'ci•den'tal
oc•cip'i•tal
oc•clude', -clud'ed,
  -clud'ing
oc•clu'sion
oc•cult'
oc'cul•ta'tion
oc•cult'ism
oc'cu•pan•cy
oc'cu•pant
oc'cu•pa'tion
oc'cu•pa'tion•al
oc'cu•pi'er
oc'cu•py', -pied',
  -py'ing
oc•cur', -curred',
  -cur'ring
oc•cur'rence
o'cean
o'ce•an'ic
o'cean•og'ra•pher
o'cean•o•graph'ic
  or o'cean•o•graph'-
  i•cal
o'cean•og'ra•phy
o•cel'lus *pl.* -li'
oc'e•lot'
o'cher *or* o'chre
o'clock'
oc'ta•gon'

oc•tag'o•nal
oc'ta•he'dron *pl.*
  -drons *or* -dra
oc'tal
oc'tane'
oc'tant
oc'tave
oc•ta'vo *pl.* -vos
oc•tet'
oc•til'lion
oc•til'lionth
Oc•to'ber
oc'to•ge•nar'i•an
oc'to•pus *pl.* -pus•es
  or -pi'
oc'u•lar
oc'u•list
o'da•lisque' *also*
  o'da•lisk'
odd'ball'
odd'i•ty
odds
ode
o'di•ous
o'di•um
o•dom'e•ter
o'dor
o'dor•if'er•ous
o'dor•ous
od'ys•sey *pl.* -seys
oed'i•pal *also*
  Oed'i•pal
o'er *(over)*
  ✔ oar, or, ore
of
of'fal *(refuse)*
  ✔ awful

off′beat′
off′-Broad′way′
off′-col′or
of·fend′
of·fend′er
of·fense′ *(violation)*
of′fense′ *(act of attacking)*
of·fen′sive
of′fer
of′fer·ing
of′fer·er *or* of′fer·or
of′fer·to·ry
off′hand′
off′hand′ed·ly
off′-hour′
of′fice
of′fice·hold′er
of′fi·cer
of·fi′cial *(authorized)*
   ✔ *officious*
of·fi′ci·ate′, -at′ed, -at′ing
of·fi′ci·a′tor
of·fi′cious *(meddlesome)*
   ✔ *official*
off′ing
off′-key′
off′-lim′its
off′-line′ *adj.*
off′load′ *or* off′-load′
off′-peak′
off′-price′
off′print′

off′-put′ting
off′-road′
off′-screen′ *or* off′screen′
off′-sea′son
off′set′, -set′, -set′ting
off′shoot′
off′shore′
off′side′ *also* off′sides′
off′-site′
off′spring′ *pl.* off′spring′
off′-stage′ *or* off′stage′
off′-the-cuff′ *adj.*
off′-the-rec′ord *adj.*
off′-the-wall′ *adj.*
off′-white′
oft
of′ten
of′ten·times′ *also* oft′times′
o′gle, o′gled, o′gling
o′gler
o′gre
oh *interj.*
   ✔ *owe*
O·hi′o·an
ohm
ohm′me·ter
oil
oil′cloth′
oil′i·ness

oil′skin′
oil′y
oink
oint′ment
O·jib′wa *pl.* -wa *or* -was
OK *or* o·kay′ *pl.* OK's *or* o·kays′
OK *or* o·kay′, OK'd *or* o·kayed′, OK'ing *or* o·kay′ing
o·ka′pi *pl.* -pi *or* -pis
O′kla·ho′man
o′kra
old
old′en
old′-fash′ioned
old′-time′
old′-tim′er
old′-world′ *also* Old′ World′ *adj.*
o′le·ag′i·nous
o′le·an′der
o′le·fin
o·le′ic
o′le·o′ *(margarine)*, *pl.* -os′
   ✔ *olio*
o′le·o·res′in
ol·fac′to·ry
ol′i·garch′
ol′i·gar′chic *or* ol′i·gar′chi·cal
ol′i·gar′chy
Ol′i·go·cene′
o′li·o′ *(stew)*, *pl.* -os′
   ✔ *oleo*

ol′ive
Ol′mec *pl.* -mec *or*
-mecs
O•lym′pi•ad′
O•lym′pi•an
O•lym′pic
O•lym′pics
O′ma•ha′ *pl.* -ha′ *or*
-has′
om′buds•man
om′buds•per′son
om′buds•wom′an
o•me′ga
om′e•let *also*
om′e•lette
o′men
om′i•cron′
om′i•nous
o•mis′sion
o•mit′, o•mit′ted,
o•mit′ting
om′ni•bus′ *pl.*
-bus′es
om•nip′o•tence *or*
om•nip′o•ten•cy
om•nip′o•tent
om′ni•pres′ence
om′ni•pres′ent
om•nis′cience *or*
om•nis′cien•cy
om•nis′cient
om′ni•vore′
om•niv′o•rous
on•board′ *adj.*
once
once′-o′ver *n.*
on′com′ing

one
O•nei′da *pl.* -da *or*
-das
one′-lin′er
one′ness
one′-on-one′
on′er•ous
one•self′ *also* one's
self′
one′-sid′ed
one′-time′ *(former)*
one′-time′ *(for one
time)*
one′-to-one′
one′-track′
one-up′man•ship′
one′-way′
on′go′ing
on′ion
on′ion•skin′
on′-line′ *adj.*
on′load′
on′look′er
on′ly
on′o•mat′o•poe′ia
on′o•mat′o•poe′ic
or on′o•mat′o•po•
et′ic
On′on•da′ga *pl.* -ga
or -gas
on′rush′
on′rush′ing
on′-screen′ *or*
on′screen′
on′set′
on′shore′
on′side′

on′-site′
on′slaught′
on-stage′ *or*
on•stage′
on′-the-job′ *adj.*
on′to′
on′to•log′i•cal
on•tol′o•gy
o′nus
on′ward *adj. & adv.*
on′wards *adv.*
on′yx
oo′dles
ooze, oozed, ooz′ing
ooz′y
o•pac′i•ty
o′pal
o′pal•es′cence
o′pal•es′cent
o•paque′
o′pen
o′pen-air′
o′pen-and-shut′
adj.
o′pen-end′ed
o′pen•er
o′pen-eyed′
o′pen•hand′ed
o′pen•heart′ed
o′pen-hearth′
o′pen-heart′
sur′ger•y
o′pen•ing
o′pen-mind′ed

o'pen·work'
op'er·a
op'er·a·ble
op'er·and
op'er·ant
op'er·ate', -at'ed, -at'ing
op'er·at'ic
op'er·a'tion
op'er·a·tive
op'er·a·tor
o·per'cu·lum *pl.* -la *or* -lums
o'e·ret'ta
oph·thal'mic *(relating to the eye)*
oph·thal'mo·log'·ic *or* oph·thal'mo·log'i·cal *(relating to ophthalmology)*
oph'thal·mol'o·gist
oph'thal·mol'o·gy
o'pi·ate
o·pine', o·pined', o·pin'ing
o·pin'ion
o·pin'ion·at'ed
o'pi·um
o·pos'sum *pl.* -sum *or* -sums
op·po'nent
op'por·tune'
op'por·tun'ism
op'por·tun'ist
op'por·tun·is'tic
op'por·tu'ni·ty

op·pos'a·ble
op·pose' *(to contend against)*, -posed', -pos'ing
✔ *appose*
op'po·site *(altogether different)*
✔ *apposite*
op'po·si'tion
op'press'
op·pres'sion
op·pres'sive
op·pres'sor
op·pro'bri·ous
op·pro'bri·um
opt
op'ti·cal
op·ti'cian
op'tics
op'ti·mal
op'ti·mism
op'ti·mist
op'ti·mis'tic
op'ti·mi·za'tion
op'ti·mize', -mized', -miz'ing
op'ti·mum *pl.* -ma *or* -mums
op'tion
op'tion·al
op·tom'e·trist
op·tom'e·try
op'u·lence
op'u·lent
o'pus *pl.* o'per·a *or* o'pus·es
or *conj.*

✔ *oar, o'er, ore*
or'a·cle *(prophet)*
✔ *auricle*
o·rac'u·lar
o'ral *(relating to the mouth)*
✔ *aural*
or'ange
or'ange·ade'
o·rang'u·tan' *also* o·rang'ou·tang'
o·rate', o·rat'ed, o·rat'ing
o·ra'tion
or'a·tor
or'a·to'ri·o' *pl.* -os'
or'a·to'ry
orb
or'bit
or'bit·al
or'chard
or'ches·tra
or·ches'tral
or'ches·trate', -trat'ed, -trat'ing
or'ches·tra'tion
or'chid
or·dain'
or·deal'
or'der
or'der·ly
or'di·nal
or'di·nance *(command)*
✔ *ordnance*
or'di·nar'i·ly
or'di·nar'y

or'di·nate'
or'di·na'tion
ord'nance *(military supplies)*
  ✔ ordinance
Or'do·vi'cian
or'dure
ore *(mineral)*
  ✔ oar, o'er, or
o·reg'a·no
Or'e·go'ni·an
or'gan
or'gan·dy
or·gan·elle'
or·gan'ic
or'gan·ism
or'gan·ist
or'gan·i·za'tion
or'gan·ize', -ized',
  -iz'ing
or'gan·iz'er
or·gan'za
or'gasm
or·gi·as'tic
or'gy
o'ri·el
o'ri·ent *(to locate)*
O'ri·ent *(Asia)*
o'ri·en·tal *also*
  O'ri·en'tal
o'ri·en·tate',
  -tat'ed, -tat'ing
o'ri·en·ta'tion
or'i·fice
o'ri·ga'mi *pl.* -mis
or'i·gin
o·rig'i·nal

o·rig'i·nal'i·ty
o·rig'i·nate',
  -nat'ed, -nat'ing
o·rig'i·na'tor
o'ri·ole'
or'i·son
or'na·ment
or'na·men'tal
or'na·men·ta'tion
or·nate'
or'ner·y
or'ni·thol'o·gist
or'ni·thol'o·gy
o'ro·tund'
or'phan
or'phan·age
or'tho·clase'
or'tho·don'tia
or'tho·don'tics
or'tho·don'tist
or'tho·dox' *also*
  Or'tho·dox'
or'tho·dox'y
or·thog'o·nal
or'tho·graph'ic
or·thog'ra·phy
or'tho·pe'dics
or'tho·pe'dist
o'ryx *pl.* o'ryx *or*
  o'ryx·es
O'sage' *pl.* O'sage'
  or O'sag'es
os'cil·late', -lat'ed,
  -lat'ing
os'cil·la'tion
os'cil·la'tor
os·cil'lo·scope'

o'sier
os'mi·um
os·mo'sis *pl.* -ses
os·mot'ic
os'prey *pl.* -preys
os'si·fi·ca'tion
os'si·fy', -fied',
  -fy'ing
os·ten'si·ble
os·ten'si·bly
os'ten·ta'tion
os'ten·ta'tious
os'te·o·path'
os'te·op'a·thy
os'te·o·po·ro'sis
os'tra·cism
os'tra·cize', -cized',
  -ciz'ing
os'trich *pl.* -trich *or*
  -trich·es
oth'er
oth'er·wise'
Ot'ta·wa *pl.* -wa *or*
  -was
ot'ter *pl.* -ter *or* -ters
ot'to·man *(furniture)*, *pl.* -mans
Ot'to·man *(people)*,
  pl. -mans
ouch
ought *aux. v.*
  ✔ aught
ounce
our *pron.*
  ✔ hour
ours
our·selves'

oust′er
out′age
out′-and-out′ *adj.*
out′back′ *adv.*
out′back′ *n.*
out•bid′, -bid′,
  -bid′den *or* -bid′,
  -bid′ding
out′board′
out′bound′
out′break′
out′build′ing
out′burst′
out′cast′
out•class′
out′come′
out′crop′
out′cry′
out•dat′ed
out•dis′tance,
  -tanced, -tanc•ing
out•do′, -did′,
  -done′, -do′ing,
  -does′
out′door′ *adj.*
out•doors′ *adv. & n.*
out′er
out′er•most′
out′field′
out′field′er
out′fit′, -fit•ted,
  -fit•ting
out′fit′ter
out•flank′
out′flow′
out′fox′
out′go′ing

out•grow′, -grew′,
  -grown′, -grow′ing
out′growth′
out•guess′
out′house′
out′ing
out•land′ish
out•last′
out′law′
out′lay′
out′let′
out′line′, -lined′,
  -lin′ing
out•live′, -lived′,
  -liv′ing
out′look′
out′ly′ing
out•ma•neu′ver
out•mod′ed
out•num′ber
out′-of-bounds′
  adv.
out′-of-date′ *adj.*
out′-of-the-way′
  adj.
out′pa′tient
out•play′
out′post′
out•pour′ing
out′put′
out′rage′, -raged′,
  -rag′ing
out•ra′geous
out•rank′
out•reach′ *v.*
out′reach′ *n.*
out′rid′er

out′rig′ger
out′right′
out•run′, -ran′,
  -run′, -run′ning
out•sell′, -sold′,
  -sell′ing
out′set′
out•shine′, -shone′,
  -shin′ing
out′side′
out•sid′er
out•size′ *also*
  out′sized′
out′skirts′
out•smart′
out•spo′ken
out•spread′,
  -spread′,
  -spread•ing
out′spread′ *n.*
out•stand′ing
out•stay′
out′stretch′
out•strip′,
  -stripped′,
  -strip′ping
out′ward
out•wear′, -wore′,
  -worn′, -wear′ing
out•weigh′
out•wit′, -wit′ted,
  -wit′ting
out′work′ *v.*
out′work′ *n.*
o′val
o•var′i•an
o′va•ry

o•va′tion
ov′en
ov′en•bird′
o′ver
o′ver•a•bun′dance
o′ver•a•bun′dant
o′ver•a•chieve′,
 -chieved′,
 -chiev′ing
o′ver•a•chiev′er
o′ver•act′
o′ver•ac′tive
o′ver•age *n.*
o′ver•age′ *adj.*
o′ver•all′ *adj.*
o′ver•alls′
o′ver•arm′ *adj.*
o′ver•arm′ *v.*
o′ver•awe′, -awed′,
 -aw′ing
o′ver•bal′ance,
 -anced, -anc•ing
o′ver•bear′ing
o′ver•bid′, -bid′,
 -bid′den *or* -bid′,
 -bid′ding
o′ver•bid′ *n.*
o′ver•bite′
o′ver•board′
o′ver•book′
o′ver•bur′den
o′ver•buy′,
 -bought′, -buy′ing
o′ver•call′ *v.*
o′ver•call′ *n.*
o′ver•ca•pac′i•ty
o′ver•cap′i•tal•ize′,

-ized′, -iz′ing
o′ver•cast′ *adj. & n.*
o′ver•cast′, -cast′,
 -cast′ing
o′ver•charge′,
 -charged′,
 -charg′ing
o′ver•charge′ *n.*
o′ver•coat′
o′ver•come′,
 -came′, -come′,
 -com′ing
o′ver•com•pen•
 sate′, -sat′ed,
 -sat′ing
o′ver•com•pen•sa′-
 tion
o′ver•con′fi•dence
o′ver•con′fi•dent
o′ver•crowd′
o′ver•de•vel′op
o′ver•do′ *(to do to*
 excess), -did′,
 -done′, -do′ing,
 -does′
 ✔ *overdue*
o′ver•dose′,
 -dosed′, -dos′ing
o′ver•draft′
o′ver•draw′,
 -drew′, -drawn′,
 -draw′ing
o′ver•dress′
o′ver•drive′ *n.*
o′ver•drive′,
 -drove′, -driv′en,
 -driv′ing

o′ver•due′ *(unpaid)*
 ✔ *overdo*
o′ver•eat′, -ate′,
 -eat′en, -eat′ing
o′ver•es′ti•mate′,
 -mat′ed, -mat′ing
o′ver•ex•ert′
o′ver•ex•pose′,
 -posed′, -pos′ing
o′ver•ex•po′sure
o′ver•ex•tend′
o′ver•flow′ *v.*
o′ver•flow′ *n.*
o′ver•grow′, -grew′,
 -grown′, -grow′ing
o′ver•growth′
o′ver•hand′ *also*
 o′ver•hand′ed
o′ver•hang′,
 -hung′, -hang′ing
o′ver•hang′ *n.*
o′ver•haul′ *v.*
o′ver•haul′ *n.*
o′ver•head′ *adj. & n.*
o′ver•head′ *adv.*
o′ver•hear′,
 -heard′, -hear′ing
o′ver•heat′
o′ver•joyed′
o′ver•kill′
o′ver•land′
o′ver•lap′, -lapped′,
 -lap′ping
o′ver•lap′ *n.*
o′ver•lay′, -laid′,
 -lay′ing
o′ver•lay′ *n.*

o'ver•leaf'

o'ver•leap',
-leaped' or -leapt',
-leap'ing

o'ver•lie', -lay',
-lain', -ly'ing

o'ver•load' v.

o'ver•load' n.

o'ver•long'

o'ver•look' v.

o'ver•look' n.

o'ver•lord'

o'ver•ly

o'ver•mas'ter

o'ver•much'

o'ver•night' adj. &
n.

o'ver•night' adv.

o'ver•pass' n.

o'ver•pass',
-passed' or -past',
-pass'ing

o'ver•pay', -paid',
-pay'ing

o'ver•play'

o'ver•pop'u•late',
-lat'ed, -lat'ing

o'ver•pop'u•la'tion

o'ver•pow'er

o'ver•print' v.

o'ver•print' n.

o'ver•pro•duce',
-duced', -duc'ing

o'ver•pro•duc'tion

o'ver•qual'i•fied'

o'ver•rate', -rat'ed,
-rat'ing

o'ver•reach'

o'ver•ride', -rode',
-rid'den, -rid'ing

o'ver•ripe'

o'ver•rule', -ruled',
-rul'ing

o'ver•run', -ran',
-run', -run'ning

o'ver•run' n.

o'ver•seas'

o'ver•see', -saw',
-seen', -see'ing

o'ver•se'er

o'ver•sell', -sold',
-sell'ing

o'ver•set', -set',
-set'ting

o'ver•shad'ow

o'ver•shoe'

o'ver•shoot',
-shot', -shoot'ing

o'ver•shot' adj.

o'ver•sight'

o'ver•sim'pli•fi•ca'-
tion

o'ver•sim'pli•fy',
-fied', -fy'ing

o'ver•size' also
o'ver•sized'

o'ver•sleep', -slept',
-sleep'ing

o'ver•state',
-stat'ed, -stat'ing

o'ver•state'ment

o'ver•stay'

o'ver•step',
-stepped',

-step'ping

o'ver•stock' v.

o'ver•stuff'

o'ver•sub•scribe',
-scribed', -scrib'ing

o'ver•sup•ply' n.

o'ver•sup•ply',
-plied', -ply'ing

o•vert'

o'ver•take', -took',
-tak'en, -tak'ing

o'ver•tax'

o'ver•tax•a'tion

o'ver-the-count'er
adj.

o'ver-the-hill' adj.

o'ver•throw',
-threw', -thrown',
-throw'ing

o'ver•throw' n.

o'ver•time'

o'ver•tone'

o'ver•top', -topped',
o•ver•top'ping

o'ver•ture'

o'ver•turn'

o'ver•use', -used',
-us'ing

o'ver•view'

o'ver•ween'ing

o'ver•weight'

o'ver•whelm'

o'ver•whelm'ing

o'ver•work' v.

o'ver•work' n.

o'ver•wrought'

o'vi•duct'

o'vine'
o•vip'a•rous
o'vi•pos'i•tor
o'void'
o'vo•lac'to•veg'e•tar'i•an
o'vo•vi•vip'a•rous
o'vu•lar
o'vu•late', -lat'ed,
  -lat'ing
o'vu•la'tion
o'vule
o'vum *pl.* o'va
owe *(to be indebted)*,
  owed, ow'ing
  ✔ *oh*
owl'et
own
own'er
own'er•ship'
ox *pl.* ox'en
ox•al'ic ac'id
ox'blood' red'
ox'bow'
ox'ford
ox'i•dant
ox'i•da'tion
ox'ide'
ox'i•dize', -dized',
  -diz'ing
ox'i•diz'er
ox'tail'
ox'y•a•cet'y•lene
ox'y•gen
ox'y•gen•ate',
  -at'ed, -at'ing
ox'y•gen•a'tion

ox'y•gen'ic *also*
  ox'yg'e•nous
ox'y•he'mo•glo'-
  bin
ox'y•mo'ron *pl.* -ra
  or -rons
o'yez'
oys'ter
o'zone'

P

pace paced, pac'ing
pace'mak'er
pac'er
pach'y•derm'
pa•cif'ic
pac'i•fi•ca'tion
pac'i•fi'er
pac'i•fism
pac'i•fist
pac'i•fy' -fied',
  -fy'ing
pack
pack'age,
  -aged, -ag•ing
pack'er
pack'et
pack'ing
pack'ing•house'
pack'sack'
pack'sad'dle
pact
pad, pad'ded,
  pad'ding
pad'dle, -dled,

  -dling
pad'dle•fish' *pl.*
  -fish' *or* -fish'es
pad'dock
pad'dy
pad'lock'
pa'dre
pae'an *(praise)*
  ✔ *peon*
pa•el'la
pa'gan
pa'gan•ism
page, paged, pag'ing
pag'eant
pag'eant•ry
page'boy'
pag'er
pag'i•nate', -nat'ed,
  -nat'ing
pag'i•na'tion
pa•go'da
pail *(bucket)*
  ✔ *pale*
pail'ful'
pain *(hurt)*
  ✔ *pane*
pain'ful
pain'kill'er
pain'less
pains'tak'ing
paint
paint'brush'
paint'ed
paint'er *(person who
  paints)*
pain'ter *(rope)*
paint'ing

pair *(set of two)*, pl.
  pair *or* pairs
  ✔ pare, pear
pais'ley
Pai·ute' *pl.* -ute' *or*
  -utes'
pa·ja'mas
Pak'i·stan'i
pal, palled, pal'ling
pal'ace
pal'an·quin'
pal'at·a·bil'i·ty
pal'at·a·ble
pal'a·tal
pal'ate *(roof of the*
  mouth)
  ✔ palette, pallet
pa·la'tial
pa·lav'er
pale *(stake)*
  ✔ pail
pale *(lacking color)*,
  pal'er, pal'est
  ✔ pail
pale *(to fence in, to*
  lose color), paled,
  pal'ing
  ✔ pail
Pa'le·o·cene'
pa'le·og'ra·pher
pa'le·o·graph'ic *or*
  pa'le·o·graph'i·cal
pa'le·og'ra·phy
Pa'le·o·lith'ic
pa'le·on·tol'o·gist
pa'le·on·tol'o·gy
Pa'le·o·zo'ic

pal'ette *(board for*
  mixing paint)
  ✔ palate, pallet
pal'frey *pl.* -freys
pal'imp·sest
pal'in·drome'
pal'ing
pal'i·sade'
pall *(covering for a*
  coffin)
  ✔ pawl
pall *(to grow tiresome)*
  ✔ pawl
pal·la'di·um
pall'bear'er
pal'let *(hard bed)*
  ✔ palate, palette
pal'li·ate', -at·ed,
  -at'ing
pal'li·a'tion
pal'li·a'tive
pal'lid
pal'lor
palm
pal'mate' *also*
  pal'mat·ed
pal·met'to *pl.* -tos
  or -toes
palm'ist
palm'is·try
pal'o·mi'no *pl.*
  -nos
Pa·louse' *pl.* -louse'
  or -lous'es
palp
pal'pa·bil'i·ty
pal'pa·ble

pal'pa·bly
pal'pate' *(to feel by*
  touching), -pat·ed,
  -pat'ing
  ✔ palpitate
pal·pa'tion
pal'pa·tor
pal'pi·tate' *(to*
  throb), -tat·ed,
  -tat'ing
  ✔ palpate
pal'pi·ta'tion
pal'pus *pl.* -pi
pal'sy, -sied, -sy·ing
pal'tri·ness
pal'try
pam'pa *pl.* -pas
pam'per
pam'phlet
pam'phlet·eer'
pan, panned,
  pan'ning
pan·a·ce'a
pa·nache'
Pan'a·ma hat'
Pan·a·ma'ni·an
Pan'-A·mer'i·can
pan'cake'
pan'chro·mat'ic
pan'cre·as
pan'cre·at'ic
pan'da
pan·dem'ic
pan'de·mo'ni·um
pan'der
pan'der·er
pane *(sheet of glass)*

✓ pain
pan'e•gyr'ic
pan'e•gyr'i•cal
pan'e•gyr'ist
pan'el -eled *or*
  -elled, -el•ing *or*
  -el•ling
pan'el•ist
pang
pan'han'dle, -dled,
  -dling
pan'ic, -icked,
  -ick•ing
pan'ick•y
pan'ic-strick'en
pan'nier
pan'o•ply
pan'o•ram'a
pan'o•ram'ic
pan'pipe'
pan'sy
pant
pan'ta•lets' *also*
  pan'ta•lettes'
pan'ta•loons'
pan'the•ism
pan'the•ist
pan'the•is'tic *or*
  pan'the•is'ti•cal
pan'the•on'
pan'ther
pant'ies
pan'to•mime',
  -mimed', -mim'ing
pan'to•mim'ist
pan'try
pants

pant'suit' *also*
  pants' suit'
pant'y•hose' *or*
  pant'y hose'
pap
pa'pa
pa'pa•cy
pa'pal
pa'pa•raz'zo *pl.* -zi
pa'paw' *also*
  paw'paw'
pa•pa'ya
pa'per
pa'per•back'
pa'per•board'
pa'per•boy'
pa'per•girl'
pa'per•weight'
pa'per•work'
pa'per•y
pa'pier-mâ•ché'
pa•pil'la *pl.* -pil'lae
pa•poose'
pa•pri'ka
Pap'u•an
Pap'u•a New
  Guin'e•an
pa•py'rus *pl.* -rus•es
  or -ri'
par
par'a•ble
pa•rab'o•la
par'a•bol'ic *also*
  par'a•bol'i•cal
par'a•chute',
  -chut'ed, -chut'ing
par'a•chut'ist

pa•rade', -rad'ed,
  -rad'ing
pa•rad'er
par'a•digm'
par'a•dise'
par'a•dox'
par'a•dox'i•cal
par'af•fin
par'a•gon'
par'a•graph'
Par'a•guay'an
par'a•keet'
par•al'de•hyde'
par•a•le'gal
par'al•lax'
par'al•lel', -leled
  also -lelled, -lel'ing
  or -lel'ling
par•'al•lel•ism
par'al•lel'o•gram'
pa•ral'y•sis *pl.* -ses'
par'a•lyt'ic
par'a•lyze', -lyzed',
  -lyz'ing
par'a•me'ci•um *pl.*
  -ci•a *or* -ci•ums
par'a•med'ic
par'a•med'i•cal
pa•ram'e•ter *(con-*
  stant, limit)
  ✓ *perimeter*
par'a•mil'i•tar'y
par'a•mount'
par'a•mour'
par'a•noi'a
par'a•noi'ac'
par'a•noid'

par'a·pet'
par'a·pher·na'lia
par'a·phrase',
  -phrased',
  -phras'ing
par'a·ple'gi·a
par'a·ple'gic
par'a·pro·fes'sion·al
par'a·psy·chol'o·gy
par'a·site'
par'a·sit'ic *also*
  par'a·sit'i·cal
par'a·sit·ism
par'a·sol'
par'a·sym'pa·thet'ic
par'a·thy'roid
par'a·troop'er
par'boil'
par'cel, -celed *also*
  -celled, -cel·ing *or*
  -cel·ling
parch
parch'ment
par'don
par'don·a·ble
pare *(to peel)*, pared,
  par'ing
  ✔ pair, pear
par'e·gor'ic
pa·ren'chy·ma
par'ent
par'ent·age
pa·ren'tal
pa·ren'the·sis *pl.*
  -ses'

par'en·thet'i·cal
  also par'en·thet'ic
par'ent·hood'
pa·re'sis
par·fait'
pa·ri'ah
pa·ri'e·tal bone'
par'i-mu'tu·el
par'ish
pa·rish'ion·er
Pa·ri'sian
par'i·ty
park
par'ka
Par'kin·son's
  dis·ease'
park'way'
par'lance
par'lay' *(to bet)*
par'ley *(conference)*,
  pl. -leys
par'lia·ment
par'lia·men·tar'i·an
par'lia·men'ta·ry
par'lor
Par'me·san'
pa·ro'chi·al
pa·ro'chi·al·ism
par'o·dy -died,
  -dy'ing
pa·role',
  -roled', -rol'ing
pa·rol·ee'
pa·rot'id
par'ox·ysm
par'ox·ys'mal

par·quet'
par·quet'ry
par'ri·cid'al
par'ri·cide'
par'rot
par'ry -ried, -ry'ing
parse, parsed,
  pars'ing
par'sec'
Par'see *pl.* -sees
par'si·mo'ni·ous
par'si·mo'ny
pars'ley *pl.* -leys
pars'nip
par'son
par'son·age
part
par·take', -took',
  -tak'en, -tak'ing
par·tak'er
par'tial
par'ti·al'i·ty
par·tic'i·pant
par·tic'i·pate',
  -pat'ed, -pat'ing
par·tic'i·pa'tion
par·tic'i·pa'tor
par·tic'i·pa·to'ry
par'ti·cip'i·al
par'ti·ci·ple
par'ti·cle
par·ti-col'ored
par·tic'u·lar
par·tic'u·lar'i·ty
par·tic'u·lar·i·za'-
  -tion
par·tic'u·lar·ize'

-ized', -iz'ing
par·tic'u·lar·ly
part'ing
par'ti·san
par·ti'tion
part'ner
part'ner·ship'
part' of speech' *pl.*
parts' of speech'
par'tridge *pl.* -tridge
or -tridg·es
part'-time' *adj.*
part'-time' *adv.*
par·tu·ri'tion
part'way'
par'ty
Pas·cal' *or* PAS·CAL'
pas'chal
pass
pass'a·ble *(capable
of being passed)*
✔ passible
pass'a·bly
pas'sage
pas'sage·way'
pass'book'
pas·sé'
pas'sen·ger
pas'ser·by' *also*
pas'ser-by' *pl.*
pas'sers·by' *also*
pas'sers-by'
pas'ser·ine'
pass'-fail'
pas'si·ble *(sensitive)*
✔ passable
pas'sim

pass'ing
pas'sion
pas'sion·ate
pas'sion·flow'er
pas'sive
pas·siv'i·ty
pass'key'
Pass'o·ver
pass'port'
pass'word'
past
pas'ta
paste, past'ed,
past'ing
paste'board'
pas·tel'
pas'tern
pas'teur·i·za'tion
pas'teur·ize', -ized',
-iz'ing
pas·tiche'
pas·tille' *also* pas'til
pas'time'
pas'tor
pas'tor·al
pas'tor·ate
pas·tra'mi *pl.* -mis
pas'try
pas'tur·age
pas'ture, -tured,
-tur·ing
past'y *(resembling
paste)*
pas'ty *(meat pie)*
pat, pat'ted, pat'ting
patch
patch'i·ness

patch·ou'li *also*
patch·ou'ly *or*
pach·ou'li *pl.* -lis
also -lies
patch'work'
patch'y
pate *(head)*
pâ·té' *(meat paste)*
pa·tel'la *pl.* -tel'lae
pat'ent
pat'ent·ee'
pa'ter·fa·mil'i·as *pl.*
pa'tres·fa·mil'i·as
pa·ter'nal
pa·ter'nal·ism
pa·ter'nal·is'tic
pa·ter'ni·ty
pa'ter·nos'ter
path
pa·thet'ic
path'find'er
path'o·gen
path'o·gen'ic
path'o·log'i·cal
also path'o·log'ic
pa·thol'o·gist
pa·thol'o·gy
pa'thos'
path'way'
pa'tience
pa'tient
pat'i·o' *pl.* -os'
pat'ois' *pl.* pat'ois'
pa'tri·arch'
pa'tri·ar'chal
pa'tri·ar'chy
pa·tri'cian

pat'ri•cid'al
pat'ri•cide'
pat'ri•lin'e•al
pat'ri•mo'ni•al
pat'ri•mo'ny
pa'tri•ot
pa'tri•ot'ic
pa'tri•ot•ism
pa•trol', -trolled',
  -trol'ling
pa•trol'man
pa•trol'wom'an
pa'tron
pa'tron•age
pa'tron•ize', -ized',
  -iz'ing
pat'ro•nym'ic
pa•troon'
pat'sy
pat'ter
pat'tern
pat'ty
pau'ci•ty
paunch'y
pau'per
pause, paused,
  paus'ing
pa•vane' also
  pa•van'
pave, paved, pav'ing
pave'ment
pa•vil'ion
paw
pawl (hinged device)
  ✓ pall
pawn
pawn'bro'ker

Paw•nee' pl. -nee'
  or -nees'
pawn'shop'
pay, paid, pay'ing
pay'a•ble
pay'check'
pay'day'
pay•ee'
pay'load'
pay'mas'ter
pay'ment
pay'off' n.
pay'-per-view' n.
pay'roll'
pea
peace (calm)
  ✓ piece
peace'a•ble
peace'a•bly
peace'ful
peace'keep'ing
peace'mak'er
peace'time'
peach
peach'y
pea'cock'
pea'fowl' pl. -fowl'
  or -fowls'
pea'hen'
peak (mountain top)
  ✓ peek, pique
peaked (pointed)
peak'ed (sickly)
peal (ringing)
  ✓ peel
pea'nut
pear (fruit)

✓ pair, pare
pearl (gem)
  ✓ purl
pearl'y
peas'ant
peas'ant•ry
peat
peat' moss'
peb'ble, -bled, -bling
peb'bly
pe•can'
pec'ca•dil'lo pl.
  -loes or -los
pec'ca•ry
peck
pec'tin
pec'to•ral
pe•cu'liar
pe•cu'li•ar'i•ty
pe•cu'ni•ar'y
ped'a•gog'ic also
  ped'a•gog'i•cal
ped'a•gogue'
ped'a•go'gy
ped'al (to operate a
  lever with the foot),
  -aled or -alled,
  -al•ing or -al•ling
  ✓ peddle
ped'ant
pe•dan'tic
ped'ant•ry
ped'dle (to sell),
  -dled, -dling
  ✓ pedal
ped'dler
ped'es•tal

pe·des'tri·an
pe'di·at'ric
pe'di·a·tri'cian
pe'di·at'rics
ped'i·cel
ped'i·cure'
ped'i·gree'
ped'i·greed'
ped'i·ment
ped'lar
pe·dom'e·ter
ped'o·phile'
ped'o·phil'i·a
pe·dun'cle
peek *(glance)*
  ✔ *peak, pique*
peel *(skin or rind)*
  ✔ *peal*
peep
peep'er
peep'hole'
peer *(to look)*
  ✔ *pier*
peer *(equal)*
  ✔ *pier*
peer'age
pecr'ess
peer'less
peeve, peeved,
  peev'ing
pee'vish
pee'wee *(small
  thing)*
  ✔ *pewee*
peg, pegged,
  peg'ging
peg'board'

peg'ma·tite'
pei·gnoir'
pe·jor'a·tive
Pe'king·ese' *also*
  Pe'kin·ese' *pl.* -ese'
pe'koe *(tea)*
  ✔ *picot*
pe·lag'ic
pelf
pel'i·can
pe·lisse'
pel·lag'ra
pel'let
pell'-mell' *also*
  pell'mell'
pel·lu'cid
pelt
pel'vic
pel'vis *pl.* -vis·es *or*
  -ves
pem'mi·can
pen *(to write)*,
  penned, pen'ning
pen *(to confine)*,
  penned *or* pent,
  pen'ning
pe'nal
pe'nal·i·za'tion
pe'nal·ize', -ized',
  -iz'ing
pen'al·ty
pen'ance
pence
pen'chant
pen'cil, -ciled *also*
  -cilled, -cil·ing *also*
  -cil·ling

pen'dant *also*
  pen'dent *n.*
pen'dent *also*
  pen'dant *adj.*
pend'ing
pen'du·lous
pen'du·lum
pen'e·tra·bil'i·ty
pen'e·tra·ble
pen'e·trate',
  -trat'ed, -trat'ing
pen'e·tra'tion
pen'guin
pen'i·cil'lin
pen·in'su·la
pen·in'su·lar
pe'nis *pl.* -nis·es *or*
  -nes
pen'i·tence
pen'i·tent
pen'i·ten'tial
pen'i·ten'tia·ry
pen'knife'
pen'man
pen'man·ship'
pen' name' *or*
  pen'name'
pen'nant
pen'ne *pl.* pen'ne
pen'ni·less
pen'non
Penn'syl·va'nian
pen'ny *(U.S. coin)*,
  pl. pen'nies
pen'ny *(British
  coin)*, *pl.* pence *or*
  pen'nies

pen'ny-pinch'ing

pen'ny•roy'al

pen'ny•weight'

pen'ny-wise' *or*
pen'ny•wise'

pen'ny•worth'

Pe•nob'scot *pl.*
-scot *or* -scots

pe•nol'o•gist

pe•nol'o•gy

pen'sion *(retirement
money)*

pen•sion' *(lodging)*

pen'sion•er

pen'sive

pen'stock'

pen'ta•cle

pen'ta•gon'

pen'tag'o•nal

pen•tam'e•ter

Pen'ta•teuch'

pen'tath'lon

pen'ta•ton'ic

Pen'te•cost'

Pen'te•cos'tal

pent'house'

pent'-up' *adj.*

pe•nu'che *also*
pe•nu'chi

pe'nult'

pe•nul'ti•mate

pe•num'bra *pl.*
-brae *or* -bras

pe•nu'ri•ous

pen'u•ry

pe'on *(menial
worker)*

✔ *paean*

pe'on•age

pe'o•ny

peo'ple *pl.* -ple *or*
-ples

peo'ple, -pled,
-pling

pep, pepped,
pep'ping

pep'per

pep'per•corn'

pep'per•mint'

pep'per•o'ni *pl.*
-nis

pep'per•y

pep'py

pep'sin *also* pep'sine

pep'tic

Pe'quot' *pl.* -quot'
or -quots'

per

per•am'bu•late',
-lat'ed, -lat'ing

per•am'bu•la'tion

per•am'bu•la'tor

per an'num

per•cale'

per cap'i•ta

per•ceiv'a•ble

per•ceive', -ceived',
-ceiv'ing

per•cent' *also*
per cent'

per•cent'age

per•cen'tile'

per•cep'ti•bil'i•ty

per•cep'ti•ble

per•cep'ti•bly

per•cep'tion

per•cep'tive

per•cep'tu•al

perch *(roost)*

perch *(fish), pl.*
perch *or* perch'es

per•chance'

per'co•late', -lat'ed,
-lat'ing

per'co•la'tion

per'co•la'tor

per•cus'sion

per di'em

per•di'tion

per'e•grine

per•emp'to•ri•ly

per•emp'to•ry

per•en'ni•al

per'fect *adj.*

per•fect' *v.*

per•fect'i•bil'i•ty

per•fect'i•ble

per•fec'tion

per•fec'tion•ism

per•fec'tion•ist

per•fid'i•ous

per'fi•dy

per'fo•rate', -rat'ed,
-rat'ing

per'fo•ra'tion

per•force'

per•form'

per•form'er

per•form'ance

per•fume' *n.*

per•fume', -fumed',

-fum'ing
per•fum'er•y
per•func'to•ri•ly
per•func'to•ry
per•haps'
per'i•car'di•um *pl.*
    -di•a
per'i•gee
per'i•he'li•on *pl.*
    -li•a
per'il
per'il•ous
pe•rim'e•ter
    (boundary)
    ✔ parameter
pe'ri•od
pe'ri•od'ic
pe'ri•od'i•cal
pe'ri•o•dic'i•ty
per'i•o•don'tal
per'i•pa•tet'ic
pe•riph'er•al
pe•riph'er•y
per'i•scope'
per'ish
per'ish•a•ble
per'i•stal'sis *pl.* -ses
per'i•stal'tic
per'i•to•ne'al
per'i•to•ne'um *pl.*
    -ne'a
per'i•to•ni'tis
per'i•wig'
per'i•win'kle
per'jure, -jured,
    -jur•ing
per'jur•er

per'ju•ry
perk *(to stick up)*
perk *(perquisite)*
perk'y
perm
per'ma•frost'
per'ma•nence
per'ma•nen•cy
per'ma•nent
per'ma•nent-
    press' *adj.*
per•man'ga•nate'
per'me•a•bil'i•ty
per'me•a•ble
per'me•ate', -at'ed,
    -at'ing
per'me•a'tion
Per'mi•an
per•mis'si•ble
per•mis'sion
per•mis'sive
per•mit', -mit'ted,
    -mit'ting
per'mit *n.*
per'mu•ta'tion
per•mute', -mut'ed,
    -mut'ing
per•ni'cious
per•nick'e•ty
per'o•rate', -rat'ed,
    -rat'ing
per'o•ra'tion
per•ox'ide',
    -id'ed, -id'ing
per'pen•dic'u•lar
per'pe•trate',
    -trat'ed, -trat'ing

per'pe•tra'tion
per'pe•tra'tor
per•pet'u•al
per•pet'u•ate',
    -at'ed, -at'ing
per•pet'u•a'tion
per'pe•tu'i•ty
per•plex'
per•plexed'
per•plex'i•ty
per'qui•site *(benefit)*
    ✔ prerequisite
per se'
per'se•cute' *(to ha-*
    rass), -cut'ed,
    -cut'ing
    ✔ prosecute
per'se•cu'tion
per'se•cu'tor
per'se•ver'ance
per'se•vere',
    -vered', -ver'ing
Per'sian
per•sim'mon
per•sist'
per•sist'ence *or*
    per•sist'en•cy
per•sist'ent
per•snick'e•ty
per'son
per•so'na *pl.* -nas *or*
    -nae
per'son•a•ble
per'son•age
per'son•al *(private)*
    ✔ personnel
per'son•al'i•ty

per'son•al•ize',
-ized', -iz'ing
per•so'na non
gra'ta
per•son'i•fi•ca'tion
per•son'i•fy', -fied',
-fy'ing
per'son•nel' *(em-
ployees)*
✔ *personal*
per•spec'tive *(view)*
✔ *prospective*
per'spi•ca'cious
per'spi•cac'i•ty
per'spi•cu'i•ty
per'spi•ra'tion
per•spire', -spired',
-spir'ing
per•suad'a•ble
per•suade',
-suad'ed, -suad'ing
per•sua'sion
per•sua'sive
pert
per•tain'
per'ti•na'cious
per'ti•nac'i•ty
per'ti•nence *or*
per'ti•nen•cy
per'ti•nent
per•turb'
per'tur•ba'tion
pe•ruke'
pe•rus'a•ble
pe•rus•al
pe•ruse', -rused',
-rus'ing

Pe•ru'vi•an
per•vade', -vad'ed,
-vad'ing
per•va'sion
per•va'sive
per•verse'
per•ver'sion
per•ver'si•ty
per•vert' *v.*
per'vert' *n.*
per•vert'ed
Pe'sach'
pe•se'ta
pes'ky
pe'so *pl.* -sos
pes'si•mism
pes'si•mist
pes'si•mis'tic
pest
pes'ter
pes'ti•cide'
pes•tif'er•ous
pes'ti•lence
pes'ti•lent
pes'ti•len'tial
pes'tle
pes'to
pet, pet'ted, pet'ting
pet'al
pe•tard'
pet'cock'
pe'ter
pet'i•ole'
pet'it *also* pet'ty
(lesser)
✔ *petty*
pe•tite' *(small)*

pet'it four' *pl.*
pet'its fours' *or*
pet'it fours'
pe•ti'tion
pet'it point'
pet'rel *(bird)*
✔ *petrol*
pe'tri dish'
pet'ri•fac'tion *also*
pet'ri•fi•ca'tion
pet'ri•fy', -fied',
-fy'ing
pet'ro•chem'i•cal
pe•trog'ra•phy
pet'rol *(gasoline)*
✔ *petrel*
pet'ro•la'tum
pe•tro'le•um
pe•trol'o•gy
pet'ti•coat'
pet'ti•fog'ger
pet'tish
pet'ti•ness
pet'ty *(trivial)*
✔ *petit*
pet'ty of'fi•cer
pet'u•lance
pet'u•lant
pe•tu'ni•a
pew
pe'wee *also* pee'wee
(bird)
✔ *peewee*
pew'ter
pfen'nig
pH
pha'e•ton

phag'o•cyte'
pha'lanx' *pl.*
  -lanx'es *or*
  pha•lan'ges
phal'lic
phal'lus
phan'tasm
phan•tas'mal *or*
  phan•tas'mic
phan'tom
Phar'aoh
phar'i•see
phar'ma•ceu'ti•cal
  also phar'ma•ceu'-
  tic
phar'ma•ceu'tics
phar'ma•cist
phar'ma•col'o•gy
phar'ma•co•poe'ia
  also phar'ma•co•
  pe'ia
phar'ma•cy
pha•ryn'ge•al
phar'ynx *pl.*
  pha•ryn'ges *or*
  phar'ynx•es
phase *(to plan in*
  stages), phased,
  phas'ing
  ✔ *faze*
pheas'ant *pl.* -ants
  or -ant
phe'no•bar'bi•tal'
phe'nol'
phe'nol•phthal'-
  ein'
phe•nom'e•nal

phe•nom'e•non'
  pl. -na *also* -nons'
phe'no•type'
phen'yl
phi
phi'al
Phil'a•del'phi•an
phi•lan'der
phil'an•throp'ic
phi•lan'thro•pist
phi•lan'thro•py
phil'a•tel'ic
phi•lat'e•list
phi•lat'e•ly
phil'har•mon'ic
  also Phil'har•
  mon'ic
phi•lip'pic
Phil'ip•pine'
Phil'is•tine
phil'o•den'dron *pl.*
  -drons *or* -dra
phi•lol'o•gist
phi•lol'o•gy
phi•los'o•pher
phil'o•soph'i•cal
  also phil'o•soph'ic
phi•los'o•phize',
  -phized', -phiz'ing
phi•los'o•phy
phil'ter *also* phil'tre
  (magic potion)
  ✔ *filter*
phle•bi'tis
phle•bot'o•mist
phle•bot'o•my
phlegm

phleg•mat'ic
phlo'em
phlox *pl.* phlox *or*
  phlox'es
pho'bi•a
phoe'be
Phoe•ni'cian
phoe'nix
phone, phoned,
  phon'ing
pho'neme'
pho•ne'mic
pho•net'ic
pho•ne•ti'cian
pho•net'ics
phon'ic
phon'ics
pho'ni•ness
pho'no•graph'
pho'no•graph'ic
pho'ny *also*
  pho'ney *pl.* -nies
  also -neys
phoo'ey
phos'phate'
phos'phor
phos'pho•res'-
  cence
phos'pho•res'cent
phos•phor'ic
phos'pho•rous *adj.*
phos'pho•rus *n.*
pho'to *pl.* -tos
pho'to•cell'
pho'to•cop'i•er
pho'to•cop'y,
  -cop'ied, -cop'y•ing

pho'to•e•lec'tric
also pho'to•e•lec'-
tri•cal

pho'to•e•lec'tron'

pho'to•en•grave',
-graved', -grav'ing

pho'to-es'say' *also*
pho'to•es'say'

pho'to•gen'ic

pho'to•graph'

pho•tog'ra•pher

pho'to•graph'ic

pho•tog'ra•phy

pho'to•gra•vure'

pho'to•jour'nal•
ism

pho'to•me•chan'-
i•cal

pho•tom'e•ter

pho•tom'e•try

pho'to•mi'cro•
graph'

pho'to•mon•tage'

pho'ton'

pho'to•re•cep'tive

pho'to•re•cep'tor

pho'to•sen'si•tive

pho'to•sen'si•tiv'-
i•ty

pho'to•sen'si•tize',
-tized', -tiz'ing

pho'to•sphere'

pho'to•syn'the•sis

pho'to•syn'the•
size', -sized',
-siz'ing

pho•tot'ro•pism

phras'al

phrase, phrased,
phras'ing

phra'se•ol'o•gy

phre•nol'o•gy

phy•lac'ter•y

phy'lum *pl.* -la

phys'ic *(to act as a
cathartic)*, -icked,
-ick•ing
✔ *physique, psychic*

phys'i•cal

phy•si'cian

phys'i•cist

phys'ics

phys'i•og'no•my

phys'i•o•log'i•cal

phys'i•ol'o•gist

phys'i•ol'o•gy

phys'i•o•ther'-
a•py

phy•sique' *(body)*
✔ *physic*

pi *(Greek letter), pl.*
pis
✔ *pie*

pi'a•nis'si•mo'

pi•an'ist

pi•an'o *(instrument),
pl.* -os

pi•a'no *(musical
direction)*

pi•an'o•for'te

pi•az'za *pl.* -zas *also*
-ze

pi'ca *(type size)*
✔ *pika*

pic'a•dor' *pl.* -dors'
or pic'a•do'res

pic'a•resque'

pic'a•yune'

pic'ca•lil'li *pl.* -lis

pic'co•lo' *pl.* -los'

pick

pick'ax' *or* pick'axe'

pick'er•el *pl.* -el *or*
-els

pick'et

pick'le, -led, -ling

pick'-me-up' *n.*

pick'pock'et

pick'up' *n.*

pick'y

pic'nic, -nicked,
-nick•ing

pic'nick•er

pi'cot *(loop)*
✔ *pekoe*

pic'ric ac'id

Pict

pic'to•gram'

pic'to•graph'

pic•tog'ra•phy

pic•to'ri•al

pic'ture

pic'tur•esque'

pid'dling

pidg'in *(form of
speech)*
✔ *pigeon*

pie *(pastry)*
✔ *pi*

pie'bald'

piece *(to join parts*

of), pieced,
piec′ing
✔ *peace*
pièce de ré•sis•
tance′ *pl.* pièces
de ré•sis•tance′
piece′meal′
piece′ of eight′ *pl.*
piec′es of eight′
piece′work′
pied
pier *(dock)*
✔ *peer*
pierce, pierced,
pierc′ing
pi′e•ty
pi•e′zo•e•lec•tric′-
i•ty
pig
pi′geon *(bird)*
✔ *pidgin*
pi′geon•hole′,
-holed′, -hol′ing
pi′geon-toed′
pig′gish
pig′gy•back′
pig′gy bank′
pig′head•ed
pig′let
pig′ment
pig′men•ta′tion
Pig′my
pig′pen′
pig′skin′
pig′sty′
pig′tail′
pi′ka *(animal)*

✔ *pica*
pike *(spear, turnpike)*
pike *(fish), pl.* pike *or*
pikes
pike′staff′
pi′laf′ *or* pi′laff′
pi•las′ter
pile *(to heap),* piled,
pil′ing
pile *(beam, loop of*
yarn)
piles
pile′up′ *or*
pile′-up′ *n.*
pil′fer
pil′grim
pil′grim•age
pil′ing
pill
pil′lage, -laged,
-lag•ing
pil′lag•er
pil′lar
pill′box′
pill′lion
pil′lo•ry, -ried,
-ry•ing
pil′low
pil′low•case′
pil′low•slip′
pi′lot
pi′lot•house′
Pi′ma *pl.* -ma *or*
-mas
pi•mien′to *also*
pi•men′to *pl.* -tos
pim′per•nel′

pim′ple
pim′ply
pin, pinned,
pin′ning
pi′ña co•la′da
pin′a•fore′
pi•ña′ta
pin′ball′
pince′-nez′ *pl.*
pince′-nez′
pin′cers *also*
pinch′ers
pinch
pinch′-hit′, -hit′,
-hit′ting
pinch′ hit′ *n.*
pinch′ hit′ter
pin′cush•ion
pine, pined, pin′ing
pin′e•al
pine′ap′ple
pin′feath•er
pin′head′
pin′hole′
pin′ion *(wing, gear-*
wheel)
✔ *piñon*
pink′eye′
pink′ie *also* pink′y
pink′ing shears′
pin′nace
pin′na•cle
pin′nate′
pi′noch′le *or*
pi′noc′le *also*
pe′nuch′le *or*
pe′nuck′le

pi′ñon′ *also*
pin′yon′ *(tree) pl.*
-ñons′ *or* pi•ño′nes
also -yons
✔ *pinion*

pin′point′

pin′prick′

pin′scher

pin′stripe′

pint

pin′to *pl.* -tos *or*
-toes

pin′to bean′

pint′-size′ *also*
pint′-sized′

pin′wale′

pin′wheel′

pin′worm′

pin′y *also* pine′y

Pin′yin′ *or* pin′yin′

pi′o•neer′

pi′ous

pip, pipped, pip′ping

pipe, piped, pip′ing

pipe′line′, -lined′,
-lin′ing

pip′er

pi•pette′ *(glass tube)*

pip′it *(bird)*

pip′pin

pip′-squeak′

pi′quan•cy *or*
pi′quant•ness

pi′quant

pique *(to provoke)*,
piqued, piqu′ing
✔ *peak, peek*

pi•qué′ *(fabric)*

pi•quet′ *also*
pic•quet′ *(card
game)*

pi′ra•cy

pi•ra′nha *also*
pi•ra′ña

pi′rate, -rat•ed,
-rat•ing

pi•rogue′

pir′ou•ette′, -et′ted,
-et′ting

pis•ca•to′ri•al *or*
pis′ca•to′ry

pis•ta•chi•o′ *pl.* -os′

pis′til *(flower organ)*
✔ *pistol*

pis•til•late′

pis′tol *(gun)*
✔ *pistil*

pis′ton

pit, pit′ted, pit′ting

pi′ta

pit′a•pat′, -pat′ted,
-pat′ting

pitch

pitch′-black′

pitch′blende′

pitch′-dark′

pitch′er

pitch′fork′

pitch′out′

pit′e•ous

pit′fall′

pith

pith′ hel′met

pith′y

pit′i•a•ble

pit′i•ful

pit′i•less

pit′tance

pit′ter-pat′ter

pi•tu′i•tar′y

pit′y, -ied, -y•ing

piv′ot

piv′ot•al

pix′el

pix′y *or* pix′ie

piz′za

piz•zazz′ *or* piz•zaz′

piz′ze•ri′a

piz′zi•ca′to

plac′ard

pla•cate′, -cat•ed,
-cat•ing

pla•cat′er

pla•ca′tion

place *(to set)*, placed,
plac′ing
✔ *plaice*

pla•ce′bo *pl.* -bos *or*
-boes

place′hold′er

place′kick′ *v.*

place′-kick′er

place′ mat′

place′ment

pla•cen′ta *pl.* -tas *or*
-tae

pla•cen′tal

plac′id

pla•cid′i•ty

plack′et

pla′gia•rism

pla′gia·rist

pla′gia·rize′,
-rized′, -riz′ing

plague, plagued,
plagu′ing

plaice *(fish)*, pl.
plaice *or* plaic′es
✔ *place*

plaid

plain *(clear, simple)*
✔ *plane*

plain *(flat, treeless
area)*
✔ *plane*

plain′chant′

plain′clothes′
man *or*
plain′clothes′man

plain′song′

plain′spo′ken

plaint

plain′tiff

plain′tive

plait *(braid, to braid)*
✔ *plat, plate*

plan, planned
plan′ning

pla′nar *(flat)*
✔ *planer*

pla·nar′i·an

plane *(surface, air-
plane, tool, tree)*
✔ *plain*

plane *(to smooth
with a plane)*,
planed, plan′ing
✔ *plain*

plan′er *(one that
planes)*
✔ *planar*

plan′et

plan′e·tar′i·um pl.
-i·ums *or* -i·a

plan′e·tar′y

plan′e·toid′

plank

plank′ton

plan′ner

plant

plan′tain

plan′tar *(relating to
the sole of the foot)*
✔ *planter*

plan·ta′tion

plant′er *(one that
plants)*
✔ *plantar*

plaque

plash

plas′ma *also* plasm

plas·mo′di·um pl.
-di·a

plas′ter

plas′ter·board′

plas′ter·work′

plas′tic

plas·tic′i·ty

plas′tid

plat *(braid, to braid)*,
plat′ted, plat′ting
✔ *plait*

plate *(to coat)*,
plat′ed, plat′ing
✔ *plait*

pla·teau′ pl. -teaus′
or -teaux′

plate′ful′

plate′let

plat′en

plat′form′

plat′i·num

plat′i·tude′

plat′i·tu′di·nous

Pla·ton′ic

Pla′to·nism

pla·toon′

plat′ter

plat′y·pus pl.
-pus·es

plau′dit

plau′si·ble

plau·si·bil′i·ty

plau′si·bly

play

pla′ya

play′a·ble

play′-act′ n.

play′back′ n.

play′bill′

play′book′

play′boy′

play′-by-play′

play′er

play′ful

play′girl′

play′go′er

play′ground′

play′house′

play′mate′

play′off′ n.

play′pen′

play'room'
play'thing'
play'wright'
pla'za
plea
plea'-bar'gain *v.*
plead, plead'ed *or*
  pled, plead'ing
pleas'ant
pleas'ant•ry
please, pleased,
  pleas'ing
pleas'ur•a•ble
pleas'ur•a•bly
pleas'ure
pleat
plebe *also* pleb
ple•be'ian
pleb'i•scite'
plec'trum *pl.*
  -trums *or* -tra
pledge, pledged,
  pledg'ing
Pleis'to•cene'
ple'na•ry
plen'i•po•ten'ti•
  ar'y
plen'i•tude'
plen'te•ous
plen'ti•ful
plen'ty
ple'num *pl.* -nums
  or -na
ple'si•o•saur' *also*
  ple'si•o•sau'rus
pleth'o•ra
pleu'ra *pl.* -rae

pleu'ral
pleu'ri•sy
plex'us *pl.* -us *or*
  -us•es
pli'a•bil'i•ty *or*
  pli'a•ble•ness
pli'a•ble
pli'an•cy
pli'ant
pli•é'
pli'ers
plight
plinth
Pli'o•cene'
plod, plod'ded,
  plod'ding
plod'der
plop, plopped,
  plop'ping
plot, plot'ted,
  plot'ting
plot'ter
plov'er *pl.* -er *or* -ers
plow *also* plough
plow'man
plow'share'
ploy
pluck'y
plug, plugged,
  plug'ging
plug'ger
plum *(fruit)*
  ✔ *plumb*
plum'age
plumb *(weight)*
  ✔ *plum*
plumb'er

plumb'ing
plumb' line'
plume, plumed,
  plum'ing
plum'met
plump
plun'der
plun'der•er
plunge, plunged,
  plung'ing
plung'er
plunk
plu•per'fect
plu'ral
plu•ral'i•ty
plus *pl.* plus'es *or*
  plus'ses
plush
plu•toc'ra•cy
plu'to•crat'ic
Plu•to'ni•an *also*
  Plu•ton'ic *(relating
  to Pluto)*
plu•to'ni•um
  (element)
plu'vi•al
ply, plied, ply'ing
ply'wood'
pneu•mat'ic
pneu•mo'nia
poach
poach'er
pock *(pustule, scar)*
  ✔ *pox*
pock'et
pock'et•book'
pock'et•ful' *pl.*

pock'et•fuls' *or*
   pock'ets•ful'
pock'et•knife'
pock'et-sized' *or*
   pock'et•size'
pock'mark'
po'co
pod
po•di'a•trist
po•di'a•try
po'di•um *pl.* -di•a *or*
   -di•ums
po'em
po'e•sy
po'et
po•et'ic
po•ct'i•cal
po'et lau're•ate *pl.*
   po'ets lau're•ate *or*
   po'et lau're•ates
po'et•ry
po'go stick'
po•grom'
poi
poign'an•cy
poign'ant
poin•set'ti•a
point
point'-blank'
point'ed
point'er
poin'til•lism
poin'til•list
point'less
poise, poised,
   pois'ing
poi'son

poi'son•er
poi'son•ous
poke, poked, pok'ing
pok'er
pok'er•faced'
po'key *(jail), pl.*
   -keys
pok'y *also* poke'y
   (slow)
po'lar
po•lar'i•ty
po'lar•i•za'tion
po'lar•ize', -ized',
   -iz'ing
pole *(axis point, rod)*
   ✔ *poll*
pole *(to propel with a*
   pole), poled,
   pol'ing
   ✔ *poll*
Pole *(inhabitant of*
   Poland)
   ✔ *poll*
pole'ax' *or* pole'axe'
pole'cat'
po•lem'ic
po•len'ta
pole'star'
pole'-vault' *v.*
pole'-vault'er
po•lice' *pl.* po•lice'
po•lice', -liced',
   -lic'ing
po•lice'man
po•lice'wom'an
pol'i•cy
pol'i•cy•hold'er

po'li•o'
po'li•o•my'e•li'tis
pol'ish *(to shine)*
Po'lish *(relating to*
   Poland)
po•lite', -lit'er,
   -lit'est
pol'i•tic *(shrewd)*
   ✔ *politick*
po•lit'i•cal
pol'i•ti'cian
pol'i•tick *(to talk*
   politics)
   ✔ *politic*
pol'i•tics
pol'i•ty
pol'ka
poll *(casting of votes)*
   ✔ *pole, Pole*
pol'len
pol'li•nate',
   -li•nat'ed,
   -li•nat'ing
pol'li•na'tion
pol'li•na'tor
pol'li•wog' *also*
   pol'ly•wog'
poll'ster
pol•lut'ant
pol•lute', -lut'ed,
   -lut'ing
pol•lu'tion
po'lo
pol'o•naise'
po•lo'ni•um
pol'ter•geist'
pol•troon'

pol'y•an'drous
pol'y•an'dry
pol'y•chro•mat'ic
    also pol'y•chro'mic
    or pol'y•chro'mous
pol'y•chrome'
pol'y•es'ter
pol'y•eth'yl•ene'
po•lyg'a•mist
po•lyg'a•mous
po•lyg'a•my
pol'y•glot'
pol'y•gon'
po•lyg'o•nal
pol'y•graph'
pol'y•he'dron *pl.*
    -drons *or* -dra
pol'y•mer
pol'y•mer'ic
po•lym'er•i•za'•
    tion
pol'y•mer•ize',
    -ized', -iz'ing
Pol'y•ne'sian
pol'y•no'mi•al
pol'yp
pol'y•phon'ic
po•lyph'o•ny
pol'y•sac'cha•ride'
    also pol'y•sac'cha•
    rid *or* pol'y•sac'•
    cha•rose'
pol'y•sty'rene
pol'y•syl•lab'ic
pol'y•syl'la•ble
pol'y•tech'nic
pol'y•the•ism

pol'y•the'ist
pol'y•the•is'tic
pol'y•un•sat'u•
    rat'ed
pol'y•va'lence *or*
    pol'y•va'len•cy
pol'y•va'lent
po•made'
pome'gran'ate
Pom'er•a'ni•an
pom'mel *(to beat
    up)*, -meled *also*
    -melled, -mel'ing
    also -mel'ling
    ✔ *pummel*
pom'mel *(part of
    saddle)*
    ✔ *pummel*
pomp
pom'pa•dour'
pom•pa'no' *pl.* -no'
    or -nos'
pom•pon' *or*
    pom'pom'
pom•pos'i•ty *or*
    pom'pous•ness
pom'pous
pon'cho *pl.* -chos
pond
pon'der
pon'der•ous
pon•gee'
pon'iard
pon'tiff
pon•tif'i•cal
pon•tif'i•cate',

-cat'ed, -cat'ing
pon•toon'
po'ny
po'ny•tail'
pooch
poo'dle
pooh
pooh'-pooh' *v.*
pool
pool'room'
pool'side'
poop
poor
poor'house'
pop, popped,
    pop'ping
pop'corn'
pope *or* Pope
pop'gun'
pop'in•jay'
pop'lar
pop'lin
pop'o'ver
pop'py
pop'py•cock'
pop'-top'
pop'u•lace *(general
    public)*
    ✔ *populous*
pop'u•lar
pop'u•lar'i•ty
pop'u•lar•i•za'tion
pop'u•lar•ize',
    -ized', -iz'ing
pop'u•late', -lat'ed,
    -lat'ing
pop'u•la'tion

pop′u·list

pop′u·lous *(thickly settled)*
  ✔ *populace*

por′ce·lain

porch

por′cine′

por′cu·pine′

pore *(to study)*, pored, por′ing
  ✔ *pour*

pore *(tiny opening)*
  ✔ *pour*

por′gy *pl.* -gy *or* -gies

pork

pork′er

pork′pie′

por·nog′ra·pher

por′no·graph′ic

por·nog′ra·phy

po·ros′i·ty

po′rous

por′phy·ry

por′poise *pl.* -poise *or* -pois·es

por′ridge

por′rin·ger

port

port′a·ble

port·age, -aged, -ag·ing

por′tal

port·cul′lis

por·tend′

por·tent′

por·ten′tous

por′ter

por′ter·house′

port·fo′li·o′ *pl.* -os′

port′hole′

por′ti·co′ *pl.* -coes′ *or* -cos′

por′tion

port′li·ness

port′ly

por′trait

por′trait·ist

por′trai·ture′

por·tray′

por·tray′al

Por′tu·guese′ *pl.* -guese′

pose, posed, pos′ing

pos′er *(one that poses, problem)*

po·seur′ *(affected person)*

posh

pos′it

po·si′tion

pos′i·tive

pos′i·tiv·ism

pos′i·tiv·ist

pos′i·tron′

pos′se

pos·sess′

pos·sessed′

pos·ses′sion

pos·ses′sive

pos·ses′sor

pos′si·bil′i·ty

pos′si·ble

pos′si·bly

pos′sum

post

post′age

post′al

post′ card′ *also* post′card′

post′date′, -dat′ed, -dat′ing

post′er

pos·te′ri·or

pos·ter′i·ty

pos′tern

post·grad′u·ate

post·haste′

post·hu·mous

post·hyp·not′ic

pos·til′ion *also* pos·til′lion

post·im·pres′sion·ism

post·im·pres′sion·ist

post·in·dus′tri·al

post′man

post′mark′

post′mas′ter

post′me·rid′i·an *(in the afternoon)*

post′ me·rid′i·em *(after noon)*

post′mis′tress

post·mod′ern *or* post-mod′ern

post·mod′ern·ism

post·mod′ern·ist

post·mor′tem

post·na′sal

post·na′tal

post•op'er•a•tive
post'paid'
post•par'tum
post•pone',
-poned', -pon'ing
post•pone'ment
post'script'
post'trau•mat'ic
pos'tu•lant
pos'tu•late', -lat'ed,
-lat'ing
pos'tu•la'tion
pos'tu•la'tor
pos'ture, -tured,
-tur'ing
post'war'
po'sy
pot, pot'ted, pot'ting
po'ta•ble
pot'ash'
po•tas'si•um
po•ta'tion
po•ta'to pl. -toes
Pot'a•wat'o•mi pl.
-mi or -mis
pot'bel'lied
pot'bel'ly
pot'boil'er
pot'bound'
po'ten•cy
po'tent
po'ten•tate'
po•ten'tial
po•ten'ti•al'i•ty
po•ten'ti•om'e•ter
pot'herb'
pot'hold'er

pot'hole'
pot'hook'
po'tion
pot'latch'
pot'luck'
pot'pie'
pot'pour•ri' pl. -ris'
pot'sherd' also
pot'shard'
pot'shot' also
pot' shot'
pot'tage
pot'ted
pot'ter
pot'ter•y
pouch
poul'tice
poul'try
pounce, pounced,
pounc'ing
pound pl. pound or
pounds
pound v.
pound'-fool'ish
pour (to flow)
✔ pore
pout
pov'er•ty
pov'er•ty-strick'en
POW pl. POW's also
POWs
pow'der
pow'der•y
pow'er
pow'er•boat'
pow'er•ful
pow'er•house'

pow'er•less
Pow'ha•tan' pl.
-tan' or -tans'
pow'wow'
pox (disease)
✔ pock
prac'ti•ca•bil'i•ty
prac'ti•ca•ble
(possible)
prac'ti•cal (useful,
sensible)
prac'ti•cal'i•ty
prac'ti•cal•ly
prac'tice, -ticed,
-tic'ing
prac•ti'tion•er
prae'tor
prae•to'ri•an
prag•mat'ic
prag'ma•tism
prag'ma•tist
prai'rie
praise, praised,
prais'ing
praise'wor'thy
pra'line'
pram
prance, pranced,
pranc'ing
prank
prank'ster
pra'se•o•dym'i•um
prate, prat'ed,
prat'ing
prat'fall'
prat'tle, -tled, -tling
prawn

pray *(to say a prayer)*
✔ prey
prayer *(petition)*
pray'er *(person who prays)*
preach
preach'er
preach'y
pre·ad·o·les'cence
pre·ad·o·les'cent
pre'am'ble
pre·am'pli·fi'er
pre·ar·range',
-ranged', -rang'ing
Pre·cam'bri·an
pre·car'i·ous
pre·cau'tion
pre·cau'tion·ar'y
pre·cede' *(to come before)*, -ced'ed,
-ced'ing
✔ proceed
prec'e·dence
prec'e·dent *(prior example)*
✔ president
pre·ced'ing
pre'cept'
pre·cep'tor
pre·ces'sion *(precedence, axial movement)*
✔ procession
pre'cinct'
pre'cious
prec'i·pice
pre·cip'i·tate',

-tat'ed, -tat'ing
pre·cip'i·tate
(hasty)
✔ precipitous
pre·cip'i·ta'tion
pre·cip'i·tous
(steep)
✔ precipitate
pre·cise'
pre·ci'sion
pre·clude',
-clud'ed, -clud'ing
pre·co'cious
pre·co'cious·ness
or pre·coc'i·ty
pre'-Co·lum'bi·an
pre·con·ceive',
-ceived', -ceiv'ing
pre'con·cep'tion
pre'con·di'tion
pre·cur'sor
pre·date', -dat'ed,
-dat'ing
pred'a·tor
pred'a·to'ry
pre'de·cease',
-ceased', -ceas'ing
pred'e·ces'sor
pre·des'ti·na'tion
pre·des'tine,
-tined, -tin·ing
pre'de·ter'mi·na'-
tion
pre'de·ter'mine,
-mined, -min·ing
pre·dic'a·ment
pred'i·cate',

-cat'ed, -cat'ing
pred'i·ca'tion
pred'i·ca'tive
pre·dict'
pre·dict'a·ble
pre·dic'tion
pred'i·lec'tion
pre'dis·pose',
-posed', -pos'ing
pre'dis·po·si'tion
pre·dom'i·nance
pre·dom'i·nant
pre·dom'i·nate',
-nat'ed, -nat'ing
pree'mie
pre·em'i·nence
pre·em'i·nent *or*
pre-em'i·nent
pre·empt' *or*
pre-empt'
pre·emp'tion *or*
pre-emp'tion
pre·emp'tive *or*
pre-emp'tive
pre·emp'to·ry *or*
pre-emp'to·ry
preen
pre'ex·ist' *or*
pre'-ex·ist'
pre'fab'
pre·fab'ri·cate',
-cat'ed, -cat'ing
pre·fab'ri·ca'tion
pref'ace, -aced,
-ac·ing
pref'a·to'ry
pre'fect'

pre'fec'ture

pre·fer', -ferred',
  -fer'ring

pref'er·a·ble

pref'er·a·bly

pref'er·ence

pref'er·en'tial

pre·fer'ment

pre·fig'ure, -ured,
  -ur·ing

pre·fix' v.

pre·fix' n.

pre'flight'

preg'nan·cy

preg'nant

pre·heat'

pre·hen'sile

pre'his·tor'ic also
  pre'his·tor'i·cal

pre'his·to·ry

pre·judge',
  -judged', -judg'ing

prej'u·dice, -diced,
  -dic·ing

prej'u·di'cial

prel'ate

pre'law'

pre·lim'i·nar'y

prel'ude, -ud'ed,
  -ud'ing

pre·mar'i·tal

pre'ma·ture'

pre'med'

pre·med'i·cal

pre·med'i·tate',
  -tat'ed, -tat'ing

pre·med'i·ta'tion

pre·mier' (first in
  importance, prime
  minister)

pre·miere' (first per-
  formance)

prem'ise, -ised,
  -is·ing

pre'mi·um

pre·mo'lar

pre'mo·ni'tion

pre·na'tal

pre·nup'tial

pre·oc'cu·pa'tion

pre·oc'cu·py',
  -pied', -py'ing

pre'or·dain'

prep

pre·pack'age,
  -aged, -ag·ing

prep'a·ra'tion

pre·par'a·to'ry

pre·pare', -pared',
  -par'ing

pre·par'ed·ness

pre·pay', -paid',
  -pay'ing

pre·pon'der·ance

pre·pon'der·ant

pre·pon'der·ate',
  -at'ed, -at'ing

prep'o·si'tion

prep'o·si'tion·al

pre·pos·sess'ing

pre·pos·ses'sion

pre·pos'ter·ous

prep'py or prep'pie
  pl. -pies

pre'puce'

Pre-Raph'a·el·ite'
  also pre-
  Raph'a·el·ite'

pre·req'ui·site
  (prior requirement)
  ✔ perquisite

pre·rog'a·tive

pres'age n.

pre·sage', -saged',
  -sag'ing

pres'by·ter

Pres'by·te'ri·an

pres'by·te'ri·an·ism

pres'by·ter'y

pre'school'

pre'sci·ence

pre'sci·ent

pre·scribe' (to im-
  pose, to order),
  -scribed', -scrib'ing
  ✔ proscribe

pre·scrip'tion

pre·scrip'tive

pres'ence

pres'ent n.

pre·sent' v.

pre·sent'a·bil'i·ty

pre·sent'a·ble

pres'en·ta'tion

pres'ent-day'

pre·sen'ti·ment
  (premonition)
  ✔ presentment

pres'ent·ly

pre·sent'ment (pres-
  entation)

✔ *presentiment*
pres'er•va'tion
pre•ser'va•tive
pre•serve', -served',
   -serv'ing
pre•serv'er
pre•set', -set',
   -set'ting
pre'shrunk'
pre•side', -sid'ed,
   -sid'ing
pres'i•den•cy
pres'i•dent (*chief
   officer*)
   ✔ *precedent*
pres'i•dent-e•lect'
   pl. pres'i•dents-
   e•lect'
pres'i•den'tial
pre•si'di•o'
pre•sid'i•um *pl.* -i•a
   or -i•ums
pre•soak'
pre•sort'
press
press'ing
press'room'
press'run'
pres'sure, -sured,
   -sur•ing
pres'sur•i•za'tion
pres'sur•ize', -ized',
   -iz'ing
pres'ti•dig'i•ta'tion
pres'ti•dig'i•ta'tor
pres•tige'
pres•ti'gious

pres•tis'si•mo'
pres'to
pre•sum'a•ble
pre•sum'a•bly
pre•sume' (*to sup-
   pose, to dare*),
   -sumed', -sum'ing
   ✔ *assume*
pre•sum'ed•ly
pre•sump'tion
pre•sump'tive
pre•sump'tu•ous
pre'sup•pose',
   -posed', -pos'ing
pre'sup•po•si'tion
pre•teen'
pre•tend'
pre•tend'er
pre•tense'
pre•ten'sion
pre•ten'tious
pret'er•it *or*
   pret'er•ite
pre•term'
pre'ter•nat'u•ral
pre'text'
pre•tri'al
pret'ti•fy', -fied',
   -fy'ing
pret'ti•ly
pret'ti•ness
pret'ty, -tied, -ty•ing
pret'zel
pre•vail'
prev'a•lence
prev'a•lent
pre•var'i•cate',

   -cat'ed, -cat'ing
pre•var'i•ca'tion
pre•var'i•ca'tor
pre•vent'
pre•vent'a•ble *or*
   pre•vent'i•ble
pre•ven'tion
pre•ven'tive *also*
   pre•ven'ta•tive
pre•view' *also*
   pre'vue'
pre'vi•ous
pre'war'
prey (*quarry, victim*)
   ✔ *pray*
price, priced,
   pric'ing
prick
prick'le, -led, -ling
prick'ly
pride, prid'ed,
   prid'ing
pri'er *also* pry'er
   (*one that pries*)
   ✔ *prior*
priest
priest'ess
priest'hood'
prig
prig'gish
prim, prim'mer,
   prim'mest
pri'ma•cy
pri'ma don'na
pri'mal
pri•mar'i•ly
pri'mar'y

pri'mate'
pri'ma•ve'ra
prime, primed,
 prim'ing
prim'er *(elementary
 textbook)*
prim'er *(one that
 primes)*
prime'-time' *adj.*
pri•me'val
prim'i•tive
pri'mo•gen'i•tor
pri'mo•gen'i•ture
pri•mor'di•al
primp
prim'rose'
prince
prince'dom
prince'ly
prin'cess
prin'ci•pal *(chief,
 money)*
 ✔ *principle*
prin'ci•pal'i•ty
prin'ci•ple *(doctrine)*
 ✔ *principal*
print
print'er
print'ing
print'out'
pri'or *(before)*
 ✔ *prier*
pri'or *(monk)*
 ✔ *prier*
pri'or•ess
pri•or'i•tize',

-tized', -tiz'ing
pri•or'i•ty
pri'or•y
prism
pris•mat'ic
pris'on
pris'on•er
pris'sy
pris'tine'
pri'va•cy
pri'vate
pri'va•teer'
pri•va'tion
priv'et
priv'i•lege
priv'i•leged
priv'i•ly
priv'y
prize, prized, priz'ing
prize'fight'
prize'fight'er
prize'win'ning
pro *pl.* pros
pro•ac'tive *or*
 pro-ac'tive
prob'a•bil'i•ty
prob'a•ble
prob'a•bly
pro'bate', -bat'ed,
 -bat'ing
pro•ba'tion
pro•ba'tion•ar'y
probe, probed,
 prob'ing
pro'bi•ty
prob'lem

prob'lem•at'ic *also*
 prob'lem•at'i•cal
pro•bos'cis *pl.*
 -cis•es *or* -ci•des'
pro'caine'
pro•ce'dur•al
pro•ce'dure
pro•ceed' *(to go for-
 ward)*
 ✔ *precede*
pro•ceed'ing
pro'ceeds'
proc'ess'
pro•ces'sion
 (parade)
 ✔ *precession*
pro•ces'sion•al
pro-choice'
pro•claim'
proc'la•ma'tion
pro•cliv'i•ty
pro•con'sul
pro•con'su•lar
pro•cras'ti•nate',
 -nat'ed, -nat'ing
pro•cras'ti•na'tion
pro•cras'ti•na'tor
pro'cre•ate', -at'ed,
 -at'ing
pro'cre•a'tion
proc•tol'o•gist
proc•tol'o•gy
proc'tor
proc'u•ra'tor
pro•cure', -cured',
 -cur'ing

pro·cure'ment
prod, prod'ded,
  prod'ding
prod'der
prod'i·gal
prod'i·gal'i·ty
pro·di'gious
prod'i·gy
pro·duce', -duced',
  -duc'ing
pro'duce' *n.*
pro·duc'er
pro·duc'i·ble *or*
  pro·duce'a·ble
prod'uct
pro·duc'tion
pro·duc'tive
pro·duc·tiv'i·ty *or*
  pro·duc'tive·ness
prof'a·na'tion
pro·fane', -faned',
  -fan'ing
pro·fan'i·ty
pro·fess'
pro·fes'sion
pro·fes'sion·al
pro·fes'sor
pro·fes·so'ri·al
prof'fer
pro·fi'cien·cy
pro·fi'cient
pro'file', -filed',
  -fil'ing
prof'it *(gain)*
  ✔ *prophet*
prof'it·a·ble

prof'it·eer'
prof'li·ga·cy
prof'li·gate
pro·found'
pro·fun'di·ty
pro·fuse'
pro·fu'sion
pro·gen'i·tor
prog'e·ny *pl.* -ny *or*
  -nies
pro·ges'ter·one'
prog·no'sis *pl.* -ses
prog·nos'tic
prog·nos'ti·cate',
  -cat'ed, -cat'ing
prog·nos'ti·ca'tion
prog·nos'ti·ca'tor
pro'gram',
  -grammed' *or*
  -gramed',
  -gram'ming *or*
  -gram'ing
pro'gram·mat'ic
pro'gram'mer *or*
  pro'gram'er
prog'ress *n.*
pro·gress' *v.*
pro·gres'sion
pro·gres'sive
pro·hib'it
pro'hi·bi'tion
pro'hi·bi'tion·ist
pro·hib'i·tive *also*
  pro·hib'i·to'ry
proj'ect *n.*
pro·ject' *v.*

pro·jec'tile
pro·jec'tion
pro·jec'tion·ist
pro·jec'tor
pro'le·tar'i·an
pro'le·tar'i·at
pro-life'
pro·lif'er·ate',
  -at'ed, -at'ing
pro·lif'er·a'tion
pro·lif'ic
pro'lix'
pro·lix'i·ty
pro'logue'
pro·long'
pro·lon·ga'tion
prom
prom'e·nade',
  -nad'ed, -nad'ing
pro·me'thi·um
prom'i·nence
prom'i·nent
prom'is·cu'i·ty
pro·mis'cu·ous
prom'ise, -ised,
  -is·ing
prom'is·so'ry
prom'on·to'ry
pro·mote',
  -mot'ed, -mot'ing
pro·mo'tion
pro·mo'tion·al
prompt
prompt'er
prom'ul·gate',
  -gat'ed, -gat'ing

prom'ul•ga'tion
prone
prong'horn' *pl.*
  -horn' *or* -horns'
pro•nom'i•nal
pro'noun'
pro•nounce',
  -nounced',
  -nounc'ing
pro•nounce'a•ble
pro•nounce'ment
pron'to
pro•nun'ci•a'tion
proof
proof'read', -read',
  -read'ing
proof'read'er
prop, propped,
  prop'ping
prop'a•gan'da
prop'a•gan'dist
prop'a•gan'dize',
  -dized', -diz'ing
prop'a•gate',
  -gat'ed, -gat'ing
prop'a•ga'tion
pro'pane'
pro•pel', -pelled',
  -pel'ling
pro•pel'lant *also*
  pro•pel'lent
pro•pel'ler
pro•pen'si•ty
prop'er
prop'er•tied'
prop'er•ty

pro'phase'
proph'e•cy *n.*
proph'e•sy', -sied',
  -sy'ing
proph'et *(seer)*
  ✔ *profit*
pro•phet'ic
pro'phy•lac'tic
pro•pin'qui•ty
pro•pi'ti•ate',
  -at'ed, -at'ing
pro•pi'tious
pro•po'nent
pro•por'tion
pro•por'tion•al
pro•por'tion•ate
pro•pos'al
pro•pose', -posed',
  -pos'ing
prop'o•si'tion
pro•pound'
pro•pri'e•tar'y
pro•pri'e•tor
pro•pri'e•ty
pro•pul'sion
pro•pul'sive
pro'pyl•ene'
pro•rate', -rat'ed,
  -rat'ing
pro•sa'ic
pro•sce'ni•um *pl.*
  -ni•ums *or* -ni•a
pro•scribe' *(to for-*
  bid), -scribed',
  -scrib'ing
  ✔ *prescribe*

pro•scrip'tion
pro•scrip'tive
prose
pros'e•cute' *(to try*
  by law), -cut'ed,
  -cut'ing
  ✔ *persecute*
pros'e•cu'tion
pros'e•cu'tor
pros'e•lyte', -lyt'ed,
  -lyt'ing
pros'e•ly•tize',
  -tized', -tiz'ing
pros'o•dy
pros'pect'
pro•spec'tive
  (likely to be or
  become)
  ✔ *perspective*
pros•pec'tor
pro•spec'tus
pros'per
pros•per'i•ty
pros'per•ous
pros'ta•glan'din
pros'tate' *(gland)*
  ✔ *prostrate*
pros•the'sis *pl.* -ses
pros•thet'ic
pros'ti•tute',
  -tut'ed, -tut'ing
pros'ti•tu'tion
pros'trate' *(to throw*
  down flat), -trat'ed,
  -trat'ing
  ✔ *prostate*

pros•tra'tion
pro'tac•tin'i•um
pro•tag'o•nist
pro'te•an
pro•tect'
pro•tec'tion
pro•tec'tive
pro•tec'tor *also*
  pro•tect'er
pro•tec'tor•ate
pro'té•gé'
pro'tein'
pro•test' *v.*
pro'test' *n.*
Prot'es•tant
Prot'es•tant•ism
prot'es•ta'tion
pro'to•col'
pro'toc'tist
pro'ton'
pro'to•plasm
pro'to•plas'mic *or*
  pro'to•plas'mal *or*
  pro'to•plas•mat'ic
pro'to•typ'al *or*
  pro'to•typ'ic *or*
  pro'to•typ'i•cal
pro'to•type'
pro'to•zo'an *also*
  pro'to•zo'on' *pl.*
  -zo'ans *or* -zo'a *also*
  -zo'ons'
pro'to•zo'an *or*
  pro'to•zo'al *or*
  pro'to•zo'ic
pro•tract'

pro•trac'tion
pro•trac'tor
pro•trude',
  -trud'ed, -trud'ing
pro•tru'sion
pro•tu'ber•ance
pro•tu'ber•ant
proud
prov'a•ble
prove, proved,
  proved *or* prov'en
  prov'ing
prov'e•nance
Pro'ven•çal'
prov'en•der
prov'erb'
pro•ver'bi•al
pro•vide', -vid'ed,
  -vid'ing
pro•vid'er
prov'i•dence
prov'i•dent
prov'i•den'tial
prov'ince
pro•vin'cial
pro•vin'ci•al'i•ty
pro•vi'sion
pro•vi'sion•al
pro•vi'so *pl.* -sos *or*
  -soes
prov'o•ca'tion
pro•voc'a•tive
pro•voke', -voked',
  -vok'ing
pro'vo•lo'ne
pro'vost'

prow
prow'ess
prowl
prowl'er
prox'i•mal
prox'i•mate
prox•im'i•ty
prox'y
prude
pru'dence
pru'dent
pru•den'tial
prud'er•y
prud'ish
prune *(fruit)*
prune *(to trim),*
  pruned, prun'ing
pru'ri•ence
pru'ri•ent
Prus'sian
prus'sic ac'id
pry, pried, pry'ing
psalm
psalm'o•dy
Psal'ter *also* psal'ter
psal'ter•y
pseu'do•nym'
pseu'do•pod'
pseu'do•sci'ence
pshaw
psi
psit'ta•co'sis
pso•ri'a•sis
psych *(to inspirit)*
psy'che *(soul or*
  spirit)

psy'che•del'ic

psy'chi•at'ric

psy•chi'a•trist

psy•chi'a•try

psy'chic *(relating to the mind)*
✔ *physic*

psy'cho•a•nal'y•sis
pl. -ses'

psy'cho•an'a•lyst

psy'cho•an'a•lyt'ic
or psy'cho•an'a•lyt'i•cal

psy'cho•an'a•lyze',
-lyzed', -lyz'ing

psy'cho•bi•ol'o•gy

psy'cho•dra'ma

psy'cho•log'i•cal

psy•chol'o•gist

psy•chol'o•gy

psy'cho•path'

psy'cho•path'ic

psy•cho'sis *pl.* -ses

psy'cho•so•mat'ic

psy'cho•ther'a•pist

psy'cho•ther'a•py

psy•chot'ic

ptar'mi•gan *pl.*
-gan *or* -gans

pter'o•dac'tyl

pter'o•saur'

Ptol'e•ma'ic

pto'maine'

pty'a•lin

pub

pu'ber•ty

pu•bes'cence

pu•bes'cent

pu'bic

pu'bis *pl.* -bes

pub'lic

pub'li•can

pub'li•ca'tion

pub'li•cist

pub•lic'i•ty

pub'li•cize', -cized',
-ciz'ing

pub'lic-spir'it•ed

pub'lish

pub'lish•er

puce

puck

puck'er

pud'ding

pud'dle

pudg'i•ness

pudg'y

pueb'lo *(community),* *pl.* -los

Pueb'lo *(people), pl.*
-lo *or* -los

pu'er•ile

pu•er'per•al

Puer'to Ri'can

puff'ball'

puff'er

puf'fin

puff'i•ness

puff'y

pug

pu'gi•lism

pu'gi•list

pug•na'cious

pug•nac'i•ty

puis'sance

puis'sant

puke, puked,
puk'ing

pul'chri•tude'

pul'chri•tu'di•nous

pule, puled, pul'ing

pull

pul'let

pul'ley *pl.* -leys

Pull'man

pull'o•ver *n.*

pull'-up' *n.*

pul'mo•nar'y

pulp

pul'pit

pulp'wood'

pulp'y

pul'sar'

pul'sate', -sat'ed,
-sat'ing

pul•sa'tion

pulse, pulsed,
puls'ing

pul'ver•i•za'tion

pul'ver•ize', -ized',
-iz'ing

pu'ma

pum'ice

pum'mel *(to beat),*
-meled *also*
-melled, -mel•ing
or -mel'ling
✔ *pommel*

pump

pum′per·nick′el
pump′kin
pun, punned,
  pun′ning
pun′cheon
punch′y
punc·til′i·o′ *pl.* -os′
punc·til′i·ous
punc′tu·al
punc′tu·al′i·ty
punc′tu·ate′,
  -at′ed, -at′ing
punc′tu·a′tion
punc′ture, -tured,
  -tur·ing
pun′dit
pun′gen·cy
pun′gent
pun′ish
pun′ish·a·ble
pu′ni·tive
punk
pun′ster
punt′er
pu′ny
pu′pa *pl.* -pae or
  -pas
pu′pal (*relating to a
  pupa*)
  ✔ *pupil*
pu′pate′, -pat′ed,
  -pat′ing
pu·pa′tion
pu′pil (*student*)
  ✔ *pupal*
pup′pet
pup′pet·eer′

pup′pet·ry
pup′py
pur′blind′
pur′chas·a·ble
pur′chase, -chased,
  -chas·ing
pure, pur′er, pur′est
pure′bred′
pu·rée′ -réed′,
  -ré′ing
pur′ga·tive
pur′ga·to′ri·al
pur′ga·to′ry
purge, purged,
  purg′ing
pu′ri·fi·ca′tion
pu′ri·fi′er
pu′ri·fy′, -fied′,
  -fy′ing
Pu′rim
pu′rine′
pur′ist
Pu′ri·tan
pu·ri·tan′i·cal
Pu′ri·tan·ism
pu′ri·ty
purl (*to flow, knitting
  stitch*)
  ✔ *pearl*
pur·loin′
pur′ple
pur·port′ *v.*
pur′port′ *n.*
pur·pose
purr
purse, pursed,
  purs′ing

purs′er
pur·su′a·ble
pur·su′ance
pur·su′ant
pur·sue′, -sued′,
  -su′ing
pur·suit′
pu′ru·lence
pu′ru·lent
pur·vey′
pur·vey′ance
pur·vey′or
pus (*yellowish
  fluid*)
  ✔ *puss*
push′-but′ton
  also push′but′ton
  adj.
push′cart′
push′o′ver *n.*
push′pin′
push′up′ *n.*
push′y
pu′sil·lan′i·mous
puss (*cat, mouth*)
  ✔ *pus*
puss′y (*cat*)
pus′sy (*full of pus*)
puss′y·foot′
pus′tule
put (*to place*), put,
  put′ting
  ✔ *putt*
pu′ta·tive
put′down′ *or*
put′-down′ *n.*
put′-on′ *adj. & n.*

pu′tre•fac′tion
pu′tre•fy′, -fied′,
 -fy′ing
pu′trid
putsch
putt *(to hit a golf
 ball)*, putt′ed,
 putt′ing
 ✔ put
putt′er *(golf club)*
putt′er *v.*
put′ty, -tied, -ty•ing
puz′zle, -zled,
 -zling
puz′zle•ment
puz′zler
Pyg′my *also* Pig′my
 pl. -mies
py•ja′mas
py′lon′
py•lo′rus *pl.* -ri
py′or•rhe′a
pyr′a•mid
py•ram′i•dal
pyre
pyr′i•dine′
pyr′i•dox′ine
py′rite′
py•ri′tes *pl.* -tes
py′ro•ma′ni•a
py′ro•ma′ni•ac′
py′ro•tech′nic *also*
 py′ro•tech′ni•cal
py′ro•tech′nics
Pyr′rhic vic′to•ry
Py•thag′o•re′an
py′thon′

Q

quack
quack′er•y
quad
quad′ran′gle
quad′rant
quad′ra•phon′ic
 also quad′ri•
 phon′ic
quad•rat′ic
quad•ren′ni•al
quad′ri•ceps′
quad′ri•lat′er•al
qua•drille′
quad•ril′lion
quad•ril′lionth
quad′ri•ple′gia
quad′ri•ple′gic
quad′ru•ped′
quad•ru′ple, -pled,
 -pling
quad•ru′plet
qua•dru′pli•cate′,
 -cat′ed, -cat′ing
quaff
quag′mire′
qua′hog′
quail *pl.* quail *or*
 quails
quail *v.*
quaint
quake, quaked,
 quak′ing
Quak′er
Quak′er•ism
qual′i•fi•ca′tion

qual′i•fi′er
qual′i•fy′, -fied′,
 -fy′ing
qual′i•ta′tive
qual′i•ty
qualm
quan′da•ry
quan′ta
quan′ti•fi•ca′tion
quan′ti•fy′, -fied′,
 -fy′ing
quan′ti•ta′tive
quan′ti•ty
quan′tum *pl.* -ta
Qua′paw *pl.* -paw *or*
 -paws
quar′an•tine′,
 -tined′, -tin′ing
quark
quar′rel, -reled *or*
 -relled, -rel•ing *or*
 -rel•ling
quar′rel•er *or*
 quar′rel•ler
quar′rel•some
quar′ry *(object of
 pursuit, excavation)*
quar′ry *(to excavate
 stone)*, -ried,
 -ry•ing
quart
quar′ter
quar′ter•back′
quar′ter•deck′
quar′ter•fi′nal
quar′ter•fi′nal•ist
quar′ter-hour′ *also*

quar'ter hour'
quar'ter•ly
quar'ter•mas'ter
quar'ter•staff' *pl.*
  -staves'
quar•tet' *also*
  quar•tette'
quar'to *pl.* -tos
quartz
quartz'ite'
qua'sar'
quash
qua'si
qua'si-stel'lar
  ob'ject'
quat'er•nar'y *(in fours)*
Qua'ter•nar'y *(geo-logic period)*
quat'rain'
qua'ver
quay *(wharf)*
  ✔ *cay, key*
quea'si•ness
quea'sy
que•bra'cho *pl.*
  -chos
Quech'ua *pl.* -ua *or*
  -uas
queen
queen'li•ness
queen'ly
queer
quell
quench
quench'a•ble
quer'u•lous

que'ry, -ried, -ry•ing
quest
ques'tion
ques'tion•a•ble
ques'tion•a•bly
ques'tion•er
ques'tion•naire'
quet•zal' *pl.* -zals' *or*
  -za'les
queue *(to get in line)*,
  queued, queu'ing
  ✔ *cue*
quib'ble, -bled,
  -bling
quib'bler
quiche
quick
quick'en
quick'-freeze',
  -froze', -fro'zen,
  -freez'ing
quick'lime'
quick'sand'
quick'sil'ver
quick'step'
quick'-tem'pered
quick'-wit'ted
quid *(piece of chew-ing tobacco)*
quid *(money)*, *pl.*
  quid *or* quids
qui•es'cence
qui•es'cent
qui'et
qui'e•tude'
quill
quilt'ing

quince
qui'nine'
quin•quen'ni•al
quin'sy
quin•tes'sence
quin•tes•sen'tial
quin•tet' *also*
  quin•tette'
quin•til'lion
quin•til'lionth
quin•tu'ple, -pled,
  -pling
quin•tu'plet
quip, quipped,
  quip'ping
quip'ster
quire *(unit of paper)*
  ✔ *choir*
quirk
quirt
quis'ling
quit, quit *or*
  quit'ted, quit'ting
quit'claim'
quite
quit'ter
quiv'er
quix•ot'ic *also*
  quix•ot'i•cal
quiz *pl.* quiz'zes
quiz, quizzed,
  quiz'zing
quiz'zi•cal
quoin *(corner)*
  ✔ *coin*
quoit
quon'dam

quo'rum
quo'ta
quot'a•bil'i•ty
quot'a•ble
quo•ta'tion
quote, quot'ed, quot'ing
quo•tid'i•an
quo'tient

R

rab'bet *also* re'bate' *(groove)*
  ✔ *rabbit*
rab'bi *pl.* -bis
rab'bi•nate'
rab•bin'i•cal
rab'bit *(animal), pl.* -bits *or* -bit
  ✔ *rabbet*
rab'ble
rab'ble-rous'er
Rab'e•lai'si•an
rab'id
ra'bies
rac•coon' *pl.* -coons' *or* -coon'
race, raced, rac'ing
race'course'
race'horse'
ra•ceme'
rac'er
race'track'
race'way'
ra'cial

rac'ism
rac'ist
rack *(frame)*
  ✔ *wrack*
rack'et *also* rac'quet *(device for striking a ball)*
rack'et *(uproar)*
rack'et•eer'
rac•on•teur'
rac'quet•ball'
rac'y
rad
ra'dar
ra'dar•scope'
ra'di•al
ra'di•ance *also* ra'di•an•cy
ra'di•ant
ra'di•ate', -at'ed, -at'ing
ra'di•a'tion
ra'di•a'tor
rad'i•cal
rad'i•cal•ism
rad'i•cand'
ra•dic'chi•o *pl.* -os
ra'di•o *pl.* -os
ra'di•o, -oed, -o•ing
ra'di•o•ac'tive
ra'di•o•ac•tiv'i•ty
ra'di•o•car'bon
ra'di•o•gram'
ra'di•o•graph'
ra'di•og'ra•pher
ra'di•o•graph'ic
ra'di•og'ra•phy

ra'di•o•i'so•tope'
ra'di•o•log'i•cal *or* ra'di•o•log'ic
ra'di•ol'o•gist
ra'di•ol'o•gy
ra'di•om'e•ter
ra'di•om'e•try
ra'di•o•pac'i•ty
ra'di•o•paque'
ra'di•o•phone'
ra'di•o•sonde'
ra'di•o•tel'e•phone'
rad'ish
ra'di•um
ra'di•us *pl.* -di•i' *or* -di•us•es
ra'dix *pl.* rad'i•ces' *or* ra'dix•es
ra'don
raf'fi•a
raff'ish
raf'fle
raft
raft'er
rag, ragged, rag'ging
rag'a•muf'fin
rage, raged, rag'ing
rag'ged
rag'ged•y
rag'lan
ra•gout'
rag'tag'
rag'time'
rag'weed'
rah
raid

raid'er

rail

rail'ing

rail'ler•y

rail'road'

rail'way'

rai'ment

rain *(precipitation)*
  ✔ reign, rein

rain'bow'

rain' check'

rain'coat'

rain'drop'

rain'fall'

rain'storm'

rain'wa'ter

rain'wear'

rain'y

raise *(to lift)*, raised,
  rais'ing
  ✔ raze

rais'er *(one that
  raises)*
  ✔ razor

rai'sin

rai'son d'ê'tre

ra'jah *or* ra'ja

rake, raked, rak'ing

rak'ish

ral'li•er

ral'ly, -lied, -ly•ing

ram, rammed,
  ram'ming

Ram'a•dan

ram'ble, -bled,
  -bling

ram'bler

ram•bunc'tious

ram'ie

ram'i•fi•ca'tion

ram'i•fy', -fied',
  -fy'ing

ra'mose'

ramp

ram'page, -paged,
  -pag•ing

ram'pant

ram'part

ram'rod'

ram'shack'le

ranch

ranch'er

ran•che'ro *pl.* -ros

ran'cho *pl.* -chos

ran'cid

ran'cor

ran'cor•ous

ran'dom

rang

range, ranged,
  rang'ing

rang'er

rang'y

ra'ni *also* ra'nee *pl.*
  -nis *also* -nees

rank'ing

ran'kle, -kled, -kling

ran'sack'

ran'som

rant

rant'er

rap *(to knock)*,
  rapped, rap'ping
  ✔ wrap

ra•pa'cious

ra•pa'cious•ness *or*
  ra•pac'i•ty

rape, raped, rap'ing

rap'id

ra•pid'i•ty *or*
  rap'id•ness

rap'id-fire'

ra'pi•er

rap'ine

rap'ist

rap•pel', -pelled',
  -pel'ling

rap'port'

rap'proche•ment'

rap•scal'lion

rapt

rap'ture

rap'tur•ous

rare, rar'er, rar'est

rare'ness

rare'bit'

rare' earth'

rare'-earth'
  el'e•ment

rar'e•fac'tion

rar'e•fi'a•ble

rar'e•fy', -fied',
  -fy'ing

rar'i•ty

ras'cal

ras•cal'i•ty

rash'er

rasp

rasp'ber'ry

rasp'y

Ras'ta•far'i•an

Ras•ta•far•i•an•ism
rat, rat'ted, rat'ting
rat'a•touille'
ratch'et
rate, rat'ed, rat'ing
rath'er
rat'i•fi•ca'tion
rat'i•fy', -fied',
  -fy'ing
ra'tio pl. -tios
ra•ti•oc'i•nate',
  -nat'ed, -nat'ing
ra•ti•oc'i•na'tion
ra•ti•oc'i•na'tive
ra'tion
ra'tion•al adj.
ra'tion•ale' n.
ra'tion•al•ism
ra'tion•al•ist
ra'tion•al•is'tic
ra'tion•al'i•ty
ra'tion•al•i•za'tion
ra'tion•al•ize',
  -ized', -iz'ing
rat'line also rat'lin
rat•tan'
rat'ter
rat'tle, -tled, -tling
rat'tler
rat'tle•snake'
rau'cous
raun'chy
rav'age, -aged,
  -ag•ing
rav'ag•er
rave, raved, rav'ing
rav'el, -eled also

-elled, -el•ing also
  -el•ling
ra'ven
rav'en•ing
rav'en•ous
ra•vine'
rav'i•o'li pl. -li or -lis
rav'ish
rav'ish•ing
raw
raw'boned'
raw'hide'
ray (beam, fish)
  ✔ re
ray'on
raze also rase (to de-
  molish), razed,
  raz'ing
  ✔ raise
ra'zor (cutting instru-
  ment)
  ✔ raiser
ra'zor•blade' also
  ra'zor blade'
razz
re (musical tone)
  ✔ ray
re (concerning)
reach
re•act'
re•ac'tant
re•ac'tion
re•ac'tion•ar'y
re•ac'ti•vate',
  -vat'ed, -vat'ing
re•ac'ti•va'tion
re•ac'tive

re•ac'tor
read (to examine
  something written),
  read, read'ing
  ✔ reed
read'a•bil'i•ty or
  read'a•ble•ness
read'a•ble
read'er
read'er•ship'
read'i•ly
read'i•ness
re•ad•just'
re•ad•just'ment
read'y, -ied, -y•ing
read'y-made' or
  read'y•made'
re•af•firm'
re•af•fir•ma'tion
re•a'gent
re•al (actual)
  ✔ reel
re•al es•tate'
re'al•ism
re'al•ist
re'al•is'tic
re'al•is'ti•cal•ly
re•al'i•ty (actuality)
  ✔ realty
re'al•iz'a•ble
re'al•i•za'tion
re'al•ize', -ized',
  -iz'ing
re'al•ly
realm
real'-time'
Re'al•tor

re'al•ty *(property)*
　✔ reality
ream *(unit of paper)*
ream *(to form a hole)*
ream'er
reap
reap'er
re'ap•por'tion
re'ap•prais'al
re'ap•praise',
　-praised', -prais'ing
rear
re'ar•range',
　-ranged', -rang'ing
re'ar•range'ment
rear'-view' mir'ror
　or rear'view'
　mir'ror
rear'ward *adv. &*
　adj.
rear'wards *adv.*
rea'son
rea'son•a•ble
rea'son•a•bly
rea'son•ing
re'as•sem'ble,
　-bled, -bling
re'as•sur'ance
re'as•sure', -sured',
　-sur'ing
re'bate', -bat'ed,
　-bat'ing
re•bel', -belled',
　-bel'ling
reb'el *n.*
re•bel'lion
re•bel'lious

re•birth'
re•born'
re•bound' *v.*
re'bound' *n.*
re•buff'
re•build', -built',
　-build'ing
re•buke', -buked',
　-buk'ing
re'bus *pl.* -bus•es
re•but', -but'ted,
　-but'ting
re•but'tal
re•cal'ci•trance *or*
　re•cal'ci•tran•cy
re•cal'ci•trant
re•call' *v.*
re'call' *n.*
re•cant'
re'can•ta'tion
re•cap' *(to replace a*
　cap), -capped',
　-cap'ping
re'cap' *(recapped tire,*
　summary)
re'cap' *(to summa-*
　rize), -capped',
　-cap'ping
re'ca•pit'u•late',
　-lat'ed, -lat'ing
re'ca•pit'u•la'tion
re•cap'ture, -tured,
　-tur•ing
re•cast', -cast',
　-cast'ing
re'cast' *n.*
re•cede' *(to ebb)*,

-ced'ed, -ced'ing
re•cede' *(to cede*
　back), -ced'ed,
　-ced'ing
re•ceipt'
re•ceiv'a•ble
re•ceive', -ceived',
　-ceiv'ing
re•ceiv'er
re•ceiv'er•ship'
re'cent
re•cep'ta•cle
re•cep'tion
re•cep'tion•ist
re•cep'tive
re'cep•tiv'i•ty
re•cep'tor
re•cess'
re•ces'sion *(with-*
　drawal)
re-ces'sion *(restora-*
　tion)
re•ces'sion•al
re•ces'sive
re•charge',
　-charged',
　-charg'ing
re'charge' *n.*
re•cid'i•vism
re•cid'i•vist
rec'i•pe'
re•cip'i•ent
re•cip'ro•cal
re•cip'ro•cate',
　-cat'ed, -cat'ing
re•cip'ro•ca'tion
rec'i•proc'i•ty

re·cit'al

rec'i·ta'tion

rec'i·ta'tive adj.

rec'i·ta·tive' n.

re·cite', -cit'ed, -cit'ing

reck'less

reck'on

reck'on·ing

re·claim' (to make usable)

re-claim' (to claim again)

re·claim'a·ble

rec'la·ma'tion

re·cline', -clined', -clin'ing

re·clin'er

re·cluse' adj.

rec'luse' n.

re·clu'sive

rec'og·ni'tion

rec'og·niz'a·ble

re·cog'ni·zance

re·cog'ni·zant

rec'og·nize', -nized', -niz'ing

re·coil' v.

re'coil' n.

rec'ol·lect' (to remember)

re'-col·lect' (to collect again)

rec'ol·lec'tion

re·com'bi·nant

rec'om·mend'

rec'om·men·da'-tion

rec'om·pense', -pensed', -pens'ing

rec'on·cil'a·ble

rec'on·cile', -ciled', -cil'ing

rec'on·cil'i·a'tion

rec'on·dite'

re'con·di'tion

re·con'nais·sance

re·con'noi'ter

re'con·sid'er

re'con·sid'er·a'-tion

re'con·struct'

re'con·struc'tion

re'con·struc'tive

re·cord' v.

rec'ord n.

re·cord'er

re·cord'ing

re·count' (to narrate)

re-count' (to count again)

re'-count' (another count)

re·coup'

re'course'

re·cov'er (to regain)

re-cov'er (to cover again)

re·cov'er·a·ble

re·cov'er·y

rec're·ant

rec're·ate' (to refresh), -at'ed, -at'ing

re'-cre·ate' (to create again), -at'ed, -at'ing

re'-cre·a'tion (new creation)

rec're·a'tion (refreshment)

rec're·a'tion·al

re·crim'i·nate', -nat'ed, -nat'ing

re·crim'i·na'tion

re·crim'i·na·to'ry

re'cru·desce', -desced', -desc'ing

re'cru·des'cence

re'cru·des'cent

re·cruit'

re·cruit'er

rec'tal

rec'tan·gle

rec·tan'gu·lar

rec'ti·fy', -fied', -fy'ing

rec'ti·lin'e·ar

rec'ti·tude'

rec'to pl. -tos

rec'tor

rec'to·ry

rec'tum pl. -tums or -ta

re·cum'bent

re·cu'per·ate', -at'ed, -at'ing

re·cu'per·a'tion

re·cu'per·a'tive or re·cu'per·a·to'ry

re•cur', -curred',
  -cur'ring
re•cur'rence
re•cur'rent
re•cuse', -cused',
  -cus'ing
re•cy'cle, -cled,
  -cling
red, red'der, red'dest
re•dact'
re•dac'tion
red'bird'
red'-blood'ed
red'breast'
red'coat'
red'den
red'dish
re•deem'
re•deem'a•ble
re•demp'tion
red'-hand'ed
red'head'
red'head'ed
red'-hot'
red'-let'ter
re•do', -did', -done',
  -do'ing, -does'
red'o•lence
red'o•lent
re•dou'ble, -bled,
  -bling
re•doubt'a•ble
re•dound'
re•dress'
re•dress'er *or*
  re•dres'sor
red'start'

re•duce', -duced',
  -duc'ing
re•duc'i•bil'i•ty
re•duc'i•ble
re•duc'tion
re•duc'tive
re•dun'dan•cy
re•dun'dant
re•dux'
red'wing'
red'wood'
re•ech'o *also*
  re-ech'o, -ocd,
  -o'ing
reed *(grass, musical*
  instrument)
  ✔ read
reef
reek *(to smell badly)*
  ✔ wreak
reel *(spool, whirling,*
  dance)
  ✔ real
re'e•lect' *also*
  re'-e•lect'
re'e•lec'tion
re'en•act' *also*
  re'-en•act'
re•en'ter *also*
  re-en'ter
re•en'trance
re•en'try *also*
  re-en'try
re'es•tab'lish
re'es•tab'lish•
  ment
re'ex•am'ine,

-ined, -in•ing
re•fec'to•ry
re•fer', -ferred',
  -fer'ring
ref'er•a•ble
ref'e•ree', -reed',
  -ree'ing
ref'er•ence
ref'er•en'dum *pl.*
  -dums *or* -da
ref'er•ent
ref'er•en'tial
re•fer'ral
re•fill' *v.*
re'fill' *n.*
re•fine', -fined',
  -fin'ing
re•fine'ment
re•fin'er•y
re•fit', re•fit'ted,
  re•fit'ting
re•flect'
re•flec'tion
re•flec'tive
re•flec'tor
re•flex' *adj. & n.*
re•flex' *v.*
re•flex'ive
re•for'est
re'for•es•ta'tion
re•form' *(to improve)*
re-form' *(to form*
  again)
ref'or•ma'tion
re•for'ma•tive
re•for'ma•to'ry
re•form'er

re·fract'
re·frac'tion
re·frac'tive
re·frac'tive·ness *or*
  re'frac·tiv'i·ty
re·frac'tor
re·frac'to·ry
re·frain'
re·fresh'
re·fresh'er
re·fresh'ing
re·fresh'ment
re'fried' beans'
re·frig'er·ant
re·frig'er·ate',
  -at'ed, -at'ing
re·frig'er·a'tion
re·frig'er·a'tor
ref'uge
ref'u·gee'
re·ful'gence *or*
  re·ful'gen·cy
re·ful'gent
re·fund' *v.*
re'fund' *n.*
re·fund'a·ble
re·fur'bish
re·fus'al
re·fuse' *(to decline),*
  -fused', -fus'ing
ref'use *(trash)*
re·fut'a·ble
ref'u·ta'tion *also*
  re·fut'al
re·fute', -fut'ed,
  -fut'ing
re·gain'

re'gal *(royal)*
re·gale' *(to delight),*
  -galed', -gal'ing
re·ga'lia
re·gard'
re·gard'ing
re·gard'less
re·gat'ta
re'gen·cy
re·gen'er·ate',
  -at'ed, -at'ing
re·gen'er·a'tion
re·gen'er·a'tive
re'gent
reg'gae
reg'i·cid'al
reg'i·cide'
re·gime' *also*
  ré·gime'
reg'i·men
reg'i·ment
reg'i·men'tal
reg'i·men·ta'tion
re'gion
re'gion·al
reg'is·ter *(record)*
  ✓ *registrar*
reg'is·tered
reg'is·trar' *(official)*
  ✓ *register*
reg'is·tra'tion
reg'is·try
re·gress'
re·gres'sion
re·gres'sive
re·gret', -gret'ted,
  -gret'ting

re·gret'ful
re·gret'ta·ble
re·group'
reg'u·lar
reg'u·lar'i·ty
reg'u·lar·ize',
  -ized', -iz'ing
reg'u·late', -lat'ed,
  -lat'ing
reg'u·la'tion
reg'u·la'tive
reg'u·la'tor
reg'u·la·to'ry
re·gur'gi·tate',
  -tat'ed, -tat'ing
re·gur'gi·ta'tion
re·ha·bil'i·tate',
  -tat'ed, -tat'ing
re·ha·bil'i·ta'tion
re·ha·bil'i·ta'tive
re·hash' *v.*
re'hash' *n.*
re·hears'al
re·hearse',
  -hearsed',
  -hears'ing
reign *(rule)*
  ✓ *rain, rein*
re·im·burs'a·ble
re·im·burse',
  -bursed', -burs'ing
re·im·burse'ment
rein *(strap, to hold
back)*
  ✓ *rain, reign*
re·in·car'nate',
  -nat'ed, -nat'ing

re•in•car•na'tion
rein'deer' *pl.* -deer'
  or -deers'
re'in•force'a•ble
re'in•force' *or*
  re'en•force',
  -forced', -forc'ing
re'in•force'ment
re'in•state',
  -stat'ed, -stat'ing
re'in•state'ment
re•it'er•ate', -at'ed,
  -at'ing
re•it'er•a'tion
re•it'er•a'tive
re•ject' *v.*
re'ject' *n.*
re•jec'tion
re•joice', -joiced',
  -joic'ing
re•join' *(to reply)*
re-join' *(to join
  again)*
re•join'der
re•ju've•nate',
  -nat'ed, -nat'ing
re•ju've•na'tion
re•lapse', -lapsed',
  -laps'ing
re'lapse' *n.*
re•late', -lat'ed,
  -lat'ing
re•la'tion
re•la'tion•ship'
rel'a•tive
rel'a•tiv'i•ty
re•lax'

re•lax•a'tion
re•laxed'
re'lay' *n.*
re'lay' *(to pass along)*
re-lay' *(to lay again)*,
  -laid', -lay'ing
re•lease' *(to let go)*,
  -leased', -leas'ing
re-lease' *(to lease
  again)*, -leased',
  -leas'ing
rel'e•gate', -gat'ed,
  -gat'ing
rel'e•ga'tion
re•lent'
re•lent'less
rel'e•vance *or*
  rel'e•van•cy
rel'e•vant
re•li'a•bil'i•ty *or*
  re•li'a•ble•ness
re•li'a•ble
re•li'a•bly
re•li'ance
re•li'ant
rel'ic
re•lief'
re•liev'a•ble
re•lieve', -lieved',
  -liev'ing
re•liev'er
re•lig'ion
re•lig'ious
re•lin'quish
rel'ish
re•live', -lived',
  -liv'ing

re•lo•cate', -cat'ed,
  -cat'ing
re'lo•ca'tion
re•luc'tance
re•luc'tant
re•ly', -lied', -ly'ing
re•main'
re•main'der
re•mains'
re•make', -made',
  -mak'ing
re'make' *n.*
re•mand'
re•mark'
re•mark'a•ble
re•mark'a•bly
re'match' *n.*
re•me'di•a•ble
re•me'di•a•bly
re•me'di•al
rem'e•dy, -died,
  -dy•ing
re•mem'ber
re•mem'brance
re•mind'
re•mind'er
rem'i•nisce',
  -nisced', -nisc'ing
rem'i•nis'cence
rem'i•nis'cent
re•miss'
re•mis'sion
re•mit', -mit'ted,
  -mit'ting
re•mit'tance
re•mit'ter
rem'nant

re•mod'el, -eled
  also -elled, -el•ing
  also -el•ling
re•mod'el•er
re•mon'strance
re•mon'strate',
  -strat'ed, -strat'ing
re'mon•stra'tion
re•mon'stra•tive
rem'o•ra
re•morse'
re•morse'ful
re•mote', -mot'er,
  -mot'est
re•mov'a•ble
re•mov'al
re•move', -moved',
  -mov'ing
re•mu'ner•ate',
  -at'ed, -at'ing
re•mu'ner•a'tion
re•mu'ner•a•tive
ren'ais•sance'
  (rebirth)
  ✔ renascence
re'nal
re•nas'cence
  (renaissance)
  ✔ renaissance
re•nas'cent
rend, rent *or*
  rend'ed, rend'ing
ren'der
ren'dez•vous' *pl.*
  -vous'
ren'dez•vous',
  -voused', -vous'ing

ren•di'tion
ren'e•gade'
re•nege', -neged',
  -neg'ing
re•new'
re•new'a•ble
re•new'al
ren'net
ren'nin
re•nounce',
  -nounced',
  -nounc'ing
re•nounce'ment
ren'o•vate', -vat'ed,
  -vat'ing
ren'o•va'tion
ren'o•va'tor
re•nown'
re•nowned'
rent *(payment)*
rent *(tear)*
rent'al
rent'er
re•nun'ci•a'tion
re•o'pen
re•or'gan•i•za'tion
re•or'gan•ize',
  -ized', -iz'ing
re•or'gan•iz'er
re•pair' *(to fix)*
re•pair' *(to go)*
re•pair'a•ble
re•pair'man
re•pair'wom'an
rep'a•ra•ble
rep'a•ra'tion
re•par'a•tive *also*

re•par'a•to'ry
rep'ar•tee'
re•past'
re•pa'tri•ate',
  -at'ed, -at'ing
re•pa'tri•a'tion
re•pay', -paid',
  -pay'ing
re•pay'a•ble
re•pay'ment
re•peal'
re•peat'
re•peat'ed
re•peat'er
re•pel', -pelled',
  -pel'ling
re•pel'lence *or*
re•pel'len•cy
re•pel'lent
re•pent'
re•pen'tance
re•pen'tant
re•per•cus'sion
rep'er•toire' *(group
  of works)*
rep'er•to'ry *(theatri-
  cal company)*
rep'e•ti'tion
rep'e•ti'tious
re•pet'i•tive
re•place', -placed',
  -plac'ing
re•place'a•ble
re•place'ment
re•play' *v.*
re'play' *n.*
re•plen'ish

re·plete'
re·ple'tion
rep'li·ca
rep'li·cate', -cat·ed,
  -cat'ing
rep'li·ca'tion
re·pli'er
re·ply', -plied',
  -ply'ing
re·port'
re·port'ed·ly
re·port'er
re·pose', posed',
  -pos'ing
re·pos'i·to·ry
re'pos·sess'
re'pos·ses'sion
rep're·hend'
rep're·hen'si·ble
rep're·hen'si·bil'-
  i·ty
rep're·hen'si·bly
rep're·hen'sion
rep're·sent'
rep're·sen·ta'tion
rep're·sen·ta'tion·
  al
rep're·sen·ta·tive
re·press'
re·press'i·ble
re·pres'sion
re·pres'sive
re·prieve',
  -prieved',
  -priev'ing
rep'ri·mand'
re'print' *n.*

re·print' *v.*
re·pri'sal
re·prise', -prised',
  -pris'ing
re·proach'
re·proach'ful
rep'ro·bate'
rep'ro·ba'tion
re'pro·duce',
  -duced', -duc'ing
re'pro·duc'i·ble
re'pro·duc'tion
re'pro·duc'tive
re·proof'
re·prove', -proved',
  -prov'ing
rep'tile
rep·til'i·an
re·pub'lic
re·pub'li·can
re·pu'di·ate',
  -at'ed, -at'ing
re·pu'di·a'tion
re·pu'di·a'tive
re·pu'di·a'tor
re·pug'nance
re·pug'nant
re·pulse', -pulsed',
  -puls'ing
re·pul'sion
re·pul'sive
rep'u·ta·ble
rep'u·ta·bly
rep'u·ta'tion
re·pute', -put'ed,
  -put'ing
re·quest'

req'ui·em
re·quire', -quired',
  -quir'ing
re·quire'ment
req'ui·site
req'ui·si'tion
re·quit'al
re·quite', -quit'ed,
  -quit'ing
re'run' *n.*
re·run', -ran', -run',
  -run'ning
re'sale'
re·scind'
re·scind'a·ble
re·scis'sion
res'cue, -cued,
  -cu·ing
res'cu·er
re·search'
re·search'er
re·sem'blance
re·sem'ble, -bled,
  -bling
re·sent'
re·sent'ful
re·sent'ment
res'er·va'tion
re·serve', -served',
  -serv'ing
re·serv'ed·ly
re·serv'ist
res'er·voir'
re·side', -sid'ed,
  -sid'ing
res'i·dence
res'i·den·cy

res'i•dent
res'i•den'tial
re•sid'u•al
res'i•due'
re•sign' *(to give up)*
re-sign' *(to sign again)*
res'ig•na'tion
re•sil'ience
re•sil'ien•cy
re•sil'ient
res'in
res'in•ous
re•sist'
re•sis'tance
re•sis'tant
re•sist'er *(one that resists)*
re•sis'tor *(electrical device)*
res'o•lute'
res'o•lu'tion
re•solv'a•ble
re•solve', -solved', -solv'ing
res'o•nance
res'o•nant
res'o•nate', -nat'ed, -nat'ing
res'o•na'tion
re•sort'
re•sound'
re•source'
re•source'ful
re•spect'
re•spect'a•bil'i•ty
re•spect'a•ble

re•spect'a•bly
re•spect'ful
re•spec'tive
re•spell', -spelled' *or* -spelt', -spell'ing
res'pi•ra'tion
res'pi•ra'tor
res'pi•ra•to'ry
re•spire', -spired', -spir'ing
res'pite
re•splen'dence *or* re•splen'den•cy
re•splen'dent
re•spond'
re•sponse'
re•spon'si•bil'i•ty
re•spon'si•ble
re•spon'si•bly
re•spon'sive
rest *(quiet, remainder)*
  ✔ wrest
re•state', -stat'ed, -stat'ing
re•state'ment
res'tau•rant
res'tau•ra•teur'
rest'ful
res'ti•tu'tion
res'tive
rest'less
res'to•ra'tion
re•stor'a•tive
re•store', -stored', -stor'ing
re•strain'
re•straint'

re•strict'
re•stric'tion
re•stric'tive
rest'room'
re•sult'
re•sul'tant
re•sume' *(to begin again)*, -sumed', -sum'ing
ré'su•mé' *or* re'su•me' *or* re'su•mé' *(summary)*
re•sump'tion
re•sur'gence
re•sur'gent
res'ur•rect'
res'ur•rec'tion
re•sus'ci•tate', -tat'ed, -tat'ing
re•sus'ci•ta'tion
re•sus'ci•ta'tor
re'tail'
re'tail'er
re•tain'
re•tain'er
re•tal'i•ate', -at'ed, -at'ing
re•tal'i•a'tion
re•tal'i•a•to'ry
re•tard'
re•tar'dant
re'tar•da'tion
re•tard'ed
retch *(to vomit)*
  ✔ wretch
re•ten'tion

re•ten'tive
ret'i•cence
ret'i•cent
re•tic'u•lar
re•tic'u•late
re•tic'u•la'tion
ret'i•na *pl.* -nas *or* -nae'
ret'i•nal
ret'i•nol'
ret'i•nue'
re•tire', -tired', -tir'ing
re•tir•ee'
re•tire'ment
re•tort'
re•touch'
re•trace', -traced', -trac'ing
re•tract'
re•tract'a•ble *or* re•tract'i•ble
re•trac'tile
re•trac'tion
re•trac'tor
re•tread' (*to fit a new tire tread*)
re'tread' *n.*
re-tread' (*to tread again*), -trod', -trod'den, -tread'ing
re•treat'
re•trench'
re'tri•al
ret'ri•bu'tion
re•trib'u•tive

re•trib'u•to'ry
re•triev'a•ble
re•triev'al
re•trieve', -trieved', -triev'ing
re•triev'er
ret'ro•ac'tive
ret'ro•grade'
ret'ro•gress'
ret'ro•gres'sion
ret'ro•gres'sive
ret'ro•rock'et
ret'ro•spect'
ret'ro•spec'tive
ret'ro•vi'rus *pl.* -rus•es
re•turn'
re•turn'a•ble
re•turn•ee'
re•un'ion
re•u•nite', -nit'ed, -nit'ing
re•us'a•ble
re•use', -used', -us'ing
rev, revved, rev'ving
re•vamp'
re•veal'
rev•eil•le
rev'el, -eled *also* -elled, -el'ing *or* -el•ling
rev'e•la'tion
rev'el•er *or* rev'el•ler
rev'el•ry
re•venge', -venged',

-veng'ing
re•venge'ful
rev'e•nue
re•verb'
re•ver'ber•ate', -at'ed, -at'ing
re•ver'ber•a'tion
re•vere', -vered', -ver'ing
rev'er•ence
rev'er•end
rev'er•ent
rev'er•en'tial
rev'er•ie
re•ver'sal
re•verse', -versed', -vers'ing
re•vers'i•ble
re•ver'sion
re•vert'
re•vert'i•ble
re•view' (*to examine*) ✔ *revue*
re•view'er
re•vile', -viled', -vil'ing
re•vis'a•ble
re•vise', -vised', -vis'ing
re•vis'er *or* re•vi'sor
re•vi'sion
re•vi'tal•i•za'tion
re•vi'tal•ize', -ized', -iz'ing
re•viv'al
re•vive', -vived', -viv'ing

rev'o•ca•ble
rev'o•ca'tion
re•voke', -voked',
  -vok'ing
re•volt'
re•volt'ing
rev'o•lu'tion
rev'o•lu'tion•ar'y
rev'o•lu'tion•ist
rev'o•lu'tion•ize',
  -ized', -iz'ing
re•volve', -volved',
  -volv'ing
re•volv'er
re•vue' *(show)*
  ✔ *review*
re•vul'sion
re•ward'
re•wind', -wound',
  -wind'ing
re'wind' *n.*
re•word'
re•work'
re•write', -wrote',
  -writ'ten, -writ'ing
re'write' *n.*
re•writ'er
Reye's' syn'drome
rhap•sod'ic *also*
  rhap'sod'i•cal
rhap'so•dize',
  -dized', -diz'ing
rhap'so•dy
rhe'a
Rhen'ish
rhe'ni•um
rhe'o•stat'

rhe'sus mon'key
rhet'o•ric
rhe•tor'i•cal
rhet'o•ri'cian
rheum *(mucus)*
  ✔ *room*
rheu•mat'ic
rheu'ma•tism
rheu'ma•toid'
Rh fac'tor
rhine'stone'
rhi'no *pl.* -nos
rhi•noc'er•os *pl.* -os
  or -os•es
rhi'zome'
rho *(Greek letter)*
  ✔ *roe, row*
Rhode' Is'land•er
Rho•de'sian
rho'di•um
rho'do•den'dron
rhom'boid'
rhom•boi'dal
rhom'bus *pl.*
  -bus•es *or* -bi
rhu'barb'
rhyme *also* rime *(to
  compose verse)*,
  rhymed *also* rimed,
  rhym'ing *also*
  rim'ing
  ✔ *rime*
rhythm
rhyth'mic *also*
  rhyth'mi•cal
rib, ribbed, rib'bing
rib'ald

rib'ald•ry
rib'bon
ri'bo•fla'vin
ri'bo•nu•cle'ic
  ac'id
ri'bose'
ri'bo•some'
rice
rich
rich'es
Rich'ter scale'
rick
rick'ets
rick'et•y
rick'rack'
rick'sha *or*
  rick'shaw
ric'o•chet'
ri•cot'ta
rid, rid *or* rid'ded,
  rid'ding
rid'dance
rid'dle, -dled, -dling
ride, rode, rid'den,
  rid'ing
rid'er
ridge, ridged,
  ridg'ing
ridge'pole'
rid'i•cule', -culed',
  -cul'ing
ri•dic'u•lous
rife, rif'er, rif'est
rif'fle *(to shuffle)*,
  -fled, -fling
  ✔ *rifle*
riff'raff'

ri′fle *(firearm)*

ri′fle *(to plunder)*,
-fled, -fling
✔ *riffle*

ri′fle•man

rift

rig, rigged, rig′ging

rig′a•to′ni

rig′ger *(one who rigs)*
✔ *rigor*

right *(correct, opposite of left)*
✔ *rite, wright, write*

right′-an′gled

right′eous

right′ful

right′-hand′ *adj.*

right′-hand′ed

right′-hand′er

right′ist

right′-mind′ed

right′ of way′ *also*
right′-of-way′ *pl.*
rights′ of way′ *or*
right′ of ways′ *also*
rights′-of-way′ *or*
right′-of-ways′

right′-side′ up′

right′-to-life′ *adj.*

right′wing′ *adj.*

right′wing′er

right′y

rig′id

ri•gid′i•ty

rig′ma•role′ *also*
rig′a•ma•role′

rig′or *(severity)*

✔ *rigger*

rig′or mor′tis

rig′or•ous

rile, riled, ril′ing

rill

rim, rimmed,
rim′ming

rime *(to cover with
frost)*, rimed,
rim′ing
✔ *rhyme*

rind

ring *(circle)*
✔ *wring*

ring *(to encircle)*,
ringed, ring′ing
✔ *wring*

ring *(to sound)*, rang,
rung, ring′ing
✔ *wring*

ring′er

ring′lead′er

ring′let

ring′mas′ter

ring′side′

ring′worm′

rink

rin′ky-dink′

rinse, rinsed, rins′ing

ri′ot

ri′ot•er

ri′ot•ous

rip, ripped, rip′ping

rip′cord′

ripe, rip′er, rip′est

rip′en

rip′-off′

ri•poste′, -post′ed,
-post′ing

rip′ple, -pled, -pling

rip′-roar′ing

rip′saw′

rise, rose, ris′en,
ris′ing

ris′er

ris′i•ble

risk′y *(dangerous)*
✔ *risqué*

ri•sot′to

ris•qué′ *(suggestive)*
✔ *risky*

ri′tar•dan′do

rite *(ceremony)*
✔ *right, wright, write*

rit′u•al

rit′u•al•ism

rit′u•al•is′tic

ritz′y

ri′val, -valed *or*
-valled, -val•ing *or*
-val•ling

ri′val•ry

riv′er

riv′er•bank′

riv′er•bed′

riv′er•boat′

riv′er•side′

riv′et, -et•ed, -et•ing

riv′et•er

riv′u•let

ri′yal′

RNA

roach *(fish)*, *pl.*
roach *or* roach′es

roach (cockroach), pl.
  roach'es
road
road'bed'
road'block'
road'house'
road'ie also road'y
road'run'ner
road'side'
road'ster
road'way'
road'work'
roam
roam'er
roan
roar
roar'ing
roast
roast'er
rob, robbed,
  rob'bing
rob'ber
rob'ber•y
robe, robed, rob'ing
rob'in
ro'bot
ro•bot'ics
ro•bust'
roc (legendary bird)
rock (stone, to move
  back and forth)
rock'er
rock'et
rock'et•eer'
rock'et•ry
rock'fish' pl. -fish'
  or -fish'es

rock'ing chair'
rock'ing horse'
rock''n'roll' or
  rock'-and-roll'
rock'-ribbed'
rock'y
ro•co'co
rod
ro'dent
ro'de•o' pl. -os'
roe (fish eggs)
  ✔ rho, row
roe (small deer), pl.
  roe or roes
  ✔ rho, row
roe'buck'
roent'gen
rog'er interj.
rogue
rogu'er•y
rogu'ish
roil
rois'ter
role also rôle (part in
  a play)
roll (to revolve)
roll (list of names,
  bread)
roll'a•way' adj.
roll'back' n.
roll'er
roll'er coast'er
roll'er skate' n.
roll'er-skate',
  -skat'ed, -skat'ing
roll'er skat'er
rol'lick

rol'lick•ing
rol'lick•some or
  rol'lick•y
roll'-on' adj. & n.
roll'out' n.
roll'o'ver n.
ro'ly-po'ly
ro•maine'
ro'man (type)
Ro'man (relating to
  Rome)
ro•mance' (to woo),
  -manced',
  -manc'ing
Ro•mance'
  (languages)
Ro'man•esque'
Ro•ma'ni•an also
  Ru•ma'ni•an
ro•man'tic
ro•man'ti•cism
ro•man'ti•cist
ro•man'ti•cize',
  -cized', -ciz'ing
Rom'a•ny
Ro'me•o' pl. -os'
romp
romp'ers
ron'do pl. -dos
rood (cross)
  ✔ rude
roof
roof'er
roof'ing
roof'top'
roof'tree'
rook

rook'er•y
rook'ie
room (space)
  ✔ rheum
room'er (lodger)
  ✔ rumor
room'ful'
room'i•ness
room'mate'
room'y
roost
roost'er
root (plant part, origin)
  ✔ route
root (to dig, to cheer)
  ✔ route
root' beer'
root'less
root'let
root'stock'
rope, roped, rop'ing
rop'er
rop'y
Ror'schach test'
ro'sa•ry
rose (flower)
ro•sé' (wine)
ro'se•ate
rose'bud'
rose'bush'
rose'-col'ored
rose'mar'y
ro•sette'
rose'wood'
Rosh' Ha•sha'nah
  also Rosh'

Ha•sha'na
Ro'si•cru'cian
ros'in
ros'i•ness
ros'ter
ros'trum pl. -trums
  or -tra
ros'y
rot, rot'ted, rot'ting
Ro•tar'i•an
ro'ta•ry
ro'tate', -tat'ed,
  -tat'ing
ro•ta'tion
ro'ta•tor
ro'ta•to'ry
rote (memorizing by
  repetition)
  ✔ wrote
ro'ti•fer
ro•tis'se•rie
ro'tor
ro'to•till'er
rot'ten
ro•tund'
ro•tun'da
ro•tun'di•ty
rouge, rouged,
  roug'ing
rough (not smooth)
  ✔ ruff
rough'age
rough'en
rough'house',
  -housed', -hous'ing
rough'neck'
rough'ness

rough'shod'
rou•lette'
round
round'a•bout'
round'ed
roun'de•lay'
round'house'
round'-the-clock'
round'trip' or
  round'-trip'
round'up' n.
round'worm'
rouse, roused,
  rous'ing
roust'a•bout'
rout (to defeat, to dig
  up)
route (to direct),
  rout'ed, rout'ing
  ✔ root
rou•tine'
roux (thickener)
  ✔ rue
rove, roved, rov'ing
rov'er (wanderer)
ro'ver (pirate)
row (line)
  ✔ rho, roe
row (to propel with
  oars)
  ✔ rho, roe
row (brawl)
row'boat'
row'di•ness
row'dy
row'el
row'lock'

roy'al
roy'al•ist
roy'al•ty
rub, rubbed,
　rub'bing
rub'ber
rub'ber band'
rub'ber•ize', -ized',
　-iz'ing
rub'ber•neck'
rub'ber stamp' *also*
　rub'ber•stamp' *n.*
rub'ber-stamp' *v.*
rub'ber•y
rub'bish
rub'ble
rub'down' *n.*
ru•bel'la
ru'bi•cund
ru•bid'i•um
ru'ble *also* rou'ble
ru'bric
ru'by
ruck'sack'
ruck'us
rud'der
rud'dy
rude *(ill-mannered)*,
　rud'er, rud'est
　✔ rood
ru'di•ment
ru'di•men'ta•ry
rue *(to feel regret for)*,
　rued, ru'ing
　✔ roux
rue'ful
ruff *(collar)*

　✔ rough
ruf'fi•an
ruf'fle, -fled, -fling
rug
Rug'by
rug'ged
ru'in
ru'in•a'tion
ru'in•ous
rule, ruled, rul'ing
rul'er
rum
rum'ba *also*
　rhum'ba
rum'ble, -bled,
　-bling
rum•bus'tious
ru'men *pl.* -mi•na *or*
　-mens
ru'mi•nant
ru'mi•nate',
　-nat'ed, -nat'ing
ru'mi•na'tion
ru'mi•na'tive
ru'mi•na'tor
rum'mage, -maged,
　-mag'ing
rum'my
ru'mor *(gossip)*
　✔ roomer
ru'mor•mon'ger
rump
rum'ple, -pled,
　-pling
rum'pus
run, ran, run,
　run'ning

run'a•bout' *n.*
run'a•round' *n.*
run'a•way' *n. & adj.*
run'down' *n.*
run'-down' *adj.*
rune
rung *(rod)*
　✔ wrung
run'ic
run'-in' *n.*
run'ner
run'ner-up' *pl.*
　run'ners-up'
run'ning
run'ny
run'off' *n.*
run'-of-the-mill'
run'-on' sen'tence
runt
run'-through' *n.*
run'way'
ru•pee'
ru•pi'ah
rup'ture, -tured,
　-tur'ing
ru'ral
ruse
rush
rush' hour' *n.*
rush'-hour' *adj.*
rus'set
Rus'sian
rust
rus'tic
rus'ti•cate', -cat'ed,
　-cat'ing
rus'ti•ca'tion

rus•tic′i•ty
rust′i•ness
rus′tle, -tled, -tling
rus′tler
rust′y
rut, rut′ted, rut′ting
ru′ta•ba′ga
ru•the′ni•um
ruth′er•ford′i•um
ruth′less
rye *(grain)*
  ✔ *wry*

S

Sab′bath
sab•bat′i•cal
sa′ber
sa′ber-toothed′
  ti′ger
sa′ble
sa•bot′
sab′o•tage′, -taged′,
  -tag′ing
sab′o•teur′
sac *(body part)*
  ✔ *sack*
sac′cha•rin *n.*
sac′cha•rine *adj.*
sac′er•do′tal
sa′chem
sa•chet′ *(perfumed*
  bag)
  ✔ *sashay*
sack *(bag, loot, wine)*
  ✔ *sac*

sack *(to fire, to rob)*
  ✔ *sac*
sack′cloth′
sack′ing
sac′ra•ment
sac′ra•men′tal
sa′cred
sac′ri•fice′, -ficed′,
  -fic′ing
sac′ri•fi′cial
sac′ri•lege
sac′ri•le′gious
sac′ris•tan
sac′ris•ty
sac′ro•sanct′
sa′crum *pl.* -cra
sad, sad′der, sad′dest
sad′den
sad′dle, -dled, -dling
sad′dle•bag′
sad′dler
sa′dism
sa′dist
sa•dis′tic
sa•fa′ri *pl.* -ris
safe, saf′er, saf′est
safe′-con′duct
safe′-de•pos′it
  box′
safe′guard′
safe′keep′ing
safe′ty
saf′flow′er
saf′fron
sag, sagged, sag′ging
sa′ga
sa•ga′cious

sa•gac′i•ty
sag′a•more′
sage, sag′er, sag′est
sage′brush′
sa′go *pl.* -gos
sa•gua′ro *pl.* -ros
Sa•hap′ti•an
Sa•hap′tin *pl.* -tin
  or -tins
sa′hib
said
sail *(canvas)*
  ✔ *sale*
sail′board′
sail′boat′
sail′cloth′
sail′fish′ *pl.* -fish′ *or*
  -fish′es
sail′ing
sail′or
saint
Saint′ Ber•nard′
saint′ed
saint′hood′
saint′li•ness
sake *(purpose)*
sa′ke *also* sa′ki
  (liquor)
sal
sa•laam′
sal′a•bil′i•ty
sal′a•ble *also*
  sale′a•ble
sa•la′cious
sal′ad
sal′a•man′der
sa•la′mi

sal'a•ried'

sal'a•ry

sale (act of selling)
  ✔ sail

sales'clerk'

sales'man

sales'man•ship'

sales'peo'ple

sales'per'son

sales'wom'an

sa•lic'y•late'

sal'i•cyl'ic ac'id

sa'li•ence also
  sa'li•en•cy

sa'li•ent

sa'line'

sa•lin'i•ty

Sa'lish

sa•li'va

sal'i•var'y

sal'i•vate', -vat'ed,
  -vat'ing

sal'i•va'tion

sal'low

sal'ly, -lied, -ly'ing

sal'ma•gun'di pl.
  -dis

salm'on pl. -on or
  -ons

sal'mo•nel'la pl.
  -nel'lae or -nel'las
  -nel'la

sa•lon' (room, gath-
  ering)

sa•loon' (tavern)

sal'sa

sal' so'da

salt

salt'box'

salt'cel'lar

sal•tine'

salt'i•ness

salt'pe'ter

salt'shak'er

salt'wa'ter or
  salt'-wa'ter adj.

salt'y

sa•lu'bri•ous

sa•lu'ki pl. -kis

sal'u•tar'y

sal'u•ta'tion

sa•lu'ta•to'ri•an

sa•lu'ta•to'ry

sa•lute', -lut'ed,
  -lut'ing

sal'va•ble

Sal'va•do'ran or
  Sal'va•do'ri•an

sal'vage, -vaged,
  -vag'ing

sal'vage•a•ble

sal'vag•er

sal•va'tion

salve, salved,
  salv'ing

sal'ver

sal'vo pl. -vos or
  -voes

Sa•mar'i•tan

sa•mar'i•um

sam'ba

sam•bu'ca

same

same'ness

Sa•mo'an

sam'o•var'

Sam'o•yed' also
  Sam•o•yede'

sam'pan'

sam'ple, -pled,
  -pling

sam'pler

sam'u•rai' pl. -rai'
  or -rais

San pl. San or Sans

san'a•to'ri•um also
  san'i•tar'i•um pl.
  -to'ri•ums or
  -to'ri•a also
  -tar'i•ums or
  -tar'i•a

sanc'ti•fi•ca'tion

sanc'ti•fy', -fied',
  -fy'ing

sanc'ti•mo'ni•ous

sanc'ti•mo'ny

sanc'tion

sanc'ti•ty

sanc'tu•ar'y

sanc'tum pl. -tums
  or -ta

sand

san'dal

san'dal•wood'

sand'bag', -bagged',
  -bag'ging

sand'bank'

sand'bar'

sand'blast'

sand'blast'er

sand'box'

sand'er
sand'lot'
sand'man
sand'pa'per
sand'pi'per
sand'stone'
sand'storm'
sand'wich
sand'y
sane *(of sound mind)*,
 san'er, san'est
 ✔ *seine*
sang-froid'
san'gri'a
san'gui·nar'y
san'guine
san·guin'i·ty
san'i·tar'y
san'i·ta'tion
san'i·tize', -tized',
 -tiz'ing
san'i·ty
sans
San'sei' *pl.* -sei' *or*
 -seis
San'skrit'
San'ta Claus'
San·tee' *pl.* -tee' *or*
 -tees'
sap, sapped,
 sap'ping
sa'pi·ence
sa'pi·ent
sap'ling
sap'o·dil'la
sa·pon'i·fi'a·ble
sa·pon'i·fi'er

sa·pon'i·fi·ca'tion
sa·pon'i·fy', -fied',
 -fy'ing
sap'phire
sap'py
sap'suck'er
sap'wood'
Sar'a·cen
sa·ran'
sar'casm
sar·cas'tic
sar·co'ma *pl.* -mas
 also -ma·ta
sar·coph'a·gus *pl.*
 -gi' *or* -gus·es
sar·dine'
Sar·din'i·an
sar·don'ic
sa'ri *pl.* -ris
sa·rong'
sar'sa·pa·ril'la
sar·to'ri·al
sash
sa·shay' *(walk
 casually)*
 ✔ *sachet*
sa·shi'mi
sass
sas'sa·fras'
sas'sy
sa·tan'ic *or*
 sa·tan'i·cal
satch'el
sate, sat'ed, sat'ing
sa·teen'
sat'el·lite'
sa'tia·bil'i·ty

sa'tia·ble
sa'ti·ate', -at'ed,
 -at'ing
sa'ti·a'tion
sa·ti'e·ty
sat'in
sat'in·y
sat'ire
sa·tir'i·cal *or*
 sa·tir'ic
sat'i·rist
sat'i·rize', -rized',
 -riz'ing
sat'is·fac'tion
sat'is·fac'to·ri·ly
sat'is·fac'to·ry
sat'is·fi'er
sat'is·fy', -fied',
 -fy'ing
sa'trap'
sa'tra·py
sat'u·ra·ble
sat'u·rate', -rat'ed,
 -rat'ing
sat'u·ra'tion
Sat'ur·day'
sat'ur·na'li·a
sat'ur·nine'
sa'tyr
sauce, sauced,
 sauc'ing
sauce'pan'
sau'cer
sauc'y
Sau'di *or* Sau'di
 A·ra'bi·an
sau'er·kraut'

Sauk *pl.* Sauk *or*
  Sauks
sau'na
saun'ter
sau'ri•an
sau'sage
sau•té', -téed',
  -té'ing
Sau•ternes' *or*
  sau•ternes'
sav'a•ble *or*
  save'a•ble
sav'age
sav'age•ry
sa•van'na *also*
  sa•van'nah
sa•vant'
save, saved, sav'ing
sav'ior
sa'voir-faire'
sa'vor
sa'vor•y
sav'vy, -vied, -vy•ing
saw, sawed, sawed *or*
  sawn, saw'ing
saw'buck'
saw'dust'
sawed'-off'
saw'fish' *pl.* -fish' *or*
  -fish'es
saw'horse'
saw'mill'
saw'yer
sax
sax'i•frage
Sax'on
sax'o•phone'

sax'o•phon'ist
say, said, say'ing
say'-so' *pl.* -sos'
scab, scabbed,
  scab'bing
scab'bard
sca'bies
scads
scaf'fold
scaf'fold•ing
scal'a•wag' *also*
  scal'ly•wag'
scald
scale, scaled, scal'ing
sca'lene'
scal'i•ness
scal'lion
scal'lop *also*
  scol'lop
sca'lop•pi'ne *also*
  sca'lop•pi'ni
scalp
scal'pel
scalp'er
scal'y
scam
scamp
scam'per
scam'pi *pl.* -pi
scan, scanned,
  scan'ning
scan'dal
scan'dal•ize',
  -ized', -iz'ing
scan'dal•mon'ger
scan'dal•ous
Scan'di•na'vi•an

scan'di•um
scan'ner
scan'sion
scant
scant'i•ly
scant'y
scape
scape'goat'
scape'grace'
scap'u•la *pl.* -las *or*
  -lae'
scar, scarred,
  scar'ring
scar'ab
scarce, scarc'er,
  scarc'est
scar'ci•ty
scare, scared,
  scar'ing
scare'crow'
scarf *pl.* scarfs *or*
  scarves
scar'let
scar'y
scat, scat'ted,
  scat'ting
scathe, scathed,
  scath'ing
scat'o•log'i•cal
sca•tol'o•gy
scat'ter
scat'ter•brain'
scat'ter•brained'
scav'enge, -enged,
  -eng•ing
scav'en•ger
sce•nar'i•o' *pl.* -os'

sce•nar′ist

scene

scen′er•y

sce′nic

scent *(odor)*
   ✔ cent, sent

scep′ter

scep′tic

scep′ti•cal

scep′ti•cism

sched′ule, -uled,
   -ul•ing

sche′ma *pl.* -ma•ta
   or -mas

sche•mat′ic

sche′ma•tize′,
   -tized′, -tiz′ing

scheme, schemed,
   schem′ing

schem′er

scher•zan′do *pl.*
   -dos

scher′zo *pl.* -zos *or*
   -zi

schil′ling *(monetary*
   unit of Austria)
   ✔ shilling

schism

schis•mat′ic

schist

schiz′oid′

schiz′o•phre′ni•a

schiz′o•phren′ic

schlep *or* schlepp
   also shlep,
   schlepped *also*
   shlepped,

schlep′ping *or*
   schlepp′ing *also*
   shlep′ping

schlock *also* shlock

schmaltz *also*
   schmalz

schmaltz′y *also*
   schmalz′y

schmo *pl.* schmoes
   or schmos

schmooze *or*
   schmoose,
   schmoozed *or*
   schmoosed,
   schmooz′ing *or*
   schmoos′ing

schmuck *also*
   shmuck

schnapps *pl.*
   schnapps

schnau′zer

schol′ar

scho•las′tic

scho•las′ti•cism

school

school′book′

school′boy′

school′ bus′

school′child′ *also*
   school′ child′

school′girl′

school′house′

school′ing

school′marm′

school′mas′ter

school′mate′

school′mis′tress

school′room′

school′teach′er

school′work′

school′yard′

schoo′ner

schot′tische

schwa

sci•at′ic

sci•at′i•ca

sci′ence

sci′en•tif′ic

sci′en•tist

sci′en•tol′o•gy

scim′i•tar

scin•til′la

scin′til•late′,
   -lat′ed, -lat′ing

scin′til•la′tion

sci′on *(descendant or*
   heir)

sci′on *also* ci′on
   (shoot or twig)

scis′sile

scis′sion

scis′sors

scle′ra

scle•ro′sis *pl.* -ses

scle•rot′ic

scoff

scoff′law′

scold

sco′li•o′sis

sconce

scone

scoop′ful′

scoot′er

scope

scor•bu′tic also
  scor•bu′ti•cal
scorch
scorch′er
score, scored,
  scor′ing
score′board′
score′card′
score′keep′er
scor′er
sco•ri•a *pl.* -ri•ae′
scorn
scorn′ful
scor′pi•on
Scot
scotch *(to stifle or wound)*
Scotch *(people, whisky)*
Scotch′man
Scotch′wom′an
scot′-free′
Scots
Scots′man
Scots′wom′an
Scot′tie
Scot′tish
scoun′drel
scour
scourge, scourged,
  scourg′ing
scourg′er
scout
scout′ing
scout′mas′ter
scow
scowl

scrab′ble, -bled,
  -bling
scrag
scrag′gy
scram, scrammed,
  scram′ming
scram′ble, -bled,
  -bling
scram′bler
scrap, scrapped,
  scrap′ping
scrap′book′
scrape, scraped,
  scrap′ing
scrap′er
scrap′pi•ness
scrap′ple
scrap′py
scratch
scratch′i•ly
scratch′i•ness
scratch′y
scrawl
scraw′ni•ness
scraw′ny
scream
scream′er
screech
screech′ing
screed
screen
screen′ing
screen′play′
screen′ test′ *n.*
screen′-test′ *v.*
screen′writ′er
screen′writ′ing

screw
screw′ball′
screw′driv′er
screw′y
scrib′al
scrib′ble, -bled,
  -bling
scrib′bler
scribe, scribed,
  scrib′ing
scrim
scrim′mage,
  -maged, -mag•ing
scrimp
scrim′shaw′ *pl.*
  -shaw′ *or* -shaws′
scrip *(paper money)*
script *(writing, text)*
Scrip′tur•al
Scrip′ture
script′writ′er
script′writ′ing
scriv′en•er
scrod
scrof′u•la
scrof′u•lous
scroll
Scrooge
scro′tal
scro′tum *pl.* -ta *or*
  -tums
scrounge,
  scrounged,
  scroung′ing
scroung′y
scrub, scrubbed,
  scrub′bing

scrub'ber
scrub'bi•ness
scrub'by
scruff
scruff'y
scrump'tious
scrunch
scru'ple, -pled,
    -pling
scru'pu•los'i•ty *or*
    scru'pu•lous•ness
scru'pu•lous
scru'ti•nize',
    -nized', -niz'ing
scru'ti•niz'er
scru'ti•ny
scu'ba
scud, scud'ded,
    scud'ding
scuff
scuf'fle, -fled, -fling
scuf'fler
scull *(oar, boat)*
    ✔ *skull*
scul'ler•y
scul'lion
sculpt
sculp'tor
sculp'tur•al
sculp'ture, -tured,
    -tur•ing
scum
scup *pl.* scup *or*
    scups
scup'per
scurf
scur•ril'i•ty

scur'ri•lous
scur'ry, -ried,
    -ry•ing
scur'vy
scutch'eon
scut'tle, -tled, -tling
scut'tle•butt'
scythe, scythed,
    scyth'ing
sea *(body of water)*
    ✔ *see, si*
sea'bed'
sea' bird'
sea'board'
sea'coast'
sea'far'er
sea'far'ing
sea'food'
sea'go'ing
sea' green'
sea'gull' *also*
    sea'gull'
sea' horse'
seal
sea'-lane'
seal'ant
seal'er
seal'ing wax'
seal'skin'
seam *(junction)*
    ✔ *seem*
sea'man *(sailor)*
    ✔ *semen*
sea'man•ship'
seam'stress
seam'y
sé'ance'

sea'plane'
sea'port'
sear *(to scorch)*
    ✔ *seer, sere*
search
search'light'
sea'scape'
sea'shell'
sea'shore'
sea'sick'
sea'side'
sea'son
sea'son•a•ble
sea'son•a•bly
sea'son•al
sea'son•ing
seat
seat'ing
sea'ward *adv. & adj.*
sea'wards *adv.*
sea'way'
sea'weed'
sea'wor'thi•ness
sea'wor'thy
se•ba'ceous
se'cant'
se•cede', -ced'ed,
    -ced'ing
se•ces'sion
se•ces'sion•ism
se•ces'sion•ist
se•clude', -clud'ed,
    -clud'ing
se•clu'sion
sec'ond
sec'on•dar'i•ly
sec'ond•ar'y

sec'ond-class' *adj. & adv.*

sec'ond-de•gree' burn'

sec'ond-guess' *v.*

sec'ond•hand' *adj. & adv.*

sec'ond-rate' *adj.*

se'cre•cy

se'cret *(hidden)*
  ✔ *secrete*

sec're•tar'i•al

sec're•tar'i•at

sec're•tar'y

sec're•tar'y-gen'er•al *pl.* sec're•tar'ies-gen'er•al

se•crete' *(to produce a substance, to hide),* -cret'ed, -cret'ing
  ✔ *secret*

se•cre'tion

se'cre•tive

se•cre'tor

se•cre'to•ry

sect

sec•tar'i•an

sec•tar'i•an•ism

sec'tion

sec'tion•al

sec'tion•al•ism

sec'tion•al•ist

sec'tor

sec'u•lar

sec'u•lar•i•za'tion

sec'u•lar•ize', -ized', -iz'ing

se•cur'a•ble

se•cure', -cur'er, -cur'est

se•cure', -cured', -cur'ing

se•cu'ri•ty

se•dan'

se•date', -dat'ed, -dat'ing

se•da'tion

sed'a•tive

sed'en•tar'i•ly

sed'en•tar'y

Se'der *pl.* -ders *or* Se•dar'im

sedge

sed'i•ment

sed'i•men'ta•ry

sed'i•men•ta'tion

se•di'tion

se•di'tious

se•duce', -duced', -duc'ing

se•duce'a•ble *or* se•duc'i•ble

se•duc'er

se•duc'tion

se•duc'tive

sed'u•lous

see *(to perceive with the eye),* saw, seen, see'ing
  ✔ *sea, si*

see *(bishop's position)*
  ✔ *sea, si*

seed *(plant part), pl.* seeds *or* seed
  ✔ *cede*

seed'ling

seed'y

seek, sought, seek'ing

seem *(to appear to be)*
  ✔ *seam*

seep

seep'age

seer *(person who fore-sees)*
  ✔ *sear, sere*

seer'suck'er

see'saw'

seethe, seethed, seeth'ing

see'-through' *adj.*

seg'ment

seg•men'tal

seg'men•ta'tion

se'go lil'y

seg're•gate', -gat'ed, -gat'ing

seg're•ga'tion

seg're•ga'tion•ist

seine *(to fish with a net),* seined, sein'ing
  ✔ *sane*

seis'mic

seis'mo•gram'

seis'mo•graph'

seis•mog'ra•pher

seis'mo•graph'ic *also* seis'mo•graph'-

i•cal

seis•mog'ra•phy

seis•mo•log'ic *also*
  seis•mo•log'i•cal

seis•mol'o•gist

seis•mol'o•gy

seiz'a•ble

seize, seized, seiz'ing

sei'zure

sel'dom

se•lect'

se•lec'tion

se•lec'tive

se•lec'tiv'i•ty

se•lect'man

se•lec'tor

se•lect'wom'an

se•le'ni•um

self *pl.* selves

self'-ab•sorbed'

self'-ad•dressed'

self'-ap•point'ed

self'-as•sur'ance

self'-as•sured'

self'-cen'tered

self'-con•fessed'

self'-con'fi•dence

self'-con'fi•dent

self'-con'scious

self'-con•tained'

self'-con•trol'

self'-con•trolled'

self'-de•fense'

self'-de•ni'al

self'-de•struct'

self'-de•ter'mi•na'-
  tion

self'-dis'ci•pline

self'-ed'u•cat'ed

self'-ef•fac'ing

self'-em•ployed'

self'-es•teem'

self'-ev'i•dent

self'-ex•plan'a•
  to'ry

self'-ex•pres'sion

self'-ful•fill'ing

self'-gov'ern•ing

self'-gov'ern•ment

self'-help'

self'-im•por'tance

self'-im•por'tant

self'-im•prove'-
  ment

self'-in•dul'gence

self'-in•dul'gent

self'-in'ter•est

self'ish

self'-knowl'edge

self'less

self'-made'

self'-pit'y

self'-pol'li•na'tion

self'-por'trait

self'-pos•sessed'

self'-pos•ses'sion

self'-pres'er•va'tion

self'-pro•pelled'

self'-re•gard'

self'-re•li'ance

self'-re•li'ant

self'-re•spect'

self'-re•straint'

self'-right'eous

self'-rule'

self'-sac'ri•fice'

self'same'

self'-sat'is•fac'tion

self'-sat'is•fied'

self'-seek'ing

self'-serv'ice

self'-serv'ing

self'-start'er

self'-styled'

self'-suf•fi'cien•cy

self'-suf•fi'cient

self'-sup•port'ing

self'-sus•tain'ing

self'-taught'

self'-will'

self'-willed'

self'-wind'ing

sell *(to exchange for
  money),* sold,
  sell'ing
  ✔ *cell*

sell'er *(person who
  sells)*
  ✔ *cellar*

sell'out' *n.*

selt'zer

sel'vage *also*
  sel'vedge

se•man'ti•cist

se•man'tics

sem'a•phore

sem'blance

se'men *(whitish
  fluid)*
  ✔ *seaman*

se•mes'ter

sem'i·an'nu·al
(twice a year)
✔ biannual, biennial, biyearly, semiyearly
sem'i·ar'id
sem'i·a·rid'i·ty
sem'i·au·'to·mat'ic
sem'i·cir'cle
sem'i·cir'cu·lar
sem'i·co'lon
sem'i·con·duc'tor
sem'i·con'scious
sem'i·de·tached'
sem'i·dry'
sem'i·fi'nal *n.*
sem'i·fi'nal *adj.*
sem'i·fi'nal·ist
sem'i·for'mal
sem'i·gloss'
sem'i·month'ly
(twice a month)
✔ bimonthly
sem'i·nal
sem'i·nar
sem'i·nar'i·an
sem'i·nar'y
Sem'i·nole' *pl.*
-nole' *or* -noles'
sem'i·of·fi'cial
sem'i·pre'cious
sem'i·pri'vate
sem'i·pro·fes'sion·al
sem'i·skilled'
sem'i·sol'id
Sem'ite'
Se·mit'ic
sem'i·tone'

sem'i·trail'er
sem'i·trop'i·cal
sem'i·vow'el
sem'i·week'ly
(twice a week)
✔ biweekly
semiyearly *(twice a year)*
✔ biannual, biennial, biyearly, semiannual
sen'ate *also* Sen'ate
sen'a·tor
sen'a·to'ri·al
send, sent, send'ing
send'off' *n.*
Sen'e·ca *pl.* -ca *or* -cas
sen'e·schal
se'nile'
se·nil'i·ty
sen'ior
sen·ior'i·ty
sen'na
se·ñor' *pl.* -ño'res
se·ño'ra
se·ño·ri'ta
sen'sate' *also* sen'sat'ed
sen·sa'tion
sen·sa'tion·al
sen·sa'tion·al·ism
sen·sa'tion·al·ize', -ized', -iz'ing
sense, sensed, sens'ing
sense'less
sen·si·bil'i·ty

sen'si·ble
sen'si·bly
sen'si·tive
sen'si·tiv'i·ty *or* sen'si·tive·ness
sen'si·ti·za'tion
sen'si·tize', -tized', -tiz'ing
sen'sor
sen'so·ry
sen'su·al
sen'su·al'i·ty
sen'su·ous
sent *past tense and past participle of* send
✔ cent, scent
sen'tence, -tenced, -tenc'ing
sen·ten'tial *(relating to a sentence)*
sen·ten'tious *(pithy, pompous)*
sen'tience
sen'tient
sen'ti·ment
sen'ti·men'tal
sen'ti·men·tal'i·ty
sen'ti·men'tal·ize', -ized', -iz'ing
sen'ti·nel
sen'try
se'pal
sep'a·ra·ble
sep'a·rate', -rat'ed, -rat'ing
sep'a·rate·ly

sep′a•ra′tion
sep′a•ra•tism
sep′a•ra•tist
sep′a•ra′tor
se′pi•a
sep′sis
Sep•tem′ber
sep•ten′ni•al
sep•tet′ *also*
  sep•tette′
sep′tic
sep′ti•ce′mi•a
sep•til′lion
sep•til′lionth
sep′tu•a•ge•nar′-
  i•an
sep′tum *pl.* -ta
sep′ul•cher
se•pul′chral
se′quel
se′quence
se•quen′tial
se′ques•tra′tion
se′quin
se′quined
se•quoi′a
se•ra′glio *pl.* -glios
se•ra′pe *also*
  sa•ra′pe
ser′aph *pl.* -a•phim
  or -aphs
se•raph′ic
Serb
Ser′bi•an
Ser′bo-Cro•a′tian
sere *(withered)*

✔ sear, seer
ser′e•nade′,
  -nad′ed, -nad′ing
ser′en•dip′i•tous
ser′en•dip′i•ty
se•rene′
se•ren′i•ty
serf *(laborer)*
  ✔ surf
serf′dom
serge *(cloth)*
  ✔ surge
ser′geant
ser′geant at arms′
  pl. ser′geants at
  arms′
ser′geant ma′jor
  pl. ser′geants
  ma′jor *or* ser′geant
  ma′jors
se′ri•al *(of or in a se-*
  ries)
  ✔ cereal
se′ri•al•i•za′tion
se′ri•al•ize′, -ized′,
  -iz′ing
se′ries *pl.* -ries
ser′if
se′ri•ous
ser′mon
ser′mon•ize′,
  -ized′, -iz′ing
ser′mon•iz′er
se′rous
ser′pent
ser′pen•tine′
ser′rate′ *or* ser′rat•ed

se′rum *pl.* -rums *or*
  -ra
ser′vant
serve, served,
  serv′ing
serv′er
serv′ice, -iced,
  -ic•ing
serv′ice•a•bil′i•ty
serv′ice•a•ble
serv′ice•man
serv′ice•per′son
serv′ice•wom′an
ser′vile
ser•vil′i•ty
ser′vi•tor
ser′vi•tude′
ses′a•me
ses′qui•cen•ten′-
  ni•al
ses′sile′
ses′sion *(meeting)*
  ✔ cession
set, set, set′ting
set′back′ *n.*
set•tee′
set′ter
set′ting
set′tle, -tled, -tling
set′tle•ment
set′tler
set′-to′ *pl.* -tos′
set′up′ *n.*
sev′en
sev′en•teen′
sev′en•teenth′
sev′enth

Sev'enth-day'
  Ad'ven'tist
sev'en·ti·eth
sev'en·ty
sev'er
sev'er·al
sev'er·ance
se·vere', -ver'er,
  -ver'est
se·ver'i·ty
sew *(to stitch)*,
  sewed, sewn *or*
  sewed, sew'ing
  ✔ *so, sow*
sew'age
sew'er
sew'er·age
sex
sex'a·ge·nar'i·an
sex'ism
sex'ist
sex'-linked'
sex'tant
sex·tet'
sex·til'lion
sex·til'lionth
sex'ton
sex·tu'ple, -pled,
  -pling
sex·tup'let
sex'u·al
sex'u·al'i·ty
shab'bi·ly
shab'bi·ness
shab'by
shack
shack'le, -led, -ling

shad *pl.* shad *or*
  shads
shade, shad'ed,
  shad'ing
shad'i·ness
shad'ow
shad'y
shaft
shag
shag'bark'
shag'gy
shah
shak'a·ble *or*
  shake'a·ble
shake, shook,
  shak'en, shak'ing
shake'down'
shake'out'
shak'er *(one that
  shakes)*
Shak'er *(member of
  a religious group)*
Shake·spear'e·an
  or Shake·spear'i·an
shake'up' *n.*
shak'i·ly
shak'o *pl.* -os *or* -oes
shak'y
shale
shall
shal'lop
shal'lot
shal'low
sham, shammed,
  sham'ming
sha'man
sham'ble, -bled,

-bling
sham'bles
shame, shamed,
  sham'ing
shame'faced'
shame'fac'ed·ly
shame'ful
shame'less
sham·poo' *pl.*
  -poos'
sham'rock'
shang·hai', -haied',
  -hai'ing
shank
shan·tung'
shan'ty *(shack)*
  ✔ *chantey*
shape, shaped,
  shap'ing
shape'less
shape'li·ness
shape'ly
shard *also* sherd
  (potsherd)
  ✔ *chard*
share, shared,
  shar'ing
share'crop'per
share'hold'er
shark
sharp'en
sharp'en·er
sharp'shoot'er
shat'ter
shat'ter·proof'
shave, shaved,
  shaved *or* shav'en,

shav'ing
shav'er
Sha'vi·an
Sha·vu'ot'
shawl
Shaw·nee' *pl.* -nee'
  or -nees'
she
sheaf *pl.* sheaves
shear *(to clip),*
  sheared, sheared *or*
  shorn, shear'ing
  ✔ *sheer*
shears
sheath *pl.* sheaths
sheathe, sheathed,
  sheath'ing
shed, shed, shed'-
  ding
shed'der
sheen
sheep *pl.* sheep
sheep'dog' *also*
  sheep' dog'
sheep'fold'
sheep'herd'er
sheep'ish
sheep'skin'
sheer *(to swerve)*
  ✔ *shear*
sheer *(transparent,*
  complete)
  ✔ *shear*
sheet
sheet'ing
sheik *also* sheikh
  (Arab leader)

✔ *chic*
shek'el
shel'duck'
shelf *pl.* shelves
shell
shel·lac', -lacked,
  -lack'ing
shelled
shell'fish'
shell'-shocked'
shel'ter
shel'tie *also* shel'ty
shelve, shelved
  shelv'ing
she·nan'i·gan
shep'herd
shep'herd·ess
sher'bet
sher'iff
sher'ry
Shet'land' po'ny
shib'bo·leth
shield
shift'i·ly
shift'less
shift'y
Shi'ite'
shil·le'lagh *also*
  shil·la'lah
shil'ling *(British*
  coin)
  ✔ *schilling*
shil'ly-shal'ly,
  -lied, -ly·ing
shim'mer
shim'my, -mied,
  -my·ing

shin, shinned,
  shin'ning
shin'bone'
shin'dig'
shine, shone *or*
  shined, shin'ing
shin'er
shin'gle, -gled,
  -gling
shin'gles
shin'i·ness
shin'ny, -nied,
  -ny·ing
shin' splints' *also*
  shin'splints'
Shin'to
Shin'to·ism
Shin'to·ist
shin'y
ship, shipped,
  ship'ping
ship'board'
ship'build'er
ship'build'ing
ship'load'
ship'mas'ter
ship'mate'
ship'ment
ship'per
ship'shape'
ship'wreck'
ship'yard'
shire
shirk
shirr
shirt
shirt'ing

shirt'tail'
shirt'waist'
shish' ke•bab' *also*
  shish' ke•bob' *or*
  shish' ka•bob'
shiv'er
shiv'er•y
shoal
shoat *also* shote
shock
shock'er
shock'ing
shod'dy
shoe (*to cover the*
  foot), shod, shod *or*
  shod'den, shoe'ing
  ✔ shoo
shoe'horn'
shoe'lace'
shoe'mak'er
shoe'string'
shoe'tree'
sho'far' *pl.* -fars *or*
  sho•froth'
sho'gun'
shoo (*to scare away*),
  shooed, shoo'ing
  ✔ shoe
shoo'-in'
shook-up' *adj.*
shoot (*to fire a*
  weapon), shot,
  shoot'ing
  ✔ chute
shoot'er
shoot'out' *also*
  shoot'-out' *n.*

shop, shopped,
  shop'ping
shop'keep'er
shop'lift'
shop'lift'er
shop'per
shop'talk'
shop'worn'
shore (*land along a*
  body of water)
shore (*to support*),
  shored, shor'ing
shore' bird'
shore'line'
short
short'age
short'bread'
short'cake'
short'change',
  -changed',
  -chang'ing
short'chang'er
short' cir'cuit *n.*
short'-cir'cuit *v.*
short'com'ing
short'cut'
short'en
short'en•ing
short'fall'
short'hand'
short'-hand'ed
short'horn'
short'-lived'
short'-or'der *adj.*
short'-range'
short'sight'ed
short'stop'

short'-tem'pered
short'wave' *adj.*
short'-wind'ed
Sho•sho'ne *pl.* -ne
  or -nes
shot
shot'gun'
shot' put'
shot'-put'er
should
shoul'der
should'n't
shout
shove, shoved,
  shov'ing
shov'el, -eled *also*
  -elled, -el•ing *also*
  -el•ling
shov'el•er *also*
  shov'el•ler
show, showed,
  shown *or* showed,
  show'ing
show'boat'
show'case'
show'down'
show'er (*one that*
  shows)
show'er (*rainfall*)
show'girl'
show'i•ness
show'man
show'man•ship'
show'off' *n.*
show'piece'
show' room'
show'time' *or*

show′ time′
show′y
shrap′nel *pl.* -nel
shred, shred′ded *or*
  shred, shred′ding
shred′der
shrew
shrewd
shrew′ish
shriek
shrike
shrill
shrimp *pl.* shrimp *or*
  shrimps
shrine
shrink, shrank *or*
  shrunk, shrunk *or*
  shrunk′en,
  shrink′ing
shrink′a•ble
shrink′age
shrink′er
shrink′-wrap′,
  -wrapped′,
  -wrap′ping
shrive, shrove *or*
  shrived, shriv′en *or*
  shrived, shriv′ing
shriv′el, -eled *or*
  -elled, -el•ing *or*
  -el•ling
shriv′er
shroud
shrub
shrub′ber•y
shrub′by
shrug, shrugged,

shrug′ging
shuck
shucks
shuck′er
shud′der
shuf′fle, -fled, -fling
shuf′fle•board′
shul
shun, shunned,
  shun′ning
shun′ner
shunt
shush
shut, shut, shut′ting
shut′down′ *n.*
shut′eye′
shut′-in′ *n.*
shut′off′ *n.*
shut′out′ *n.*
shut′ter
shut′ter•bug′
shut′tle, -tled, -tling
shut′tle•cock′
shy, shi′er *or* shy′er,
  shi′est *or* shy′est
shy, shied, shy′ing
shy′ster
si *(musical tone)*
  ✔ sea, see
Si′a•mese′ *pl.* -mese′
Si•be′ri•an
sib′i•lance *or*
  sib′i•lan•cy
sib′i•lant
sib′ling
sib′yl
sic *(thus)*

✔ sick
sic *also* sick *(to at-*
  tack), sicced *also*
  sicked, sic′cing *also*
  sick′ing
✔ sick
Si•cil′ian
sick *(ill)*
  ✔ sic
sick′bay′
sick′bed′
sick′en
sick′en•ing
sick′le
sick′li•ness
sick′ly
sid′dur *pl.*
  sid•du′rim
side, sid′ed, sid′ing
side′arm′ *adj. & adv.*
side′ arm′ *n.*
side′board′
side′burns′
side′car′
sid′ed
side′kick′
side′light′
side′line′
side′long′
si•de′re•al
side′sad′dle
side′show′
side′split′ting
side′step′,
  -stepped′, -step′ping
side′step′per
side′stroke′

side'swipe',
-swiped', -swip'ing
side'track'
side'walk'
side'wall'
sideward *adv. & adj.*
sidewards *adv.*
side'ways' *also*
side'way'
side'wind'er
sid'ing
si'dle, -dled, -dling
siege
si•en'na
si•er'ra
si•es'ta
sieve, sieved, siev'ing
sift
sift'er
sigh
sight *(ability to see)*
✓ *cite, site*
sight'ed
sight'less
sight'-read', -read',
-read'ing
sight'see'ing
sight'se'er
sig'ma
sign *(indication)*
✓ *sine*
sig'nal, -naled *or*
-nalled, -nal•ing *or*
-nal•ling
sig'nal•er *or*
sig'nal•ler
sig'nal•i•za'tion

sig'nal•ize', -ized',
-iz'ing
sig'na•to'ry
sig'na•ture
sign'board'
sig'net *(seal)*
✓ *cygnet*
sig•nif'i•cance
sig•nif'i•cant
sig•ni•fi•ca'tion
sig'ni•fy, -fied,
-fy'ing
si•gnor' *pl.* -gno'ri
also -gnors'
si•gno'ra *pl.* -gno're
or -gnoras'
si•gno're *pl.* -gno'ri
si'gno•ri'na *pl.* -ne
or -nas
sign'post'
Sikh
si'lage
si'lence, -lenced,
-lenc•ing
si'lent
sil'hou•ette',
-et'ted, -et'ting
sil'i•ca
sil'i•cate'
sil'i•con *(element)*
sil'i•cone' *(polymer)*
silk'en
silk'i•ness
silk'-screen' *or*
silk'screen' *n.*
silk'-screen' *v.*
silk'worm'

silk'y
sill
sil'li•ness
sil'ly
si'lo *pl.* -los
silt
Si•lu'ri•an
sil'ver
sil'ver•fish' *pl.* -fish'
or -fish'es
sil'ver•smith'
sil'ver-tongued'
sil'ver•ware'
sil'ver•y
sim'i•an
sim'i•lar
sim'i•lar'i•ty
sim'i•le
si•mil'i•tude'
sim'mer
si'mo•ny
sim'per
sim'ple, -pler, -plest
sim'ple-mind'ed
or sim'ple•mind'ed
sim'ple•ton
sim•plic'i•ty
sim'pli•fi•ca'tion
sim'pli•fi'er
sim'pli•fy', -fied',
-fy'ing
sim'ply
sim'u•late', -lat'ed,
-lat'ing
sim'u•la'tion
sim'u•la•tive
sim'u•la'tor

si'mul·cast'
si'mul·ta·ne'i·ty
si'mul·ta'ne·ous
sin, sinned, sin'ning
since
sin·cere', -cer'er,
  -cer'est
sin·cere'ly
sin·cer'i·ty
sine (*mathematical function*)
  ✔ sign
si'ne·cure'
sin'ew
sin'ew·y
sin'ful
sing, sang *or* sung,
  sung, sing'ing
singe, singed,
  singe'ing
sing'er
Sin'gha·lese' *or*
  Sin'ha·lese' *pl.*
  -lese'
sin'gle, -gled, -gling
sin'gle-breast'ed
sin'gle-hand'ed
sin'gle-mind'ed
sin'gle-space',
  -spaced', -spac'ing
sin'gly
sing'song'
sin'gu·lar
sin'gu·lar'i·ty
sin'is·ter
sin'is·tral
sink, sank *or* sunk,

sunk, sink'ing
sink'a·ble
sink'hole'
sin'ner
sin'u·os'i·ty
sin'u·ous
si'nus
si'nus·i'tis
Siou'an
Sioux *pl.* Sioux
sip, sipped, sip'ping
si'phon *also*
  sy'phon
si'phon·al *or*
  si·phon'ic
sir
sire, sired, sir'ing
si'ren
sir'loin'
si·roc'co *pl.* -cos
sis
si'sal
sis'sy
sis'ter
sis'ter·hood'
sis'ter-in-law' *pl.*
  sis'ters-in-law'
sis'ter·li·ness
sis'ter·ly
sit, sat, sit'ting
si·tar'
sit'com' *also*
  sit'-com'
sit'-down' strike'
site (*location*)
  ✔ cite, sight
sit'-in' *n.*

sit'ter
sit'ting
sit'u·ate', -at'ed,
  -at'ing
sit'u·a'tion
sit'-up' *n.*
sitz' bath'
six
six'-gun'
six'-pack'
six'pence
six'-shoot'er
six'teen'
six'teenth'
sixth
six'ti·eth
six'ty
siz'a·ble *also*
  size'a·ble
siz'a·bly
size, sized, siz'ing
siz'zle, -zled, -zling
skate, skat'ed,
  skat'ing
skate'board'
skate'board'er
skate'board'ing
skat'er
skeet
skein
skel'e·tal
skel'e·ton
skep'tic *also* scep'tic
skep'ti·cal *also*
  scep'ti·cal
skep'ti·cism *also*
  scep'ti·cism

sketch
sketch'book'
sketch'i•ly
sketch'i•ness
sketch'pad'
sketch'y
skew
skew'er
ski *pl.* skis
ski, skied, ski'ing
skid, skid'ded,
  skid'ding
ski'er
skiff
skill
skilled
skil'let
skill'ful
skim, skimmed,
  skim'ming
skim'mer
skimp'i•ness
skimp'y
skin, skinned,
  skin'ning
skin'-deep'
skin'-dive', -dived',
  -div'ing
skin' div'er
skin' div'ing *n.*
skin'flint'
skin'ner
skin'ni•ness
skin'ny
skin'tight'
skip, skipped,
  skip'ping

skip'per
skir'mish
skirt
skit
skit'ter
skit'tish
skit'tles
skoal
skulk
skull *(head bones)*
  ✔ *scull*
skull'cap'
skull•dug'ger•y *or*
  skul•dug'ger•y
skunk
sky
sky' blue'
sky'box'
sky'dive', -dived',
  -div'ing
sky'div'er
Skye' ter'ri•er
sky'-high'
sky'jack'
sky'jack'er
sky'lark'
sky'light'
sky'line'
sky'rock'et
sky'scrap'er
sky'ward *adv. & adj.*
sky'wards *adv.*
sky'writ'er
sky'writ'ing
slab
slack
slack'en

slack'er
slag
slake, slaked,
  slak'ing
sla'lom
slam, slammed,
  slam'ming
slam'-dunk' *or*
  slam' dunk'
slan'der
slan'der•ous
slang
slang'y
slant
slant'wise'
slap, slapped,
  slap'ping
slap'dash'
slap'hap'py
slap'stick'
slash
slat
slate, slat'ed, slat'ing
slath'er
slat'tern
slaugh'ter
slaugh'ter•house'
Slav
slave, slaved,
  slav'ing
slave' driv'er
slave'hold'er
slav'er *(to drool)*
slav'er *(ship engaged
  in slave traffic)*
slav'er•y
Slav'ic

slav'ish

slaw

slay *(to kill)*, slew,
slain, slay'ing
✔ sleigh

slea'zi•ness

slea'zy

sled, sled'ded,
sled'ding

sledge

sledge'ham'mer

sleek

sleep, slept, sleep'ing

sleep'i•ly

sleep'i•ness

sleep'o'ver

sleep'walk'ing

sleep'walk'er

sleep'y

sleep'y•head'

sleet

sleeve, sleeved,
sleev'ing

sleigh *(sledge)*
✔ slay

sleight *(dexterity,
trick)*
✔ slight

slen'der

sleuth

slew *also* slue *(large
amount)*
✔ slough, slue

slice, sliced, slic'ing

slice'a•ble

slic'er

slick

slick'er

slide, slid, slid'ing

slight *(small)*
✔ sleight

slight *(to snub)*
✔ sleight

slim, slim'mer,
slim'mest

slim, slimmed,
slim'ming

slime

slim'i•ness

slim'y

sling, slung,
sling'ing

sling'shot'

slink, slunk *also*
slinked, slink'ing

slip, slipped,
slip'ping

slip'case'

slip'cov'er

slip'knot'

slip'-on' *n. & adj.*

slip'o'ver

slip'page

slip'per

slip'per•i•ness

slip'per•y

slip'shod'

slip'-up' *n.*

slit, slit, slit'ting

slith'er

slit'ter

sliv'er

slob

slob'ber

sloe *(fruit)*
✔ slow

slog, slogged,
slog'ging

slo'gan

slog'ger

sloop

slop, slopped,
slop'ping

slope, sloped,
slop'ing

slop'pi•ly

slop'pi•ness

slop'py

slosh

slot, slot'ted,
slot'ting

sloth

sloth'ful

slouch

slouch'y

slough *also* slew
(hollow, swamp)
✔ slew, slue

slough *(to shed)*

Slo'vak'

slov'en

Slo'vene'

slov'en•li•ness

slov'en•ly

slow *(not quick)*
✔ sloe

slow'down' *n.*

slow'-mo'tion *adj.*

slow'poke'

slow'-wit'ted *or*
slow'wit'ted

sludge
sludg'y
slue *also* slew *(to turn)*, slued *also* slewed, slu'ing *or* slew'ing
  ✔ slew, slough
slug, slugged, slug'ging
slug'gard
slug'ger
slug'gish
sluice, sluiced, sluic'ing
slum
slum'ber
slum'ber•er
slum'ber•ous *or* slum'brous
slump
slur, slurred, slur'ring
slurp
slush'i•ness
slush'y
slut
sly, sli'er *also* sly'er, sli'est *or* sly'est
sly'ness
smack
smack'-dab' *adv.*
small
small'ish
small'-mind'ed
small'pox'
small'-scale' *adj.*
small'time' *or* small'-time' *adj.*

smarm'y
smart
smart' al'eck n.
smart'-al'eck *or* smart'-al'eck•y *adj.*
smart'en
smash
smash'ing
smash'up' n.
smat'ter•ing
smear
smell, smelled *or* smelt, smell'ing
smell'y
smelt *(to melt)*
smelt *(fish)*, *pl.* smelts *or* smelt
smelt'er
smid'gen *also* smid'geon *or* smid'gin
smile, smiled, smil'ing
smil'er
smirch
smirk
smite, smote, smit'ten *or* smote, smit'ing
smith
smith'er•eens'
smith'y
smock
smock'ing
smog
smog'gy
smoke, smoked,

smok'ing
smoke'house'
smoke'less
smok'er
smoke' screen' *or* smoke'screen'
smoke'stack'
smok'i•ness
smok'y
smol'der *also* smoul'der
smooth
smooth'bore' *also* smooth' bore'
smor'gas•bord'
smoth'er
smudge, smudged, smudg'ing
smudg'y
smug, smug'ger, smug'gest
smug'gle, -gled, -gling
smug'gler
smut
smut'ty
snack
snaf'fle, -fled, -fling
snag, snagged snag'ging
snail
snake
snake'bite'
snake'root'
snake'skin'
snak'y
snap, snapped,

snap'ping
snap'drag'on
snap'per
snap'pi•ly
snap'pi•ness
snap'pish
snap'py
snap'shot'
snare, snared,
  snar'ing
snarl
snatch
sneak, sneaked *also*
  snuck, sneak'ing
sneak'er
sneak'i•ly
sneak'i•ness
sneak'y
sneer
sneeze, sneezed,
  sneez'ing
snick'er
snide, snid'er,
  snid'est
sniff
snif'fle, -fled, -fling
snif'ter
snig'ger
snip, snipped,
  snip'ping
snipe *pl.* snipe *or*
  snipes
snipe, sniped,
  snip'ing
snip'er
snip'pet
snip'py

snit
snitch
sniv'el, -eled *or*
  -elled, -el'ing *or*
  -el'ling
sniv'el•er *or*
  sniv'el•ler
snob
snob'ber•y
snob'bish
snob'bism
snood
snook'er
snoop
snoop'y
snoot'i•ly
snoot'i•ness
snoot'y
snooze, snoozed,
  snooz'ing
snore, snored,
  snor'ing
snor'kel
snort
snout
snow
snow'ball'
snow'bird'
snow'-blind' *or*
  snow'-blind'ed
snow'bound'
snow'cap'
snow'capped'
snow'drift'
snow'drop'
snow'fall'
snow'flake'

snow'man'
snow'mo•bile'
snow'plow'
snow'shoe',
  -shoed', -shoe'ing
snow'storm'
snow'suit'
snow'y
snub, snubbed,
  snub'bing
snub'-nosed'
snuff
snuff'box'
snuf'fle, -fled, -fling
snug, snug'ger,
  snug'gest
snug'gle, -gled,
  -gling
so *(thus)*
  ✔ sew, sow
soak
so'-and-so' *pl.* -sos'
soap
soap'box'
soap'i•ness
soap'stone'
soap'suds'
soap'y
soar *(to rise)*
  ✔ sore
sob, sobbed,
  sob'bing
so'ber
so•bri'e•ty
so'bri•quet'
so'-called'
soc'cer

so'cia·bil'i·ty *or*
  so'cia·ble·ness
so'cia·ble
so'cia·bly
so'cial
so'cial·ism
so'cial·ist
so'cial·is'tic
so'cial·ite'
so'cial·i·za'tion
so'cial·ize', -ized',
  -iz'ing
so·ci'e·tal
so·ci'e·ty
so·ci·o·cul'tur·al
so·ci·o·ec'o·nom'ic
so·ci·o·log'ic *or*
  so·ci·o·log'i·cal
so·ci·ol'o·gist
so·ci·ol'o·gy
so·ci·o·path'
so·ci·o·po·lit'i·cal
sock *pl.* socks *or* sox
sock'et
sock'eye' salm'on
So·crat'ic
sod, sod'ded,
  sod'ding
so'da
so·dal'i·ty
sod'den
so'di·um
so'di·um-va'por
  lamp'
sod'om·y
so'fa
soft

soft'ball'
soft'-boiled'
soft'-core'
soft'cov'er
soft'en
soft'en·er
soft'heart'ed
soft'-ped'al, -aled
  or -alled, -al·ing *or*
  -al·ling
soft'-shell' *also*
  soft'-shelled'
soft'-shoe' *n.*
soft'-soap' *v.*
soft'-spo'ken
soft'ware'
soft'wood'
soft'y *or* soft'ie *pl.*
  -ies
sog'gi·ness
sog'gy
soil
soi·ree' *also* soi·rée'
so'journ'
so'journ·er
sol *also* so (*musical
  tone*)
  ✔ sole, soul
sol'ace, -aced,
  -ac·ing
so'lar
so·lar'i·um *pl.* -i·a
  or -i·ums
sol'der
sol'dier
sole (*bottom of a
  shoe*)

  ✔ sol, soul
sole (*to put a sole on*),
  soled, sol'ing
  ✔ sol, soul
sole (*single*)
  ✔ sol, soul
sole (*fish*), *pl.* sole *or*
  soles
  ✔ sol, soul
sol'e·cism
sole'ly
sol'emn
so·lem'ni·ty
sol'em·ni·za'tion
sol'em·nize',
  -nized', -niz'ing
so'le·noid'
so·lic'it
so·lic'i·ta'tion
so·lic'i·tor
so·lic'i·tous
so·lic'i·tude'
sol'id
sol'i·dar'i·ty
so·lid'i·fi·ca'tion
so·lid'i·fy', -fied',
  -fy'ing
so·lid'i·ty
sol'id-state' *adj.*
so·lil'o·quize',
  -quized', -quiz'ing
so·lil'o·quy *pl.*
  -quies
sol'ip·sism
sol'ip·sis'tic
sol'i·taire'
sol'i·tar'y

sol'i•tude'
so'lo *pl.* -los
sol'lo•ist
sol'stice
sol'u•bil'i•ty
sol'u•ble
sol'ute
so•lu'tion
solv'a•ble
solve, solved,
   solv'ing
sol'ven•cy
sol'vent
So•ma'li *pl.* -li *or* -lis
so•mat'ic
som'ber
som•bre'ro *pl.* -ros
some *(a few)*
   ✔ sum
some'bod'y
some'day'
some'how'
some'one'
some'place'
som'er•sault' *also*
   sum'mer•sault'
some'thing'
some'time'
some'times'
some'way' *also*
   some'ways'
some'what'
some'where'
som•nam'bu•late',
   -lat'ed, -lat'ing
som•nam'bu•lism
som•nam'bu•list

som•nam'bu•lis'-
   tic *also* som•nam'-
   bu•lar
som'no•lence
som'no•lent
son *(male child)*
   ✔ sun
so'nar'
so•na'ta
song
song'bird'
song'writ'er
son'ic
son'-in-law' *pl.*
   sons'-in-law'
son'net
son'net•eer'
son'ny *(boy)*
   ✔ sunny
so•nor'i•ty
so•no'rous
soon
soot
sooth *(truth)*
soothe *(to calm)*,
   soothed, sooth'ing
sooth'say'er
soot'y
sop, sopped,
   sop'ping
soph'ism
soph'ist
so•phis'ti•cate',
   -cat'ed, -cat'ing
so•phis'ti•ca'tion
soph'is•try
soph'o•more'

soph'o•mor'ic
sop'o•rif'ic
sop'py
so•pran'o *pl.* -os
sor'cer•er
sor'cer•ess
sor'cer•y
sor'did
sore *(painful)*, sor'er,
   sor'est
   ✔ soar
sor'ghum
so•ror'i•ty
sor'rel
sor'row
sor'row•ful
sor'ry
sort'er
sor'tie
so'-so'
sot
sou
souf•flé'
sough
soul *(spirit)*
   ✔ sol, sole
soul'ful
soul'less
soul'-search'ing
sound
sound'ing
sound'proof'
sound'track'
soup
soup'spoon'
soup'y
sour

source
sour'dough'
sou'sa•phone'
souse, soused,
  sous'ing
south
South' Af'ri•can
South' A•mer'i•
  can
south'bound'
South' Car'o•
  lin'i•an
South' Da•ko'tan
south•east'
south•east'er
south•east'er•ly
south•east'ern
south•east'ward
  adj. & adv.
south•east'wards
  adv.
south'er•ly
south'ern
south'ern•er
south'ern•most'
south'paw
south'ward *adv. &*
  adj.
south'wards *adv.*
south•west'
south•west'er *also*
  sou'•west'er
south•west'er•ly
south•west'ern
south•west'ward
  adv. & adj.
south•west'wards

adv.
sou've•nir'
sov'er•eign
sov'er•eign•ty
so'vi•et'
sow (to plant),
  sowed, sown *or*
  sowed, sow'ing
  ✔ *sew, so*
sow (female pig)
soy
soy'a
soy'bean'
soy' sauce'
spa
space, spaced,
  spac'ing
space'craft' *pl.*
  -craft'
space'ship'
space'-time'
spa'cious
spade, spad'ed,
  spad'ing
spa'dix *pl.* -di•ces'
spa•ghet'ti
span, spanned,
  span'ning
span'dex
span'gle, -gled,
  -gling
Span'iard
span'iel
Span'ish
Span'ish
  A•mer'i•can *n.*
Span'ish-

A•mer'i•can *adj.*
spank'ing
span'ner
spar (pole)
spar (to box),
  sparred, spar'ring
spare, spared,
  spar'ing
spare, spar'er,
  spar'est
spare'ribs'
spark
spar'kle, -kled,
  -kling
spar'kler
spar'row
sparse, spars'er,
  spars'est
spar'si•ty
Spar'tan
spasm
spas•mod'ic
spas'tic
spat (oyster spawn),
  pl. spat *or* spats
spat (to spawn, to
  quarrel), spat'ted,
  spat'ting
spat (shoe covering)
spate
spa'tial
spat'ter
spat'u•la
spav'in
spav'ined
spawn
spay

speak, spoke,
  spo•ken, speak'ing
speak'eas'y
speak'er
speak'er•phone'
spear
spear'fish' *v.*
spear'head'
spear'mint'
spe'cial
spe'cial•ist
spe•ci•al'i•ty *(distin-
  guishing feature)*
  ✔ *specialty*
spe'cial•i•za'tion
spe'cial•ize', -ized',
  -iz'ing
spe'cial•ty *(special
  occupation or skill)*
  ✔ *speciality*
spe'cie *(coin)*
spe'cies *(kind),* pl.
  -cies
spe•cif'ic
spe•cif'i•cal•ly
spec'i•fi•ca'tion
spec'i•fy', -fied',
  -fy'ing
spec'i•men
spe'cious
speck
speck'le
speck'led
spec'ta•cle
spec•tac'u•lar
spec'ta'tor
spec'ter

spec'tral
spec'tro•gram'
spec'tro•graph'
spec'tro•graph'ic
spec•trog'ra•phy
spec•trom'e•ter
spec•trom'e•try
spec'tro•scope'
spec'tro•scop'ic *or*
  spec'tro•scop'i•cal
spec•tros'co•py
spec'trum pl. -tra *or*
  -trums
spec'u•late', -lat'ed,
  -lat'ing
spec'u•la'tion
spec'u•la•tive
spec'u•la'tor
speech'less
speech'mak'er
speech'mak'ing
speech'writ'er
speech'writ'ing
speed, sped *or*
  speed'ed,
  speed'ing
speed'boat'
speed'er
speed•om'e•ter
speed'-read'ing
speed'up' *n.*
speed'way'
speed'well'
speed'y
spe'le•ol'o•gist
spe'le•ol'o•gy
spell, spelled *or*

spelt, spell'ing
spell'bind',
  -bound', -bind'ing
spell'er
spell'ing bee'
spe•lunk'er
spe'lunk'ing
spend, spent,
  spend'ing
spend'thrift'
sperm pl. sperm *or*
  sperms
sper'ma•ce'ti pl.
  -tis
sper•mat'o•phyte'
sper•mat'o•zo'on'
  pl. -zo'a
spew
sphag'num
sphe'noid'
sphe•noi'dal
sphere
spher'i•cal
sphe'roid'
sphinc'ter
sphinx pl. sphinx'es
  or sphin'ges'
sphyg'mo•ma•
  nom'e•ter
spice, spiced,
  spic'ing
spic'i•ness
spick'-and-span'
spic'ule
spic'y
spi'der
spiel

spiff'y
spig'ot
spike, spiked,
  spik'ing
spike'nard'
spik'i·ness
spik'y
spill, spilled *or* spilt,
  spill'ing
spill'age
spill'o·ver
spill'way'
spin, spun,
  spin'ning
spin'ach
spi'nal
spin'dle, -dled,
  -dling
spin'dly
spin'drift'
spine
spine'less
spin'et
spin'na·ker
spin'ner
spin'ner·et'
spin'off' *or*
  spin'-off'
spin'ster
spin'y
spir'a·cle
spi'ral, -raled *also*
  -ralled, -ral·ing *also*
  -ral·ling
spire
spi·ril'lum *pl.* -la
spir'it

spir'it·ed
spir'it·less
spir'i·tu·al
spir'i·tu·al·ism
spir'i·tu·al·ist
spir'i·tu·al'i·ty
spi'ro·chete'
spi'ro·gy'ra
spit *(to eject from the
  mouth)*, spat *or* spit,
  spit'ting
spit *(to place on a
  rod)*, spit'ted,
  spit'ting
spit'ball'
spite, spit'ed,
  spit'ing
spite'ful
spit'fire'
spit'tle
spit·toon'
spitz
splash
splash'down'
splash'y
splat'ter
splay
splay'foot'
splay'foot'ed
spleen
splen'did
splen'dor
splice, spliced,
  splic'ing
splic'er
splint
splin'ter

split, split, split'ting
split'-lev'el
split'ter
splotch
splotch'y
splurge, splurged,
  splurg'ing
splut'ter
spoil, spoiled *or*
  spoilt, spoil'ing
spoil'age
spoil'er
spoil'sport'
spoke, spoked,
  spok'ing
spo'ken
spokes'man
spokes'per'son
spokes'wom'an
spo'li·a'tion
spo'li·a'tor
spon'dee'
sponge, sponged,
  spong'ing
spong'i·ness
spong'y
spon'sor
spon'sor·ship'
spon·ta'ne'i·ty
spon·ta'ne·ous
spoof
spook
spook'i·ness
spook'y
spool
spoon
spoon'bill'

spoon'-feed', -fed', -feed'ing
spoon'ful'
spoor *(animal track)*
   ✔ spore
spo•rad'ic
spo•ran'gi•um *pl.* -gi•a
spore *(reproductive organ)*
   ✔ spoor
spo'ro•phyte'
spo'ro•zo'an
spor'ran
sport
sport'ing
spor'tive
sports'man
sports'man•like'
sports'man•ship'
sports'wear'
sports'wom'an
sports'writ'er
sport'y
spot, spot'ted, spot'ting
spot'-check' *v.*
spot'less
spot'light', -light'ed *or* -lit', -light'ing
spot'ti•ness
spot'ty
spouse
spout
spout'er
sprain
sprat

sprawl
spray
spread, spread, spread'ing
spread'a•bil'i•ty
spread'a•ble
spread'-ea'gle, -gled, -gling
spread'er
spread'sheet'
spree
sprig, sprigged, sprig'ging
spright'li•ness
spright'ly
spring, sprang *or* sprung, sprung, spring'ing
spring'board'
spring'bok' *pl.* -bok' *or* -boks'
spring'time'
spring'y
sprin'kle, -kled, -kling
sprin'kler
sprint
sprint'er
sprit
sprite
sprit'sail
spritz
spritz'er
sprock'et
sprout
spruce *(tree)*
spruce *(neat)*,

spruc'er, spruc'est
spruce *(to make neat)*, spruced, spruc'ing
spry, spri'er *or* spry'er, spri'est *or* spry'est
spry'ly
spry'ness
spud
spume, spumed, spum'ing
spu•mo'ni *or* -ne
spunk
spunk'y
spur, spurred, spur'ring
spu'ri•ous
spurn
spurt
sput'nik
sput'ter
spu'tum *pl.* -ta
spy, spied, spy'ing
spy'glass'
squab
squab'ble, -bled, -bling
squab'bler
squad
squad'ron
squal'id
squall
squall'y
squal'or
squa'mous *also* squa'mose'

squan'der

square, squar'er, squar'est

square, squared, squar'ing

square' dance' *n.*

square'-dance', -danced', -danc'ing

square'-rigged'

square'-rig'ger

squash

squash'y

squat, squat'ted, squat'ting

squat, squat'ter, squat'test

squat'ter

squawk

squeak

squeak'y

squeal

squea'mish

squee'gee

squeez'a•ble

squeeze, squeezed, squeez'ing

squeez'er

squelch

squib

squid *pl.* squids *or* squid

squig'gle, -gled, -gling

squint

squire, squired, squir'ing

squirm

squir'rel, -reled *or* -relled, -rel'ing *or* -rel•ling

squirt

squish

stab, stabbed, stab'bing

stab'ber

sta•bil'i•ty

sta'bi•li•za'tion

sta'bi•lize', -lized', -liz'ing

sta'bi•liz'er

sta'ble, -bler, -blest

sta'ble, -bled, -bling

sta'bly

stac•ca'to

stack

sta'di•um *pl.* -di•ums *or* -di•a

staff *(rod), pl.* staffs *or* staves

staff *(group of assis-tants), pl.* staffs

staff'er

stag

stage, staged, stag'ing

stage'coach'

stage'hand'

stage'-struck'

stag'ger

stag'ger•ing

stag'ing

stag'nan•cy

stag'nant

stag•nate', -nat'ed, -nat'ing

stag•na'tion

stag'y *also* stag'ey

staid

stain

stain'less

stair *(steps)* ✔ stare

stair'case'

stair'way'

stair'well'

stake *(to mark the limits of, to gamble),* staked, stak'ing ✔ steak

stake'out'

sta•lac'tite' *(down-ward deposit)*

sta•lag'mite' *(up-ward deposit)*

stale, stal'er, stal'est

stale'mate', -mat'ed, -mat'ing

Sta'lin•ism

Sta'lin•ist

stalk'er

stall

stal'lion

stal'wart

sta'men *pl.* -mens *or* -mi•na

stam'i•na

sta'mi•nate'

stam'mer

stamp

stam•pede', -ped'ed, -ped'ing

stance

stanch *also* staunch
(*to check the flow*)
✔ staunch

stan'chion

stand, stood,
stand'ing

stand'-a·lone' *adj.*

stan'dard

stan'dard-bear'er

stan'dard·i·za'tion

stan'dard·ize',
-ized', -iz'ing

stand'by' *pl.* -bys'

stand·ee'

stand'-in' *n.*

stand'ing

stand'off' *n.*

stand·off'ish

stand'out' *n.*

stand'pipe'

stand'point'

stand'still'

stand'up' *or*
stand'-up' *adj.*

stan'nic

stan'nous

stan'za

sta'pes *pl.* -pes *or*
-pe·des'

staph'y·lo·coc'cus
pl. -coc'ci

sta'ple, -pled, -pling

sta'pler

star, starred,
star'ring

star'board

starch'y

star'-crossed'

star'dom

stare (*to gaze fixedly*),
stared, star'ing
✔ stair

star'fish' *pl.* -fish' *or*
-fish'es

star'gaze', -gazed',
-gaz'ing

stark

star'let

star'light'

star'ling

star'lit'

star'ry

star'ry-eyed'

star'struck' *or*
star'-struck'

start'er

star'tle, -tled, -tling

star·va'tion

starve, starved,
starv'ing

starve'ling

stash

sta'sis *pl.* -ses

state, stat'ed, stat'ing

state'hood'

state'house' *also*
state' house'

state'li·ness

state'ly

state'ment

state'-of-the-art'
adj.

state'room'

state'side'

states'man

states'man·ship'

states'wom'an

stat'ic

stat'ics

sta'tion

sta'tion·ar'y (*not
moving*)
✔ stationery

sta'tion·er

sta'tion·er'y (*paper
and envelopes*)
✔ stationary

sta'tion·mas'ter

sta·tis'tic

sta·tis'ti·cal

stat·is·ti'cian

sta·tis'tics

sta'tor

stat'u·ar'y

stat'ue

stat'u·esque'

stat'u·ette'

stat'ure

sta'tus

sta'tus quo'

stat'ute

stat'u·to'ry

staunch *also* stanch
(*steadfast*)
✔ stanch

stave, staved *or*
stove, stav'ing

stay

stay'sail'

stead

stead'fast' *also*
  sted'fast'
stead'i•ly
stead'i•ness
stead'y, -ied, -y•ing
stead'y-state'
  theo'ry
steak *(meat)*
  ✔ stake
steal *(to take without
  permission)*, stole,
  sto'len, steal'ing
  ✔ steel
stealth
stealth'i•ly
stealth'y
steam
steam'boat'
steam'er
steam'fit'ter
steam'roll'er
steam'ship'
steam'y
ste'a•tite'
steed
steel *(metal)*
  ✔ steal
steel'work'
steel'work'er
steel'y
steel'yard'
steep
steep'en
stee'ple
stee'ple•chase'
stee'ple•jack'
steer

steer'age
steers'man
steg'o•saur' *also*
  steg'o•sau'rus
stein
stel'lar
stem, stemmed,
  stem'ming
stem'ware'
stem'wind'er
stench
sten'cil, -ciled *or*
  -cilled, -cil•ing *or*
  -cil•ling
ste•nog'ra•pher
sten'o•graph'ic *or*
  sten'o•graph'i•cal
ste•nog'ra•phy
sten•to'ri•an
step *(to walk)*,
  stepped, step'ping
  ✔ steppe
step'broth'er
step'child'
step'daugh'ter
step'-down' *adj. &
  n.*
step'fa'ther
step'-in' *adj. & n.*
step'lad'der
step'moth'er
step'par'ent
steppe *(plain)*
  ✔ step
stepped'-up' *adj.*
step'ping•stone'
step'sis'ter

step'son'
step'-up' *adj. & n.*
ster'e•o' *pl.* -os'
ster'e•o•phon'ic
ster'e•o•scope'
ster'e•o•scop'ic
ster'e•o•type',
  -typed', -typ'ing
ster'e•o•typ'ic *or*
  ster'e•o•typ'i•cal
ster'ile
ste•ril'i•ty
ster'il•i•za'tion
ster'il•ize', -ized',
  -iz'ing
ster'il•iz'er
ster'ling
stern
ster'num *pl.* -nums
  or -na
stern'-wheel'er
ster'oid *n.*
ster'oid' *or*
  ste•roi'dal *adj.*
ster'ol'
steth'o•scope'
ste've•dore'
stew
stew'ard
stew'ard•ship'
stewed
stick, stuck, stick'ing
stick'ball'
stick'er
stick'i•ness
stick'le, -led, -ling
stick'le•back'

stick′ler
stick′pin′
stick′up′ n.
stick′y
stiff
stiff′en
stiff′-necked′
sti′fle, -fled, -fling
stig′ma pl.
  stig•ma′ta or
  stig′mas
stig′ma•ti•za′tion
stig′ma•tize′,
  -tized′, -tiz′ing
stile (steps)
  ✔ style
sti•let′to pl. -tos or
  -toes
still
still′birth′
still′born′
still′ life′ pl. still′
  lifes′
still′-life′ adj.
stilt
stilt′ed
stim′u•lant
stim′u•late′, -lat′ed,
  -lat′ing
stim′u•lat′er or
  stim′u•la′tor
stim′u•la′tion
stim′u•la′tive
stim′u•lus pl. -li′
sting, stung,
  sting′ing
stin′gi•ness

sting′ray′
stin′gy
stink, stank or stunk,
  stunk, stink′ing
stint
sti′pend
stip′ple, -pled,
  -pling
stip′u•late′, -lat′ed,
  -lat′ing
stip′u•la′tion
stip′u•la′tor
stip′ule
stir, stirred, stir′ring
stir′rer
stir′rup
stitch
stoat pl. stoat or
  stoats
stock
stock•ade′
stock′bro′ker
stock′hold′er
stock′i•ness
stock′i•nette′ also
  stock′i•net′
stock′ing
stock′man
stock′pile′, -piled′,
  -pil′ing
stock′room′ also
  stock′ room′
stock′-still′
stock′y
stock′yard′
stodg′i•ly
stodg′i•ness

stodg′y
sto′gy or sto′gie pl.
  -gies
sto′ic also sto′i•cal
sto′i•cism
stoke, stoked,
  stok′ing
stok′er
stole
stol′id
sto•lid′i•ty
sto′lon′
sto′ma pl. -ma•ta or
  -mas
stom′ach
stom′ach•ache′
stomp
stone, stoned,
  ston′ing
stone′-blind′
stone′cut′ter
stone′-deaf′
stone′ma′son
stone′wall′
stone′ware′
stone′work′
stone′work′er
ston′i•ness
ston′y
stooge
stool
stool′ pi′geon
stoop (to bend for-
  ward)
  ✔ stoup
stoop (staircase)
  ✔ stoup

stop, stopped,
  stop′ping
stop′gap′
stop′light′
stop′o′ver
stop′page
stop′per
stop′watch′
stor′age
store, stored, stor′ing
store′-bought′ *adj.*
store′front′
store′house′
store′keep′er
store′room′
sto′ried
stork
storm
storm′i•ness
storm′y
sto′ry
sto′ry•book′
sto′ry•tell′er
stoup *(basin)*
  ✔ *stoop*
stout
stout′heart′ed
stove
stove′pipe′
stow
stow′a•way′ *n.*
strad′dle, -dled,
  -dling
strad′dler
strafe, strafed,
  straf′ing
strag′gle, -gled,

-gling
strag′gler
strag′gly
straight *(erect)*
  ✔ *strait*
straight′a•way′
straight′edge′
straight′en *(to make straight)*
  ✔ *straiten*
straight•for′ward
  adj. & adv.
straight•for′wards
  adv.
straight′way′
strain
strained
strain′er
strait *(channel)*
  ✔ *straight*
strait′en *(to make narrow)*
  ✔ *straighten*
strait′jack′et *also*
  straight′jack′et
strait′-laced′
strand
strange, strang′er,
  strang′est
stran′gle, -gled,
  -gling
stran′gler
stran′gu•late′,
  -lat′ed, -lat′ing
stran′gu•la′tion
strap, strapped,
  strap′ping

strat′a•gem
stra•te′gic
strat′e•gist
strat′e•gy
strat′i•fi•ca′tion
strat′i•fy′, -fied′,
  -fy′ing
stra′to•cu′mu•lus
  pl. -li′
strat′o•sphere′
strat′o•spher′ic
stra′tum *pl.* -ta *or*
  -tums
stra′tus *pl.* -ti
straw
straw′ber′ry
stray
streak′y
stream′er
stream′let
stream′line′,
  -lined′, -lin′ing
street′car′
street′-smart′
strength
strength′en
stren′u•ous
strep′to•coc′cal
strep′to•coc′cus *pl.*
  -coc′ci
strep′to•my′cin
stress
stretch
stretch′a•ble
stretch′er
streu′sel
strew, strewed,

strewn *or* strewed,
strew'ing
stri'a *pl.* -ae
stri'ate' *also*
stri'at'ed
stri•a'tion
strick'en
strict
stric'ture
stride, strode,
strid'den, strid'ing
stri'dence *or*
stri'den•cy
stri'dent
strife
strike, struck, struck
or struck'en,
strik'ing
strike'break'er
strike'out'
strik'er
string, strung,
string'ing
strin'gen•cy
strin'gent
string'er
string'i•ness
string'y
strip, stripped,
strip'ping
stripe, striped,
strip'ing
strip'ling
strip'-mine',
-mined', -min'ing
strip'-search' *v.*
strip'tease' *also*

strip' tease' *n.*
strive, strove,
striv'en *or* strived,
striv'ing
strobe
stro'ga•noff'
stroke, stroked,
strok'ing
stroll
stroll'er
strong'-arm'
adj. & v.
strong'box'
strong'hold'
stron'ti•um
strop, stropped,
strop'ping
stro'phe
struc'tur•al
struc'ture, -tured,
-tur•ing
stru'del
strug'gle, -gled,
-gling
strum, strummed,
strum'ming
strut, strut'ted,
strut'ting
strych'nine'
stub, stubbed,
stub'bing
stub'bi•ness
stub'ble
stub'born
stub'by
stuc'co *pl.* -coes *or*
-cos

stuck'-up' *adj.*
stud, stud'ded,
stud'ding
stu'dent
stu'di•o' *pl.* -os
stu'di•ous
stud'y, -ied, -y•ing
stuff'i•ness
stuff'ing
stuff'y
stul'ti•fi•ca'tion
stul'ti•fy', -fied',
-fy'ing
stum'ble, -bled,
-bling
stum'bler
stump'y
stun, stunned,
stun'ning
stunt'man'
stunt'wom'an
stu'pe•fac'tion
stu'pe•fy', -fied',
-fy'ing
stu•pen'dous
stu'pid
stu•pid'i•ty
stu'por
stur'di•ness
stur'dy
stur'geon
stut'ter
stut'ter•er
sty *(pigpen), pl.* sties
sty *also* stye *(inflam-*
mation), pl. sties
also styes

style *(to design)*,
  styled, styl'ing
  ✔ *stile*
styl'ish
styl'ist
sty·lis'tic
styl'ize', -ized',
  -iz'ing
sty'lus *pl.* -lus·es *or*
  -li
sty'mie, -mied,
  -mie·ing *also*
  -my·ing
styp'tic
sty'rene'
sua'sion
suave, suav'er,
  suav'est
suav'i·ty *or*
  suave'ness
sub, subbed,
  sub'bing
sub·al'tern
sub'a·tom'ic
sub'cen'ter
sub'class'
sub·com·mit'tee
sub·com·pact'
sub·con'scious
sub·con'ti·nent
sub·con'tract'
sub·con'trac'tor
sub·cu·ta'ne·ous
sub'di·vide',
  -vid'ed, -vid'ing
sub'di·vi'sion
sub·dom'i·nant

sub·due', -dued',
  -du'ing
sub·fam'i·ly
sub·ge'nus *pl.*
  -gen'er·a
sub'group'
sub'head'
sub·hu'man
sub'ject *adj. & n.*
sub·ject' *v.*
sub·jec'tion
sub·jec'tive
sub'jec·tiv'i·ty
sub·join'
sub'ju·gate',
  -gat'ed, -gat'ing
sub'ju·ga'tion
sub'ju·ga'tor
sub·junc'tive
sub'king'dom
sub'lease', -leased',
  -leas'ing
sub'lease' *n.*
sub'let', -let',
  -let'ting
sub'let' *n.*
sub'li·mate',
  -mat'ed, -mat'ing
sub'li·ma'tion
sub·lime'
sub·lim'i·nal
sub·lim'i·ty
sub'ma·chine'
  gun'
sub'ma·rine'
sub·merge',
  -merged',

  -merg'ing
sub·mer'gence
sub·mer'gi·bil'i·ty
sub·mer'gi·ble
sub·merse',
  -mersed', -mers'ing
sub·mers'i·ble
sub·mer'sion
sub·mis'sion
sub·mis'sive
sub·mit', -mit'ted,
  -mit'ting
sub·mit'tal
sub·or'der
sub·or'di·nate',
  -nat'ed, -nat'ing
sub·or'di·na'tion
sub·orn'
sub·or·na'tion
sub·phy'lum
sub'plot'
sub·poe'na, -naed,
  -na'ing
sub'rou·tine'
sub·scribe',
  -scribed', -scrib'ing
sub·scrib'er
sub'script'
sub·scrip'tion
sub'se·quence
sub'se·quent
sub·serve', -served',
  -serv'ing
sub·ser'vi·ence
sub·ser'vi·ent
sub'set'
sub·side', -sid'ed,

-sid'ing
sub•si'dence
sub•sid'i•ar'y
sub•si•dize', -dized',
  -diz'ing
sub•si•diz'er
sub•si•dy
sub•sist'
sub•sis'tence
sub'soil'
sub•son'ic
sub'spe'cies *pl.* -cies
sub'stance
sub•stan'dard
sub•stan'tial
sub•stan'ti•al'i•ty
sub•stan'ti•ate',
  -at'ed, -at'ing
sub•stan'ti•a'tion
sub'stan•tive
sub•sta'tion
sub'sti•tut'a•bil'i•ty
sub'sti•tut'a•ble
sub'sti•tute',
  -tut'ed, -tut'ing
sub'sti•tu'tion
sub•stra'tum *pl.* -ta
  or -tums
sub•struc'ture
sub•sum'a•ble
sub•sume',
  -sumed', -sum'ing
sub'ter•fuge'
sub•ter•ra'ne•an
sub'text'
sub'ti'tle
sub'tle, sub'tler,

sub'tlest
sub'tle•ty
sub'tly
sub•ton'ic
sub•to'tal, -taled
  also -talled, -tal•ing
  also -tal•ling
sub•tract'
sub•trac'tion
sub•trac'tive
sub•tra•hend'
sub•trop'i•cal
sub•trop'ics
sub'urb'
sub•ur'ban
sub•ur'ban•ite'
sub•ur'bi•a
sub•ver'sion
sub•ver'sive
sub•vert'
sub'way'
suc•ceed'
suc•cess'
suc•cess'ful
suc•ces'sion
suc•ces'sive
suc•ces'sor
suc•cinct'
suc'cor *(relief)*
  ✔ *sucker*
suc'co•tash'
Suc'coth *also*
  Suk'koth
suc'cu•lence *or*
  suc'cu•len•cy
suc'cu•lent
suc•cumb'

such
suck
suck'er *(one that
  sucks, lollipop, dupe)*
  ✔ *succor*
suck'le, -led, -ling
suck'ling
su'cre
su'crose'
suc'tion
Su'da•nese' *pl.*
  -nese'
sud'den
sud'sy
sue, sued, su'ing
suede *also* suède
su'et
suf'fer
suf'fer•a•ble
suf'fer•ance
suf•fice', -ficed',
  -fic'ing
suf•fi'cien•cy
suf•fi'cient
suf'fix
suf'fo•cate', -cat'ed,
  -cat'ing
suf'fo•ca'tion
suf'frage
suf'fra•gette'
suf'fra•gist
suf•fuse', -fused',
  -fus'ing
suf•fu'sion
sug'ar
sug'ar•coat' *v.*
sug'ar•plum'

sug'ar•y
sug•gest'
sug•gest'i•bil'i•ty
sug•gest'i•ble
sug•ges'tion
sug•ges'tive
su'i•cid'al
su'i•cide'
suit *(set of clothes, playing cards, legal action)*
  ✓ *suite*
suit'a•bil'i•ty
suit'a•ble
suit'a•bly
suit'case'
suite *(series of rooms)*
  ✓ *suit, sweet*
suit'or
su'ki•ya'ki
sul'fate'
sul'fide'
sul'fite'
sul'fur *also* sul'phur
sul•fu'ric
sul'fur•ous *also* sul'phur•ous
sulk'y
sul'len
sul'ly, -lied, -ly•ing
sul'tan
sul•tan'a
sul'tan•ate'
sul'try
sum *(to add)*, summed, sum'ming

✓ *some*
su'mac *also* su'mach
Su•me'ri•an
sum'ma cum lau'de
sum•mar'i•ly
sum'ma•ri•za'tion
sum'ma•rize', -rized', -riz'ing
sum'ma•ry *(brief statement)*
  ✓ *summery*
sum•ma'tion
sum'mer
sum'mer•house'
sum'mer•time'
sum'mer•y *(of summer)*
  ✓ *summary*
sum'mit
sum'mon
sum'mons *pl.* -mons•es
sump'tu•ous
sun *(star)*
  ✓ *son*
sun *(to bask in the sun)*, sunned, sun'ning
  ✓ *son*
sun'bathe', -bathed', -bath'ing
sun'beam'
sun'bon'net
sun'burn', -burned' *or* -burnt',

-burn'ing
sun'burst'
sun'dae *(ice cream dessert)*
Sun'day *(day of the week)*
sun'der
sun'di'al
sun'down'
sun'dress'
sun'dries
sun'dry
sun'fish' *pl.* -fish' *or* -fish'es
sun'flow'er
sun'glass'es
sunk'en
sun'light'
sun'lit'
Sun'na
Sun'ni
Sun'nite'
sun'ny *(full of sunshine, cheerful)*
  ✓ *sonny*
sun'rise'
sun'room'
sun'screen'
sun'set'
sun'shade'
sun'shine'
sun'spot'
sun'stroke'
sun'tan'
sun'tanned'
sun'up'
sun'ward *adv. &*

adj.

sun'wards *adv.*

sup, supped,
  sup'ping

su'per

su'per·a·bun'-
  dance

su'per·a·bun'dant

su'per·an'nu·at·ed

su·perb'

su'per·charge'
  -charged',
  -charg'ing

su'per·cil'i·ous

su'per·com·put'er

su'per·con·duc·
  tiv'i·ty

su'per·con·duc'tor

su'per·con'ti·nent

su'per·cool' *v.*

su'per·e'go

su'per·e·rog'a·
  to'ry

su'per·fi'cial

su'per·fi'ci·al'i·ty

su'per·fine'

su'per·flu'i·ty

su·per'flu·ous

su'per·heat'

su'per·high'
  fre'quen·cy

su'per·high'way'

su'per·hu'man

su'per·im·pose',
  -posed', -pos'ing

su'per·im·po·si'-
  tion

su'per·in·tend'

su'per·in·ten'-
  dence

su'per·in·ten'dent

su·pe'ri·or

su·pe'ri·or'i·ty

su·per'la·tive

su'per·man'

su'per·mar'ket

su·per'nal

su'per·nat'u·ral

su'per·no'va *pl.*
  -vae *or* -vas

su'per·nu'mer·ar'y

su'per·pow'er

su'per·sat'u·rate',
  -rat'ed, -rat'ing

su'per·sav'er

su'per·script'

su'per·scrip'tion

su'per·sede',
  -sed'ed, -sed'ing

su'per·sen'si·tive

su'per·son'ic

su'per·star'

su'per·sti'tion

su'per·sti'tious

su'per·store'

su'per·struc'ture

su'per·tank'er

su'per·ton'ic

su'per·vene',
  -vened', -ven'ing

su'per·vise', -vised',
  -vis'ing

su'per·vi'sion

su'per·vi'sor

su'per·vi'so·ry

su·pine'

sup'per

sup·plant'

sup'ple, -pler, -plest

sup'ple·ment

sup'ple·men'ta·ry
  or sup'ple·men'tal

sup'pli·ant

sup'pli·cant

sup'pli·cate',
  -cat'ed, -cat'ing

sup'pli·ca'tion

sup·pli'er

sup·ply', -plied',
  -ply'ing

sup·port'

sup·port'a·ble

sup·por'tive

sup·pos'a·ble

sup·pose', -posed',
  -pos'ing

sup·pos'ed·ly

sup'po·si'tion

sup·pos'i·to'ry

sup·press'

sup·press'er *also*
  sup·pres'sor

sup·press'i·ble

sup·pres'sion

sup'pu·rate',
  -rat'ed, -rat'ing

sup'pu·ra'tion

su'pra·re'nal

su·prem'a·cist

su·prem'a·cy

su·preme'

sur'cease', -ceased',
-ceas'ing
sur'charge',
-charged',
-charg'ing
sur'coat'
surd
sure, sur'er, sur'est
sure'-fire'
sure'-foot'ed *or*
sure'foot'ed
sur'e•ty
surf *(waves)*
✔ *serf*
sur'face, -faced,
-fac•ing
surf'board'
sur'feit
surge *(to move with
gathering force)*,
surged, surg'ing
✔ *serge*
sur'geon
Sur'geon
Gen'er•al *pl.*
Sur'geons
Gen'er•al
sur'ger•y
sur'gi•cal
sur'li•ness
sur'ly
sur•mise', -mised',
-mis'ing
sur•mount'
sur•mount'a•ble
sur'name'

sur•pass'
sur'plice *(robe)*
sur'plus *(excess)*
sur•prise', -prised',
-pris'ing
sur•re'al
sur•re'al•ism
sur•re'al•ist
sur•re'al•is'tic
sur•ren'der
sur'rep•ti'tious
sur'rey *pl.* -reys
sur•ro•ga•cy
sur'ro•gate
sur•round'
sur•round'ings
sur'tax'
sur•veil'lance
sur•vey' *v.*
sur'vey' *pl.* -veys
sur•vey'ing
sur•vey'or
sur•viv'al
sur•viv'al•ist
sur•vive', -vived',
-viv'ing
sur•vi'vor
sus•cep'ti•bil'i•ty
sus•cep'ti•ble
sus•cep'tive
su'shi
sus•pect' *v.*
sus'pect' *n. & adj.*
sus•pend'
sus•pend'ers
sus•pense'

sus•pen'sion
sus•pi'cion
sus•pi'cious
sus•tain'
sus•tain'able
sus'te•nance
su'ture, -tured,
-tur•ing
su'ze•rain
su'ze•rain•ty
svelte, svelt'er,
svelt'est
swab *also* swob,
swabbed *also*
swobbed,
swab'bing *also*
swob'bing
swad'dle, -dled,
-dling
swag
swag'ger
Swa•hi'li *pl.* -li *or*
-lis
swain
swal'low
swal'low•tail'
swal'low-tailed'
swa'mi *pl.* -mis
swamp'land'
swamp'y
swan
swank
swank'y
swan's'-down' *also*
swans'down'
swap *also* swop,

swapped *also*
swopped,
swap'ping *also*
swop'ping
sward *(turf)*
  ✔ *sword*
swarm
swarth'y
swash'buck'ler
swash'buck'ling
swas'ti•ka
swat, swat'ted,
  swat'ting
swatch
swath *also* swathe
  (width, strip)
swathe *(to wrap)*,
  swathed, swath'ing
swat'ter
sway
sway'back'
sway'backed'
swear, swore, sworn,
  swear'ing
sweat, sweat'ed *or*
  sweat, sweat'ing
sweat'er
sweat'pants'
sweat'shirt'
sweat'shop'
sweat'y
swede *(rutabaga)*
Swede *(inhabitant of
  Sweden)*
Swed'ish
sweep, swept,

sweep'ing
sweep'stakes'
sweet *(sugary)*
  ✔ *suite*
sweet'bread'
sweet'bri'er *also*
  sweet'bri'ar
sweet'en
sweet'en•er
sweet'heart'
sweet'ie
sweet'meat'
swell, swelled,
  swelled *or* swol'len,
  swell'ing
swel'ter
swept'back'
swerve, swerved,
  swerv'ing
swift
swig, swigged,
  swig'ging
swill
swim, swam, swum,
  swim'ming
swim'mer
swim'mer•et'
swim'suit'
swim'wear'
swin'dle, -dled,
  -dling
swin'dler
swine *pl.* swine
swine'herd'
swing, swung,
  swing'ing

swin'ish
swipe, swiped,
  swip'ing
swirl
swish
Swiss *pl.* Swiss
Swiss' chard'
Swiss' cheese'
switch
switch'blade'
switch'board'
switch'er
switch'man
switch'o'ver *n.*
switch'yard'
swiv'el, -eled *or*
  -elled, -el•ing *or*
  -el•ling
swoon
swoop
swoosh
sword *(weapon)*
  ✔ *sward*
sword'fish' *pl.* -fish'
  or -fish'es
sword'play'
swords'man
swords'man•ship'
sword'tail'
Syb'a•rite' *also*
  syb'a•rite'
syb'a•rit'ic *also*
  Syb'a•rit'ic
syc'a•more'
syc'o•phan•cy
syc'o•phant

syc'o•phan'tic or
  syc'o•phan'ti•cal
syl•lab'ic
syl•lab'i•ca'tion
syl•lab'i•fi•ca'tion
syl•lab'i•fy' or
  syl•lab'i•cate',
  -fied' or -cat'ed,
  -fy'ing or -cat'ing
syl'la•ble
syl'la•bus pl. -bus•es
  or s-bi'
syl'lo•gism
sylph
syl'van also sil'van
sym•bi'o'sis pl. -ses
sym'bi•ot'ic
sym'bol (sign)
  ✔ cymbal
sym•bol'ic also
  sym•bol'i•cal
sym•bol•ism
sym•bol•i•za'tion
sym•bol•ize', -ized',
  -iz'ing
sym•met'ri•cal also
  sym•met'ric
sym'me•try
sym'pa•thet'ic
sym'pa•thize',
  -thized', -thiz'ing
sym'pa•thiz'er
sym'pa•thy
sym•phon'ic
sym'pho•ny
sym•po'si•um pl.
  -si•ums or -si•a

symp'tom
symp'to•mat'ic
syn'a•gogue' also
  syn'a•gog'
syn'apse'
sync or synch
syn•chron'ic
syn'chro•nic'i•ty
syn'chro•ni•za'-
  tion
syn'chro•nize',
  -nized', -niz'ing
syn'chro•nous
syn'chro•tron'
syn•cli'nal
syn'cline'
syn'co•pate',
  -pat'ed, -pat'ing
syn'co•pa'tion
syn'co•pe
syn'cre•tism
syn'cre•tize',
  -tized', -tiz'ing
syn'di•cate',
  -cat'ed, -cat'ing
syn'di•ca'tion
syn'drome'
syn'er•gism
syn'er•gis'tic
syn'er•gy
syn'fu'el
syn'od
syn'o•nym'
syn•on'y•mous
syn•on'y•my
syn•op'sis pl. -ses'
syn•op'size',

-sized', -siz'ing
syn•tac'tic or
  syn•tac'ti•cal
syn'tax'
syn'the•sis pl. -ses'
syn'the•size',
  -sized', -siz'ing
syn'the•siz'er
syn•thet'ic
syph'i•lis
syph'i•lit'ic
Syr'i•an
sy•rin'ga
sy•ringe'
syr'inx' pl.
  sy•rin'ges or
  syr'inx'es
syr'up also sir'up
syr'up•y
sys'tem
sys•tem•at'ic also
  sys•tem•at'i•cal
sys'tem•a•ti•za'tion
sys'tem•a•tize',
  -tized', -tiz'ing
sys•tem'ic
sys'to•le
sys•tol'ic

T

tab, tabbed, tab'bing
tab'ard
tab'bou•leh
tab'by
tab'er•na•cle

ta′ble, -bled, -bling
tab•leau′ *pl.* -leaux′
 or -leaus′
ta′ble•cloth′
ta′ble•land′
ta′ble•spoon′
ta′ble•spoon•ful′
tab′let
ta′ble•top′
ta′ble•ware′
tab′loid′
ta•boo′ *also* ta•bu′
 pl. -boos′ *also* -bus′
ta′bor
tab′u•lar
tab′u•late′, -lat′ed,
 -lat′ing
tab′u•la′tion
tab′u•la′tor
ta•chom′e•ter
tac′it
tac′i•turn′
tac′i•tur′ni•ty
tack
tack′le, -led, -ling
tack′ler
tack′y
ta′co *pl.* -cos
tac′o•nite′
tact
tact′ful
tac′tic
tac′ti•cal
tac•ti′cian
tac′tile
tact′less
tad′pole′

taf′fe•ta
taf′fy
tag, tagged, tag′ging
Ta•ga′log *pl.* -log *or*
 -logs
Ta•hi′tian
tail *(hind part)*
 ✔ *tale*
tail *(to follow)*
 ✔ *tale*
tail′board′
tail′coat′
tail′gate′, -gat′ed,
 -gat′ing
tail′light′
tai′lor
tail′pipe′
tail′spin′
Tai′no *pl.* -no *or*
 -nos
taint
take, took, tak′en,
 tak′ing
take′down′ *adj. & n.*
take′off′ *n.*
take′out′ *also*
 take′-out′ *n.*
take′o′ver *also*
 take′-o′ver *n.*
tak′er
talc
tal′cum
tale *(story)*
 ✔ *tail*
tale′bear′er
tal′ent
tal′ent•ed

tale′tell′er
tal′is•man
tal′is•man′ic
talk
talk′a•tive
talk′back′ *n.*
talk′ie *(movie)*
 ✔ *talky*
talk′ing-to′ *pl.* -tos′
talk′y *(talkative)*
 ✔ *talkie*
tall
tal′lith *pl.* -liths *or*
 tal•lith′im
tal′low
tal′ly, -lied, -ly•ing
tal′ly•ho′
Tal′mud
Tal•mu′dic *also*
 Tal•mu′di•cal
tal′on
ta′lus *(bone),* *pl.* -li′
ta′lus *(debris),* *pl.*
 -lus•es
tam
ta•ma′le
tam′a•rack′
tam′a•rind′
tam′a•risk′
tam′bour′
tam′bou•rine′
tame, tam′er,
 tam′est
tame, tamed,
 tam′ing
tam′er
Tam′il *pl.* -il *or* -ils

tam'-o'-shan'ter

tamp

tam'per (to interfere)

tamp'er (neutron
  reflector)

tam'pon'

tan, tanned,
  tan'ning

tan, tan'ner,
  itan'nest

tan'a•ger

Ta•nakh'

tan'bark'

tan'dem

tang

tan'ge•lo' pl. -los'

tan'gent

tan•gen'tial

tan'ger•ine'

tan'gi•bil'i•ty

tan'gi•ble

tan'gi•bly

tan'gle, -gled, -gling

tan'go pl. -gos

tan'go, -goed,
  -go•ing

tang'y

tank'ard

tank'er

tan'ner

tan'ner•y

tan'nic

tan'nin

tan'ning

tan'sy

tan'ta•lite'

tan'ta•lize', -lized',

-liz'ing

tan'ta•lum

tan'ta•mount'

tan'trum

Tao'ism

Tao'ist

tap, tapped,
  tap'ping

ta'pa

tap'-dance',
  -danced', -danc'ing

tap' danc'er

tape, taped, tap'ing

ta'per (candle, to
  diminish)
  ✔ tapir

tape'-re•cord' v.

tape' re•cord'er

tap'es•try

tape'worm'

tap'i•o'ca

ta'pir (animal)
  ✔ taper

tap'root'

taps

tar, tarred, tar'ring

tar'an•tel'la

ta•ran'tu•la pl. -las
  or -lae'

tar'di•ness

tar'dy

tare (weed, weight)
  ✔ tear

tar'get

tar'iff

tar'mac'

tar'nish

ta'ro (plant), pl. -ros

tar'ot (card)

tarp

tar'pa'per

tar'pau•lin

tar'pon pl. -pon or
  -pons

tar'ra•gon'

tar'ry (to delay),
  -ried, -ry•ing

tar'ry (like tar)

tar'sal

tar'sus pl. -si

tart

tar'tan

tar'tar (deposit on
  the teeth, acid
  compound, violent
  person)

Tar'tar also Ta'tar
  (people)

tar•tar'ic

tar'tar sauce'

task

task'mas'ter

Tas•ma'ni•an

tas'sel, -seled or
  -selled, -sel•ing or
  -sel•ling

taste, tast'ed,
  tast'ing

taste'ful (showing
  good taste)
  ✔ tasty

taste'less

tast'y (having good
  flavor)

✔ *tasteful*

tat, tat'ted, tat'ting

tat'ter

tat'tle, -tled, -tling

tat'tler

tat'tle•tale'

tat•too' *pl.* -toos'

tat•too', -tooed',
  -too'ing

tau *(Greek letter)*
  ✔ *taw*

taunt

taupe *(color)*
  ✔ *tope*

taut

tau•to•log'i•cal *or*
  tau'to•log'ic

tau•tol'o•gy

tav'ern

taw *(marble)*
  ✔ *tau*

taw'dry

taw'ny

tax'a•ble

tax•a'tion

tax'-de•duct'i•ble

tax'-ex•empt'

tax'i *pl.* -is *or* -ies

tax'i, -ied, -i•ing *or*
  -y•ing

tax'i•cab'

tax'i•der'mist

tax'i•der'my

tax'i•me'ter

tax•o•nom'ic *also*
  tax'o•nom'i•cal

tax•on'o•my

tax'pay'er

T'-ball' *also*
  tee'-ball'

tea *(beverage)*
  ✔ *tee, ti*

teach, taught,
  teach'ing

teach'a•ble

teach'er

tea'cup'

tea'house'

teak

tea'ket'tle

teal *pl.* teal *or* teals

team *(group)*
  ✔ *teem*

team'mate'

team'ster

team'work'

tea'pot'

tear *(to pull apart)*,
  tore, torn, tear'ing
  ✔ *tare*

tear *(drop of liquid)*
  ✔ *tier*

tear'drop'

tear'ful

tear'jerk'er

tea'room'

tease, teased,
  teas'ing

tea'sel

tea'spoon'

tea'spoon•ful'

teat

tea'time'

tech•ne'ti•um

tech'ni•cal

tech'ni•cal'i•ty

tech•ni'cian

tech•nique'

tech'no•log'i•cal
  also tech'no•log'ic

tech•nol'o•gist

tech•nol'o•gy

ted'dy bear' *also*
  Ted'dy bear'

Te' De'um

te'di•ous

te'di•um

tee *(small peg)*
  ✔ *tea, ti*

teem *(to abound)*
  ✔ *team*

teen'age' *or* teen'-
  age' *also* teen'aged'
  or teen'-aged'

teen'ag'er *also*
  teen'-ag'er

tee'ny *also* teen'sy

tee'ter

tee'ter-tot'ter

teethe, teethed,
  teeth'ing

tee'to'tal•er *or*
  tee'to'tal•ler

tek'tite'

tel'e•cast', -cast' *or*
  -cast'ed, -cast'ing

tel'e•com•mu'ni•
  ca'tion

tel'e•com•mut'ing

tel'e•gram'

tel'e•graph'

te·leg'ra·pher *or*
  te·leg'ra·phist
tel'e·graph'ic *also*
  tel'e·graph'i·cal
te·leg'ra·phy
tel'e·ki·ne'sis
tel'e·ki·net'ic
tel'e·mar'ket·ing
tel'e·me'ter
tel'em'e·try
tel'e·path'ic
te·lep'a·thy
tel'e·phone',
  -phoned',
  -phon'ing
tel'e·phon'ic
te·leph'o·ny
tel'e·pho'to·
  graph'
tel'e·pho·tog'ra·
  phy
tel'e·pho'to lens'
tel'e·scope',
  -scoped', -scop'ing
tel'e·scop'ic
tel'e·thon'
tel'e·type'writ·er
tel'e·vise', -vised',
  -vis'ing
tel'e·vi'sion
tell, told, tell'ing
tell'er
tell'tale'
tel'lu·ride'
tel·lu'ri·um
tel'o·phase'
te·mer'i·ty

tem'per
tem'per·a
tem'per·a·ment
tem'per·a·men'tal
tem'per·ance
tem'per·ate
tem'per·a·ture
tem'pered
tem'pest
tem·pes'tu·ous
tem'plate *also*
  tem'plet
tem'ple
tem'po *pl.* -pos *or*
  -pi
tem'po·ral
tem'po·rar'y
tem'po·ri·za'tion
tem'po·rize',
  -rized', -riz'ing
temp·ta'tion
tempt'ing
tem'pu·ra
ten
ten'a·bil'i·ty
ten'a·ble
te·na'cious
te·nac'i·ty
ten'an·cy
ten'ant
tend
ten·den·cy
ten·den'tious *also*
  ten·den'cious
ten'der *(fragile)*
ten'der *(to offer)*
tend'er *(one that*

  tends)
ten'der·foot' *pl.*
  -foots' *or* -feet'
ten'der·heart'ed
ten'der·ize', -ized',
  -iz'ing
ten'der·iz'er
ten'der·loin'
ten'don
ten'dril
ten'e·ment
ten'et
ten'-gal'lon hat'
Ten'nes·se'an
ten'nis
ten'on
ten'or
ten'pin'
tense, tens'er,
  tens'est
tense, tensed,
  tens'ing
ten'sile
ten'sion
ten'sor
tent
ten'ta·cle
ten'ta·tive
ten'ter
ten'ter·hook'
tenth
ten'u·ous
ten'ure
te'pee *also* tee'pee
tep'id
te·qui'la
ter'a·byte'

ter'bi•um
ter'i•ya'ki
term
ter'ma•gant
ter'mi•na•ble
ter'mi•nal
ter'mi•nate', -nat'ed, -nat'ing
ter'mi•na'tion
ter'mi•na'tive
ter'mi•na'tor
ter'mi•nol'o•gy
ter'mi•nus *pl.* -nus•es *or* -ni'
ter'mite'
tern *(bird)*
  ✔ *turn*
ter'race, -raced, -rac•ing
ter'ra cot'ta *n.*
ter'ra-cot'ta *adj.*
ter'ra fir'ma
ter•rain'
ter'ra•pin
ter•rar'i•um *pl.* -i•ums *or* -i•a
ter•res'tri•al
ter'ri•ble
ter'ri•bly
ter'ri•er
ter•rif'ic
ter'ri•fy', -fied', -fy'ing
ter'ri•to'ri•al
ter'ri•to'ri•al'i•ty
ter'ri•to'ry
ter'ror

ter'ror•ism
ter'ror•ist
ter'ror•ize', -ized', -iz'ing
ter'ry
terse, ters'er, ters'est
ter'ti•ar'y *(third)*
Ter'ti•ar'y *(geologic period)*
tes'se•late', -lat'ed, -at'ing
tes'se•la'tion
test
tes'ta•ment
tes'tate'
tes'ta'tor
test'-drive', -drove', -driv'en, -driv'ing
test'er *(one that tests)*
tes'ter *(canopy)*
tes'ti•cle
tes'ti•fy', -fied', -fy'ing
tes'ti•mo'ni•al
tes'ti•mo'ny
tes'tis *pl.* -tes
tes•tos'ter•one'
test'-tube' ba'by
tes'ty
tet'a•nus
tetch'y *also* tech'y
tête'-à-tête'
teth'er
teth'er•ball'
Te'ton' *pl.* -ton' *or* -tons'

tet'ra
tet'ra•cy'cline'
tet'rad'
tet'ra•he'dron *pl.* -drons *or* -dra
te•tram'e•ter
tet'rarch'
tet'rar'chy
Teu'ton
Teu•ton'ic
Tex'an
text
text'book'
tex'tile'
tex'tu•al
tex'tur•al
tex'ture
Thai *pl.* Thai *or* Thais
thal'a•mus *pl.* -mi'
thal'li•um
thal'lo•phyte'
thal'lus *pl.* -li *or* -lus•es
than
thane
thank'ful
thank'less
thanks
thanks•giv'ing
that *pl.* those
thatch
thaw
the *article*
  ✔ *thee*
the'a•ter *or* the'a•tre

the·at′ri·cal *also*
  the·at′ric
the·at′rics
thee *pron.*
  ✔ *the*
theft
their *possessive form*
  of they
  ✔ *there, they're*
theirs
them
the·mat′ic
theme
them·selves′
then
thence
thence·forth′
thence·for′ward
  also thence·
  for′wards
the·oc′ra·cy
the′o·crat′ic *or*
  the′o·crat′i·cal
the′o·lo′gi·an
the′o·log′i·cal *also*
  the′o·log′ic
the·ol′o·gy
the′o·rem
the′o·ret′i·cal *also*
  the′o·ret′ic
the′o·re·ti′cian
the′o·rist
the′o·rize′, -rized′,
  -riz′ing
the′o·ry
the′o·soph′i·cal
the·os′o·phist

the·os′o·phy
ther′a·peu′tic *also*
  ther′a·peu′ti·cal
ther′a·peu′tics
ther′a·pist
ther′a·py
there *(at that place)*
  ✔ *their, they're*
there′a·bouts′ *also*
  there′a·bout′
there·af′ter
there·at′
there·by′
there′fore′
there·from′
there·in′
there·of′
there·on′
there·to′
there′to·fore′
there·un′der
there·un′to′
there·up·on′
there·with′
ther′mal
ther′mic
therm′i·on
ther′mo·cou′ple
ther′mo·dy·nam′ic
ther′mo·e·lec′tric
  also ther′mo·e·lec′-
  tri·cal
ther′mo·e·lec·tric′-
  i·ty
ther′mo·graph′
ther·mom′e·ter
ther′mo·nu′cle·ar

ther′mo·plas′tic
ther′mo·sphere′
ther′mo·stat′
the·sau′rus *pl.*
  -sau′rus·es *or*
  -sau′ri
these *sing.* this
the′sis *pl.* -ses
thes′pi·an
the′ta
thew
they
they're *contraction of*
  they are
  ✔ *their, there*
thi′a·mine *also*
  thi′a·min
thick
thick′en
thick′en·er
thick′et
thick′set′
thick′-skinned′
thief *pl.* thieves
thieve, thieved,
  thiev′ing
thiev′er·y
thigh′bone′
thim′ble
thin, thin′ner,
  thin′nest
thin, thinned,
  thin′ning
thine
thing
thing′a·ma·bob′ *or*
  thing′u·ma·bob′

also thing'um•bob'
thing'a•ma•jig' *also*
  thing'u•ma•jig'
think, thought,
  think'ing
think'a•ble
thin'-skinned'
third'-class' *adv. &*
  adj.
third'-de•gree'
  burn'
thirst'y
thir•teen'
thir•teenth'
thir'ti•eth
thir'ty
this *pl.* these
this'tle
this'tle•down'
thith'er
thole' pin'
thong
tho•rac'ic
tho'rax' *pl.* -rax'es
  or -ra•ces'
tho'ri•um
thorn'y
thor'ough
thor'ough•bred'
thor'ough•fare'
thor'ough•go'ing
those *sing.* that
thou
though
thought
thought'ful
thought'less

thou'sand
thou'sandth
thrash
thread
thread'bare'
thread'y
threat
threat'en
three
three'-
  di•men'sion•al
three'-piece' *adj.*
three'-ply' *adj.*
three'score'
three'some
thren'o•dy
thresh'er
thresh'old'
thrice
thrift'i•ly
thrift'y
thrill'er
thrive, thrived *or*
  throve, thrived *or*
  thriv'en, thriv'ing
throat
throat'y
throb, throbbed,
  throb'bing
throe *(pang)*
  ✔ *throw*
throm'bin
throm•bo'sis *pl.*
  -ses
throm'bus *pl.* -bi
throne
throng

throt'tle, -tled,
  -tling
through
through•out'
throw *(to hurl)*,
  threw, thrown,
  throw'ing
  ✔ *throe*
throw'a•way' *adj.*
  & n.
throw'back'
thrum, thrummed,
  thrum'ming
thrush
thrust
thru'way' *also*
  through'way'
thud, thud'ded,
  thud'ding
thug
thu'li•um
thumb'nail'
thumb'screw'
thumb'tack'
thump
thun'der
thun'der•bird'
thun'der•bolt'
thun'der•clap'
thun'der•cloud'
thun'der•head'
thun'der•ous
thun'der•show'er
thun'der•storm'
thun'der•struck'
Thurs'day
thus

thwack
thwart
thy
thyme *(plant)*
  ✓ *time*
thy'mine'
thy'mus *pl.* -mus•es
thy'roid'
thy•rox'ine' *also*
  thy•rox'in
thy•self'
ti *(musical tone)*
  ✓ *tea, tee*
ti•ar'a
Ti•bet'an
tib'i•a *pl.* -i•ae' *or*
  -i•as
tic *(muscle contrac-*
  tion)
tick *(clicking sound,*
  mark, arachnid,
  cloth case)
tick'bird'
tick'er
tick'et
tick'ing
tick'le, -led, -ling
tick'ler
tick'lish
tick'tack'toe' *also*
  tick'-tack'-toe'
tid'al
tid'bit'
tid'dly•winks'
tide, tid'ed, tid'ing
tide'land'
tide'wa'ter

ti'di•ly
tid'ings
ti'dy, -died, -dy•ing
tie, tied, ty'ing
tie'back' n.
tie'break'er
tie'-dye', -dyed',
  -dye'ing
tie'-in' n.
tier *(row)*
  ✓ *tear*
tie'-up' n.
tiff
ti'ger
ti'ger-eye' *also*
  ti'ger's-eye'
tight
tight'en
tight'fist'ed
tight'lipped' *also*
  tight'-lipped'
tight'rope'
tights
tight'wad'
ti'gress
til'de
tile, tiled, til'ing
till *(to prepare land)*
till *(until)*
till *(drawer, glacial*
  deposit)
till'a•ble
till'age
till'er *(one that tills)*
til'ler *(lever)*
tilt
tilth

tim'ber *(trees)*
  ✓ *timbre*
tim'ber•land'
tim'ber•line'
tim'bre *(sound*
  quality)
  ✓ *timber*
tim'brel
time *(to clock),*
  timed, tim'ing
  ✓ *thyme*
time'card'
timed'-re•lease'
  also time'-re•lease'
time'-hon'ored
time'keep'er
time'-lapse' *adj.*
time'less
time'ly
time'-out' *also*
  time' out'
time'piece'
tim'er
time'sav'ing
time'serv'er *also*
  time'-serv'er
time'-share'
time'-shar'ing
time'ta'ble
time'-test'ed
time'worn'
tim'id
ti•mid'i•ty
tim'or•ous
tim'o•thy
tim'pa•ni *also*
  tym'pa•ni

tin, tinned, tin'ning
tinc'ture
tin'der
tin'der•box'
tine
tin'foil' *also*
   tin' foil'
ting *(to make a light*
   metallic sound),
   tinged, ting'ing
tinge *(to tint),*
   tinged, tinge'ing *or*
   ting'ing
tin'gle, -gled, -gling
tin'ker
tin'kle, -kled, -kling
tin'ny
tin'-plate', -plat'ed,
   -plat'ing
tin'sel, -seled *or*
   -selled, -sel•ing *or*
   -sel•ling
tin'smith'
tint
tin'tin•nab'u•la'-
   tion
ti'ny
tip, tipped, tip'ping
tip'-off' *n.*
tip'per
tip'pet
tip'ple, -pled, -pling
tip'pler
tip'sy
tip'toe', -toed',
   -toe'ing
tip'top'

ti'rade'
tire, tired, tir'ing
tire'less
tire'some
'tis
tis'sue
tit
ti'tan *(great person)*
Ti'tan *(giant)*
ti•tan'ic
ti•ta'ni•um
tithe, tithed,
   tith'ing
ti'tian
tit'il•late', -lat'ed,
   -lat'ing
tit'il•la'tion
ti'tle, -tled, -tling
tit'mouse'
tit'ter
tit'tle
tit'tle-tat'tle, -tled,
   -tling
tit'u•lar
tiz'zy
Tlin'git *pl.* -git *or*
   -gits
to *(toward)*
   ✔ too, two
toad *(animal)*
   ✔ toed
toad'stool'
toad'y, -ied, -y•ing
toast
toast'er
toast'mas'ter
toast'mis'tress

to•bac'co *pl.* -cos *or*
   -coes
to•bac'co•nist
to•bog'gan
toc•ca'ta
toc'sin *(alarm)*
   ✔ toxin
to•day'
tod'dle, -dled,
   -dling
tod'dler
tod'dy
to-do' *pl.* -dos'
toe *(digit)*
   ✔ tow
toed *(having toes)*
   ✔ toad
toe'hold'
toe'nail'
tof'fee
to'fu
tog, togged, tog'ging
to'ga
to•geth'er
tog'gle, -gled, -gling
toil *(labor)*
toile *(fabric)*
toi'let
toi'let•ry
toi•lette'
toil'some
to'ken
to'ken•ism
tol'er•a•ble
tol'er•a•bly
tol'er•ance
tol'er•ant

tol'er•ate', -at'ed,
  -at'ing
tol'er•a'tion
toll'booth'
toll'gate'
Tol'tec' *pl.* -tec' or
  -tecs'
Tol•tec'an
tol'u•ene'
tom'a•hawk'
to•ma'to *pl.* -toes
tomb
tom'boy'
tomb'stone'
tom'cat'
tome
tom•fool'er•y
to•mor'row
tom'tit'
tom'-tom' *also*
  tam'-tam'
ton (*unit of weight*)
  ✓ tun
ton'al
to•nal'i•ty
tone, toned, ton'ing
Ton'gan
tongs
tongue, tongued,
  tongu'ing
tongue'-in-cheek'
tongue'-lash'ing
tongue'-tied'
ton'ic
to•night'
ton'nage
ton'sil

ton'sil•lec'to•my
ton'sil•li'tis
ton•so'ri•al
ton'sure, -sured,
  -sur'ing
ton'tine'
too (*also*)
  ✓ to, two
tool (*device*)
  ✓ tulle
tool'box'
tool'ing
toot
tooth *pl.* teeth
tooth'ache'
tooth'brush'
toothed
tooth'paste'
tooth'pick'
tooth'pow'der
tooth'some
tooth'y
top, topped,
  top'ping
to'paz'
top'coat'
top'drawer' *adj.*
tope (*to drink*),
  toped, top'ing
  ✓ taupe
top'flight' *adj.*
top•gal'lant
top'-heav'y
to'pi•ar'y
top'ic
top'i•cal
top'knot'

top'mast
top'most'
top'notch'
to•pog'ra•pher
top'o•graph'ic *or*
  top'o•graph'i•cal
to•pog'ra•phy
top'o•log'ic *or*
  top'o•log'i•cal
to•pol'o•gy
top'ping
top'ple, -pled,
  -pling
top'sail
top'-se'cret *adj.*
top'side'
top'soil'
top'spin'
top'stitch'
top'sy-tur'vy
toque
To'rah *also* to'rah
torch
tor'e•a•dor'
tor'ment' *n.*
tor•ment' *v.*
tor•men'tor *also*
  tor•ment'er
tor•na'do *pl.* -does
  or -dos
tor•pe'do *pl.* -does
tor'pid
tor'por
torque
tor'rent
tor•ren'tial
tor'rid

tor'sion

tor'so *pl.* -sos *or* -si

tort *(wrongful act)*

torte *(cake)*

tor•til'la

tor'toise

tor'toise•shell'

tor'tu•ous *(winding)*
   ✔ *torturous*

tor'ture, -tured,
   -tur•ing

tor'tur•ous *(painful)*
   ✔ *tortuous*

To'ry

toss'up' *n.*

tos•ta'da *or*
   tos•ta'do *pl.* -das *or*
   -dos

tot

to'tal, -taled *or*
   -talled, -tal•ing *or*
   -tal•ling

to•tal'i•tar'i•an

to•tal'i•tar'i•an•
   ism

to•tal'i•ty

tote, tot'ed, tot'ing

to'tem

to•tem'ic

tot'ter

tou'can'

touch

touch'-and-go'
   adj.

touch'back' *n.*

touch'down' *n.*

tou•ché'

touch'ing

touch'-me-not'

touch'stone'

touch'-tone'

touch'-type',
   -typed', -typ'ing

touch'-up' *n.*

touch'y

tough *(rugged)*
   ✔ *tuff*

tough'en

tou•pee'

tour

tour' de force' *pl.*
   tours' de force'

tour'ism

tour'ist

tour'ma•line *also*
   tur'ma•line

tour'na•ment

tour'ne•dos' *pl.*
   -dos'

tour'ney *pl.* -neys

tour'ni•quet

tou'sle, -sled, -sling

tout

tow *(to pull along)*
   ✔ *toe*

tow *(flax)*
   ✔ *toe*

to•ward' *also*
   to•wards'

tow'el, -eled *or*
   -elled, -el•ing *or*
   -el•ling

tow'er

tow'head'

tow'head•ed

tow'hee

town

towns'folk'

town'ship'

towns'peo'ple

tow'path'

tox•e'mi•a

tox'ic

tox•ic'i•ty

tox'i•co•log'i•cal *or*
   tox'i•co•log'ic

tox'i•col'o•gist

tox'i•col'o•gy

tox'in *(poison)*
   ✔ *tocsin*

toy

trace, traced,
   trac'ing

trace'a•ble

trac'er

trac'er•y

tra'che•a *pl.*
   -che•ae' *or* -che•as

tra'che•ot'o•my

tra•cho'ma

track *(path)*
   ✔ *tract*

track'-and-field'
   adj.

track'ball'

tract *(area, pamphlet)*
   ✔ *track*

trac'ta•ble

trac'ta•bly

trac'tion

trac'tor

trade, trad'ed,
  trad'ing
trade'-in' *n.*
trade'mark'
trade'off' *n.*
trades'man
trades'peo'ple
tra·di'tion
tra·di'tion·al
tra·duce', -duced',
  -duc'ing
traf'fic, -ficked,
  -fick·ing
traf'fick·er
tra·ge'di·an
tra·ge'di·enne'
trag'e·dy
trag'ic
trag'i·cal
trag'i·com'e·dy
trag'i·com'ic *or*
  trag'i·com'i·cal
trail'blaz'er
trail'er
train
train·ee'
train'er
train'load'
train'man
traipse, traipsed,
  traips'ing
trait
trai'tor
trai'tor·ous
tra·jec'to·ry
tram
tram'mel, -meled *or*

-melled, -mel·ing
  or -mel·ling
tramp
tram'ple, -pled,
  -pling
tram'po·line'
trance
tran'quil
tran'quil·ize' *also*
  tran'quil·lize',
  -quil·ized' *also*
  -quil·lized',
  -quil·iz'ing *also*
  -quil·liz'ing
tran'quil·iz'er
tran·quil'li·ty *or*
  tran·quil'i·ty
trans·act'
trans·ac'tion
trans·at·lan'tic
tran·scend'
tran·scen'dent
tran'scen·den'tal
trans'con·ti·nen'-
  tal
tran·scribe',
  -scribed', -scrib'ing
tran'script'
tran·scrip'tion
tran'sept'
trans·fer', -ferred',
  -fer'ring
trans'fer *also*
  trans·fer'al *n.*
trans·fer'a·ble
trans·fer'ence
trans·fig'u·ra'tion

trans·fig'ure, -ured,
  -ur·ing
trans·fi'nite'
trans·fix'
trans·form' *v.*
trans'form' *n.*
trans'for·ma'tion
trans'for·ma'tion·
  al
trans·form'a·tive
trans·form'er
trans·fuse', -fused',
  -fus'ing
trans·fu'sion
trans·gress'
trans·gres'sion
trans·gres'sor
tran'sience *or*
  tran'sien·cy
tran'sient
tran·sis'tor
tran·sis'tor·ize',
  -ized', -iz'ing
tran'sit
tran·si'tion
tran·si'tion·al
tran'si·tive
tran'si·to'ry
trans·lat'a·ble
trans·late', -lat'ed,
  -lat'ing
trans·la'tion
trans·la'tor
trans·lit'er·ate',
  -at'ed, -at'ing
trans·lit'er·a'tion
trans·lu'cence *or*

trans•lu'cen•cy
trans•lu'cent
trans•mi'grate',
-grat'ed, -grat'ing
trans•mi•gra'tion
trans•mis'si•ble
trans•mis'sion
trans•mit',
-mit'ted, -mit'ting
trans•mit'ta•ble
trans•mit'tal
trans•mit'ter
trans•mut'a•ble
trans•mu•ta'tion
trans•mute',
-mut'ed, -mut'ing
trans•o•ce•an'ic
tran'som
tran•son'ic
trans•pa•cif'ic
trans•par'en•cy
    also trans•par'ence
trans•par'ent
tran•spi•ra'tion
tran•spire', -spired',
-spir'ing
trans•plant' *v.*
trans•plant' *n.*
trans•plan•ta'tion
trans•po'lar
trans•port' *v.*
trans•port' *n.*
trans•por•ta'tion
trans•pos'a•ble
trans•pose',
-posed', -pos'ing
trans•po•si'tion

trans•sex'u•al
trans•ship',
-shipped',
-ship'ping
trans•ship'ment
tran•sub•stan'ti•
ate', -at'ed, -at'ing
tran•sub•stan'ti•
a'tion
trans•u•ran'ic
trans•ver'sal
trans•verse'
trans•ves'tite'
trap, trapped,
trap'ping
tra•peze'
tra•pe'zi•um *pl.*
-zi•ums *or* -zi•a
trap'e•zoid'
trap'e•zoi'dal
trap'per
trap'ping
Trap'pist
trap'shoot'ing
trash'i•ness
trash'y
trau'ma *pl.* -mas *or*
-ma•ta
trau•mat'ic
trau'ma•tize',
-tized', -tiz'ing
tra•vail'
trav'el, -eled *or*
-elled, -el'ing *or*
-el•ling
trav'el•er *or*
trav'el•ler

trav'e•logue' *also*
trav'e•log'
tra•verse', -versed',
-vers'ing
trav'erse *n.*
trav'es•ty, -tied,
-ty•ing
tra•vois' *pl.* -vois'
also -vois'es
trawl'er
tray
treach'er•ous
treach'er•y
trea'cle
tread, trod, trod'den
or trod, tread'ing
tread'le, -led, -ling
tread'mill'
trea'son
trea'son•a•ble
trea'son•ous
treas'ure, -ured,
-ur•ing
treas'ur•er
treas'ure-trove'
treas'ur•y
treat
treat'a•ble
trea'tise
treat'ment
trea'ty
treb'le, -led, -ling
treb'ly
tree, treed, tree'ing
tree'-of-heav'en
tree'top'
tre'foil'

trek, trekked,
  trek'king
trel'lis
trem'a•tode'
trem'ble, -bled,
  -bling
tre•men'dous
trem'o•lo' *pl.* -los'
trem'or
trem'u•lous
trench
trench'an•cy
trench'ant
trend'y
tre•pan', -panned',
  -pan'ning
trep'a•na'tion
treph'i•na'tion
tre•phine',
  -phined', -phin'ing
trep'i•da'tion
tres'pass
tres'pass•er
tress
tres'tle
tri'ad'
tri'age'
tri'al
tri•an'gle
tri•an'gu•lar
tri•an'gu•late',
  -lat'ed, -lat'ing
tri•an'gu•la'tion
Tri•as'sic
tri•ath'lon
trib'al
tribe

trib'u•la'tion
tri•bu'nal
trib'une'
trib'u•tar'y
trib'ute
trice
tri'ceps' *pl.* -ceps'es
  also -ceps'
tri•cer'a•tops'
tri•chi'na *pl.* -nae *or*
  -nas
trich'i•no'sis
trick'er•y
trick'le, -led, -ling
trick'ster
trick'y
tri'col'or
tri'cot
tri•cus'pid
tri•cus'pi•dal *or*
  tri•cus'pi•date'
tri'cy'cle
tri'dent
tried
tri•en'ni•al
tri'fle, -fled, -fling
tri•fo'cal
tri•fo'li•ate *also*
  tri•fo'li•at'ed
tri•fur'cate *also*
  tri•fur'cat'ed
trig'ger
trig'o•no•met'ric *or*
  trig'o•no•met'ri•cal
trig'o•nom'e•try
trill
tril'lion

tril'lionth
tril'li•um
tri•lo'bate'
tri'lo•bite'
tri'lo•gy
trim, trimmed,
  trim'ming
trim, trim'mer,
  trim'mest
tri•mes'ter
tri•ni'tro•tol'u•ene'
trin'i•ty
trin'ket
tri•no'mi•al
tri'o *pl.* -os
tri'ode'
tri•ox'ide'
trip, tripped,
  trip'ping
tri•par'tite'
tripe
tri'ple, -pled, -pling
trip'let
trip'li•cate *adj.*
trip'li•cate', -cat'ed,
  -cat'ing
tri'pod'
trip'tych
tri'sect'
tri•sec'tion
trite, trit'er, trit'est
trit'i•um
tri'ton
tri'umph
tri•um'phal
tri•um'phant
tri•um'vir *pl.* -virs

or -vi•ri'
tri•um'vi•rate
tri•va'lent
triv'et
triv'i•a
triv'i•al
triv'i•al'i•ty
tRNA
tro'che *(lozenge)*
tro'chee *(metrical foot in poetry)*
trog'lo•dyte'
Tro'jan
troll
trol'ley *pl.* -leys
trol'lop
trom•bone'
trom•bon'ist
troop *(group, group of soldiers)*
   ✔ troupe
troop'er
troop'ship'
trope
tro'phy
trop'ic
trop'i•cal
tro'pism
tro'po•pause'
tro'po•sphere'
trot, trot'ted, trot'ting
troth
trot'ter
trou'ba•dour'
trou'ble, -led, -ling
trou'ble•mak'er

trou'ble•shoot'er
trou'ble•some
trough
trounce, trounced, trounc'ing
troupe *(group of actors)*
   ✔ troop
trou'sers
trous'seau *pl.* -seaux *or* -seaus
trout *pl.* trout *or* trouts
trow'el
troy
tru'an•cy
tru'ant
truce
truck'er
truck'le, -led, -ling
truck'load'
truc'u•lence
truc'u•lent
trudge, trudged, trudg'ing
true, tru'er, tru'est
true, trued, tru'ing *or* true'ing
true'-blue'
true'-life' *adj.*
true'love' *n.*
truf'fle
tru'ism
tru'ly
trump'er•y
trum'pet
trum'pet•er

trun'cate', -cat'ed, -cat'ing
trun•ca'tion
trun'cheon
trun'dle, -dled, -dling
trunk
truss
trust
trus•tee' *(guardian)*
   ✔ trusty
trust'ful
trust'wor'thy
trust'y *(dependable)*
   ✔ trustee
truth
truth'ful
try, tried, try'ing
try'out' *n.*
try•pan'o•some'
tryp'sin
tryst
tset'se fly'
T'-shirt' *also* tee' shirt'
T'-square'
tsu•na'mi *pl.* -mis
tu'ba
tub'by
tube
tu'ber
tu'ber•cle
tu•ber'cu•lar
tu•ber'cu•late'
tu•ber'cu•lin
tu•ber'cu•lo'sis
tu•ber'cu•lous

tube′rose′

tu′ber•ous

tub′ing

tu′bu•lar

tu′bule

tuck′er

Tu′dor

Tues′day

tu′fa

tuff *(rock)*
  ✔ *tough*

tuft

tug, tugged,
  tug′ging

tug′boat′

tu•i′tion

tu•la•re′mi•a

tu′lip

tulle *(net)*
  ✔ *tool*

tum′ble, -bled,
  -bling

tum′ble•down′ *adj.*

tum′bler

tum′ble•weed′

tum′brel *or*
  tum′bril

tu•mes′cence

tu•mes′cent

tu′mid

tum′my

tu′mor

tu′mult′

tu•mul′tu•ous

tun *(cask)*
  ✔ *ton*

tu′na *pl.* -na *or* -nas

tun′a•ble *also*
  tune′a•ble

tun′dra

tune, tuned, tun′ing

tune′ful

tun′er

tune′-up′ *n.*

tung′sten

tu′nic

Tu•ni′sian

tun′nel, -neled *or*
  -nelled, -nel•ing *or*
  -nel•ling

tun′ny *pl.* -ny *or*
  -nies

tu′pe•lo′ *pl.* -los′

Tu′pi *pl.* -pi *or* -pis

tur′ban *(headdress)*
  ✔ *turbine*

tur′bid

tur′bid•ness *or*
  tur•bid′i•ty

tur′bine *(engine)*
  ✔ *turban*

tur′bo•charg′er

tur′bo•jet′

tur′bo•prop′

tur′bot *pl.* -bot *or*
  -bots

tur′bu•lence

tur′bu•lent

tu•reen′

turf *pl.* turfs *also*
  turves

tur′gid

tur•gid′i•ty *or*
  tur′gid•ness

Turk

tur′key *pl.* -keys

Turk′ic

Turk′ish

tur′mer•ic

tur′moil′

turn *(to rotate)*
  ✔ *tern*

turn′a•bout′ *n.*

turn′a•round′ *n.*

turn′buck′le

turn′coat′

tur′nip

turn′key′ *pl.* -keys′

turn′off′ *n.*

turn′out′ *n.*

turn′o′ver *n.*

turn′pike′

turn′stile′

turn′ta•ble

tur′pen•tine′

tur′pi•tude′

tur′quoise′

tur′ret

tur′tle

tur′tle•dove′

tur′tle•neck′

Tus′ca•ro′ra *pl.*
  -ra *or* -ras

tusk

tus′sle

tus′sock

tu′te•lage

tu′tor

tu•to′ri•al

tut′ti-frut′ti *pl.* -tis

tu′tu

tux
tux•e′do *pl.* -dos *or*
  -does
TV *pl.* TVs *or* TV′s
twad′dle, -dled,
  -dling
twain
twang
'twas
tweak
tweed
tweet′er
tweez′ers
twelfth
twelve
twelve′month′
twelve′-tone′ *adj.*
twen′ti•eth
twen′ty
twerp
twice
twice′-told′
twid′dle, -dled,
  -dling
twig
twi′light′
twill
twin
twine, twined,
  twin′ing
twinge, twinged,
  twing′ing
twin′kle, -kled,
  -kling
twirl′er
twist′a•ble
twist′er

twit, twit′ted,
  twit′ting
twitch
twit′ter
two *(number)*
  ✔ to, too
two′-bit′
two′-by-four′
two′-di•men′-
  sion•al
two′-faced′
two′-fist′ed
two′-hand′ed
two′-ply′
two′-seat′er
two′some
two′-step′
two′-time′, -timed′,
  -tim′ing
two′-tim′er
two′-way′
two′-wheel′er
ty•coon′
tyke *also* tike
tym•pan′ic
tym′pa•num *also*
  tim′pa•num *pl.* -na
  or -nums
type, typed, typ′ing
type′cast′, -cast′,
  -cast′ing
type′face′
type′script′
type′set′, -set′,
  -set′ting
type′set′ter
type′write′, -wrote′,

-writ′ten, -writ′ing
type′writ′er
ty′phoid′
ty•phoon′
ty′phous *adj.*
ty′phus *n.*
typ′i•cal
typ′i•fy′, -fied′,
  -fy′ing
typ′ist
ty′po *pl.* -pos
ty•pog′ra•pher
ty′po•graph′i•cal
  or ty′po•graph′ic
ty•pog′ra•phy
ty•pol′o•gy
ty•ran′ni•cal *also*
  ty•ran′nic
tyr′an•nize′,
  -nized′, -niz′ing
ty•ran′no•saur′ *also*
  ty•ran′no•saur′us
tyr′an•nous
tyr′an•ny
ty′rant
ty′ro *pl.* -ros

U

u•biq′ui•tous
u•biq′ui•ty
ud′der
UFO *pl.* UFOs *or*
  UFO′s
ugh
ug′li•ness

ug′ly
uh
uh-huh′
U·krain′i·an
u′ku·le′le
ul′cer
ul′cer·ate′, -at·ed,
 -at′ing
ul′cer·a′tion
ul′cer·a·tive
ul′cer·ous
ul′na *pl.* -nas *or* -nae
ul′nar
ul·te′ri·or
ul′ti·mate
ul′ti·ma′tum *pl.*
 -tums *or* -ta
ul′tra·con·ser′va·
 tive
ul′tra·high′
ul′tra·lib′er·al
ul′tra·light′ *n. &*
 adj.
ul′tra·ma·rine′
ul′tra·mod′ern
ul′tra·son′ic
ul′tra·sound′
ul′tra·vi′o·let
ul′u·late′, -lat′ed,
 -lat′ing
ul′u·la′tion
um′bel
um′ber
um·bil′i·cal
um·bil′i·cus *pl.* -ci′
um′bra *pl.* -bras *or*
 -brae

um′brage
um·brel′la
u′mi·ak′
um′laut′
um′pire′, -pired′,
 -pir′ing
ump′teen′
ump′teenth′
un·a·bashed′
un·a′ble
un′a·bridged′
un·ac′cent·ed
un′ac·cept′a·ble
un′ac·com′pa·nied
un′ac·count′a·ble
un′ac·cus′tomed
un′ac·quaint′ed
un′a·dorned′
un′a·dul′ter·at·ed
un′af·fect′ed
un·al′ien·a·ble
un′a·ligned′
un·al′loyed′
un·al′ter·a·ble
un′-A·mer′i·can
u′na·nim′i·ty
u·nan′i·mous
un·an′swer·a·ble
un′an·tic′i·pat·ed
un′ap·peal′ing
un′ap·pre′ci·at·ed
un′ap·proach′a·ble
un·apt′
un′a·shamed′
un′as·sail′a·ble
un′as·sem′bled

un′as·sist′ed
un′as·sum′ing
un′at·tached′
un′at·tain′a·ble
un′at·test′ed
un′a·vail′a·ble
un′a·vail′ing
un′a·void′a·ble
un′a·void′a·bly
un′a·ware′
un′a·wares′
un·bal′anced
un·bar′, -barred′,
 -bar′ring
un·bear′a·ble
un·bear′a·bly
un·beat′a·ble
un·beat′en
un′be·com′ing
un′be·known′
un′be·knownst′
un′be·lief′
un′be·liev′a·ble
un′be·liev′a·bly
un′be·liev′er
un·bend′, -bent′,
 -bend′ing
un·bi′ased *also*
 un·bi′assed
un·bid′den
un·bind′, -bound′,
 -bind′ing
un·blessed′ *also*
 un·blest′
un·blink′ing
un·blush′ing
un·bolt′

un·born'
un·bos'om
un·bound'
un·bound'ed
un·bowed'
un·bri'dled
un·bro'ken
un·buck'le, -led,
  -ling
un·bur'den
un·but'ton
un·called'-for'
un·can'ni·ly
un·can'ny
un·cap', -capped',
  -cap'ping
un·car'ing
un·ceas'ing
un·cer'e·mo'ni·ous
un·cer'tain
un·cer'tain·ty
un·chain'
un·change'a·ble
un·char'i·ta·ble
un·chart'ed
un·chris'tian
un'cial
un'ci·form'
un·cir'cum·cised'
un·civ'il
un·civ'i·lized'
un·clad'
un·clasp'
un'cle
un·clean'
un·clear'
un·clog', -clogged',

-clog'ging
un·close', -closed',
  -clos'ing
un·clothe',
  -clothed',
  -cloth'ing
un·coil'
un·com'fort·a·ble
un·com'fort·a·bly
un'com·mit'ted
un·com'mon
un'com·mu'ni·ca'-
  tive
un'com·pro·
  mis'ing
un'con·cern'
un'con·cerned'
un'con·di'tion·al
un'con·di'tioned
un'con'quer·a·ble
un'con'scion·a·ble
un·con'scious
un'con·sid'ered
un'con·sti·tu'tion·
  al
un'con·sti·tu'tion·
  al'i·ty
un'con·trol'la·ble
un'con·trol'la·bly
un'con·trolled'
un'con·ven'tion·al
un'con·ven'tion·
  al'i·ty
un'co·or'di·nat'ed
un·cork'
un·count'ed
un·coup'le, -pled,

-pling
un·couth'
un·cov'er
un·cross'
unc'tion
unc'tu·ous
un·cul'ti·vat'ed
un·cul'tured
un·cut'
un·daunt'ed
un·de·cid'ed
un·de·clared'
un·de·mon'stra·
  tive
un'de·ni'a·ble
un'de·ni'a·bly
un'der
un'der·a·chieve',
  -chieved',
  -chiev'ing
un'der·act'
un'der·age'
un'der·arm'
un'der·bel'ly
un'der·bid', -bid',
  -bid'ding
un'der·brush'
un'der·buy',
  -bought', -buy'ing
un'der·cap'i·tal·
  ize', -ized', -iz'ing
un'der·car'riage
un'der·charge',
  -charged',
  -charg'ing
un'der·charge' *n.*
un'der·clothes'

un′der•cloth′ing
un′der•coat′
un′der•cov′er
un′der•cur′rent
un′der•cut′, -cut′,
-cut′ting
un′der•de•vel′oped
un′der•dog′
un′der•done′
un′der•dressed′
un′der•em•ployed′
un′der•es′ti•mate′,
-mat′ed, -mat′ing
un′der•ex•pose′,
-posed′, -pos′ing
un′der•ex•po′sure
un′der•feed′, -fed′,
-feed′ing
un′der•foot′
un′der•gar′ment
un′der•go′, -went′,
-gone′, -go′ing,
-goes′
un′der•grad′u•ate
un′der•ground′
adj.
un′der•ground′
adv.
un′der•growth′
un′der•hand′ *also*
un′der•hand′ed
un′der•lay′, -laid′,
-lay′ing
un′der•lie′, -lay′,
-lain′, -ly′ing
un′der•line′,
-lined′, -lin′ing

un′der•ling
un′der•mine′,
-mined′, -min′ing
un′der•most′
un′der•neath′
un′der•nour′ished
un′der•pants′
un′der•pass′
un′der•pin′ning
un′der•priv′i•leged
un′der•rate′,
-rat′ed, -rat′ing
un′der•score′,
-scored′, -scor′ing
un′der•sea′ *adj.*
un′der•sea′ *also*
un′der•seas′ *adv.*
un′der•sec′re•tar′y
un′der•sell′, -sold′,
-sell′ing
un′der•shirt′
un′der•shoot′,
-shot′, -shoot′ing
un′der•shot′ *adj.*
un′der•side′
un′der•signed′ *pl.*
-signed′
un′der•sized′ *also*
un′der•size′
un′der•staffed′
un′der•stand′,
-stood′, -stand′ing
un′der•stand′a•ble
un′der•stand′a•bly
un′der•state′,
-stat′ed, -stat′ing
un′der•state′ment

un′der•stud′y, -ied,
-y•ing
un′der•take′,
-took′, -tak′en,
-tak′ing
un′der•tak′er
un′der•tak′ing *n.*
un′der-the-
count′er *adj.*
un′der-the-ta′ble
adj.
un′der•tone′
un′der•tow′
un′der•val′ue,
-ued, -u•ing
un′der•wa′ter *adj.*
un′der•wa′ter *adv.*
un′der way′ *or*
un′der′way′
un′der•wear′
un′der•weight′
un′der•world′
un′der•write′,
-wrote′, -writ′ten,
-writ′ing
un′der•writ′er
un′de•sir′a•bil′i•ty
un′de•sir′a•ble
un′de•ter′mined
un′dies
un•dig′ni•fied′
un′dis•crim′i•nat′-
ing
un′dis•tin′guished
un•do′ *(to reverse),*
-did′, -done′,
-do′ing, -does′

✔ *undue*
un·doc'u·ment'ed
un·doubt'ed
un·dreamed' *also*
  un·dreamt'
un·dress'
un·due' *(excessive)*
  ✔ *undo*
un'du·lant
un'du·late', -lat'ed,
  -lat'ing
un'du·la'tion
un·du'ly
un·dy'ing
un·earned'
un·earth'
un·earth'ly
un·eas'y
un·ed'u·cat'ed
un'em·ploy'a·ble
un'em·ployed'
un'em·ploy'ment
un·e'qual
un·e'qualed *also*
  un·e'qualled
un'e·quiv'o·cal
un·err'ing
un'es·sen'tial
un·e'ven
un·e'vent·ful
un'ex·am'pled
un'ex·cep'tion·
  a·ble
un'ex·cep'tion·al
un'ex·pect'ed
un·fail'ing
un·fair'

un·faith'ful
un'fa·mil'iar
un'fa·mil·iar'i·ty
un·fas'ten
un·fa'vor·a·ble
un·fa'vor·a·bly
un·feel'ing
un·feigned'
un·fet'ter
un·fin'ished
un·fit'
un·flap'pa·ble
un·fledged'
un·flinch'ing
un·fold'
un'fore·seen'
un'for·get'ta·ble
un·formed'
un'for·tu·nate
un·found'ed
un'fre'quent·ed
un·friend'ly
un·frock'
un·fruit'ful
un·furl'
un·gain'ly
un·glued'
un·god'ly
un·gov'ern·a·ble
un·gra'cious
un'gram·mat'i·cal
un·grate'ful
un·guard'ed
un'guent
un'gu·late
un·hal'lowed
un·hand'

un·hap'py
un·har'ness
un·health'y
un·heard'
un·heard'-of'
un·hes'i·tat'ing
un·hinge',
  -hinged', -hing'ing
un·hitch'
un·ho'ly
un·hook'
un·horse', -horsed',
  -hors'ing
u'ni·cam'er·al
u'ni·cel'lu·lar
u'ni·corn'
u'ni·cy'cle
un'i·den'ti·fied'
u'ni·di·rec'tion·al
u'ni·fi·ca'tion
u'ni·form'
u'ni·for'mi·ty
u'ni·fy', -fied',
  -fy'ing
u'ni·lat'er·al
un'im·peach'a·ble
un'im·por'tance
un'im·por'tant
un'im·proved'
un'in·formed'
un'in·hab'it·ed
un'in·hib'it·ed
un'in·spired'
un'in·tel'li·gent
un'in·tel'li·gi·bil'-
  i·ty
un'in·tel'li·gi·ble

un'in•tel'li•gi•bly
un'in•tend'ed
un'in•ten'tion•al
un•in'ter•est•ed
un'in•vit'ed
un'ion
un'ion•i•za'tion
un'ion•ize', -ized',
  -iz'ing
u•nique'
u'ni•sex'
u'ni•son
u'nit
U'ni•tar'i•an
U'ni•tar'i•an•ism
U'ni•tar'i•an
  U'ni•ver'sal•ism
u'ni•tar'y
u•nite', u•nit'ed,
  u•nit'ing
u•ni•ty
u'ni•va'lent
u'ni•valve'
u'ni•ver'sal
U'ni•ver'sal•ist
u'ni•ver•sal'i•ty
u'ni•verse'
u'ni•ver'si•ty
un•just'
un•jus'ti•fi'a•ble
un•kempt'
un•kind'
un•know'a•ble
un•know'ing
un•known'
un•lace', -laced',

-lac'ing
un•latch'
un•law'ful
un•lead'ed
un•learn', -learned'
  also -learnt',
  -learn'ing
un•learn'ed *adj.*
un•leash'
un•leav'ened
un•less'
un•let'tered
un•li'censed
un•like'
un•like'ly
un•lim'ber
un•lim'it•ed
un•list'ed
un•load'
un•lock'
un•looked'-for'
un•loose', -loosed',
  -loos'ing
un•loos'en
un•love'ly
un•luck'y
un•made'
un•man'age•a•ble
un•man'ly
un•manned'
un•man'nered
un•man'ner•ly
un•mar'ried
un•mask'
un•men'tion•a•ble
un•mer'ci•ful

un•mind'ful
un•mis•tak'a•ble
un•mis•tak'a•bly
un•mit'i•gat'ed
un•mor'al
un•moved'
un•nat'u•ral
un•nec'es•sar'i•ly
un•nec'es•sar'y
un•nerve',
  -nerved', -nerv'ing
un•num'bered
un'ob•served'
un'ob•tru'sive
un•oc'cu•pied'
un•of•fi'cial
un'op•posed'
un•or'gan•ized'
un•or'tho•dox'
un•pack'
un•paid'
un•par'al•leled'
un•pin', -pinned',
  -pin'ning
un•pleas'ant
un•plug', -plugged',
  -plug'ging
un•pop'u•lar
un•prac'ticed
un•prec'e•dent'ed
un'pre•dict'a•ble
un'pre•dict'a•bly
un'prej'u•diced
un'pre•med'i•
  tat'ed
un'pre•pared'

un'pre·pos·sess'ing
un'pre·ten'tious
un·prin'ci·pled
un·print'a·ble
un'pro·duc'tive
un'pro·fes'sion·al
un·prof'it·a·ble
un'pro·voked'
un·qual'i·fied'
un·ques'tion·a·ble
un·ques'tion·a·bly
un·ques'tioned
un·quote'
un·rav'el, -eled or
  -elled, -el·ing or
  -el·ling
un·read'
un·read'a·ble
un·read'y
un·re'al
un·re·al·is'tic
un·rea'son·a·ble
un·rea'son·a·bly
un're·con·struct'ed
un·reel'
un're·gen'er·ate
un're·hearsed'
un're·lent'ing
un're·li'a·bil'i·ty
un're·li'a·ble
un're·mit'ting
un're·pent'ant
un're·quit'ed
un're·served'
un're·serv'ed·ly
un·rest'

un're·strained'
un·ripe'
un·ri'valed or
  un·ri'valled
un·roll'
un·ruf'fled
un·ru'ly
un·sad'dle, -dled,
  -dling
un·safe'
un·said'
un·san'i·tar'y
un·sat'is·fac'to·ry
un·sat'u·rat'ed
un·sa'vor·y
un·scathed'
un·schooled'
un·sci·en·tif'ic
un·scram'ble,
  -bled, -bling
un·screw'
un·scru'pu·lous
un·seal'
un·sea'son·a·ble
un·sea'soned
un·seat'
un·seem'ly
un·seen'
un·self'ish
un·set'tle, -tled,
  -tling
un·shack'le, -led,
  -ling
un·shak'a·ble
un·shak'a·bly
un·sheathe',

  -sheathed',
  -sheath'ing
un·shod'
un·sight'ly
un·skilled'
un·skill'ful
un·snap',
  -snapped',
  -snap'ping
un·snarl'
un·so'cia·bil'i·ty or
  un·so'cia·ble·ness
un·so'cia·ble
un'so·phis'ti·cat'ed
un·sound'
un·spar'ing
un·speak'a·ble
un·speak'a·bly
un·spoiled'
un·spo'ken
un·sta'ble
un·stead'y
un·stop', -stopped',
  -stop'ping
un·stressed'
un·struc'tured
un·strung'
un·stud'ied
un'sub·stan'tial
un'suc·cess'ful
un·suit'a·bil'i·ty
un·suit'a·ble
un·suit'a·bly
un·sung'
un'sus·pect'ed
un'sus·pect'ing

un·tan'gle, -gled,
 -gling
un·tapped'
un·taught'
un·ten'a·ble
un·think'a·ble
un·think'ing
un·ti'dy
un·tie', -tied',
 -ty'ing
un·til'
un·time'ly
un·tir'ing
un'to
un·told'
un·touch'a·ble
un·to·ward'
un·tried'
un·trod'den
un·true'
un·truth'
un·truth'ful
un·tu'tored
un·used'
un·u'su·al
un·ut'ter·a·ble
un·ut'ter·a·bly
un·var'nished
un·veil'
un·voiced'
un·war'rant·ed
un·war'y
un·well'
un·whole'some
un·wield'y
un·will'ing
un·wind', -wound',

 -wind'ing
un·wise', -wis'er,
 -wis'est
un·wit'ting
un·wont'ed
un·world'ly
un·wor'thy
un·wrap',
 -wrapped',
 -wrap'ping
un·writ'ten
un·yield'ing
un·yoke', -yoked',
 -yok'ing
un·zip', -zipped',
 -zip'ping
up, upped, up'ping
up'-and-com'ing
up'beat'
up·braid'
up·bring'ing
up'com'ing
up'coun'try n. &
 adj.
up·coun'try adv.
up·date', -dat'ed,
 -dat'ing
up'date' n.
up'draft'
up·end'
up'-front' or
 up'front'
up·grade', -grad'ed,
 -grad'ing
up·heav'al
up'hill'
up·hold', -held',

 -hold'ing
up·hol'ster
up·hol'ster·y
up'keep'
up'land
up·lift' v.
up'lift' n.
up'load'
up'mar'ket
up·on'
up'per
up'per·case'
up'per-class' adj.
up'per·cut'
up'per·most'
up'pi·ty
up·raise', -raised',
 -rais'ing
up'right'
up'ris'ing
up'riv'er
up'roar'
up·roar'i·ous
up·root'
up'scale', -scaled',
 -scal'ing
up·set', -set',
 -set'ting
up'set' n.
up'shot'
up'side' down'
up'si·lon
up'stage' adv. & adj.
up·stage', -staged',
 -stag'ing
up'stairs' adv.
up'stairs' adj. & n.

up·stand′ing
up′start′
up′state′
up′stream′
up·surge′, -surged′,
  -surg′ing
up′surge′ n.
up′sweep′, -swept′,
  -sweep′ing
up′swing′
up′take′
up′tight′
up′-to-date′
up′town′ n.
up′town′ adv. &
  adj.
up′turn′
up′ward adv. & adj.
up′wards adv.
up′wind′ adv.
u′ra·cil
u·ra′ni·um
ur′ban (relating to a
  city)
ur·bane′ (refined)
ur′chin
Ur′du
u·re′a
u·re′ter
u·re′thra pl. -thras
  or -thrae
urge, urged, urg′ing
ur′gen·cy
ur′gent
u′ric
u′ri·nal
u′ri·nal′y·sis pl.

-ses′
u′ri·nar′y
u′ri·nate′, -nat′ed,
  -nat′ing
u′ri·na′tion
u′rine
urn (vase)
  ✔ earn
us
us′a·ble also
  use′a·ble
us′age
use, used, us′ing
use′ful
us′er
us′er-friend′ly
ush′er
u′su·al
u′su·rer
u·su′ri·ous
u·surp′
u′sur·pa′tion
u′su·ry
U′tah·an
Ute pl. Ute or Utes
u·ten′sil
u′ter·ine
u′ter·us pl. u′ter·i or
  u′ter·us·es
u·til′i·tar′i·an
u·til′i·ty
u′ti·li·za′tion
u′til·ize′, -ized′,
  -iz′ing
ut′most′
U′to-Az′tec′an
u·to′pi·a

u·to′pi·an
ut′ter
ut′ter·ance
ut′ter·most′
U′-turn′
u′vu·la
u′vu·lar

V

va′can·cy
va′cant
va′cate′, -cat′ed,
  -cat′ing
va·ca′tion
vac′ci·nate′,
  -nat′ed, -nat′ing
vac′ci·na′tion
vac·cine′
vac′il·late′, -lat′ed,
  -lat′ing
vac′il·la′tion
vac′il·la′tor
va·cu′i·ty
vac′u·o′lar
vac′u·ole′
vac′u·ous
vac′u·um pl.
  -u′ums or -u·a
vac′u·um-packed′
vag′a·bond′
va′ga·ry
va·gi′na pl. -nas or
  -nae
vag′i·nal
va′gran·cy

va'grant

vague, vagu'er, vagu'est

vain *(fruitless, conceited)*
  ✔ vane, vein

vain•glo'ri•ous

vain'glo'ry

val'ance *(drapery)*
  ✔ valence

vale *(valley)*
  ✔ veil

val'e•dic'tion

val'e•dic'to•ri•an

val'e•dic'to•ry

va'lence *also*
  va'len•cy *(capacity to combine)*
  ✔ valance

val'en•tine'

val'et

val'e•tu'di•nar'i•an

val'iant

val'id

val'i•date', -dat'ed, -dat'ing

val'i•da'tion

va•lid'i•ty

val'ise'

val'ley *pl.* -leys

val'or

val'or•ous

val'u•a•ble

val'u•a'tion

val'ue, -ued, -u•ing

valve

val'vu•lar

va•moose', -moosed', -moos'ing

vamp

vam'pire'

vam'pir•ism

van

va•na'di•um

Van Al'len belt'

van'dal *(person who defaces)*

Van'dal *(tribe member)*

van'dal•ism

van'dal•ize', -ized', -iz'ing

Van•dyke' beard'

vane *(weathervane)*
  ✔ vain, vein

van'guard'

va•nil'la

va•nil'lin

van'ish

van'i•ty

van'quish

van'tage

vap'id

va•pid'i•ty

va'por

va'por•iz'a•ble

va'por•i•za'tion

va'por•ize', -ized', -iz'ing

va'por•iz'er

va'por•ous

va•que'ro *pl.* -ros

var'i•a•bil'i•ty *or*

var'i•a•ble•ness

var'i•a•ble

var'i•a•bly

var'i•ance

var'i•ant

var'i•a'tion

var'i•cel'la

var'i•col'ored

var'i•cose'

var'ied

var'i•e•gat'ed

va•ri'e•ty

var'i•ous

var'let

var'mint

var'nish

var'si•ty

var'y *(to change)*, -ied, -y•ing
  ✔ very

vas'cu•lar

vase

va•sec'to•my

vas'sal

vas'sal•age

vast

vat

Vat'i•can

vaude'ville'

vault

vault'er

vaunt

VCR *pl.* VCRs *or* VCR's

VDT *pl.* VDTs *or* VDT's

veal

vec'tor
veer
veg'e·ta·ble
veg'e·tal
veg'e·tar'i·an
veg'e·tar'i·an·ism
veg'e·tate', -tat'ed,
  -tat'ing
veg'e·ta'tion
veg'e·ta'tive *also*
  veg'e'tive
ve'he·mence *or*
  ve'he'men·cy
ve'he·ment
ve'hi·cle
ve·hic'u·lar
veil *(covering)*
  ✔ vale
vein *(blood vessel,*
  strip)
  ✔ vain, vane
ve'lar
veldt *also* veld
vel'lum *(parchment)*
  ✔ velum
ve·loc'i·ty
ve·lour'
ve'lum *(membrane,*
  soft palate), pl. -la
  ✔ vellum
vel'vet
vel'vet·een'
vel'vet·y
ve'nal *(open to*
  bribery)
  ✔ venial
ve·na'tion

vend
vend'er *or* ven'dor
ven·det'ta
ve·neer'
ven'er·a·ble
ven'er·a·bly
ven'er·ate', -at'ed,
  -at'ing
ven'er·a'tion
ven'er·a'tor
ve·ne're·al
ve·ne'tian blind'
  or Ve·ne'tian
  blind'
ven'geance
venge'ful
ve'ni·al *(minor)*
  ✔ venal
ven'i·son
Venn' di'a·gram'
ven'om
ven'om·ous
ve'nous
vent
ven'ti·late', -lat'ed,
  -lat'ing
ven'ti·la'tion
ven'ti·la'tor
ven'tral
ven'tri·cle
ven·tric'u·lar
ven·tril'o·quism
  also ven·tril'o·quy
ven·tril'o·quist
ven'ture, -tured,
  -tur·ing
ven'ture·some

ven'ue
Ve·nu'sian
Ve'nus's-fly'trap'
ve·ra'cious *(truth-*
  ful)
  ✔ voracious
ve·rac'i·ty
ve·ran'da *or*
  ve·ran'dah
verb
ver'bal
ver'bal·i·za'tion
ver'bal·ize', -ized',
  -iz'ing
ver·ba'tim
ver·be'na
ver'bi·age
ver·bose'
ver·bos'i·ty
ver'dant
ver'dict
ver'di·gris'
ver'dure
verge, verged,
  verg'ing
ver'i·fi'a·ble
ver'i·fi·ca'tion
ver'i·fy', -fied',
  -fy'ing
ver'i·ly
ver'i·si·mil'i·tude'
ver'i·ta·ble
ver'i·ty
ver'mi·cel'li
ver'mi·form'
ver·mil'ion *also*
  ver·mil'lion

ver′min *pl.* -min
ver′min•ous
Ver•mont′er
ver•mouth′
ver•nac′u•lar
ver′nal
ver′sa•tile
ver′sa•til′i•ty
verse
versed
ver′si•fi•ca′tion
ver′si•fi′er
ver′si•fy′, -fied′,
  -fy′ing
ver′sion
ver′sus
ver′te•bra *pl.* -brae′
  or -bras
ver′te•bral
ver′te•brate′
ver′tex′ *pl.* -tex′es *or*
  -ti•ces′
ver′ti•cal
ver•tig′i•nous
ver′ti•go′ *pl.* -goes′
  or -gos′
verve
ver′y *(extremely)*
  ✔ *vary*
ves′i•cle
ve•sic′u•lar
ves′per *(bell)*
Ves′per *(star)*
ves′pers *also*
  Ves′pers
ves′sel
vest

ves′tal
vest′ed
ves′ti•bule′
ves′tige
ves•tig′i•al
vest′ment
ves′try
ves′try•man
ves′try•wom′an
vet, vet′ted, vet′ting
vetch
vet′er•an
vet′er•i•nar′i•an
vet′er•i•nar′y
ve′to *pl.* -toes
ve′to, -toed, -to•ing
vex•a′tion
vex•a′tious
vexed
vi′a
vi′a•bil′i•ty
vi′a•ble
vi′a•duct′
vi′al *(glass container)*
  ✔ *viol*
vi′and
vi′brant
vi′bra•phone′
vi′bra•phon′ist
vi′brate′, -brat′ed,
  -brat′ing
vi•bra′tion
vi•bra′to *pl.* -tos
vi′bra′tor
vi′bra•to′ry
vi•bur′num
vic′ar

vic′ar•age
vi•car′i•ous
vice *(wickedness)*
  ✔ *vise*
vice′-pres′i•den•cy
vice′ pres′i•dent *or*
  vice′-pres′i•dent
vice′-pres′i•den′-
  tial
vice′roy′
vi′ce ver′sa
vi′chys•soise′
Vi′chy wa′ter
vic′i•nage
vi•cin′i•ty
vi′cious
vi•cis′si•tude′
vic′tim
vic′tim•i•za′tion
vic′tim•ize′, -ized′,
  -iz′ing
vic′tim•iz′er
vic′tor
vic•to′ri•a
Vic•to′ri•an
vic•to′ri•ous
vic′to•ry
vict′ual
vi•cu′ña *also*
  vi•cu′na
vid′e•o′ *pl.* -os′
vid′e•o•cas•sette′
vid′e•o•disk′ *also*
  vid′e•o•disc′
vid′e•og′ra•pher
vid′e•og′ra•phy
vid′e•o•tape′,

-taped′, -tap′ing
vie, vied, vy′ing
Vi′en•nese′ *pl.*
-nese′
Vi•et′cong′ *also*
Vi•et′ Cong′
Vi•et′minh′ *also*
Vi•et′ Minh′
Vi•et′nam•ese′ *pl.*
-ese′
view
view′find′er
view′point′
vig′il
vig′i•lance
vig′i•lant
vig′i•lan′te
vi•gnette′
vig′or
vig′or•ous
Vi′king
vile, vil′er, vil′est
vil′i•fi•ca′tion
vil′i•fi′er
vil′i•fy′, -fied′,
-fy′ing
vil′la
vil′lage
vil′lag•er
vil′lain *(wicked*
person)
✔ *villein*
vil′lain•ous
vil′lain•y
vil′lein *also* vil′lain
(serf)
✔ *villain*

vil′lus *pl.* -li
vim
vin′ai•grette′
vin′di•cate′,
-cat′ed, -cat′ing
vin′di•ca′tion
vin′di•ca′tor
vin•dic′tive
vine
vin′e•gar
vin′e•gar•y *also*
vin′e•gar•ish
vine′yard′
vin′i•cul′ture
vin′tage
vint′ner
vi′nyl
vi′ol *(musical instru-*
ment)
✔ *vial*
vi•o′la
vi•o′la•bil′i•ty *or*
vi′o•la•ble•ness
vi′o•la•ble
vi′o•late′, -lat′ed,
-lat′ing
vi′o•la′tion
vi′o•la′tor
vi′o•lence
vi′o•lent
vi′o•let
vi′o•lin′
vi′o•lin′ist
vi•o′list
vi′o•lon•cel′list
vi′o•lon•cel′lo *pl.*
-los

VIP *pl.* VIPs *or* VIP′s
vi′per
vi′per•ous
vi•ra′go *pl.* -goes *or*
-gos
vi′ral
vir′gin
vir′gin•al
Vir•gin′ian
vir•gin′i•ty
vir′gule
vir′ile
vi•ril′i•ty
vi•rol′o•gist
vi•rol′o•gy
vir•tu′ *also* ver•tu′
(fine arts)
✔ *virtue*
vir′tu•al
vir′tue *(goodness)*
✔ *virtu*
vir′tu•os′i•ty
vir′tu•o′so *pl.* -sos
or -si
vir′tu•ous
vir′u•lence *or*
vir′u•len•cy
vir′u•lent
vi′rus *pl.* -rus•es
vi′sa
vis′age
vis′-à-vis′
vis′cer•a
vis′cer•al
vis′cid
vis•cos′i•ty
vis′count′

vis′count′ess
vis′cous
vise *also* vice *(clamp)*
    ✔ vice
vis·i·bil′i·ty
vis′i·ble
vis′i·bly
Vis′i·goth′
vi′sion
vi′sion·ar′y
vis′it
vis′i·tant
vis′i·ta′tion
vis′i·tor
vi′sor *also* vi′zor
vis′ta
vi′su·al
vi′su·al·i·za′tion
vi′su·al·ize′, -ized′,
    -iz′ing
vi′ta *pl.* -tae
vi′tal
vi·tal′i·ty
vi′tal·i·za′tion
vi′tal·ize′, -ized′,
    -iz′ing
vi′tals
vi′ta·min
vi′ti·ate′, -at′ed,
    -at′ing
vi′ti·a′tion
vit′i·cul′ture
vit′i·cul′tur·ist
vit′re·ous
vit′ri·fi′a·ble
vit′ri·fi·ca′tion
vit′ri·fy′, -fied′,
    -fy′ing
vit′ri·ol′
vit′ri·ol′ic
vi·tu′per·ate′,
    -at′ed, -at′ing
vi·tu′per·a′tion
vi·tu′per·a·tive
vi′va
vi·va′cious
vi·vac′i·ty
viv′id
viv′i·fi·ca′tion
viv′i·fy′, -fied′,
    -fy′ing
vi·vip′a·rous
viv′i·sect′
viv′i·sec′tion
vix′en
viz′ard *also* vis′ard
vi·zier′
vo·cab′u·lar′y
vo′cal
vo·cal′ic
vo′cal·ist
vo′cal·i·za′tion
vo′cal·ize′, -ized′,
    -iz′ing
vo·ca′tion
voc′a·tive
vo·cif′er·ate′,
    -at′ed, -at′ing
vo·cif′er·a′tion
vo·cif′er·ous
vod′ka
vogue
voice, voiced,
    voic′ing
voice′less
voice′ mail′
voice′-o′ver *or*
    voice′o′ver
void
voi·là′
voile
vol′a·tile
vol′a·til′i·ty
vol·can′ic
vol·ca′no *pl.* -noes
    or -nos
vole
vo·li′tion
vol′ley *pl.* -leys
vol′ley·ball′
volt′age
vol·ta′ic
volt·am′me′ter
volt′-am′pere′
volt′me′ter
vol′u·bil′i·ty
vol′u·ble
vol′u·bly
vol′ume
vol′u·met′ric
vo·lu′mi·nous
vol′un·tar′i·ly
vol′un·tar′y
vol′un·teer′
vo·lup′tu·ar′y
vo·lup′tu·ous
vo·lute′
vol′vox′
vom′it
voo′doo *pl.* -doos
voo′doo·ism

vo•ra′cious
  (ravenous)
  ✔ *veracious*
vo•rac′i•ty *or*
  vo•ra′cious•ness
vor′tex′ *pl.* -tex′es *or*
  -ti•ces′
vo′ta•ry
vote, vot′ed, vot′ing
vot′er
vo′tive
vouch
vouch′er
vouch•safe′,
  -safed′, -saf′ing
vow
vow′el
voy′age, -aged,
  -ag•ing
voy′ag•er
voy•eur′
voy′eur•ism
voy′eur•is′tic
vul′ca•nite′
vul′can•i•za′tion
vul′ca•nize′,
  -nized′, -niz′ing
vul′gar
vul•gar′i•an
vul′gar•ism
vul•gar′i•ty
vul′gar•i•za′tion
vul′gar•ize′, -ized′,
  -iz′ing
vul′gate′ *(vernac-
  ular)*
Vul′gate′ *(Bible)*

vul′ner•a•ble
vul′ner•a•bil′i•ty
vul′ner•a•bly
vul′pine′
vul′ture
vul′va *pl.* -vae

W

wack′y *also*
  whack′y
wad, wad′ded,
  wad′ding
wad′dle, -dled,
  -dling
wade, wad′ed,
  wad′ing
wad′ers
wa′di *pl.* -dis *also*
  -dies
wa′fer
waf′fle, -fled, -fling
waft
wag, wagged,
  wag′ging
wage, waged,
  wag′ing
wa′ger
wag′gish
wag′gle, -gled,
  -gling
wag′on
wag′on•er
waif
wail *(cry)*
  ✔ *wale, whale*

wain *(wagon)*
  ✔ *wane*
wain′scot
wain′scot•ing
waist *(body part)*
  ✔ *waste*
waist′band′
waist′coat
waist′line′
wait *(to remain)*
  ✔ *weight*
wait′er
wait′ing
wait′per′son
wait′ress
wait′ staff′ *also*
  wait′staff′
waive *(to relinquish),*
  waived, waiv′ing
  ✔ *wave*
waiv′er *(relinquish-
  ment)*
  ✔ *waver*
wake, woke *or*
  waked, waked *or*
  wok′en, wak′ing
wake′ful
wak′en
wale *(to mark with
  ridges),* waled,
  wal′ing
  ✔ *wail, whale*
walk
walk′ie-talk′ie *pl.*
  -ies
walk′-in′ *adj. & n.*
walk′-on′ *n.*

walk'out' *n.*
walk'o'ver *n.*
walk'-through' *n.*
walk'up' *also*
  walk'-up' *n.*
walk'way'
wall
wal'la•by *pl.* -bies *or*
  -by
wall'board'
wal'let
wall'eye'
wall'eyed'
wall'flow'er
Wal•loon'
wal'lop
wal'low
wall'pa'per
wall'-to-wall'
wal'nut
wal'rus *pl.* -rus *or*
  -rus•es
waltz
Wam'pa•no'ag *pl.*
  -ag *or* -ags
wam'pum
wan, wan'ner,
  wan'nest
wand
wan'der
wan'der•lust'
wane *(to decrease),*
  waned, wan'ing
  ✔ *wain*
wan'gle, -gled,
  -gling
Wan'kel en'gine

wan'ly
want *(lack)*
  ✔ *wont*
wan'ton
wap'i•ti *pl.* -ti *or* -tis
war, warred,
  war'ring
war'ble, -bled,
  -bling
war'bler
ward
war'den
ward'er
ward'robe'
ware *(goods)*
  ✔ *wear, where*
ware'house'
war'fare'
war'head'
war'horse' *also*
  war'-horse'
war'like'
war'lock'
war'lord'
warm
warm'-blood'ed
warm'-heart'ed
war'mon'ger
warmth
warm'-up' *or*
  warm'up'
warn
warn'ing
warp
war'path'
war'rant
war'ran•ty

war'ren
war'ri•or
wart
wart' hog'
war'time'
war'y
wa'sa•bi
wash'a•ble
wash'-and-wear'
wash'ba'sin
wash'board'
wash'bowl'
wash'cloth'
washed'-out'
washed'-up'
wash'er
wash'ing
Wash'ing•to'ni•an
wash'out'
wash'rag'
wash'room'
wash'stand'
wash'tub'
was'n't
wasp'ish
was'sail
waste *(to squander),*
  wast'ed, wast'ing
  ✔ *waist*
waste'bas'ket
waste'ful
waste'land'
waste'pa'per
wast'rel
watch
watch'band'
watch'dog'

watch'ful
watch'mak'er
watch'man
watch'tow'er
watch'word'
wa'ter
wa'ter•borne'
wa'ter•buck' *pl.*
  -buck' *or* -bucks'
wa'ter•col'or
wa'ter-cool'
wa'ter•course'
wa'ter•craft'
wa'ter•cress'
wa'ter•fall'
wa'ter•fowl' *pl.*
  -fowl' *or* -fowls'
wa'ter•front'
wa'ter•logged'
wa'ter•mark'
wa'ter•mel'on
wa'ter•pow'er
wa'ter•proof'
wa'ter•proof'ing
wa'ter-re•pel'lent
wa'ter-re•sis'tant
wa'ter•shed'
wa'ter ski' *n.*
wa'ter-ski', -skied',
  -ski'ing
wa'ter•spout'
wa'ter•tight'
wa'ter•way'
wa'ter•works'
wa'ter•y
watt
watt'age

watt'-hour'
wat'tle
wave *(to move back
  and forth)*, waved,
  wav'ing
  ✔ *waive*
wave'length'
wave'let
wav'er *(one that
  waves)*
  ✔ *waiver*
wa'ver *(to vacillate)*
  ✔ *waiver*
wav'i•ness
wav'y
wax
wax'en
wax'wing'
wax'work'
wax'y
way *(course)*
  ✔ *weigh, whey*
way'far'er
way'far'ing
way'lay', -laid',
  -lay'ing
way'-out' *adj.*
way'side'
way'ward
we *pron.*
  ✔ *wee*
weak *(feeble)*
  ✔ *week*
weak'en
weak'fish' *pl.* -fish'
  or -fish'es
weak'ling

weak'ly *(sickly)*
  ✔ *weekly*
weak'-mind'ed
weal *(prosperity, welt)*
  ✔ *wheal, wheel*
wealth
wealth'y
wean
weap'on
weap'on•ry
wear *(to have on, to
  erode)*, wore, worn,
  wear'ing
  ✔ *ware, where*
wear'a•ble
wea'ri•ly
wea'ri•ness
wea'ri•some
wea'ry, -ried,
  -ry•ing
wea'sel, -seled *also*
  -selled, -sel•ing *also*
  -sel•ling
weath'er *(climate)*
  ✔ *wether, whether*
weath'er-beat'en
weath'er•cock'
weath'ered
weath'er•glass'
weath'er•ing
weath'er•proof'
weath'er-strip',
  -stripped',
  -strip'ping
weath'er
  strip'ping *n.*
weath'er•vane'

weave, wove also
weaved, wo'ven,
weav'ing
weav'er
weav'er•bird'
web, webbed,
web'bing
web'-foot'ed
wed, wed'ded, wed
or wed'ded,
wed'ding
wedge, wedged,
wedg'ing
wed'lock'
Wednes'day
wee (tiny), we'er,
we'est
✔ we
weed
weed'y
week (calendar
period)
✔ weak
week'day'
week'end'
week'long'
week'ly (once a
week)
✔ weakly
ween'ie
weep, wept,
weep'ing
wee'vil
weft
weigh (to determine
weight)
✔ way, whey

weight (measure of
heaviness)
✔ wait
weight'less
weight'lift'ing
weight'y
weir
weird
weird'o pl. -oes
welch
wel'come, -comed,
-com•ing
weld
weld'er
wel'fare'
wel'kin
well (deep hole)
well (to rise up)
well (in a good man-
ner), bet'ter, best
well'-ap•point'ed
well'-bal'anced
well'-be'ing
well'born'
well'-bred'
well'-de•fined'
well'-done'
well'-fa'vored
well'-fed'
well'-fixed'
well'-found'ed
well'-groomed'
well'-ground'ed
well'head'
well'-heeled'
well'-known'
well'-man'nered

well'-mean'ing
well'-nigh'
well'-off'
well'-read'
well'-round'ed
well'-spo'ken
well'spring'
well-thought'-of'
well'-timed'
well'-to-do'
well'-wish'er
well'-worn'
welsh also welch (to
swindle)
Welsh (relating to
Wales)
Welsh' cor'gi
Welsh'man
Welsh' rab'bit also
Welsh' rare'bit
Welsh'wom'an
welt
wel'ter
wel'ter•weight'
wen (cyst)
✔ when
wench
wend
were'n't
were'wolf'
west
west'bound'
west'er•ly
west'ern
west'ern•er
west'ern•ize',
-ized', -iz'ing

west'ern·most'
West' In'di·an
West' Vir·gin'ian
west'ward *adv. & adj.*
west'wards *adv.*
wet *(damp)*, wet'ter, wet'test
✔ *whet*
wet *(to dampen)*, wet *or* wet'ted, wet'ting
✔ *whet*
weth'er *(sheep)*
✔ *weather, whether*
wet'land'
whack
whale *(mammal)*
✔ *wail, wale*
whale'boat'
whale'bone'
whal'er
whal'ing
wham, whammed, wham'ming
wharf *pl.* wharves *or* wharfs
what
what·ev'er
what'not'
what'so·ev'er
wheal *(swelling)*
✔ *weal, wheel*
wheat
wheat'en
whee'dle, -dled, -dling
wheel *(circular frame)*
✔ *weal, wheal*
wheel'bar'row
wheel'base'
wheel'chair' *also* wheel' chair'
wheeled
wheel'er-deal'er
wheel'house'
wheel'wright'
wheeze, wheezed, wheez'ing
wheez'y
whelk
whelm
whelp
when *(at what time)*
✔ *wen*
whence
when·ev'er
when'so·ev'er
where *(at what place)*
✔ *ware, wear*
where'a·bouts'
where·as'
where·at'
where·by'
where'fore'
where·in'
where·of'
where·on'
where'so·ev'er
where'to'
where'up·on'
wher·ev'er
where'with'
where'with·al'
whet *(to hone)*, whet'ted, whet'ting
✔ *wet*
wheth'er *(if)*
✔ *weather, wether*
whet'stone'
whew
whey *(watery part of milk)*
✔ *way, weigh*
which *pron.*
✔ *witch*
which·ev'er
whiff
whif'fle·tree'
Whig
while *(period of time)*
✔ *wile*
while *(to spend time idly)*, whiled, whil'ing
✔ *wile*
whim
whim'per
whim'si·cal
whim'si·cal'i·ty
whim'sy *also* whim'sey *pl.* -sies *or* -seys
whine *(to complain)*, whined, whin'ing
✔ *wine*
whin'ny, -nied, -ny·ing
whin'y *or* whin'ey

whip, whipped *or*
   whipt, whip'ping
whip'cord'
whip'lash'
whip'per•snap'per
whip'pet
whip'poor•will'
whip'stitch'
whir, whirred,
   whir'ring
whirl
whirl'i•gig'
whirl'pool'
whirl'wind'
whirl'y•bird'
whisk
whisk'broom'
whisk'er
whis'key *also*
   whis'ky *pl.* -keys
   also -kies
whis'per
whist
whis'tle, -tled,
   -tling
whis'tle stop' *n.*
whis'tle-stop',
   -stopped',
   -stop'ping
whit *(particle)*
   ✔ *wit*
white, whit'er,
   whit'est
white'cap'
white'-col'lar *adj.*
white'fish' *pl.* -fish'
   or -fish'es

white'head'
white'-hot'
whit'en
whit'en•er
white'ness
white'out' *n.*
white'-tailed'
   deer'
white'wall'
white'wash'
whith'er *(where)*
   ✔ *wither*
whit'ing *(chalk)*
whit'ing *(fish), pl.*
   -ing *or* -ings
whit'ish
Whit'sun•day
Whit'sun•tide'
whit'tle, -tled,
   -tling
whit'tler
whiz *also* whizz,
   whizzed, whiz'zing
who
whoa
who•dun'it
who•ev'er
whole *(complete)*
   ✔ *hole*
whole'heart'ed
whole'sale'
whole'sal'er
whole'some,
   -som•er, -som•est
whole'-wheat'
whol'ly *(totally)*
   ✔ *holey, holy*

whom
whom•ev'er
whom'so•ev'er
whoop *(cry, cough)*
   ✔ *hoop*
whoop'ing cough'
whoop'ing crane'
whoops
whop'per
whore *(prostitute)*
   ✔ *hoar*
whorl
whose
who'so•ev'er
why *pl.* whys
Wich'i•ta' *pl.* -ta'
wick
wick'ed
wick'er
wick'et
wick'i•up'
wide, wid'er, wid'est
wide'-an'gle *adj.*
wide'-a•wake'
wide'-bod'ied
wide'-eyed'
wid'en
wide'-o'pen
wide'spread'
wid'geon *pl.* -geon
   or -geons
wid'ow
wid'ow•er
wid'ow's peak'
wid'ow's walk'
width
wield

wie′ner
Wie′ner schnit′zel
wie′ner•wurst′
wife *pl.* wives
wife′ly
wig
wig′gle, -gled,
  -gling
wig′gler
wig′wag′, -wagged′,
  -wag′ging
wig′wam′
wild
wild′cat′
wil′de•beest′ *pl.*
  -beests′ *or* -beest′
wil′der•ness
wild′-eyed′
wild′fire′
wild′flow′er *also*
  -flow′er
wild′fowl′ *pl.* -fowl′
  or -fowls′
wild′-goose′
  chase′
wild′life′
wild′wood′
wile *(to lure),* wiled,
  wil′ing
  ✔ *while*
will *(volition)*
will *aux. v., past tense*
  would
will′ful *also* wil′ful
will′ing
will′-o′-the-wisp′
wil′low

wil′low•y
will′pow′er *or* will′
  pow′er
wil′ly-nil′ly
wilt
wi′ly
wimp
wim′ple
win, won, win′ning
wince, winced,
  winc′ing
winch
wind *(to cause to be*
  out of breath),
  wind′ed, wind′ing
wind *(to wrap*
  around), wound,
  wind′ing
wind′bag′
wind′blown′
wind′break′
wind′burn′
wind′-chill′ fac′-
  tor
wind′fall′
wind′flow′er
wind′jam′mer
wind′lass
wind′mill′
win′dow
win′dow-dress′ing
  also win′dow
  dress′ing
win′dow•pane′
win′dow-shop′,
  -shopped′,
  -shop′ping

win′dow•sill′
wind′pipe′
wind′row′
wind′shield′
wind′sock′
Wind′sor chair′
wind′storm′
wind′surf′ing
wind′swept′
wind′-up′ *or*
  wind′up′ *n. & adj.*
wind′ward
wind′y
wine *(beverage)*
  ✔ *whine*
wine′ cel′lar
wine′press′
win′er•y
wing
winged
wing′span′
wing′spread′
wink
win′ner
win′ning
win′now
win′some
win′ter
win′ter•green′
win′ter•ize′, -ized′,
  -iz′ing
win′ter•time′
win′try *also*
  win′ter•y
wipe, wiped,
  wip′ing
wiped′-out′ *adj.*

wipe'out' *n.*
wip'er
wire, wired, wir'ing
wire'haired'
wire'less
wire'tap', -tapped',
  -tap'ping
wire'worm'
wir'i•ness
wir'ing
wir'y
wis'dom
wise, wis'er, wis'est
wise'a'cre
wise'crack'
wish'bone'
wish'ful
wish'y-wash'y
wisp
wist
wis•ter'i•a *also*
  wis•tar'i•a
wist'ful
wit *(intelligence,*
  humor)
  ✔ whit
witch *(woman with*
  supernatural powers)
  ✔ which
witch'craft'
witch'-hunt'
with
with•al'
with•draw', -drew',
  -drawn', -draw'ing
with•draw'al
with'er *(to shrivel)*

✔ whither
with'ers
with•hold', -held',
  -hold'ing
with•in'
with'-it' *adj.*
with•out'
with•stand',
  -stood', -stand'ing
wit'less
wit'ness
wit'ti•cism
wit'ti•ly
wit'ti•ness
wit'ting
wit'ty
wiz'ard
wiz'ard•ry
wiz'ened
wob'ble, -bled,
  -bling
wob'bly
woe
woe'be•gone'
woe'ful
wok
wolf *pl.* wolves
wolf'hound'
wolf'ram
wolfs'bane'
Wo'lof'
wol'ver•ine'
wom'an *pl.* wom'en
wom'an•hood'
wom'an•ish
wom'an•ize',
  -ized', -iz'ing

wom'an•iz'er
wom'an•kind'
womb
wom'bat'
wom'en•folk' *also*
  wom'en•folks'
won'der
won'der•ful
won'der•land'
won'der•ment
won'drous
wont *(accustomed)*
  ✔ want
wont'ed *(usual)*
won' ton' *or*
  won'ton'
woo
wood *(lumber)*
  ✔ would
wood'bine'
wood'carv'ing
wood'chuck'
wood'cock' *pl.*
  -cock' *or* -cocks'
wood'craft'
wood'cut'
wood'cut'ter
wood'ed
wood'en
wood'land
wood'man
wood'peck'er
wood'pile'
wood'shed'
woods'man
woods'y
wood'wind'

wood'work'
wood'work'ing
wood'y
woo'er
woof
woof'er
wool
wool'en *also*
  wool'len
wool'gath'er•er
wool'gath'er•ing
wool'ly
wooz'i•ness
wooz'y
word'book'
word' for word'
  adv.
word'-for-word'
  adj.
word'i•ness
word'ing
word'-of-mouth'
  adj.
word' proc'ess'ing
word' proc'es'sor
word'y
work, worked *also*
  wrought, work'ing
work'a•bil'i•ty *or*
  work'a•ble•ness
work'a•ble
work'a•day'
work'bench'
work'book'
work'day'
work'er
work' force' *or*

work'force'
work'horse'
work'house'
work'ing class' *n.*
work'ing-class' *adj.*
work'ing•man'
work'ing•wom'an
work'load'
work'man
work'man•ship'
work'out' *n.*
work'place' *also*
  work' place'
work'room'
work'shop'
work'space'
work'ta'ble
work'week'
world
world'li•ness
world'ly
world'ly-wise'
world'wide'
worm
worm'-eat'en
worm'wood'
worm'y
worn'-out'
wor'ri•er
wor'ri•some
wor'ry, -ried, -ry•ing
wor'ry•wart'
worse
wors'en
wor'ship, -shiped *or*
  -shipped, -ship•ing
  or -ship•ping

wor'ship•er *or*
  wor'ship•per
wor'ship•ful
worst *(most inferior)*
  ✔ *wurst*
wor'sted
worth
wor'thi•ness
worth'while'
wor'thy
would *past tense of*
  will
  ✔ *wood*
would'-be'
would'n't
wound
wow
wrack *(ruin, wreck-*
  age)
  ✔ *rack*
wraith *(ghost)*
  ✔ *wrath*
wran'gle, -gled,
  -gling
wrang'ler
wrap *(to enclose),*
  wrapped *or* wrapt,
  wrap'ping
  ✔ *rap*
wrap'a•round' *adj.*
wrap'per
wrap'-up' *n.*
wrath *(anger)*
  ✔ *wraith*
wrath'ful
wreak *(to inflict)*
  ✔ *reek*

wreath *n.*

wreathe, wreathed,
  wreath'ing

wreck

wreck'age

wren

wrench

wrest (*to obtain by
  force*)
  ✔ rest

wres'tle, -tled, -tling

wres'tler

wretch (*miserable
  person*)
  ✔ retch

wretch'ed

wrig'gle, -gled,
  -gling

wright (*person who
  constructs*)
  ✔ right, rite, write

wring (*to squeeze*),
  wrung, wring'ing
  ✔ ring

wring'er

wrin'kle, -kled,
  -kling

wrist

wrist'band'

wrist'watch'

writ (*order*)

write (*to compose*),
  wrote *also* writ,
  writ'ten *also* writ,
  writ'ing
  ✔ right, rite, wright

write'-in' *n.*

write'-off' *n.*

writ'er

write'-up' *n.*

writhe, writhed,
  writh'ing

wrong

wrong'do'er

wrong'do'ing

wrong'ful

wrong'-head'ed

wrought' i'ron

wry (*ironic, twisted*),
  wri'er *or* wry'er,
  wri'est *or* wry'est
  ✔ rye

wry'ly

wun'der·kind' *pl.*
  -kind'er

wurst (*sausage*)
  ✔ worst

X

Xan'a·du'

x'-ax'is *pl.* -ax'es

X'-chro'mo·some'

xe'bec'

xe'non'

xen'o·phobe'

xen'o·pho'bi·a

xen'o·pho'bic

xe·rog'ra·pher

xer'o·graph'ic

xe·rog'ra·phy

Xho'sa *pl.* -sa

xi

X'mas

x'-ra'di·a'tion

X'-rat'ed

x'-ray' *also* X'-ray'
  also x' ray' *or*
  X' ray'

xy'lem

xy'lo·phone'

Y

yacht

yacht'ing

yachts'man

yachts'wom'an

ya'hoo *pl.* -hoos

yak (*animal*)

yak (*talk*), yakked,
  yak'king

yam'mer

yank (*to jerk*)

Yank (*Yankee*)

Yan'kee

yap, yapped,
  yap'ping

Ya'qui *pl.* -qui *or*
  -quis

yard'age

yard'arm'

yard'mas'ter

yard'stick'

yar'mul·ke *also*
  yar'mel·ke

yarn

yar'row

yaw

yawl

yawn

yawp

yaws

y'-ax'is *pl.* -ax'es

Y'-chro'mo•some'

ye

yea

yeah

year

year'book'

year'-end' *also*
  year'end'

year'ling

year'long'

yearn

yearn'ing

year'-round'

yeast

yell

yel'low

yel'low•ham'mer

yel'low•ish

yel'low•legs' *pl.*
  -legs'

yelp

yen (*longing*)

yen (*monetary unit*),
  pl. yen

yeo'man

yeo'man•ry

yer'ba ma•té'

yes *pl.* yes'es

ye•shi'va *or*
  ye•shi'vah

yes'ter•day'

yes'ter•year'

yet

ye'ti *pl.* -tis

yew (*tree*)
  ✔ ewe, you

Yid'dish

yield

yield'ing

yip, yipped,
  yip'ping

yip'pee

yo'del, -deled *or*
  -delled, -del•ing *or*
  -del•ling

yo'ga

yo'gi *pl.* gis

yo'gurt *also*
  yo'ghurt

yoke (*to join*), yoked,
  yok'ing
  ✔ yolk

yo'kel

yolk (*yellow of an
  egg*)
  ✔ yoke

Yom' Kip•pur'

yon

yon'der

yore

York'shire pud'-
  ding

you *pron.*
  ✔ ewe, yew

you'-all' *also* y'all

young

young'ish

young'ster

your *possessive form*

  of you

you're *contraction of*
  you are

yours

your•self' *pl.*
  -selves'

youth

youth'ful

yowl

yo'-yo' *pl.* -yos'

yt•ter'bi•um

yt'tri•um

yu•an' *pl.* -an' *or*
  -ans'

yuc'ca

Yu'go•sla'vi•an

Yule

Yule'tide'

Yu'ma *pl.* -ma *or*
  -mas

Yu'man

yum'my

yup'pie

yurt

Z

za'ny

zap, zapped,
  zap'ping

Za'po•tec' *pl.* -tec'
  or -tecs'

z'-ax'is *pl.* -ax'es

zeal

zeal'ot

zeal'ous

ze′bra
ze′bu *pl.* -bus
zed
Zen′ Bud′dhism
Zen′ Bud′dhist
ze′nith
zeph′yr
zep′pe•lin *also*
  Zep′pe•lin
ze′ro *pl.* -ros *or*
  -roes
zest′ful
ze′ta
zig′gu•rat′
zig′zag′, -zagged′,
  -zag′ging
zil′lion
Zim•bab′we•an
zinc
zin′fan•del *also*

Zin′fan•del′
zing
zing′er
zin′ni•a
Zi′on *also* Si′on
Zi′on•ism
Zi′on•ist
zip, zipped, zip′ping
zip′per
zip′py
zir′con′
zir•co′ni•um
zith′er
zlo′ty *pl.* -ty *or* -tys
zo′di•ac′
zom′bie *also* zom′bi
  pl. -bies *also* -bis
zon′al
zone, zoned,
  zon′ing

zoo *pl.* zoos
zoo′keep′er
zo′o•log′i•cal *also*
  zo′o•log′ic
zo•ol′o•gist
zo•ol′o•gy
zoom
zo′o•phyte′
Zo′ro•as′tri•an
Zo′ro•as′tri•an•ism
zounds
zuc•chi′ni *pl.* -ni *or*
  -nis
Zu′lu *pl.* -lu *or* -lus
Zu′ni *also* Zu′ñi *pl.*
  -ni *or* -nis *also* -ñi
  or -ñis
zwie′back′
zy′gote′
zy•got′ic